BRITISH MOTOR CYCLES SINCE 1950

XWY 417

BRITISH MOTOR CYCLES SINCE 1950

VOLUME 4

Panther, Royal Enfield, Scott, Silk, Sunbeam, Sun and Tandon Roadsters of 250cc and Over

Steve Wilson

Patrick Stephens, Wellingborough

First published in 1987

British Library Cataloguing in Publication Data

Wilson, Steve,
British motor cycles since 1950.
Vol. 4
1. Motorcycle, British—History
I. Title
629.2'275'0941 TL440

ISBN 0-85059-830-3

Frontispiece *1960, and* Motorcycling's *Bernal Osborne gets down to it on a Model 50 Panther Grand Sports 350, on a wet day at MIRA.*

Other books in this series by Steve Wilson
British motor cycles since 1950 Vol 1: *AJW, Ambassador, AMC (AJS and Matchless) and Ariel roadsters of 250cc and over.*
British motor cycles since 1950 Vol 2: *BSA, Cotton, Douglas, DMW, Dot, EMC, Excelsior and Francis Barnett roadsters of 250cc and over.*
British motor cycles since 1930 Vol 3: *Greeves, Hesketh, Indian, James, Norman and Norton roadsters of 250cc and over.*

Patrick Stephens Limited is part of the Thorsons Publishing Group, Denington Estate, Wellingborough, Northamptonshire, NN8 2RQ, England.

Printed in Great Britain by Adlard and Son, The Garden City Press, Letchworth, Herts

10 9 8 7 6 5 4 3 2 1

Contents

Acknowledgements

Thanks for their efforts on this one to Bill Coulson, Tony Lynch, Dave Bogg, Doug Young, Dave Benson, Ian Abrahams and especially Andy Berry and Jim Chalk, all of the Royal Enfield Owners Club, also Jeff Lewis of L and D Motors for the loan of material and patience with my pestering. Thanks also to Scott Owners man John Underhill, George Silk of that ilk, Panther expert Barry Jones, Sunbeam specialist Bob Stewart, and for all matters two-stroke, Nick Kelly. To Graham Sanderson of the late lamented *Motor Cycle Weekly* for kind permission for the use of photos, as also to Cyril Ayton of *Motor Cycle Sport* and others too numerous to mention. Last but not least to Sandra den Hertog, boss typist and much else besides, whose patience with this ongoing saga of matters mechanical appears to be nearly (but not quite) unlimited; and as before, to the original hacks and snappers without whose careful work this short synthesis would not be possible.

140

How to use this book

The book is arranged by marques in the following way:

1 A brief history of the marque.
2 More detailed consideration of the major categories within the factory's road-going output during the period (ie, usually broken down into single and twin cylinder machines, but with separate sections for unusual and exceptional designs like the Gold Star).
3 These are followed by a table of *production dates*. Here, though production generally shifted during August and a new machine would usually be on display in November at the annual show of say, 1950, I have followed the makers' intentions and referred to it as the 1951 model or model for 1951. Next comes some necessarily brief *technical specifications* for each range of machines.
4 These are followed by a detailed *year-by-year survey* of each range, noting developments and modifications. (Like the book, these are 'British', as with information available it has not been possible to include export specifications.) This should help with the identification of particular models, but it should be noted that sometimes there were changes made either gradually or mid-year.
5 A final section gives details of the marque's *engine and frame numbers* (where available), *colour schemes, publications and manuals, spares shops,* and *owners' clubs* for each marque. (With the publications, o/p signifies 'out of print'.)

The following further points should be borne in mind. The *production dates* quoted are in general those for availability in the UK rather than for export. *Weights:* all weights quoted in the technical specifications are the weight dry (unless otherwise stated). They have usually derived from *Motor Cycling* magazine's Buyer's Guide section, and occasionally inaccuracies have come to light, either from a failure to update or from optimism by the factory which supplied the figures. *Speeds:* top and cruising speeds for most models are to be found in the text not the specifications, and are approximate figures. This is because not all machines were road-tested, and not all those tested underwent timed runs at MIRA. Also the author feels that top speeds on road test machines were not always representative, as they could feature non-standard high-performance parts fitted by the factories. *MPG:* petrol consumption figures are also approximate, being subject to the variables of state of tune, prevailing conditions and the hand at the throttle.

Owners' clubs: if the addresses provided here have changed, phone the BMF (01-942-7914), or write to them at Jack Wiley House, 129 Seaforth Avenue, Motspur Park, New Malden, Surrey. Please note that the above telephone number is not the same as the one which was provided in Vol 2.

Please also note that in the interests of space-saving, the following abbreviations have been used for periodicals throughout the text:
MCS—Motor Cycle Sport; MCN—Motor Cycle News; MCW—Motor Cycle Weekly; and *MCM—Motor Cycle Mechanics.*

One further point: in the fuller version of this section in Vol 1, mention was made in the 'Frame and Engine Numbers' section of the existence of records held by the Metropolitan Police Stolen Vehicles Office. These records have now been handed over to the Science Museum Library, Exhibition Road, South Kensington, London SW7 2DD (Tel: 01-581-4734). Enquiries to them should be accompanied by an SAE.

For an amplified version of this introduction, see Volume 1.

Left *Johnny Brittain aboard a Royal Enfield Bullet, in action during the 1956 ISDT in Bavaria.*

OEC

OEC Ltd, Atlanta Works, Stamshaw Road, Portsmouth

Before the war OEC (which stood for Osborn Engineering Company) had been a real name to reckon with. Not only did John Osborn and Fred Wood build big models with JAP or British Anzani engines that broke Brooklands and world speed records, but, as befitted an enterprise situated so far from the Midlands mainstream of the industry, out of their works at Gosport, across the water from Portsmouth, came a number of models with chassis designs that went from the unusual via the unorthodox to the downright odd.

There had even been something queer about their ultimate world record, though in a different sense. In 1922 Claude Temple, aboard the OEC Temple-British Anzani 1000 cc twin, took the 'World's Fastest' motor cycle record at over 108 mph: three years later he was the first to cover a hundred miles in one hour, and in 1926 went on to another world motor cycle record, topping 120 mph. The problem came on the last go-round, in 1930, when Joe Wright on a Temple-prepared supercharged OEC-JAP 1000 cc V-twin hoisted the world motor cycle speed record to an astonishing 150.736 mph. Trouble was an amateur photographer had snapped the record-breaking machine, which, due to the OEC's engine-shaft key shearing, had actually been Wright's own Zenith. Wright's hot pursuit of the bonus money from OEC was probably the cause of the deception and subsequent scandal.

The extremely quick would-be record breaker had been equipped with the best known of Osborn's far-out designs, namely duplex steering. This involved two vertical stanchions on each side of the wheel, one pair holding the wheel and the other joined with steering linkage to a sort of basket of tubes behind the wheel and connected to the frame's lower engine rails. Though unlikely-looking, duplex steering provided above-average stability.

It was just one of a line of devices including a sidecar taxi outfit with a steering wheel for the driver; a caterpillar-tracked military prototype; and the Atlanta duo, one of the early examples of feet-forward motor cycling, which today has attracted a devout following. With duplex steering and a horizontal engine, it was claimed to be just about impossible to fall off, something demonstrated by a pair of stunt-riding *Motor Cycling* journalists. Finally there was the ultra-weird OEC-built Whitworth Monocar, a two-wheeled automobile with a headlamp on its nose, a folding hood, a rear seat that appeared to involve the passenger gripping the driver around the waist with his or her legs, and a pair of tiny outrigger stabilizing wheels that lowered to prevent the Monocar falling over when halting or starting!

By now OEC had moved across to Portsmouth, and when war came again, their first Atlanta works was bombed out. They re-established themselves at another one, and post-war concentrated on competition machines, IOD 125 and 6E 197 cc Villiers-engined Trials and scrambles bikes. They had some successes with the latter including a victory at the 1949 Cotswold scramble, and they also made a JAP-engined 500 cc speedway bike. These were supplemented by utility Villiers-engined lightweight roadsters and then, briefly and in small quantities, by the 250 side-valve four-stroke model under consideration below.

Flashes of the old ingenuity and quality were evident in the use of their own compression-spring telescopic front forks and all-welded square-section frames, with rear suspension for the scramblers, as well as a two-chain rear drive system. This involved a sleeve on the swinging-arm with two sprockets mounted on ball races, which ensured constant tension whatever the angle of the swinging-arm. But by the end of 1954, not even a foray into tubular furniture could save the company, and production ceased.

OEC: The Apollo STI 250

For a try at a larger capacity than their previous Villiers 125 and 197 cc utility roadster, OEC were unfortunate in their choice of powerplant. A firm which had had their pick of superior Matchless and JAP motors pre-war, they now had to settle for a side-valve engine of legendary awfulness from Brockhouse, as used to power the Brockhouse Indian Brave.

Further details can be found in the Indian section of Vol 3, but here it can be said that the 250 single engine was handicapped for the home market by an American-style left-side gearchange, as well as having the rear chain on the right, and more fundamentally by a stiff and noisy three-speed gearbox, rudimentary coil ignition, and a wet-sump side-valve layout with a crankshaft that was prone to breakages. When it was running—it was chronically underpowered—the Indian Brave's top speed being less than 60 mph.

OEC's cycle parts probably deserved better, with the competition-proved single down-tube frame and slim forks with load and rebound springs, a respectable low weight at 220 lb, and on the STI the spindle of its 19-in front wheel off-set forward. The catalogued version, illustrated here, was rigid frame, though it is said that the scrambler's sprung frame with Girling rear units was offered as an option. What the straight-through pipe of the silencer was all about, or what it sounded like, history doesn't relate. A local source thought that though fair numbers of the 193 cc machines were produced, only about ten of the Apollo STI were built before the company collapsed. This would undoubtedly give it a certain cachet in British bike circles, should a surviving example be unearthed.

OEC: The Apollo STI 250—dates and specifications

Production dates
STI—1952–54

Specifications
Capacity, bore and stroke—248 cc (65.5 × 76 mm)
Type of engine—side-valve single
Ignition—coil
Weight—(1954) 220 lb

Colour schemes

1952 Black frame, forks and headlamp; polychromatic silver mudguards, chainguard, toolbox, fuel tank, which had panels in blue. Chromed wheel rims.
1953–54 As 1952 but tank blue-lined, not panelled; wheel rims painted silver, handlebars black.

OEC Apollo 250 for 1953.

Panther

Phelon and Moore Ltd, Horncastle Street Works, Cleckheaton, West Yorkshire
Joah Carver Phelon—a rugged name of almost biblical resonance, and completely apposite for the product with which this innovator was primarily associated. That product was the long-stroke, sloping single cylinder P and M Panther, a machine whose direct origins occurred in the antediluvian mists of the pioneer era, a motorcycle that thundered out of history more often than not linked to a sidecar which it pulled like a train, a bike that by reputation at least could tear down the side of a house. Out of the past and out of Cleckheaton, 'Cleck' or 'down t'Spen' (Valley) as they said locally, up from the local weaving towns and over the barren Yorkshire moors of the West Riding, the 'big pussies' have roared their way slogging into legend: from Uruguay to Uppsala, like the socks you can buy near Hadrian's Wall, these monolithic motorbikes, sired by hard times and designed and put together with engineering of true worth, have proved 'almost unwearoutable'.

Cleckheaton is located near the middle of that triangle of industrial cities made up of Bradford, Leeds and Huddersfield, and the roots of the story are entwined with Northern Industry. In the 1890s Joah Phelon had a small precision wire drawing die and gauge business for the textile trade, and in his spare time experimented with various forms of motor transport on a hobby basis, in collaboration with his cousin Harry Rayner. In 1901 he hit upon his first and most definitive major breakthrough. On a motorized bicycle, instead of slapping the engine at one of the various peripheral locations currently being experimented with by the pioneer designers, Joah went to the heart of the matter and integrated his machine, by making the powerplant part of the structure of the bicycle itself.

The engine bolts holding the sloping cylinder to the crankcase were extended both above and below, and the engine became the machine's front down tube. It was not quite the first example of this idea—a German design of the 1890s, and one from the USA's Indian Company in 1900 had also come up with it, but Phelon and Rayner's

Post-war logo — 'The mighty Panther.

tensioned through-engine bolts provided better frame strength and rigidity, and their design was original enough to merit a patent—as did Phelon's method of ignition control, as well as an engine starting device that would mutate into the firm's characteristic half-compression system once kickstarts were introduced. A final notable feature of this significant innovator's first machine was its use of chain drive.

At first the slopers were produced under licence by the Humber concern, whose devious mastermind Harry Lawson, known for hoarding patented designs, was, happily for P and R, pressured by circumstances into actually manufacturing this one: though Phelon had to resort to the law to get the balance of his royalties. These machines dominated the early world of reliability trials. P and R maintained a tiny manufacturing set-up of their own, but in 1903 Rayner died.

This brought Phelon into contact with a young steam engineer named Richard Moore. From 1904 they were in partnership, and P and M was born. The licensing rights to Humber lapsed and reverted to them, and one of their first moves was to take out a further joint patent on Moore's ground-

Joah Carver Phelon and Richard Moore — P and M.

breaking design for a two-speed gear. This was a double primary chain drive, using different sizes of sprocket to give different ratios, and wedge-controlled expanding clutches to engage either gear. By 1911 most makes had adopted variable gears, but in the meantime P and M's machines had established a record of the highest successes in ACU and MCC reliability trials, with Richard Moore himself a frequent competitor. This attracted orders, and hence in 1908 a new partner in the shape of Bertram (Bertie) Marians, whose family would be associated with the concern until the end. Working from London offices, Marians' role would be to transform a local industry into a business—soon exporting to the Commonwealth and to even more exotic fleet customers such as the Mexican Postal Service.

Back in Yorkshire the Horncastle Street site was first occupied in 1910, and two years later a purpose-built factory was operating, with a bridge over adjacent Commercial Street connecting the new and old buildings. Moore designed a 770 cc V-twin which also used its front cylinder as a stressed member, but World War 1 intervened, with production concentrating on the proven 500 cc single. Since 1911 this had been referred to as 'the perfected motor cycle', with features like control cables inside the handlebars and full enclosure for the chain drive to justify the boast. So it was the 500 cc two-speeder which the fledgling Royal Flying Corps and Royal Naval Air Service selected as their standard transport. In 1915 the factory came under government control and went on 24-hour production. Despite this forcing of the pace, the P and M machines, mostly with sidecar attached, were of a legendary reliability; so much so that in 1917, Service testing of the newly delivered machines was ordered stopped, as so few were ever defective.

Post-war saw improved versions of the green-liveried singles, and in 1922, the year Joah Phelon retired and shortly afterwards sold out to Moore and Marians, a new 555 cc 4½ hp side-valve single, which began to transmute the company's reliable-but-plodding image to that of swift roadsters and lusty sidecar haulers, with their own chairs now being manufactured at Cleckheaton. The 555 cc initially featured a four-speed version of the P and M two-speed system with a further two-speed countershaft, and a first use of the characteristic crude but effective dip-and-splash lubrication, with the piston dipping into the crankcase and getting a splash of oil from the spinning flywheel. This sports model was called, for the first time, the Panther. Shortly after the name had extended to embrace the whole range.

1924 saw the company engaging the colourful designer Granville Bradshaw for their first ohv machine. For Panther, Bradshaw was good and bad, and the good came first. The 500 cc ohv model retained the P and M chassis arrangement with its integral inclined cylinder, but much else changed. The four-speed gearbox became a conventional layshaft design. Visually the engine resembled an overhead cam motor, as the two pushrods were enclosed in a large, prominent tubular steel cover up the side of the barrel, which would henceforth be another 'signature' of the marque. The lubrication system was revised to feature a simple eccentric plunger oil pump but with the cylinder walls and piston still relying upon splash lubrication, (this time from massive 28 lb flywheels operating in a semi-dry crankcase which threw the excess oil forward over a weir into the equally massive oil-bearing sump—another new feature which would be characteristic of the marque's four-stroke singles from now on). Triangular, and cast integrally with the crankcase, so that the bottom end shape resembled a broad arrow head with the inclined cylinder as the shaft, the forward sump grew in size (to four pints' capacity) and shape, to a final deeply-finned form in 1934. The rudiments of the legend had now been laid down.

Although Granville Bradshaw had done the groundwork for the ohv sloper's design, much of the built-in strength was due to development work by Frank Leach, P and M's own draughtsman and experimental engineer. It was Leach who in 1926 revised the lubrication system, and in 1927 introduced the first two-port cylinder head, cooler-running with its deep finning. Above all it was Leach who in the following year lengthened the 498 cc's 90 mm stroke and bored it out marginally to achieve the classic 598 cc (87 × 100 mm) dimensions of the Model 100. In tuned Redwing sports versions, or as the cooking Model 3 or 60, the 600 cc engine would prove to be the optimum Big Pussy.

There seemed to be something of a jinx connected with twins as far as P and M were

Jolly Coppers. 1927, and Bradford City Police 'Flying Squad' aboard their Model 60 slopers.

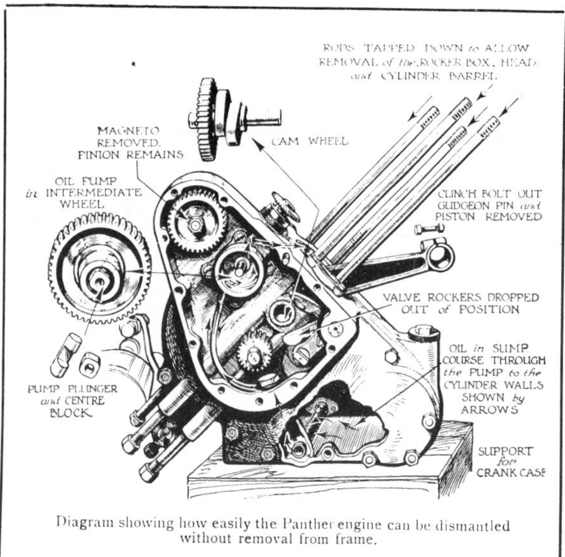

Diagram showing how easily the Panther engine can be dismantled without removal from frame.

concerned (later, neither a pre-Second World War in-line twin nor a post-war parallel twin would come to fruition). In 1927, Bradshaw's latest brainchild, the Panthette, was a transverse V-twin, like today's Moto Guzzis or the Honda CX machines. Unlike them however, it had only a 250 cc motor, and while ahead of its time in adopting unit construction and many other ingenious features, it was poorly styled, expensive and underpowered: this fatal combination—unorthodox and gutless—gave the Panthette all the sales appeal of pork in Jerusalem. One saving grace was that the cycle parts, including the unorthodox massive forged-steel frame backbone which had been severely over-ordered, were hastily adapted to take Villiers two-stroke engines. This provided the start of an economy range that would help the firm through hard times both sooner and later. On the Panthette itself, which was withdrawn after 1928, P and M suffered badly, and the financial reverse coincided with the onset of the great thirties Depression, which would annihilate many British manufacturers.

P and M's salvation came from further work done by Frank Leach, from inspired marketing and from sheer hard graft. As disaster loomed in 1932 and the staff were placed on half wages, with the London service centre closed, Leach developed a miniature heavyweight, a lighter 250 and then also a 350 version of the big sloping four-stroke, housed in a conventional frame. Numbers of these were provided for the big south London dealers, Pride and Clarke. In the face of the Depression, in the interests of cash-flow, that firm resorted to price-slashing, and found that the middleweights then sold like hot cakes. A deal was struck between P and C, and P and M, and for 1933 one of the legends of the British industry emerged; the 250 cc Red Panther, in all-red finish and featuring the 'Pride and Clarke' script beneath the Panther legend on the timing chest. This was a fully equipped, brand new motor cycle for less than £30 (£29 17s 6d was the figure that stuck, though it could be had for £1 less if the customer opted for gas instead of electric lighting). This outstanding feat of economy was achieved by both trimming specification and substituting of cheaper alternatives for components such as tyres on the model, and spray painting not stoving for components such as mudguards; and by the use of cheap outworkers, young apprentices and women, for intensive production. While the output of heavyweights rarely exceeded a thousand a year, something like 3,000 Red Panthers were made and sold each year for several seasons.

The Red Panther output was all the more extraordinary because the Cleckheaton factory's basic staff numbered just 200. It is not too fanciful to venture that the Horncastle Street works and the P and M enterprise had a flavour all their own, and a West Yorkshire one at that—tough, practical, thrifty, masculine, not given lightly to change or the new-fangled, and a curious mixture of the exotic and the homely: rather like the stuffed panther which had crouched, snarling, inside the entrance since 1927, but whose nose became worn away by countless hands touching it for luck. The factory was presided over by the upright and capable Richard Moore, a practical engineer often involved at shop-floor level.

P and M were not a large enough concern to carry out all processes in-house. In later years their plating plant was closed down, and as well as the usual ancillaries like lights, tanks and carburettors, most components including engine castings were brought in from the Midlands. The accumulation of components had some bizarre effects. There was once a crisis when it was discovered that rats had eaten all the saddles, and production was suspended while they sent down to Terrys for replacement. On the other hand, in the sixties, it was largely the accumulation of parts in stock (and these went as far back as the beam-frames for the Panthette!) which allowed production to continue for five years after the Receiver had been called in.

But despite this, self-reliance was the keynote, since after the frames had been brazed in the cellars and components turned on the belt-driven lathes on the ground floor, the building of each machine on the first floor was the responsibility of one man. This was the ultimate in quality control—if there were any complaints they were taken back to source. The despatch books are held by the MPOC (it used to be Midlands Panther Owners' Club, but after they went national the 'M' is generally accepted as standing for 'Mighty'). So today it is possible to discover if your sloper was built by Mr Clegg, Mr Oldroyd, Mr Bass or Mr Dale.

Horncastle Street was not, however, an all-male preserve. Women frequently did a man's job, for something like half a man's wages. One such was Alice Wharton, who arrived in the lean year of 1932 and left 45 years later, having earned the affectionate title of 'Auntie' from the multitude of Panther owners she dealt with from 1966 to 1977 after the factory had turned over to other activities, and she worked with the legendary ex-Chief Tester Joe Mortimer to handle the mail-order of the still remaining motor cycle spares, selling them, in addition, over the counter on Wednesdays.

Such a small, tightly knit unit would be bound to resent anyone whom they perceived as an outsider, and after the Second War many felt that P and M's destiny was too much in outsiders' hands.

Above left *The works. 1929 bottom end explained. Little changed for the next forty years.*

Right *1931 'Redwing 90' 500cc Panther, a de luxe model with twin headlamps, tail lamp and tank instrument panel.*

Right *The 1939 ACU test which covered 10,000 miles non-stop. Tall chap in white is P and M's legendary chief tester, Joe Mortimer.*

Disappointingly the war itself had involved no motor cycle production, even after the Red Panther had turned the company's fortunes around, and despite the steady development of the Model 100 which was seen in the pre-war years. Frank Leach had left Cleckheaton, at first to work at P and M's then London distributor, George Clarke Motors, but despite his absence, the 'perfecting' of the big pussy continued.

Then came the war: it saw the works turned over to sub-contract work for the Avro and Blackburn aircraft companies, and making control columns for Swordfish torpedo planes and the like. It is noticeable that no British motor cycle company which did not enjoy continuity of production making military bikes during the war would really prosper past the post-war boom. In large measure this was because of the absence of the profitable 'army surplus' business which immediately followed it, with the MOD, after purchasing them at full rate, selling back large excess stocks of spares and machines to the factories at a nominal price, for immediate and profitable resale to a transport-hungry public.

Panther were no exception; they lost the continuity and the profit, and without the capital to retool, had to rely once again on the cheap labour of young apprentices, and on the old-fashioned virtues of economy and ruggedness in their products when re-entering the market-place. Their appeal was now just to the family sidecar rider and the commuter, as there was no question of road race involvement, and Trials success had tapered off in the late thirties.

Off-road victory would not be revived by the Stroud trials versions of revamped 250 and 350 singles. The Models 65 and 75, even after the latter had been quite effectively revamped for 1954, were not great successes, and development ceased on them in 1956. The post-war phenomenon of purchase tax meant that while their price stayed competitive, they could never provide the economy biking of the Red Panther, and at just 10.5 bhp for the 250, were badly down on power against most contemporary ohv four-stroke singles; though the 15.5 bhp 350 was said to have sold fairly well in Europe.

So the main sales thrust was still with the Model 100. North America was served by one outlet, the American Motorcycle Company, which in 1949 came up with a flamboyant piece of marketing: they offered a free passage over to England to collect any Panther ordered in the States (the offer did not, however, include the return fare!). Otherwise Scandinavia displaced the Commonwealth countries as a prime export market, and not just for complete machines. From 1952 to '56, the Swedish Maskin A.B. cycle company of Falun marketed the Svalan 50 Matcher machine, with their own frame but a 250 Model 65 engine and Dowty forks. It was joined in 1953 by the Svala 75 Lyx, this time with NSU teles but the Model 75 350 powerplant.

But back at Cleckheaton, more significant changes had taken place shortly after the war. Chief among these was the retirement in 1947 of Richard Moore, with his shares going to local man Colonel Sydney Smith, and an onset of the lack of vigour which always accompanied the departure of the founder members of British motor cycle firms. This is not to say that the motor cycle side stagnated: Panther remained heavily committed to continuing development work, as we shall see, even to the extent that it exacerbated their cash-flow problems. These problems intensified an always present tendency to extreme economies, even tight-fistedness, at Cleckheaton.

In 1945 Peter Marians, the son of business

Below left *Panther's lone sporting success story, Fred Whittle, powers away on his Model 100 Trials outfit.*

Right *350 Stroud Trials Mk II. Good looking, but no success.*

Right *The essential animal: late 1951 Model 100 in harness with typically ample Garrard sidecar.*

partner Bertie, had been made a director, and from Moore's retirement onward he took an active role in the running of the company. However, as a London-based figure with something of a playboy reputation, he was regarded as an outsider by the Cleckheaton stalwarts, and never entirely accepted. In 1952 Bertie Marians and company secretary Fred Brown retired, with Bertie's shares going to his son, and Brown's to Colonel Smith. Finally, when the latter died in March of the following year, his shares in turn passed to Peter Marians, who became managing director and began to spend more time in the North.

Marians brought in the pre-war engineer Frank Leach as a fellow director. Leach had set up his own workshop in Bradford, as well as briefly producing his own FLM machines from his garages in Leeds until 1953; and even after taking up his new position at P and M, he chose to keep himself to himself, and in strong contrast to Richard Moore, to keep separate from the shop floor. By 1952 he had already been refurbishing worn Cleckheaton machinery and producing top class jigs and tools for the works, the laudable intention being to achieve finer tolerances, quieter running and longer life for P and M's engines. A continuous conveyor system was instituted in the enamelling department, which largely did away with the

1953 Model 75 350. Slow but reliable, these middleweights outsold the big 'uns in post-war Europe.

previous carrying and lifting. Bonderizing tanks were installed and gave a tough, rust resistant finish and a good base for subsequent enamelling. In another example of the maintenance of P and M quality, all nuts and bolts were Cosletized, a phosphate process producing a durable gun-metal black finish. A further conveyor system was put in to handle all the spraying, and together with the faster drying times of modern synthetic paints, helped to increase productivity in the enamelling shop. This was echoed in the works as a whole, with up to fifty heavyweights a week being produced in the peak year of 1955. At £193 16s for a solid-frame Model 100 and £211 16s for a swinging-arm version, prices were still comparable with equivalent mounts like a rigid 500 cc Model 18 Matchless single at £187, or a rear-sprung Model 19 600 cc Norton banger at £208 4s.

But according to Panther historian Barry Jones, the second phase of the factory's modernization effort had been less happy. In 1953 Leach supervised the replacement of the old belt and shaft-driven machinery in the machine shops by electrically driven equivalents. Many of the workforce felt that it was a mistake to scrap the very accurate and well-built traditional machinery for inferior modern equipment; certainly many of them could not get on with the new gear, and this was reflected to some extent in the quality of work on the motor cycles. In addition, P and M's good reputation for precision engineering meant a quantity of profitable contract work, which tended to interest Peter Marians and to downgrade the bike operation. As a consequence, no-one at Cleckheaton quite had their heart in it.

Leach's arrival also signalled some internal shake-ups, with, as noted, the Stroud dropped, the Model 35 redeveloped, and Ben Heyes, P and M's current chief draughtsman, departing for AMC. The Model 100 acquired a swinging-arm frame for 1954, and by 1956 the company estimated that a large majority of the slopers were pulling chairs, and had settled for sidecar gearing and fork trail as standard. With the Model 65 and 75 not proving too successful, Leach sensibly let them be, in favour of genuine utility models with Villiers engines, Earles front forks and a £120 price tag. The 9E-engined 197 cc Model 10/4 (this was in pre-Citizen's Band days, though 'Dragnet' was current) did well, and was followed by the pokier 2T-powered Model 35 250 twin, and later the 324 cc 3T engined Model 45 and 50 twins, some even with Siba electric starts.

All this was fine, but in the second half of the decade the management were to make two bad errors of judgement, both relating to that quagmire for the British industry, the scooter. Since the early fifties there had been permeating among our manufacturers a definite but rather vague and uneasy awareness of both the potential of this unisex non-enthusiast market, and the way the damned foreigners seemed to be monopolizing it. The problem was that the monopoly was more or less complete by the time home-grown offerings became available.

P and M's first response to this was reasonably intelligent: in 1957 they settled for importing two of the foreign products from the French Terrot company, who had a good reputation for pre-war ohv machines. But they missed two essential points: that though a German-inspired heavyweight scooter market did exist, it was limited; and that the appeal of the really popular Vespa or Lambretta, a scooter as opposed to a motor cycle with small wheels, was their stylish appearance and relatively light weight, as well as good reliability. The 'Scooterrot' was a 125 cc heavyweight, with a grotesquely bulbous nose-cone luggage compartment. It was furthermore not encouraging for Cleckheaton folk like Alice Wharton to discover that the first batches of Scooterrots arrived at the works rusty after a lengthy sojourn in damp warehouse conditions and had to be stripped and re-enamelled, an expensive process which cost the company dear. Also, there had apparently been insufficient market research on price. Partly due to the relative strength of the Franc and the pound, the brute went on sale for 1957 at £159, when a graceful state-of-the-art 125 Douglas Vespa could be had for exactly that sum: no prizes for guessing which one most scooterists chose. Despite a drop in price the following year due to devaluation of the Franc, the Scooterrot sold poorly. Its companion the Terrot moped was handicapped here, but not in its country of origin, by Britain's legal prohibition on under-16 riders, and according to Barry Jones, failed to sell at all!

Undeterred, Frank Leach proceeded to initiate P and M's own scooter project. Once again, the initial thinking seemed sensible. The company had been associated with Ernie Earles due to the use of Reynolds-Earles front forks on their Villiers-engined machines (there was also an Earles-forked Model 100 prototype, but it had not been successful, and even the bigger Villiers motors had overstressed the pivoted forks). Earles had come up with a method of tooling-up economically for the steel pressings necessary in scooter manufacture, using an alloy, Kirksite, with a low melting point. Press tools could be sand-cast from Kirksite for a fraction of the cost of doing it with traditional machine finish tools, and then afterwards melted down and re-used.

So after some costly and unsuccessful experimental work with a 125 cc Villiers-engined version with fibreglass bodywork, P and M collaborated on the steel pressings for a 175 Villiers-powered scooter with two other small firms, Sun and Dayton (the latter the progenitors of the immortally named 'Albatross' range—someone clearly had not read their *Rime of the Ancient Mariner*). But once again, with the Panther Princess, as it was dubbed, there were costly and delaying teething troubles, particularly in the handling department, and though the 254 lb production version was apparently a pleasant enough heavy scooter, the market did not justify it. Jon Stevens, editor of *Scooter World* magazine, estimated at the time that no less than ten British manufacturers were contesting what in reality, due to foreign penetration to the tune of 80,000 imported machines, was only a third of the 120,000 p/a market for new scooters (which since 1957 had been outselling motor cycles). These were slim pickings, and the Princess' 1960 launch also coincided neatly with the discouraging effects of 1959 hire-purchase restrictions. This scooter failure was a further major financial setback for P and M; components for a thousand scooters were stockpiled, but only 250 built and sold.

Villiers power, with the 1960 Model 50 Grand Sports 350. Rear fairing won Frank Leach a Design Council award: but few were made.

The company kept trying, however, with the Villiers-engined machines as well as with the heavyweight, which was supplemented for 1959 by a superior own-brand sidecar chassis. This was made in the same strong tubing as the slopers' frames, and featured an Armstrong suspension unit, a sidecar wheel brake, a jacking point, a towing point for a trailer, and provision for a spare wheel (the wheels were interchangeable with the motor cycle's). The big Panther also entered its final incarnation for 1959. P and M had realized that the Model 100 despite its undoubted virtues as a sidecar hack, at 23 bhp and at the beginning of the motorway age, was looking a little undergunned beside family outfits being harnessed to powerful twins, many of which were 650s by now. So with faultless logic P and M expanded the Model 100 to the 27 bhp 645 cc Model 120s, 'the biggest aspidistra in the world' (the phrase was actually quoted in *Motor Cycling* as describing the 120 when harnessed to a Busmar Astral 'full double-adult fixed head saloon sidecar', a monster no less than 7½ ft long!). The Model 120 was again beset by teething troubles, and for reasons that will be explained in the appropriate section, P and M had overstretched a good design; this resulted in restricted oil circulation, leading to high oil consumption, and clutch and other troubles. Despite this, the increased capacity proved to be a sales aid, with the Model 100 eclipsed by its bigger brother.

The end was in sight, however, with the bottom falling out of the traditional British motor cycle market at the beginning of the sixties. Panther sales dropped hard in 1961, rallied briefly and unexpectedly during 1962/63, but fell dramatically from then on. By October 1962 the company's situation had deteriorated sufficiently for the Receiver, in the shape of accountant Ken Davidson, to be called in.

He found, in the words of Alice Wharton, 'so many parts left on the floor, and he had to make them into money, so they made 'em into bikes'. About a thousand more heavyweights were built, the Model 100 being produced until 1963 and the Model 120 to 1966, according to factory sources, despite engine numbers indicating production continuing for 1967. Problems arose with the failing supplies of Lucas magnetos (absence of which was alleged to have done for BSA's

A10 range) and Burman gearboxes (ditto for the Ariel four-strokes—Burmans had turned over production to hair clippers and, all too symbolically, steering mechanisms for British Leyland cars). A prototype Model 120 was built with a Lucas alternator on an extended timing shaft, and an AMC gearbox, but the latter component proved a prohibitive factor, being four times as expensive as the Burman box. Peter Marians redeemed his previous record on the motorcycle side by fighting vigorously to ensure continuing supply of the traditional components: by the end, reconditioned magnetos were being used, as well as reconditioned gearboxes, since Burman had gone the whole hog and scrapped the tooling.

The Model 35 two-stroke outlived the Model 45 by a couple of years, using off-the-shelf components, including 2T engines no longer available from Villiers since 1964 but stockpiled by P and M. Marketed in the UK by Pride and Clarke and latterly George Grose of London EC4, the Model 35 became the latterday Red Panther, with a (poorly-applied) off-red finish, a red seat top, red ht leads and plug cap, red badge on the carburettor and so on. But though a fully equipped electric-start motor cycle was being offered for just £149 10s, sixties affluence ruled out a repeat of the 1930s success story, and the last of them were sold off at cut prices during 1969.

Two years before that, the general precision engineering side of the P and M business had been sold off to local firm Samuel Birkett Ltd, who mainly made valves for pipelines, and had no interest in motor cycles. Joe Mortimer and Alice Wharton continued to dispense the remaining spares until 1977, but Samuel Birkett Ltd was absorbed by the giant Imperial Metals Industry group, and the Horncastle Street works shut down in 1982.

Given the Panthers' durability and charm, however, that could not be the end of the story. There were exotic postscripts such as a very quick sixties sprinter run by the early Team Pegasus, a sloper converted to ohc; and the famously scruffy but competitive Classic racing outfit run by Autocycle's Chris Williams into the eighties, and christened 'Aunty Alice' in honour of the redoubtable Alice Wharton. On a heretical note for purists, one can also add that, almost alone among single cylinder motor cycles, the slopers can make extremely handsome choppers, possibly because that big inclined cylinder has the line of one half of a 'V'; and several fine examples of this sub-spieces may be seen at the shows today.

But the Panther spirit is kept alive most surely by the happy-go-lucky 500 strong Mighty Panther Owners' Club. Members include the notable eccentric Simon Desorgher, a musician and composer who performs Bach's 'Toccata in D' with an ensemble which includes his Model 100; the bike also features, alongside a computer, in his work 'The Chains and Cogs of Beelzebub.' With Autocycle, the Club also represents virtually the only source of spares, with items such as valve guides, previously supplied by a proprietary firm with marginally incorrect tolerances, now being made up in special batches of the precise dimensions and the correct grade of cast iron with sufficient carbon. Sid Wilkinson, the Club's machine registrar, summed up the Cleckheaton machines' appeal as follows: 'Panther seemed to stop at a stage where everything was simple. They're easy to work on and if they're screwed together correctly, they just keep on going.'

The kind of service a good Panther outfit can provide was spelled out for me when I ran a small Readers' Bikes-type competition in the 'Classic Days' column of the late *Motorcycling Weekly*. The winner had to be Margaret Handover, with the following description of her family's big slogger:

'Our bike is a 1961 600 cc Panther model 100, with a Canterbury Javelin D/A sidecar mounted on a Panther chassis' wrote Margaret. 'The Handover bike has many names: ''Bismarck'', so-called by scornful parking attendants at Himself's workplace (they're tin box wallahs who think she should be sunk); ''that thing'', by bike-hating mother-in-law; ''that fantastic conveyance'', by the local Minister's amused/ bemused

Above left *Details of Panther's own-brand sidecar chassis for 1959, with both Armstrong damper and wheel interchangeable with the machine's.*

Right *Heart of the matter. Handsome sloper engine here seen in 1952 rigid incarnation.*

wife. And all of them fit. ''Bismarck'' ploughs through the waves of traffic into Central London every day, torpedoeing from lane to lane, and every week battles down to the supermarket for the shopping, where she is held in such high repute she has her own parking space.

'At the weekends she turns into ''that fantastic conveyance'' transporting two adults, three children, one cat-in-a-basket, tent and camping gear all over the country to rallies, shows, and camping weekends.

'The Panther has proved to be extremely reliable and great fun, and while not the most elegant vehicle she has never failed to arrive at her destination, and with an average annual mileage of 10,000 miles at an average 45 mpg, our Panther makes for very economical travel.

'We have twice taken the outfit round Brands Hatch Circuit as part of the 1,000 Bike Festival, and what could possibly compare with slithering sideways round a wet Paddock Bend on a Panther combo with the throttle stuck open! And what more ''convenient'' way could there be to transport family, tea-urn, raffle prizes and an old lavatory pan (for the smash-the-crockery stall) to the school's spring fete? Or to cart boxes of autojumble stuff around, including an upended table strapped to the roof rack; or to tow a solo Panther to a show (front wheel out, forks bolted to the tow bar); or to bring home a second sidecar (roof rack again)—a double-decker sidecar raised a few eyebrows! . . .

'The Panther is sturdy enough to stand out in all weathers (the garage is needed for more delicate bikes) and to withstand attacks by local vandals—and still start first time and perform comfortably all that we ask of her.'

Margaret was writing in 1985, about a 24-year-old motor cycle. I think the case for Panther slopers, and for P and M's workmanship, can rest there.

Panther: The Model 65 and Model 75

The middleweights of the P and M range, these ohv 250 and 350 machines first appeared for 1949. Despite now adopting upright cylinders, they were very obviously the heirs of the pre-and immediate post-war Model 60 and Model 70, and hence the baby brothers of the big boppers.

The simple long-stroke (88 mm) engines reflected this. The Models 60 and 70 had already benefited from a 1938 improved crankcase breather (integral with the nut securing the chain sprocket to the engine shaft inside the crankcase), and a transmission shock absorber: both were as fitted on the Model 100, and these continued on the new machines. The substantial built-up crankshaft ran on lead-bronze bushes (roller bearings had been tried on the '48 Stroud Trials version, but dropped due to 'excessive mechanical noise', though expense may have been the truer reason!). The cams sat high, and the cylinder barrel was deeply spigoted into the top of the crankcase, with the slightly domed Hepolite piston giving compression ratios of 6.5:1 for both models.

Lubrication was by the semi-dry sump system, with pressure lubrication to the main bearings, and the flywheel rims returning surplus oil to the oil compartment cast integrally with the sump. The sump was redesigned to suit the range's new cradle frame, and had a capacity of 2½ pints. Like the heavyweights, both pushrods were concealed behind a single large polished cover, and the detachable rocker cover was of a similar kidney shape. The single-row primary chain was concealed in its oil bath behind a pressed steel cover with a sealing rim: this was the same as on the pre-war big ones, though post-war they had regained their alloy covers.

The 250 Model 65's initial standard version was joined for 1950 by a de luxe variant with superior trim—chromed saddle springs and primary chaincase sealing rims. More fundamentally, the former featured in its separate gearbox only a three-speed CP-series Burman, while both the latter and the Model 75 had a four-speed CP box (though their ratios were different). Ignition on the 250 was by Lucas coil with automatic advance and retard mechanism, and the rest of the sparks were taken care of by a gear-driven Lucas dynamo mounted forward of the cylinder and provided with a regulator. The 350 shared this dynamo arrangement but ignition for it was by Lucas magneto, mounted behind the cylinder and driven by a revised version of its predecessor's gear train. Amal carburettors and Burgess silencers were fitted.

The middleweights featured a new frame, still rigid, with straight tubes throughout and with a single front down-tube, but now having a full cradle beneath the engine, and a large single saddle down-tube. At the front, as optionally on their predecessors since 1947, they fitted a lighter version of the same Dowty Oleomatic air forks that were found on the Model 100 and will be described fully in the Heavyweight section. Here it can be said that they gave an adjustable, comfortable ride and progressive damping; but when wear occurred or if they were left standing and dried out, they would leak. The synthetic rubber seals of the single Kilner valve were linked to both fork legs to provide for inflation, but if a leak occurred the forks would lose their air and subsides as there were no springs inside to keep them extended. The headlamp sat forward of these forks on a gawky-looking arrangement of tubes, while behind them was mounted the Smiths Chronometric speedometer. Brakes on the 19 in wheels were on the insubstantial side at 6 in front and 6½ in rear.

Panther rider touches were present in the hinged rear mudguard, and a neat triangular toolbox mounted on the offside. Terry or Lycett saddles were standard, with chromed springs on the de luxe 65 and the 75. The 250s fitted a centrestand, while the 350 had

Above far left *Panther riders can be a little weird. A bathtub fairing, fine, but a bathtub sidecar?*

Above left *Typical mighty Panther owners' club member Drew Grant, with thirties big pussy. Note centre stand, and how man and machine are in perfect harmony on thirst for lubricant.*

Right *1952 Model 75 350.*

a spring-up prop stand in addition to a rear roller-cam roll-on stand. While solid-looking machines, weights were reasonably low at 304 lb for the 250, against a BSA C11 at 284 lb. Both bikes were down on power, however, with a claimed 10.42 at 5,000 rpm for the 250; this was strictly 40 mph commuting territory. The de luxe and the 350 at least were quite good-looking machines with their cream-panelled chromed 2⅞ gallon petrol tanks, and all sported the Panther 'escutcheon' tank badge with the model number in a little shield, below lettering that was no less handsome for echoing Triumph's logo.

There was little initial development on the models, many of which went for export to Europe, where demand for utility machines meant that the 350 in particular now outsold the heavyweights. Mid-1951 saw the chroming restrictions knock the bright-work off all but export or Stroud tanks, but the finish for 1952 rallied, with a new polychromatic blue paint job, and the same smart horizontal cream band forward of the kneepads as was featured on the Model 100. The factory reorganization of '52 precluded change in that year, and during it the Model 65 became temporarily unavailable due to the volume of engines being exported to the Swedish Svalan range.

1953 was a big change year, with swinging-arm versions of both machines being offered as alternatives to the rigid machines, which remained available until 1954 for the 350 and 1955 for the 250. On these rear-sprung machines, but not on the remaining rigids, the limitations of the Dowty fork were recognized and Panther's own first design of telescopic was substituted, with neater conventional headlamp brackets. Externally, the clue was that the air forks' bottom tubes were of polished alloy while those on the P and M oil-damped coil spring items, which featured two-way hydraulic control by means of a double taper plug, were enamelled black. The new frame was a fairly crude graft job on to the existing rigid one, with a malleable casting brazed onto the saddle down-tube, and a fulcrum shaft for the swinging arm on its lead-bronze bushes passing through the casting. A triangular rear frame of straight tubes supported a new mudguard with partial deep valances rather crudely tacked on to the existing guard's shape, and P and M's own attempt at rear dampers which gave 2½ inches of movement, and significantly were withdrawn the following year. According to marque historian Barry Jones, the original P and M prototype swinging-arm design when applied to a prototype Model 100 was 'so bad that

Left *Early competition variant. 1948 350 Stroud Trials prototype of Charles Markham.*

Right *Model 65 250 powerplant for 1953. Note also 'escutcheon' tank badge.*

the Press was not keen on publicizing details until the production version appeared', but when it did so it was improved.

For 1953 the standard Model 65 was dropped, and on the de luxe, whether rigid or spring-frame, magneto ignition became an option from now on, with the mag replacing the normal contact-breaker unit, and taking its drive from the intermediate gear driven by the cam pinion. The swinging-arm frames featured a centre-stand for both 250s and now also the 350, in place of its previous rear stand, as well as an additional toolbox on the near-side.

The 250 may have been grey porridge, but the 350 was potentially a good seller in markets like Scandinavia and the USA where its solid build was appreciated. So Frank Leach set about redesigning it for 1954 with a will. The engine was developed, with a new barrel which, like the head, had its finning area considerably enlarged; it was said to be in the light of experience with the now defunct Stroud Trials model, which had gained an alloy head and barrel in its final year—in a spurious allusion to this, the new Model 75's head was given a baked-on alloy-look finish! The inlet valve diameter was increased and stronger springs fitted on both valves, again from the Stroud. In the interest of mechanical quietness, the left-hand side of the cylinder head fins were tied by two substantial vertical cast-in pillars. Also, a new engine steady ran from the front down tube to the front of the head.

The improved engine was slotted into a redesigned spring frame, with a reinforced malleable casting for the swinging-arm, and a better-proportioned and more shapely looped rear sub-frame, with movements now controlled by Armstrong dampers, non-adjustable but still an improvement. The onset of spring frames for the Model 100 too, was celebrated by a new finish, with chrome returning to a new petrol tank: shallower but slightly larger at three gallons, over which the enamelled portion, blue for the 75, flowed back in two broad gold-lined bands of a swelling V-shape. This contained the new-style slanting capital letters tank badge, while on the chrome portion, the kneegrips also featured the Panther name. The rear-sprung 65, still with the old frame, adopted the Armstrong dampers and the tank colour scheme, while retaining the old badges and kneegrips. A final distinguishing feature between the two was a new pear-shaped silencer for the 350, similar to that year's Nortons. Dual-seats were optional for both models, as were pancake-shaped air cleaners.

Whether or not the breathed-on engine was substantially more powerful is

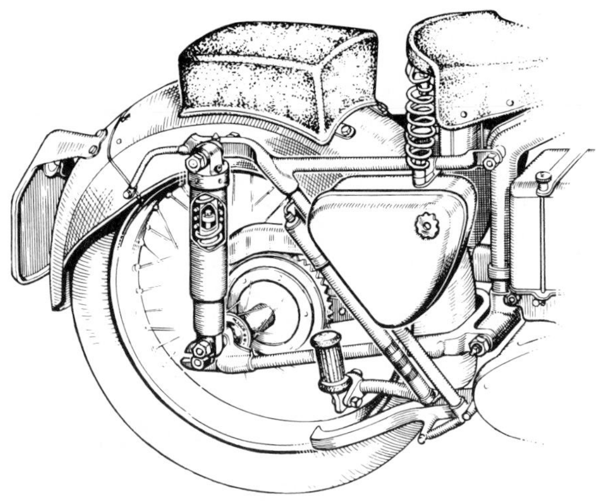

debatable—15.4 bhp at 5,000 rpm had been claimed in 1951, while from now on 15.5 at 5,500 was the given figure. Claimed weight had risen some 25 lb to 340 lb. A *Motor Cycling* road test late in the year revealed a top speed of just over 70 mph. They described its performance as 'good rather than sporty', its essential character as a 'robust constitution', and proceeded to make much of the fuel economy (65 mpg at a steady 60, rising to 110 mpg at 40)—all usually indications of lack of poke. They found the bike moderately overgeared with a 5.26:1 top, but said that this suited the engine. Faults included clack from the valve gear and piston slap when cold, brakes that were only adequate, over-flexible rubber washers in the headlamp mounting so that the light was always dipped in use, suspension 'inclined to be sluggish' (presumably harsh) 'until after considerable mileage', and a riding position spoiled by footrests mounted too high. Although these were adjustable, all positions could not be used as the exhaust pipe and rear brake pedal got in the way.

The following year, they tried out a rigid Model 65 linked to a lightweight Watsonian 'Eton' sidecar, since tax concessions for combinations of 250 cc and under had just come into force. With a steering damper fitted, and geared down by means of a 16T engine and 52T rear wheel sprocket, the little outfit proved capable of sustained 40 mph cruising. The rear brake needed frequent adjustment and oil seeped from the lower pushrod tube flange, but otherwise they were happy with the plot's sturdiness and its economy, both the initial outlay of £206 for an outfit equipped with panniers, leg-shields and a windscreen, and the 78 mpg at 40 mph which it returned on test.

1955 saw the rear-sprung Model 65S adopt the 350's frame. The Model 75, now spring-frame only, adopted a full-width front hub incorporating a 7 in brake in a tubular aluminium-alloy ribbed shell: this was optional for the 250 from now on. The rigid-framed Model 65, now in its last year, acquired the P and M telescopic front fork, and all models fitted a new Lucas MCH55 headlamp shell incorporating the speedometer, ammeter and light switch.

1956 saw the rigid frame 250 dropped. The Model 100's front forks were revised and the lighter models' forks echoed this, with the mechanism redesigned to give softer springing around the static load position, but still with adequate hydraulic checks under hard load and recoil; evidently the criticism about the 'sluggish' suspension had been absorbed. However, the middleweight fork springs were 17 in long as opposed to the Model 100's 22 in, and their wheel spindle lugs were not offset from the centre line as the slopers were. Both 250 and 350 adopted Amal Monobloc carbs with optional air filters (the latter with oil-wetted worsted elements) and enclosed rear number plates. The Model 75 adopted the elongated Lucas MCH58 headlamp shell as on that year's Model 100, as well as a new 3¼ gallon fuel tank in chrome and Sherwood Green, a welcome return to a traditional Panther finish: the 250 settled for a gold-lined maroon finish. Both adopted the new Diakon circular plastic red and silver tank badges.

And there things really stayed for the Panther middleweights, as the factory's efforts were directed to the Villiers-engined bikes and the ill-fated scooter. Leach had really tried to get the 350 right, but even so, sales were not encouraging, and thus production ran on at a low level with only minor changes relating to the rest of the range. 1957 saw dual-seats become standard for both machines, chrome side-panels introduced for the 250's tank, and as on the heavyweights, a rubber oil seal adopted in the lower portion of the big telescopic pushrod cover. Only the 250 adopted the Model 100's Burgess absorption-type silencers. From then on there seems to have

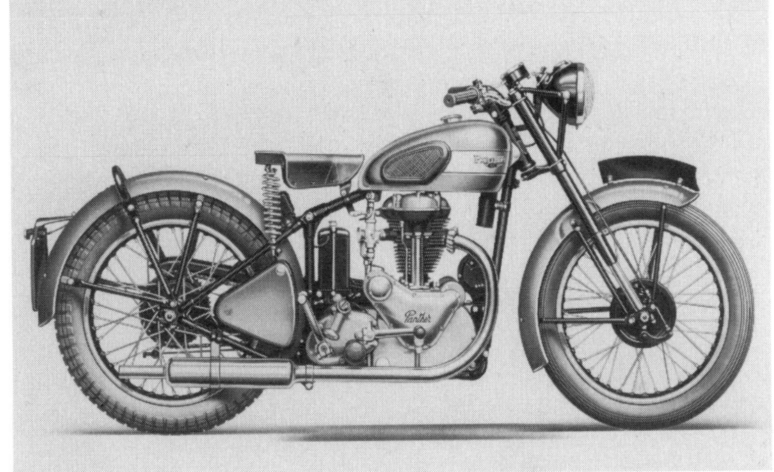

Left *First P and M swinging arm suspension, with own-brand dampers for 1953 only. Seen here on Model 65 250 — the 350's rear frame was curved.*

Right *Rigid 1953 Model 65 250 De Luxe, with four-speed gearbox and Model 75 spec finish.*

Right *Nice finish for the revised 1954 Model 75 350, with shallower tank and baked-on aluminium finish to simulate alloy head.*

Right *1957 Model 65 250. It plodded on unchanged for three more years.*

been no change, until with the shadows lengthening, the 250 was discontinued for 1961 and the 350 for 1962.

They are enigmatic bikes—utility models touched with the Panther aura—but also mysterious because they are now extremely scarce: I cannot remember ever seeing one on the road. The 250s do seem to have been uninspiring plodders with a poor power to weight ratio, but if the 350s were never roadburners, they do have a reputation for reliability, and both were well-finished machines. While probably of interest to committed Panther freaks only, like their Stroud Trials cousins, their very scarcity gives them rarity value. The downside of that is a severe absence of spares.

Panther: The Model 65 and Model 75—dates and specifications

Production dates
Model 65 standard—1949–52
Model 65 de luxe (rigid)—1949–55
Model 65S (rear sprung)—1953–60
Model 75 (rigid)—1949–54
Model 75S (rear-sprung)—1953–61

Specifications
Model 65
Capacity, bore and stroke—248 cc (60 × 88 mm)
Type of engine—ohv single
Ignition—Coil (from 1953, Magneto optional)
Weight—(1950) 304 lb (1957) 330 lb

Model 75
Capacity, bore and stroke—348 cc (71 × 88 mm)
Type of engine—ohv single
Ignition—Magneto
Weight—(1950) 314 lb (1957) 340 lb

Panther: The Model 65 and Model 75—annual development and modifications

1951
For Model 65 and 75
1 From May, chromed petrol tank panels.

1953
For Model 65 and 75
1 Swinging arm suspension (for details see text) with Panther rear units. On rear-sprung models, previous Dowty front forks replaced by Panther telescopic, with conventional headlamp brackets, centre stand, and additional toolbox on nearside.

Another view of the well-equipped 1957 Model 65 250. Good-looking but down on power.

For Model 65
2 Magneto ignition as option.

1954
For s/arm Model 65 and 75
1 Armstrong rear units fitted.
2 Dual-seats and pancake air cleaners optional.
For Model 75
3 Engine revised; more finning for head and barrel, larger diameter inlet valve, stronger springs for both valves, baked-on alloy-look finish for cylinder head.
4 New chromed 3 gallon petrol tank, shallower, with V-band of cream paint, capital letters tank badge and kneegrips marked 'PANTHER'.
5 New pear-shaped silencer.
For Model 75S
6 Revised rear sub-frame; strengthened malleable casting for swinging-arm, looped rear sub-frame.

1955
For Model 65 and 75
1 New Lucas MCH 55 headlamp shell incorporating speedo, light switch, ammeter.
2 Full-width front hub incorporating 7 in brake; standard for Model 75, optional for Model 65.
For Model 65S
3 Previous year's Model 75 spring-frame adopted.
For Model 65 (rigid)
4 Panther teles replace Dowty forks.

1956
For Model 65S and 75
1 Mechanism of front forks revised.
2 Amal Monobloc carb with optional air filters.
3 Enclosed rear number plates.
4 Diakon circular plastic red and silver tank badges.
For Model 75
5 New 3¼ gallon petrol tank with chrome side-panels.
6 Elongated Lucas MCH 58 headlamp shell.

1957
For Model 65S and 75
1 Dual-seats standard.
2 Rubber oil seals for lower portion of telescopic pushrod cover.
For Model 65S
3 Petrol tank with chrome side panels.
4 Burgess absorption-type silencer as on Model 100.

Panther: The Models 35, 35 Sports, (1956–62), 45, 45 Sports, 50 Grand Sports, and Model 35 Sports and ES Sports (1964–68)

P and M returned to Villiers power for 1956 after a 24-year lay-off. The pre-war Villiers range had gone some way to redeeming the Panthette fiasco, and the post-war machines also helped the company in its declining years as sales of the traditional four-stroke middleweights fell off. Production, however, would never be high: the total figure for the thirteen years involved was just over 4,000, and that included the Princess scooter.

Frank Leach got the ball rolling with a pair of 197 cc machines, the 8E-engined three-speed 10/3 and the 9E-powered four-speed 10/4. For 1957 they were joined by the Model 35 with the popular 2T 249 cc twin cylinder engine introduced by Villiers the previous year. (A Model 25, powered by 2H 246 cc single cylinder engine was also proposed, but never reached production: at 11.5 bhp, it was reckoned under-powered.) Since the 2T unit and its very similar 3T larger brother formed the basis of the Cleckheaton two-strokes for over ten years, some description is in order.

The 2T unit produced a claimed 15 bhp at 5,500 rpm, with the later Sports version rated at 16 bhp, and the ES Dynastart at 17 bhp to compensate for the starter's drag. Within its power-egg shape it featured a built-up crankshaft with a middle main bearing, cleverly arranged so that overall engine width was no greater than the previous single cylinder motor. A centre disc was bolted to the crankcase to separate the two chambers, and the middle journal of the shaft had an enlarged mid-section, bearing a synthetic rubber oil seal. The drive side main was a ball bearing, the timing side and the middle ones were unlipped rollers. Lubrication was assisted by oil-drain holes in the crankcase casting. Con-rods were of steel, and ran on uncaged roller big-end bearings.

The iron barrels were separate castings with air space between them, and were

inclined forward at a slight angle to the aluminium crankcase. Finning extended right down to crankcase level, and was shaped to give each cylinder an oval appearance. At the base of each barrel was a spigot about 1 in deep and cut away front and rear to clear the con-rod. Transfer passages were in the accepted Villiers mode, inclining slightly rearward. The inboard passages curved less far from the cylinder walls than did the outboard, because of the close cylinder centres. To minimize ring, the upper cylinder fins were linked front and rear by cast-in ties. The heads were separate, and of Y-alloy: they had half-pear shaped combustion chambers, with spark plugs facing to the rear, tilted back at an angle of about 30° to the cylinder axis. Head gaskets were of solid aluminium, and there were four studs and sleeve nuts per cylinder. Flat-topped pistons with two pegged compression rings gave a compression ratio of 8.2:1. On the Sports versions this would be raised to 8.7 or 9.4:1, on the Super Sports and Dynastart to 10:1.

The 6 volt electrics were supplied by an adaptation of the Villiers flywheel magneto-generator system introduced for the 1953 1H, with the magneto much smaller than its predecessors, so that external remote coils had to be used. The flywheel magneto, mounted on the right-hand side, had a remote outboard single-lobe cam keyed to an extension of the mainshaft. This cam protruded through the right-hand engine cover into a recess, closed by a detachable oval-shaped end cover, in which were installed twin contact breakers. (The end cover was echoed by an identical one on the drive side chaincase, and one or both of these sometimes carried the logo of the marque using the Villiers engine: but in the case of Panther, it was 'Villiers' on either side.)

There was a separate ignition circuit for each cylinder, energized via one of the two condensers on the armature plate, which meant that each cylinder could be timed independently. The lighting circuit was independent of the ignition; and a selenium rectifier was used to convert alternating current from the magneto's lighting coils to direct current. The headlamp switch was fitted with a middle 'L' position, with only one lighting coil in use, as well as a further 'H' position giving the full output of the generator. A detachable key to operate the ignition switch poked out of the top of the right-hand generator casting in the crankcase.

Both cylinders were served by a single Villiers S22/2 carburettor, with the air slide worked in the Panther's case by cable from the handlebars. The carb was fitted onto a cast-iron induction manifold, insulated by a washer from the cylinder, and acting as a vertical bar to divide air flow evenly between the two ports. The complete carburettor was concealed beneath a smooth cast-aluminium cover into which was built a part-conical mesh and fabric air filter. Located by dowels and secured by a knurled screw, the rounded cover did not sit flush on top of the crankcase and gearbox, as there was an air gap about ¼ in deep on each side to prevent heat building up. A four-speed gearbox was bolted to the crankcase to form a unit, with ratios of 6.2:1, 8.2:1, 11.7:1 and 19:1. Primary drive was by single strand ⅜ in pitch chain running in an oil bath. The 4½ in diameter clutch fitted four plates with Neolangite friction segments. The engine had four frame attachment lugs in positions identical to those on the single cylinder engines, so that they were interchangeable, and in the lugs were fitted proprietary rubber-bonded bushes to minimize engine vibration. All-up weight of the unit was 94 lb, rising to 114 lb with the Dynastart version. The 2T is generally reckoned to be one of the pleasantest units Villiers came up with.

Panther fitted this powerplant into cycle parts identical to their previous smaller Villiers singles, though for that year, brakes were increased from 5 in to 6 in. The frame was a fully welded job, with its elliptical swinging-arm cross-braced. The swinging-arm pivoted on Silentbloc bushes, and was controlled by non-adjustable Armstrong units tilted forward to match the angle of the front-downtube and to cleverly echo that of the tilted parallelogram-shaped side-panels, which were hinged and set in the well-panelled mid-section, concealing battery, rectifier, and toolbox, with the horn set in the panelling facing forward. These pressed steel components were produced for Cleckheaton by Ernie Earles.

Above left *One that never was. Prototype 1957 Villiers 2H-powered single, rejected for lack of poke.*

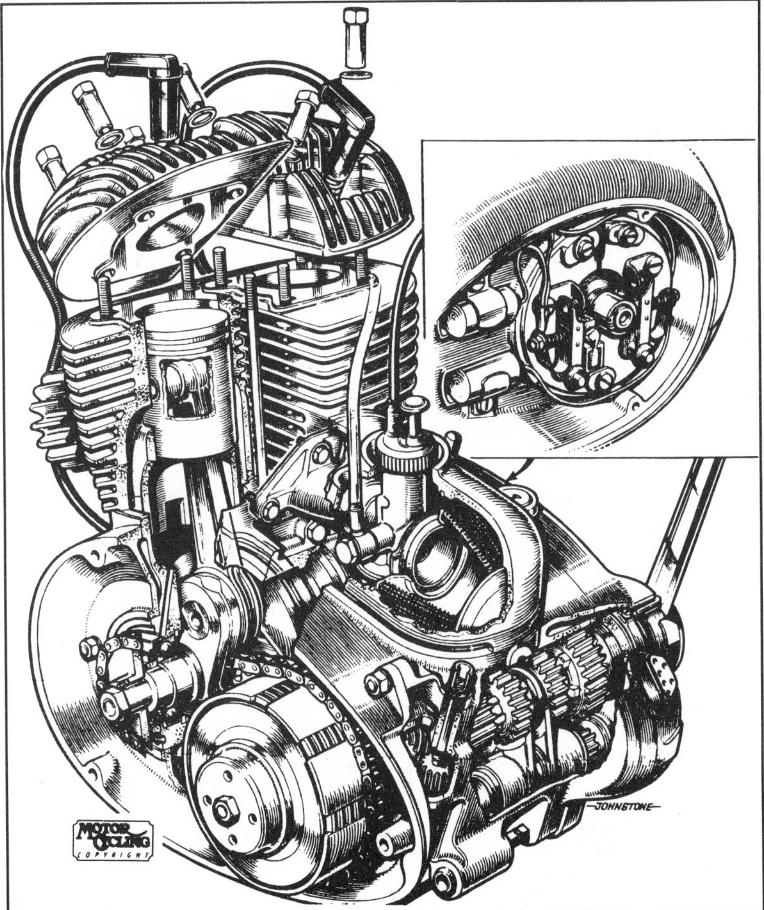

Right *Villiers 249cc 2T twin anatomized. Inset shows twin contact breakers and condensers.*

At the front end were what appeared on first glance to be conventional telescopic forks, but on closer inspection proved to be Reynolds-Earles pivoted front forks, with a swinging-arm pivoting at the back on steel-encased rubber bushes, and curvy pivot support tubes following the line of the rear of the mudguard. The suspension units, carried where a conventional fork's bottom tubes would have been, were initially Girlings but changed after two months to 'Armstrong units, to Panther specification'. The upper portions of the fabricated fork stanchions were open, and enshrouded the top of the shock absorbers, with which they were substantially co-axial.

However, there is a question mark over these forks, as though perfectly adequate with the lighter singles, they did not prove strong enough for the larger Villiers engines and were known to snap near the pivot point. This was confirmed for me by British two-stroke expert Nick Kelly, who states that he personally knows of three Panther riders whose forks snapped; one, to whom it happened even though the bike was travelling in a straight line, limps permanently as a result. These breakages occurred at a time when the machines were new or near-new. Certainly the Earles forks were shortly strengthened, and replaced by conventional forks before very long.

Otherwise, for the early Model 35, valanced mudguards for its 18 in wheels were ample without being excessive, the 2½ gallon maroon petrol tank was gold-lined and fitted the plastic tank badge, and a large dual-seat was standard. These smooth-running machines gave good service up to a top speed of around 70 mph, and at 290 lb were solid without being ponderous. At a price of just below £180 they represented reasonable value.

For 1958 Panther followed up with a Sports version with the compression raised to 9.4:1, and the engines, as historian Barry Jones dubiously puts it, 'supposedly tuned' individually before leaving the Cleckheaton works, with polished ports and 'precision assembly'. This purported to produce a top speed of 76 mph. A 7 in front brake was fitted, and the front fork for the Sports was modified; the upper portions of the stanchions were longer, raising the front of the machine, and the position of the fork pivots was altered to ensure that the fork arms were less steeply inclined. Finish of the Sports was Sea Mist/Pearl Grey, and chromed side panels were fitted on the tank.

1959 saw the ante upped again with the Model 45 Sports, using the Villiers 324 cc 3T twin unit—identical to the 2T but bored out from 50 to 57 mm. Developed for use in cars, the 3T had been adapted for motor cycles the previous year, losing the fan cooling, reverse gear, and the Siba Dynastart motor which gave the reverse capability by allowing the engine to run backwards: the Dynastart could also be wired to work as an electric start. The same applied to the 2T, which could be supplied with the Dynastart, fan cooling, and electric start for use in invalid carriages, three-wheelers, and scooters. It too could be started in either direction, though in reverse the use of first gear only was recommended!

The 325's cycle parts were identical with the 250, but to cope with the extra power of

Left *Panther 35 Sports for 1959. Note discrete Earles forks, which had already been (discretely) strengthened.*

Above right *1960, and* Motor-cycling*'s Bernal Osborne gets down to it on a Model 50 Grand Sports 350, on a wet day at MIRA.*

the tuned engine (the 45 Sports' claimed output being 18 bhp at 5,500 rpm) the front forks for both the 250s and the newcomer were strengthened, with a curved tube connecting the two stanchions immediately above the fork pivot, and two U-shaped 16-gauge steel pressings welded as gussets into the angle formed between the stanchion upper and lower members. The rear fork too was beefed up by the welding of ⅛ in thick steel plates across the pivot and cross tubes, and the joining of the plates to the fork arms by gussets. All the joints in the bolted-on rear sub-frame were also connected to the rear engine plates by two 1 × ¼ in steel plates. The Model 45 had a compression ratio of 8.0:1, and pulled higher overall gearing than the 35 by the use of a 25-tooth engine sprocket, with ratios of 18, 11, 7.8 and 5.9:1 top against the 35's 6.2:1; it was a genuine 75 mph motor cycle.

Though another 3T-engined Panther had appeared at the 1958 Show as the Model 50 Sports, it was not until late October 1959 that 'the first production job', now known as the Grand Sports, after 'very careful development' was available for a *Motor Cycling* test. The most immediately striking feature was the rear enclosure, matched by a front mudguard suitably valanced to give a curious crescent shape, and with a lifting handle behind the imitation hide-covered dual-seat. The enclosure was done by extending the existing panelling back to the rear number plate; it wasn't badly proportioned, as such things went, and won Leach a Design Council award. Owners were less impressed when the time came for tyre or wheel work, as there was an obstructive cut-down version of the standard Model 35/45's rear mudguard beneath the panelling.

The next point of note was that the Earles forks had been replaced by Panther's own heavyweight telescopic forks as used on the Model 120, with their two-way hydraulic damping and internal springs fitted inside the main stanchion tubes. This was not the only big Panther component on the Model 50, which was claimed to be the fruit of collaboration between P and M and Villiers. While the prototype's initial siamezed exhaust system had been abandoned on the grounds of 'better cooling and reliability' (though it will be noted that they were fitted to the later Model 35s) in favour of separate exhaust pipes and Villiers' own silencers with

seams, heavyweight Panther gear included a 7 in Lucas headlamp, and (on 18 in rims) big full-width hub 8 in brakes, both as fitted on the Model 120, though with much less satisfactory results. This was because, at the rear, to enable the big hub to be used, P and M bolted a sprocket to the left side and had the drum on the right operated by a cable looping under the engine rather than a cross-over linkage—making for spongy operation. (It also lacked the heavyweight's sealed rear drum, which meant interesting behaviour in the wet, with both front and rear badly affected by water fade—and then the 8 in rear suddenly coming into action.) Down-turned handlebars were a further Grand Sports peculiarity.

Motor Cycling's Bernal Osborne duly tested this middleweight 325 in late 1959 and found that while it handled and steered well, putting the new motor and front fork on a frame originally designed for a 197 cc engine led to noticeably high ground clearance, an awkwardly high position of the kick start, and a high footrest position 'to which the rider had necessarily to accustom himself'—

adjustable controls helped him to do so. (This 'garden gate' frame aspect actually applied to all rear-sprung Panthers.) The change from siamezed exhaust to twin pipes meant that the prop stand was screened by the nearside pipe: since neither it nor the centre stand had extension pieces, they were inaccessible, and the centre stand needed a lot of effort to use.

Otherwise, he praised the unit's smoothness and good acceleration, which he correctly deemed more important than top speed. The latter was just over 75 mph: the 3T had been de-tuned, with 8:1 compression retained, but standard settings on its ignition and S25/3 carburettor. Consequently, power was down on the 45 Sports, at 16.5 bhp at 5,000 rpm, and with all the heavyweight goodies, the weight was up by nearly 45 lb at 333 lb dry, making it the heaviest Villiers-powered motor cycle of all time! Both the headlamp and brakes did prove good however, the latter stopping the middleweight in 30 ft from 30 mph in the dry.

In the event, only 372 Model 50s were produced, but 1960 also saw the Model 35 adopt the 50's rear enclosure and dual-seat, though not the big front mudguard. More significantly, all the 250 and 324 cc two-strokes also acquired Panther telescopic front forks, although these were versions of the ones from the middleweight Model 65/75 range, with cheap and nasty pressed steel yokes in place of the middleweight's forged yokes. For sidecar work the Model 50's fork was reversed, and a block welded on to centralize the wheel. All but the Model 50 (and the 197s) changed their Lucas electrical gear for Miller equipment—on the grounds of a familiar Cleckheaton preoccupation, namely economy.

There was no development for the next couple of years on the models that concern us, though on the withdrawal of the 9E engine, the 10/3 went for 1961, and for 1962 the standard Model 35 was discontinued: with the arrival of the Official Receiver in October 1962, the Model 50 was quickly axed. 1963 saw the Sports 35 axed, but the standard 35 with its puny 6 in front brake, was reintroduced, probably to use up stocks. The 45 soldiered on through 1964 but was no longer available after the end of it.

Production of Panther two-strokes had

actually ceased in December 1962, but then restarted during April 1964, in a bizarre example of the involved Lilliputian politics of the British two-stroke. Details were supplied to me by the indefatigable Nick Kelly. It will be recalled that during 1962/63, Kaye Don's Ambassador concern had gone out of motor cycle production, selling up to DMW. The latter, although pleased to acquire the extra spares and tooling, had little interest in continuing the name, and though Ambassador models were still catalogued for 1963 and 1964, only about twenty were actually built. One Ambassador model had been the 2T-engined Electra 75 250 with Siba Dynastart which at £217 had proved too expensive to sell much. When DMW followed Villiers production and switched to 4T engines for 1964, a job lot of ex-Ambassador electric-start 2T motors became available, extremely cheaply.

P and M, to whom the prospect of a bargain was always like blood in the water to a shark, snapped them up. This explains both discrepancies in the engine numbers of apparently '1965' and later Panther models; and why Panther two-stroke production restarted in mid-1964.

Distribution of the new model was turned over to Pride and Clarke, who not unnaturally marketed it as the Red Panther, and in all 512 were built, 215 of them with electric start, indicated by an 'S' prefix; the first engine number was W101A. It now came in two forms, the standard, using up P and M's stock of kickstart engines, or the Model 35ES with 12 volt electrics and the Siba Dynastart electric start. Although this device has not enjoyed the best of reputations, usually because owners neglected to clean off the carbon dust and change the brushes every 8,000 miles, Nick Kelly confirmed that on his own Red Panther, it worked well and was simple to maintain.

The frames of these late two-strokes were said to have been revised to give improved handling, though the only differences Kelly could discern were a reduction in the steering head angle of around 3 degrees, and at the rear on the 1964 machines only an extra bar welded in to take attachment screws for the toolboxes, because the midriff panelling was now deleted. The 35 Sports had a single 6-volt battery box and a toolbox topped by a steel plate, while the 12 volt ES had a pair of 6 volt batteries in series, and a tin tool tray bolted to the steel plate and located under the seat. ES models had no ammeter. A larger front fork was fitted with full damping: this was the actual Model 65/75 fork, with the forged yoke in place of the previous pressed steel. The electric start models had no kickstart, though several were fitted with one as they helped turn the engine over. Off-the-shelf cycle parts included chromed steel sports mudguards, a tiny flyscreen carrying the mandatory front number plate across its bottom half, a slimmer, lower-mounted dual-seat with a red top, and a Speedwell kidney-shaped fuel tank (as seen on contemporary James and Francis-Barnett sports models, the Royal Enfield Continental and later DMW Sports twin), but with the Panther plastic badges.

As mentioned, the midriff enclosure went in favour of conventional triangular tool and battery boxes off the Model 65/75, and they, like the frame, forks, headlamp, tank, chainguard and suspension units were covered with poorly applied coats of Devil Red paint which varied in colour from batch to batch, with red plug leads and caps, and to complete the theme, a red badge on the now-exposed carburettor, which was an S25 on these later 35 models, with a 170 main jet for the kickstart and 190 for the ES models. An additional forty or so went out with black cycle parts and a green or a yellow petrol tank. While the engine remained the familiar 2T, it had had its compression raised to 10:1, and a siamezed exhaust system was fitted. Nick Kelly claims to have seen 80 mph on his 35ES, says it handled well, and with the exception of the puny 5½ in front brake as on the 197 cc models,

Above left *Nice pearl-grey Model 35 Sports for 1960.*

Right *Red Panther! Much-revised Model 35ES for 1965. Both bike and company were in the red.*

reckons it one of the best of the many two-stroke Brits he has ridden.

For 1966 when Panther's own stockpile of kickstart 2Ts was exhausted, only the electric start version was available, and these appear to have continued to be made until October 1968, the last Villiers-powered twins. The last known example was sold by Whitby's of Acton, part of the Pride and Clarke chain, during 1969; the asking price had been cut to £90, but the purchaster managed to beat them down to just £69! Today, though thin on the ground, a Panther two-stroke would make a good choice for utility transport with a touch of the unusual. While Villiers spares are plentiful enough, the cycle parts, especially for the problematic Earles forks, are not. The '65-on bikes are favourite; the 12 volt ES versions with 90 watts output and 50 per cent overload meant reliable starting as well as lights in the remarkable category for a sixties Brit. The pre-'63 7 in Motobrake hub can be fitted easily as the mountings are the same, and a sportier look achieved by the use of a 19 in hub for the front wheel as on the Model 65/75. All in all, a 1965–68 Red Panther, with the superior front fork and simplified ancillaries, and its blend of history, the workaday and the exotic, would probably be the favourite addition to anyone's collection.

Panther: The Model 35, Model 45 and Model 50—dates of specifications

Production dates

Model 35—1957–61, 1963, 1964–65
Model 35 Sports—1958–62
Model 45 Sports—1959–62
Model 50 Grand Sports—1960–62
Model 35ES—Mid-1964–68

Specifications

Model 35, 35 Sports, 35ES

Capacity, bore and stroke—249 cc (50 × 63.5 mm)
Type of engine—Two-stroke twin
Ignition—Flywheel magneto
Weight—Model 35 (1959) 290 lb

Model 45 Sports, Model 50 Grand Sports

Capacity, bore and stroke—324 cc (57 × 63.5 mm)
Type of engine—Two-stroke twin
Ignition—Flywheel magneto
Weight—Model 45 Sports (1959) 309 lb, Model 50 Grand Sports (1960) 333 lb

Panther: The Model 35, Model 45 and Model 50—annual development and modifications

1959

For Model 35, Model 35 Sports and Model 45 Sports

1 Earles front forks, rear swinging-arm and rear sub-frame strengthened (for details see text).

1960

For Model 35, 35 Sports and 45 Sports

1 Telescopic forks adopted, as on Model 65/75 but with pressed steel yokes.
2 Previous Miller electrical equipment changed to Lucas.

For Model 35 Sports and 45

3 Rear enclosure as on Model 50.

1964

For Model 35 and Model 35ES

1 Mid-year, on reintroduced 250s (for details of which see text), front fork steering head angle reduced by around 3° and extra bar welded at rear to take toolbox attachment screws.
2 Front forks with yokes as on Model 65/75.

Panther: The Model 100R, Model 100S, Model 100S de luxe, and Model 120S

It is very often the sound that first hooks a person on Panthers, the deep steady double donk (if it's a twin-port head) that gives a whole new meaning to the phrase 'the earth moved'. 'I knew instinctively', wrote marque historian Barry Jones of his first encounter with a P and M sloper, 'that the gentle thump-thump of the big lazy engine was what I would require of a machine built to last.' As virtually the only twin-port head single built post-war, it's a distinctive sound, too.

The development of the sloper before the war has been sketched in the marque history section, and the post-war product represented pretty much the perfected article that the company claimed. Not in the sense of being the fastest, the best handling, or the most elegant motorcycle, but meaning that

Model 100, still girder-forked, for 1946. World War 2? No problem.

with one or two exceptions it was very well suited to its main intended purpose, pulling a sidecar economically on the roads of the day with their 30–40 mph average journey times: if something broke it was not a matter of major engineering work to put it right. So it would go on doing what it did, with a style that was all its own, for a very long time indeed.

Naturally, the characteristics that made an engine suitable for sidecar work were good pulling power in the lower and middle ranges, and here the Model 100 excelled. Paradoxically the torque figure on paper is a not unduly impressive 20–23 ft/lb, but while the Model 100's similarly modest maximum power figure of 23.3 bhp is developed at 5,300 rpm, maximum torque is reached at 3,500 rpm, with a virtually flat curve from there back to zero. Add the motive power of a pair of 14 lb flywheels and it will be understood that the feeling of low and medium urge is no illusion, while the lack of outright power has the positive benefit of ensuring low and slow rates of wear within the engine.

It was exactly the right power for pulling a sidecar; and the economy was achieved by the use of a single small bore (1⅛ in) carburettor, initially an Amal Type 276. The additional fact that the carb was mounted level and thus at a 40° *updraught* angle to the slanted cylinder, discouraged any gulping on the part of the big one lung. A 1946 sloper returned 86 miles to the gallon on average in solo trim, while a 1949 combination gave 60 mph overall—between 10 and 20 more miles to the gallon than a twin or any other 500 single could be expected to return in harness. The later 650 Model 120, by the use of the early type Model 100's smaller exhaust valuve, a squish head and an only slightly larger carburettor, achieved an even more impressive average of 70 mpg. This fuel economy was coupled with an initial outlay that was always kept relatively low. A 1957 rear-sprung Model 100 cost £223, exactly the same as a Matchless G80S 500 single, and some £30 less than a 650 twin like the Ariel Huntmaster. The downside, more costly today than then, was oil consumption, which while around 200 mpp on a new Model 100, as we shall see fell dramatically on the Model 120, where figures of 120 mpp were recorded on near-new test machines, and it could go as low as 80 miles to the pint once an engine was worn.

Inside the engine, the built-up crank with those substantial flywheels, on the drive-side ran on a roller and, separated by a wall, a deep-groove ball-bearing, with a roller bearing only on the timing side; the engine sprocket was simply pressed up on the taper of the

Left *Model 100, circa 1952 — cutaway view.*

Right *Heavyweight lubrication system.*

drive shaft. There were occasionally problems associated with these main bearings. A recent rebuild described in *Classic Bike* reckoned that P and M must have machined the crankcases individually to achieve the correct tolerances; and the Model 100 always had a problem with main bearings for rumble, and occasionally with location, when the bearings, particularly on the drive-side, would rotate on the crankshaft. The reason was the cylinder/crankcase clamping method, which will be dealt with later; there were no cylinder base flange nuts. The clamping method would be tackled, though not successfully, with the later, more powerful, 650.

The flywheels played a part in the unusual lubrication system. This featured a conventional reciprocating plunger-type oil pump, but its function was limited to the feed side. Both the camshaft and the magneto were gear-driven, and this pump was driven by an intermediate timing gear which was integral with the pump's rotor. The oil was drawn from the four-pint finned sump compartment jutting out from the front of the crankcase, but internally separated from it. (There was a flaw associated with the sump compartment; it could occasionally leak internally, causing a badly smoking engine, as if the valve guides were well-worn.) The oil passed through a gauze strainer on the drain plug and was then fed via an oilway, from the rear of the cylinder and from the timing gears, to lubricate the big end and to spray the cylinder walls.

A perennial trouble with an inclined engine was due to gravity, with oil starvation to the inlet valve, located at its uppermost point. P and M's eventual answer was an external pipe running up on the timing side from the pump to spray the inlet valve-gear (though it still missed the valve stem) and the rest of the conventional breathing set-up, which was located in the iron cylinder head beneath a distinctive one-piece kidney-shaped alloy rocker cover. The latter was fastened on by seven ¼ in and two ⅜ in bolts, and care had to be taken not to overtighten them when replacing it if leaks were to be avoided.

From there the pump's role was over, as the return part of the system relied on other means. Oil mist from the head was channelled down inside the thick chromed telescopic pushrod cover, which was in two parts, a broader, shorter, bottom half covering the two tappets, and a longer, narrow top portion concealing the pushrods themselves; the lubricant served all that and the camshaft en route. There was also a second external metal oil line to drain oil back from the exhaust valve pocket; this pipe tended to be a source of oil leaks. Once the oil was back down in the crankcase, the really vintage part of the system came into play, with the big flywheels scooping the lubricant over a knife-edge weir and back into its compartment. Crankcase pressure was taken care of by a ball-and-spring type by-pass valve activated at 20 psi, but it rarely came to that. Barry Jones thinks that with the roller big end bearings, oil pressure on average was only about 10 psi, certainly never enough to operate an oil pressure gauge. To check circulation, with the engine running one unfastens a small hexagon-headed screw behind the cylinder, on the nearside in front of the magneto, to reveal the oilway from the pump to the cylinder wall; no more than a slow ooze of oil says that all is well, and the same slow ooze is the only evidence necessary if you then undo the top of the inlet feed up to the rockers. The system really worked by mist lubrication rather than oil circulation, and functioned best when the engine was pulling hard.

But work it did, in the same way that the head and cylinder, though sparsely finned, nevertheless experienced little overheating or rapid wear. Gradual and progressive running-in were necessary, however, on a new or rebuilt motor, and like a pre-unit BSA twin, the big Panthers took time to settle in, and ran sweeter as the mileage accumulated. A potential trouble spot on the cylinder head, whether single or twin port, was the finned iron cooling ring at the port, which either worked loose, or rusted and caused corrosion around the port inserts and the surrounding fins. The twin port heads were there primarily to tackle the problem of silencing a big single of this type, with the single port option for sidecarrists who didn't want an extra silencer between them and the chair. To save money and trouble, many owners simply blanked off the nearside port when the time came for replacement, and reportedly this causes no problems. The single port set-up is said to be marginally

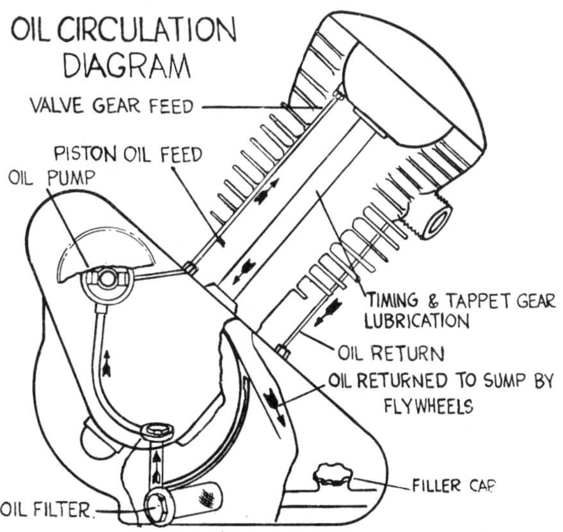

faster, though very noisy! The twin pipes do look handsome, though.

The method of fixing the engine at the front down tube was similarly crude but effective. In the crankcase, two bosses were cast in on either side of the main bearings, and up through them passed two massive ⅜ in diameter U-bolts, with the bottom U-portion a saddle fit beneath the cases. At their top end the bolts located in a massive lug positioned beneath the bottom of the steering stem just behind the forward sidecar mounting lug, with cylinder head nuts clamping down the whole assembly, and a copper ring beneath the head. With conventional rear engine plates, and the added presence of six cylinder head retaining bolts, two of which passed down into the cylinder to provide fore-and-aft support, the top of the engine could be worked on without removing it from the frame.

The separate gearbox was a BA series Burman, dubbed BAP, which in some respects was adapted for Panther requirements. 'P' denoted a top-pivoting box, and the only other model to use it was the Vincent Comet; and even that used very different internal ratios, and a different clutch. Panther codes appear to be G71 before 1950, GB50 from 1950–58, and GB29A from 1958-on. Few components were interchangeable with the bottom-pivoting boxes used by AMC, Velocette and Ariel. There were small but significant internal differences, one such being the size of the clutch's roller bearings; these looked like the conventional 0.25 × 0.25 rollers, but in fact were 0.25 × 0.35 items, and the clutch could seize if the former were mistakenly used. The box was lubricated by grease as well as a pint of oil, and from cold there was some drag until it warmed up to its working temperature.

The small diameter three-plate, five-spring clutch was in fact a major weak point, unexpected in a sidecar bike. It could slip easily, though some examples don't. Today the Ferodo inserts for the plates are not available, so some use cork inserts and run the clutch dry, with an occasional squirt to lubricate the primary chain. Furthermore, the spot where the clutch centre was splined onto the gearbox mainshaft was a bad point for wear, with the centre retained on an inadequate portion right at the end of the shaft. The situation would worsen with the more powerful 650s; but today Loctite on the splines is a partial solution, and the POC have details of modifications necessary when retoothing the centre. The clutch incorporated cush-drive rubbers, with six steel discs with deep elliptical recesses sitting inside the six cush rubbers; these discs are currently difficult to obtain.

The kickstart quadrants also tended to soften at one end and then shed their teeth. A final minus point about the Burman box was the method of adjusting it to tension the single strand primary chain behind its two-part alloy chaincase cover. The box pivoted on its top mounting when the latter was loosened off, and was moved back by twin small-diameter adjuster bolts at the bottom. If the box was anything less than perfectly free to move on its pivot, the resistance would rapidly cause the small cycle-threads of the adjuster bolts to strip.

The Pussies' electrics consisted of the gear-driven Lucas magneto, mounted rearward of the cylinder, and initially post-war incorporating automatic advance and retard, in the interests of easier starting. This was betokened by a bulge in the primary chaincase, which stayed even after the system reverted to the manual control that most Panther pilots then preferred. The dynamo was at first located separately above the magneto, and chain-driven by it.

The cycle parts included 3.25 × 19 in wheels front and rear, though not yet interchangeable, with 7 in front and 8 in rear single-sided brakes; the brake cams ran on iron bushes, and once again were vulnerable to rusting up. The rigid frame was essentially the one adopted in 1939, with triangulated tank-top tubes, and a massive single-saddle down-tube with brazed-on battery support bracket; a toolbox was mounted on the offside only. Though a long-looking set-up due to the sloping engine, actual wheelbase was a conventional 54 in, and the bike was not as heavy as the massive powerplant implied either, with a reasonable dry weight of 385 lb.

From 1947, the pre-war girder forks had given way to Dowty Oleomatic air forks, with the 7 in headlamp sitting forward of them on tubular mounts. Developed from wartime work with aircraft undercarriages, this fork used air as the sole springing medium, with about half a pint of oil providing damping. It was reckoned

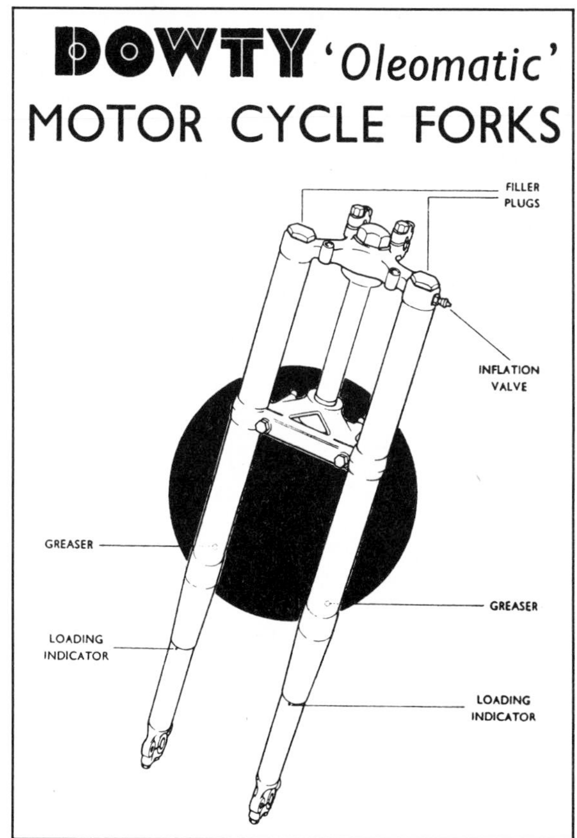

especially suitable for sidecar work, due to the ability to alter the height with increased air. The Panther version would also involve the use of a patented BSA wheel spindle clamp allowing the bottom members to be turned through 180°, giving either solo or sidecar trail.

Springing was progressive, with the fork showing 42 psi with a rider mounted, 250 psi with the fork fully compressed, and 20 psi on full rebound. The forks were light, they afforded 5½ in of movement and the system when new worked well enough to be adopted by Velocette, Scott and EMC. After 20,000 miles of testing to (characteristically) make up their own mind, the Cleckheaton folk adopted it for the Model 100, with a lighter version going on the Model 65 and 75.

What the tests could not involve, however, was a sufficient period to judge deterioration with time; and it was time that would attack the seal material on the forks and on the single Kilner valve which for the Panther version was used to top them up. Topping up would prove a tiresomely frequent chore, which also provided an opportunity to let dust and dirt in and wear the seals further; though the worst deterioration happened when a bike was left to stand for a period, and the seals dried out. The Japanese use of air forks is now widespread, but not only is modern seal material effective, but their forks also include springs as a back-up. Not so the Oleomatic, so when the forks leaked badly enough, the thing subsided into unridability. It would be replaced after a mere seven years, a gnat-bite in Cleckheaton terms.

As mentioned, the Panther was a handsome and well-finished bike, with wide handlebars and an ample Terrys saddle. For 1950 it fitted a chromed tank with lined Cream or optional Panther Green panels, the 'escutcheon' tank badge with its looped script and tiny shield beneath containing the model number, and kneegrips with the Panther name in a rectangular box. But it was far from just a pretty face, and abounded in functional rider touches. These included eccentric cam rear chain adjustment, cush drive in the Enfield rear hub, and the unique and easy-to-use Panther roller-cam rear stand, working off the rear wheel spindle bracket. This stand, in conjunction with a hinged rear mudguard, and with the mudguard-stay-cum-stand bolted to the front guard, minimized the chores at puncture time. The rear chain was lubricated, via a needle-valve, from the primary chaincase. No special tools were needed to work on the bikes, not even a feeler gauge, as valve clearance was set with the tappets just free to spin. Another convenience, introduced in pre-war days, was an ingenious coupling which allowed the magneto, and later the magdyno, to be rapidly removed without disturbing the drive or timing. This was managed by having the magneto drive shaft driven not by a gear or sprocket, but by a pair of facing dogs with a square slice of Ferodo material sandwiched between them. This fibre dog coupling was a cruciform shape up to the introduction of the magdyno for 1951, after which a square-shaped fibre dog was adopted. Both types of dog are now difficult to obtain.

So there sat your handsome Model 100, but there was still the problem of starting it. Sharing a 6:5:1 compression ratio with the other post-war Panther four-strokes past and future, the task doesn't sound too daunting, but it acquired legendary status. The problem was the inertia of the flywheels, coupled with the long stroke, so that thrust was lost before it could generate a useful reciprocating motion. Cyril Ayton described it as 'like stamping on an old-fashioned tyre inflater with a leak; but more tiring'. Some relief was at hand, however, not only in the shape of an exhaust valve lifter, but with its companion, another of P and M's patented wheezes, the half-compression device. This was worked by a small toe-operated lever protruding from the timing cover. A small third lobe or pawl on the exhaust camshaft was thereby brought into operation and so raised the exhaust valve slightly, letting the

Above left *The Dowty 'Oleomatic' forks.*

Right *Model 100 for 1949. Note bump for auto-advance on the timing chest.*

Left *1954 Rigid Model 100, with first Panther telescopics.*

Below right *Earlier type Armstrong rear shock absorber.*

Below far right *Possibly the handsomest model, though some prefer the rigid. Rear sprung 600 for 1954.*

engine turn over the compression stroke, and by halving the compression made starting easier. Equally important, unlike a conventional valve lifter, the device would stay in operation with the engine running, until it had caught properly.

Model 100s did not have performance—they worked. A solo version's top speed was 70 mph, but then again, one with a chair attached could very nearly equal that also. Optimum cruising, sorry, working speed was around the 50 mph mark, and a Panther outfit, fully or even excessively loaded, would maintain this literally up hill and down dale, with only the steepest grades making it necessary to drop from top to third. It did what it did.

Development was necessarily sparse. For 1950 manual ignition control for the magneto returned by popular demand, allowing those versed in its operation even more extensive use of top gear. In 1951, the triangular toolbox lids became slightly domed, in contrast to the previous flat ones. The rear tyre was now of 3.50 × 19 in dimensions, and an improved rear light was fitted. In mid-year, chrome restrictions led to painted tanks for all but export models, but by 1952 these were attractively styled in grey enamel, with a horizontal cream band forward of the knee-pads. For that year a Lucas magdyno replaced the previous arrangement of the separate dynamo mounting with its two-stage drive; and full tubular mudguard stays replaced the previous half-round stampings. Nothing much happened for 1953, the year of factory reorganization, though the first rear-springing was being tried out on the middleweights, and followed shortly for the Model 100.

So 1954 saw the Dowty fork replaced by a relatively crude new heavyweight telescopic, with a large diameter upper tube and shroud. It featured coil springs and two-way hydraulic damping by means of a double-taper plug; and was strengthened for sidecar work by double clamps on either side of the steering column lower lug where it held the main stanchion tubes. It no longer had the BSA spindle arrangement, so the trail was non-adjustable, and at the top end the tubular headlamp stays were replaced with conventional brackets. With the swinging-arm frame the roller-cam stand was moved from the rear hub to a central position, operating off the engine/gearbox plate assembly. A second triangular toolbox was fitted, on the nearside, and both were repositioned in the new rear frame loop, midway beneath the dual-seat. With sidecars ever in mind, either of the two 7 in long bolts retaining the lower ends of the new sub-frame could be removed, together with the bottom of the pivot bracket and the rear end of the engine plates. These could then be replaced by a ball-joint assembly to suit either left or right (for export) sidecar fixture.

The rear frame itself added 2 in to the wheelbase, which was now 56 in. It very closely resembled a conversion kit offered since mid-1952 by privateer David Gow; and indeed, though the factory too offered for 1954 a conversion for rigid-framed machines, those taking them up were referred to Gow's workshop. The production version spring-frame bolted to the existing rear frame location lugs, and consisted of a single rear fork in the form of a 10g tube bent to form a 'U', with the closed end milled to a suitable radius so that the massive pivot housing could be welded to it. This pivot housing was a very large 7 × 1 in diameter, and held substantial lead-bronze bushes. There was full adjustment for end play, and in fact owners were sometimes known to take advantage of this and inhibit free movement of the pivot. Armstrong dampers were used, of the type with an external clamp and knurled adjuster to separate the two internal coil springs if one only was required for sidecar use.

These first swinging-arm models were fitted with a single-port head as standard, which was also availabe as an option for the rigid bike. For both models, there was a handsome new chromed tank with plain knee grips, a new red and gold badge with the Panther name in slanted capitals, and a V-shaped band of cream enamel (V-shaped when seen from the saddle, with the top of the V's arms at the handlebar end of the tank). This tank's capacity was increased to four gallons, and it was standard for both rigid and swinging-arm frames, with the steering heads of both modified to accommodate it. A dual-seat became optional for both models, and with the swinging-arm frame, this dragged the sloper's appearance into the mid-50s. Finally, both models, for this year only, fitted a valanced section rear mudguard, and their 7 in front brake, while remaining half-width, was fitted with a riveted-on aluminium cover plate.

For 1955 the company recognized that the large majority of Model 100s were bought to pull chairs (for 1960 they would put the figure at 90 per cent). The sloper's solo handling was known as ponderous and an acquired taste at best. So now they offered sidecar gearing as standard, with solo available as optional; ratios for both changed a little, with the solo gearing slightly lowered overall and the sidecar third and fourth raised a bit. At the same time, the size of both valves was increased from 1 11/16 to 1⅞ in. The carburettors became Amal 376/30

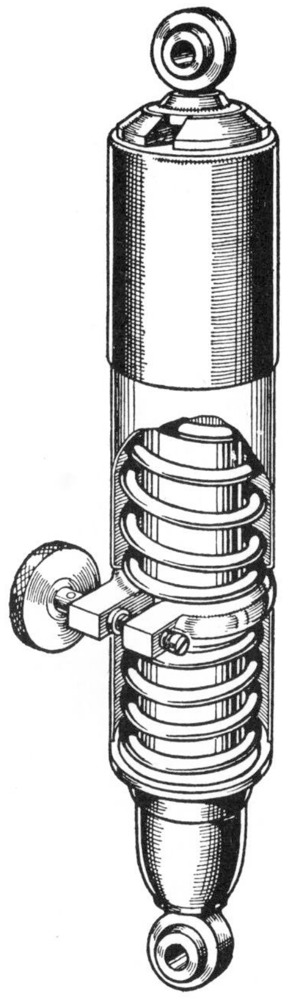

Monoblocs, with an optional Vokes air filter. The headlamp became the Lucas MCH55, with the speedometer still separate above the forks, and a combined dual stop-tail light was fitted. The dual-seat became standard on the swinging-arm model, and the previous C-section rear mudguard was reinstated for that year only.

1956 was a year with many changes. For a start, the bikes looked different, striving to keep up with BSA, Norton, AMC and Royal Enfield in employing chrome side-panels on the petrol tank, with thinner kneegrips and a new circular tank badge of red and silver Diakon plastic, with 'Panther—England' in a circle around a raised panther's head in the centre. Finish was now black. The dual-seat, still optional on the rigid, became of an improved shallower pattern. The modernizing process continued with an elongated Lucas MCH58 headlamp shell, containing the speedometer. Mudguards were now fully valanced D-section with tubular stays, and a horizontal lifting handle/grab-rail was also fitted. Number plates for all were faired in. The swinging-arm machine's appearance now rather resembled the contemporary BSA A10 twin.

More functionally, while the rigid front brake was modified to accept a knock-out spindle, the swinging-arm machines adopted new big cast-alloy full-width hubs front and rear, which were deeply finned and interchangeable; although the similar-looking brake plates differed slightly from front to rear, since the rear one housed the speedometer drive. At the rear also the cush-hub was modified, with both hubs featuring a thicker inner flange on the left side of the hub, with six large diameter holes in it. When the wheel was used in the rear position, these took the drive from six bonded-rubber shock absorber units on the chain sprocket. Brake diameter on these wheels was increased to 8 in, and the linings of the cast-in Meehanite brake shoes were 1½ in wide. As with the previous brakes, the fact that their cams ran in iron bushes meant that if they were neglected, they could rust and seize.

Suspension was also improved. The rear units changed to Armstrong AT6 or 7 (they

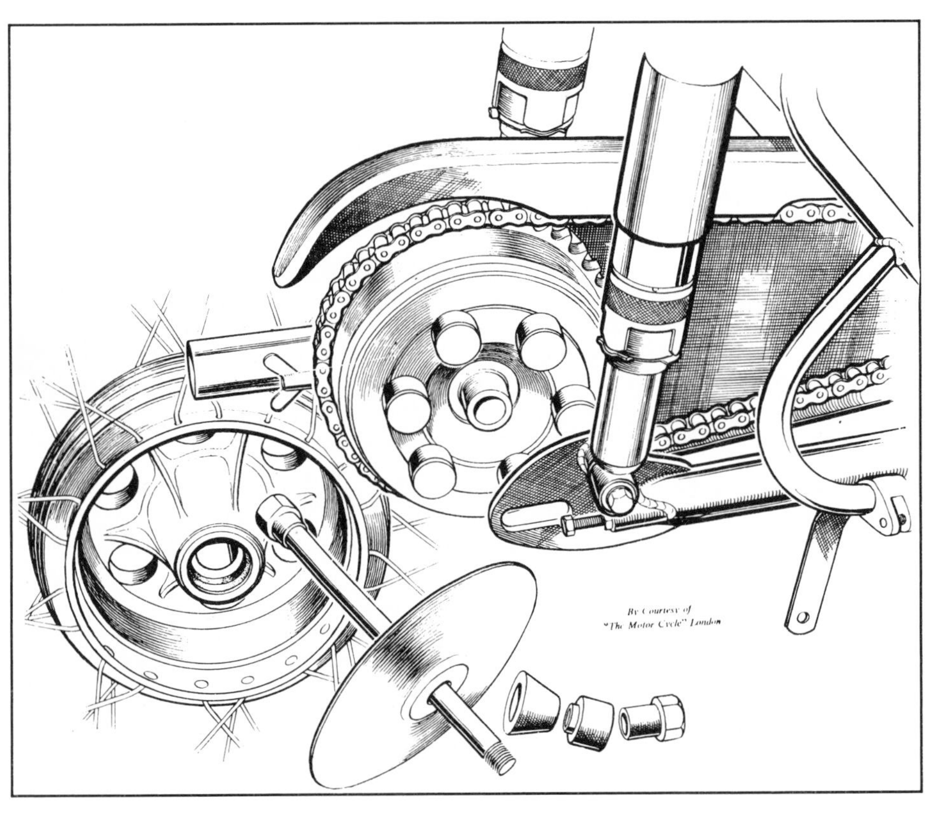

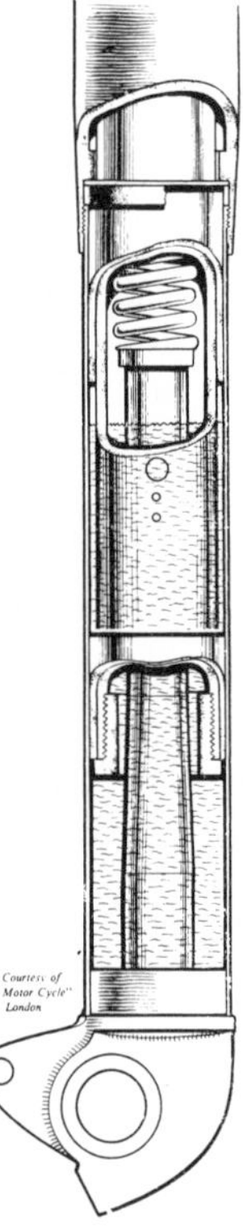

Below far left *Revised cush hub for 1956.*

Below left *Detail of Panther heavyweight fork with spindle offset forward.*

Right *Revised forks, tank panels, dual-seat. Orthodox-looking Model 100 for 1956.*

differed only in the dimension of their parts) now with a single forged-steel split ring and a knurled adjusting screw to make one of the internal springs inoperative if required. The front fork for both models was also strengthened and improved. Again, in recognition of the primary sidecar role, the trail was reduced by off-setting the wheel spindle lug ⅝ in forward from the centre line of the fork legs. Internally, the springs were now of full 1⅜ in diameter and 22 in long, as opposed to the previous half-length springs. The hydraulic damping was improved by a modified conical flow restrictor. As mentioned, the rigid's fork end was also modified to accept a quickly-detachable, knock-out ¼ in spindle. This fork lasted longer and gave better handling, and was identifiable by fork shrouds even larger than those used previously.

Again, on the sidecar front, the lower front sidecar connection was moved from the crankcase to the engine plates, while the lower rear connection was shifted to the sub-frame. This permitted the use of a two-port exhaust system on the swinging-arm frame when a sidecar was fitted, and the two-port head now became standard for both versions. Both fitted Amal Monobloc 389/21 carburettors, with as an option, a thin P and M car-type pancake filter, on an angled stub so that it sat parallel with the ground. It had oil-wetted worsted internals. Finally, for the swinging-arm model only, the rear chainguard now extended the full length of the drive and had a bottom section turning upward at the end of the run, in addition to an upper section turning down over the top of the chain.

1957 was the last year for the rigid, and it saw the sprung model separated into a cheaper standard Model 100S and a Model 100S de luxe. The former now fitted the single-port head as standard, and featured a plain black-enamel petrol tank with gold lining on the shape where the chromed side-panels would have been. More significantly it stingily reverted to a 7 in front brake and the earlier pattern hubs, so that now only the de luxe variant's wheels were interchangeable. The de luxe reversed all the above. All the Model 100s acquired a rubber oil seal in the lower portion of the telescopic push-rod cover, but the rear sprung models now had wheel-rims no longer with lined and painted centres, but plain chrome-plated; a new Lucas MCH58 headlamp shell was also fitted.

1958 saw the Model 100 rigid gone, and for the remainder the pivoted fork redesigned and strengthened. It now comprised a substantial one-piece forged steel pivot yoke, into which the tubular fork arms were brazed. In a logical development from the interchangeable wheels, the de luxe 100's front tyre became like its rear at 3.50 x 19 in. But there was little real development, as all efforts were concentrated on the last leap forward, the enlarged 646cc Model 120S— and the development process was to prove problematical.

After prototype testing, an initial batch of between thirty and forty Model 120s were produced, with the cycle parts those of the de luxe 100, and the engine bored and stroked but its design resembling the 600. Major problems immediately ensued. The increase in power, at first claimed as 28 bhp but subsequently referred to as 27 bhp, exacerbated the old 100's problem with main bearings. These were only just adequately clamped by the U-bolts sandwiching the engine together and retaining the cylinder head. The crankcase did not prove man enough for the increased stresses from the roller main bearings on the flywheel shaft, which caused hairline fractures in the case, particularly around the drive-side bearing housing.

The production 120s dealt with this in several ways. Most prominently, for the 650, the U-bolt arrangement was deleted after 26 years. The four long high-tensile rods were now separate, with their diameter increased from ⅜ to 7/16 in. The two on the particularly troublesome drive-side no longer passed straight into the crankcase, but into reinforced hexagonal adaptors screwed into the case: while the right-hand pair went directly into 1½ in long BSF threads to the crankcase. This was to reduce the stresses on the case itself. The bearing arrangement changed: the bearings themselves were of similar type to the Model 100, with a drive-side roller and a deep groove ball bearing, and a roller only on the timing side. But the extra power meant the use of heavier RM10L and RMS10 roller and ball journal bearings, and while pistons and barrels were machined from the 600's castings, the method of housing the drive-side bearings was revised. Instead of the ball and roller being separated by a wall as previously, they lay side by side in a common housing, retained by a circlip, with their inner races clamped against the flywheel cheek by the sprocket retaining nut. These arrangements were not entirely satisfactory in service, and the rollers would prove a source of trouble. Significantly, the aborted prototype 650 with the AMC gearbox also fitted plain bearings, and with a direct oil supply to them.

A further problem would come from the revised crankshaft. Though the parallel timing shaft was unchanged, the drive shaft was now also parallel, not tapered as previously, with the engine sprocket keyed on to it, not as before a press-up fit. Also, as announced, the 120's Meehanite flywheels had their diameter reduced by ¼ inch to give clearance for the longer engine's piston skirt. But the flywheels had to precisely suit the 650's balance characteristics—previously, for instance, the crank assemblies for rigid and spring-frame machines had different balance factors for this reason of suitability. So the weight loss from the ¼ in diameter reduction, it would appear, was made up for by an increase in width of section in the wheels, and since the existing flywheel casings were used, this obstructed oil circulation, in which the flywheels, of course, had an integral part to play. This contributed to the engine's notably high oil consumption mentioned earlier (once the internals are worn consumption can fall well below the 100 miles to the pint mark). Another factor was simply more modern roads and increased

The Big Yin. 650 Model 120 for 1959.

journey distances, which were more than the engine, with its optimum 30–40 mph journey averages, had been intended for; hot running thinned the oil, and increased consumption still further.

In contrast to this, though, care had been taken to combine even better petrol economy with the same excellent low down pulling power as previously. Compression from the high-domed, full-skirted piston was unchanged at 6.5:1. It will be recalled that the Model 100's valve size had increased to 1⅞ in for 1955, but now the Model 120's exhaust valve reverted to the previous small size of 1 11/16 in. The cylinder was topped with a squish head, with the sparking plug now slightly recessed, and a pear-shaped cavity extending from it across the head between the valves. This arrangement was said to prevent knock by promoting the early burning of the gases furthest from the plug and thus prevent their being trapped and detonated by the advancing flame front. P and M also fitted a slightly larger carburettor, a 1 13/16 in Monobloc 389/33, and they really seemed to have achieved their object; a 70 mpg average with sidecar attached is an impressive figure, while the extra four or so horsepower were claimed to peak at just 4,500 rpm, 800 rpm less than its predecessor. Certainly, the 650 was reputed to be no less of a lusty puller than the 600.

Externally, it was virtually identical to the 100 de luxe except for a silver petrol tank (red would later be an option) and the missing '100', which Cleckheaton had economically simply ground off the red wing on the timing case. On the nearside, the primary chaincase for all models was now in three parts, as the dome over the clutch became detachable for access to the plates; the needle rear chain lubricator from there was deleted. For this year the interchangeable front wheel's brake plate embodied a left-hand scroll on its periphery, with a close-running clearance in the mouth of the hub. The intention was to exclude rainwater, but it was said to be not very effective.

The 120's final Achilles' heel was the clutch, which remained the same as for the smaller engine and was now seriously over-stressed. It was no longer simply a matter of slip and wear, since as well as tending to burn out its clutch, the 120 was also known to literally shear the clutch centre where it was splined on to the gearbox mainshaft. However this reportedly happened most often with older and neglected machines, and it would be wrong to dismiss the Model 120, plenty of which did and do settle in and give good service. An *MCM* tester, as late as 1964, while admitting that the 120S lacked twin-cylinder smoothness, or the acceleration and top speed of a big twin, nevertheless called it 'the most practical and functional combination I have ever ridden', finding it surprisingly quick away from the traffic lights, and even with two passengers, 'belting out the revs like a marine diesel, pounding up hills as if they didn't exist, and always ready to see 70 mph off on the straight'. He was also impressed that even with the absence of a sidecar brake on the test chair, the big brakes pulled up the fully-loaded outfit in 36 ft from 30 mph. However, time has shown up the Model 120's flaws, and it is hard to escape the judgement of Barry Jones (who owned one) that with it P and M had overstretched a good design, and that the Model 100 was more of what a Panther should be.

It was offered for 1959 in conjunction with the company's own sidecar chassis. Made from the same heavy 1¾ in 12 gauge tubing as the frame, it married quickly and simply to the sloper with no alignment problems, via two conically faced bushes that took massive bolts and ball joints. There were two further attachment points via extending braces fitted to the seat and engine plates. The chassis was sprung by a single example of the same Armstrong units which controlled the bike's pivoted fork, and the wheel was interchangeable with those of the machine. Braking was offered by cable either independently, or linked to the motor cycle's rear brake pedal. The chassis also featured a built-in jacking point clipped to the underside of the outer rail, and an integral towing eye for the trailer which many well-worked Panther outfits towed full of camping gear, or even for one of the diminutive motor cycle caravans, a Penguin perhaps, or a Rambler, which had become available in the late forties and fifties. During 1960 the chassis was modified with its mudguard becoming slightly flared front and rear, and the towing point changing from a single hook to an attachment point for the spare wheel which was then offered as an extra. At a basic price of £20, this frame was a good buy, and

Made for each other. Model 120 plus P and M side-car chassis, slightly modified for 1961.

today a feature to look for if purchase of a Panther outfit is being contemplated.

That was really the end of development for the slopers, which now characteristically just ran on and on. As mentioned earlier, the 120 was a very striking concept—the biggest single in the world then, and for a long time before or since, and it caught potential buyers' imaginations, so that despite its flaws it easily outsold the Model 100. The standard 600 ended when the Receiver arrived at the end of 1962, and the de luxe a year later. Some 900 more 120s were built from existing components, however, until the end of 1966, and due to lack of demand, at George Clarke of Acton they remained on sale, motor cycling's Gila Monster, increasingly exotic and outmoded, for years after that. There is a picture of a line-up of bikes outside the dealers in 1969—a Honda 750-4, a BSA Rocket III, and poking between them, the inclined cylinder of a Model 120S—and all were brand new machines! Prices were never exorbitant (£279 got you a fully equipped Panther chassis and Model 120S outfit in 1964) and latterly became extremely silly. There is even a story, possibly apocryphal, of an offer that if on a certain day you arrived at George Clarke's on a Panther, he would give you another one free!

As is increasingly recognized, the slopers deserved better, and today a nice Panther outfit will fetch up to £1000; though this is still not exorbitant by 'classic' standards, and appropriately enough the big Panthers remain one of the bargains on the scene. About 12,000 of the Model 100 and 2,500 of the Model 120 were built. A rigid machine may be the most stylish, but a 1956 standard or 1957-on de luxe 100 are probably the most practical choices, preferably with a P and M sidecar chassis. Spares are sparse, but the Owners' Club seemed to be keeping up with essentials, though delays can be experienced. On the cycle side, the basics are hardy, and your characteristic Panther owner is not too bothered about strict originality, and will adapt other marques' components where necessary. Keeping them running is a different story, though, and the club's magazine *Sloper* carries details of useful modifications. The owners quoted at the end of the marque history section were probably typical in carrying out a couple themselves: they were doing a 12-volt conversion, had installed a pressurized oil feed to the big end and substituted a standard heavy-gauge washer for the original clutch lockwasher (to prevent damage from the clutch falling off if the splines stripped, and smashing the chaincase). Oil consumption can be improved by the use of straight, high-viscosity oil, since with the low pressure system, viscosity also has to be relied on for lubrication. With intelligent maintenance steps like these, it is still true that a Panther will, as *MCM* wrote

24 years ago, 'meet the requirements of the modern family sidecar man just as surely now as it always did'. As a written tribute said of Joah Phelon on his death, 'We have here a true example of real British grit'.

Panther: The Model 100 and Model 120—dates and specifications

Production dates (post-war)
Model 100R (rigid)—1946–57
Model 100S (swinging-arm)—1954–62
Model 100S de luxe—1957–63
Model 120S—1959–67

Specifications
Model 100 R, Model 100S, Model 100S de luxe
Capacity, bore and stroke—598 cc (87 × 100 mm)
Type of engine—ohv single
Ignition—Magneto
Weight—Model 100R (1951) 385 lb, Model 100S (1955) 406 lb, Model 100 de luxe (1959) 426 lb

Model 120S
As Model 100 except
Capacity, bore and stroke—645 cc (88 × 106 mm)
Weight—(1959) 426 lb

Panther: Model 100 and 120—annual developments and modifications

1950
For Model 100
1 Manual ignition control returned for the magneto.

1951
For Model 100
1 Rear tyre enlarged to 3.50 × 19 in.
2 Previous flat tool box lid replaced by slightly domed one.
From May 1951
3 Petrol tanks now enamelled not chromed.

1952
For Model 100
1 Lucas Magdyno Type MO-IL replaced previous separate magneto and dynamo, with fibre dog coupling between timing gears and magneto changing from cruciform to square shape.
2 Full tubular mudguard stays replace previous half-round stampings.

1954
For Model 100R rigid, Model 100S swinging-arm
1 Previous Dowty Oleomatic front forks replaced by P and M two-way hydraulically damped telescopics (for details see text). Trail no longer adjustable, and headlamp brackets replace previous tubular stays.
2 New chromed 4 gallon petrol tank with 'V'-band cream paint strip, plain kneegrips, new red and gold slanted capitals Panther tank badge (with both frames' steering head modified to accommodate it).
3 Valanced section rear mudguard.
4 7 in front brakes fitted with riveted-on aluminium cover plate.
5 Dual-seats become optional.
For Model 100S
6 Spring-frame adopted, with U-shaped swinging arm bolted to existing rear frame location lugs, and Armstrong dampers (for details see text). Bolts, bottom of pivot bracket and rear end of engine plates removable on either side for sidecar attachment.
7 Roller-cam stand moved from rear hub to centre, operating off sidecar attachment.
8 Second triangular toolbox was fitted, on the nearside, and both repositioned higher up in the new rear frame loop.
9 Single-port cylinder head fitted as standard.

1955
For Model 100R, Model 100S
1 Sidecar gearing now standard, solo optional. Sidecar-gearing altered from (5.1, 6.4, 8.7, 13.6:1) to (5.1, 6.4, 7.9, 13.5:1); solo from (4.3, 5.8, 7.3, 11.55:1) to (4.4, 6.2, 7.3, 12.4:1).
2 Size of both valves increased from previous 1 11/16 to 1 7/8 in.
3 Amal 376/30 Monobloc carb fitted, with optional Vokes air filter.
4 Headlamp shell now Lucas MCH55.
5 Combined dual stop/tail light fitted.
6 Previous (from 1953) C-section rear mudguard replaced 1954 valanced type.
For Model 100S
7 Dual-seat becomes standard.

1956
For Model 100R, Model 100S
1 Front fork strengthened, damping improved with modified conical flow restrictor, springs longer (22 in) and of 1 3/8 in diameter, and wheel spindle lug offset 5/8 in forward so that sidecar trail now standard.

2 Petrol tank now with chrome side-panels, thinner kneegrips, new circular red and silver plastic tank badge.
3 Dual-seat (still optional on rigid) becomes shallower pattern.
4 Elongated headlamp shell, now containing speedometer.
5 Fully valanced D-section mudguards with tubular stays front and rear.
6 Horizontal grab-rail/lifting handle fitted behind dual-seat.
7 Rear number plates faired in at side.
8 Amal 389/21 Monobloc carbs, with optional P and M pancake air filter with oil-wetted worsted internals.
For Model 100S
9 Front and rear wheels fully interchangeable, with full-width finned alloy hubs and 8 × 1½ in brakes. Rear cush hub modified (for details see text).
10 Armstrong suspension units altered to AT6 or 7 type.
11 Lower front sidecar connection moved from crankcase to engine plate and lower rear to the sub-frame.
12 Hence two-port exhaust system could be used with sidecar attached, and two-port head becomes standard for Model 100S, as it was already for Model 100R.
13 New rear chainguard extends full length of drive, and with bottom section up-turned at end plus top section down-turned at its end.
For Model 100R
14 Fork end modified to accept knock-out type front spindle.

1957
For Model 100R, Model 100S, Model 100S de luxe
1 Rubber seal in lower portion of telescopic pushrod cover.
2 Lucas MCH58 headlamp shell.
For Model 100S
3 Single-port head as standard, plain enamelled petrol tank with gold lining round shape of previous chrome panels, front wheel with 7 in brake, earlier pattern hubs with 1956 knock-out type front spindle, wheels not interchangeable. Model 100S de luxe as 1956 Model 100S.
For Model 100S, Model 100S de luxe
4 Plain all-chromed wheel rims.

1958
For Model 100S, Model 100S de luxe
1 Pivoted rear fork redesigned and strengthened, with substantial one-piece forged-steel pivot yoke with tubular-arms brazed into it.
For Model 100S de luxe
2 Front tyre section becomes 3.50 × 19 in, as interchangeable rear.

1959
For Model 100S, Model 100S de luxe, Model 120S
1 Three-part primary chaincase, with detachable circular clutch inspection plate; and rear chain lubricator deleted.
For Model 100 de luxe, Model 100S de luxe
2 Interchangeable front wheel embodies water-excluding left-hand scroll on its periphery.

Panther: engine and frame numbers

Post-war Panther engines used a letter and number code to indicate (1) assembler's code, (2) year of manufacture, (3) model identity code, (4) a batch number for the engine itself (engine and frame numbers did not tally) and (5) modification code for that year's production.

A typical code instanced by Barry Jones was E60ZA-608A.
(1) E = assembler's code
(2) 60 = year of manufacture
(3) ZA = model identity code
(4) 608 = engine's number in its batch
(5) A = modification code, in this instance indicating Lucas electrics.

Post-1950 Engine Model Identity Codes (3) were as follows:
GS = Model 50
J = Model 65 250 cc
K = Model 75 350 cc
M = Model 100 600 cc rigid
MS = Model 100 standard s/arm, half-width hubs
MSN = as MS above, 1957 and on
MS = Model 100 s/arm de luxe, 1957 and on
VT = Model 35 250 ts
VTS = Model 35 Sport 250 ts
VTT = Model 45
W = Model 35 1964 and on—Red Panther
X = Stroud Trials
ZA = Model 120

Some two-stroke modification codes (5) were as follows:
For Model 35 Standard and Sports 45
A = Amal handlebar controls

For Model 35 standard
B = new petrol tank design with cap moved from right to centre
For Standard and Sports
C = Armstrong units
For Standard and Sports
D = Miller electrics
For Sports
E = Lucas electrics
For Sports
B = teleforks (from January 1959)

Listed below are incomplete (and for the two strokes, inconsistent) engine and frame numbers. If in doubt, the Owners' Club holds the complete despatch books from Cleckheaton and can identify a machine accurately.

	Engine	Frame
For 1957		
Model 35	950A	VT001
For 1958		
Model 35	950A	VT261C
For 1959		
Model 35	950A	VT266C
Model 35 Sports	950A	VTS281A
Model 45	847B	VTT101A
Model 50	847B	GS101A
For 1960		
Model 35 Standard ends	—	VT427E
Model 45	847B	VTT299B
Model 50	893B	GS200B
For 1961		
Model 35	004D	VT419E
Model 35 Sports	004D	VTS554E
Model 45	893B	VTT375B
Model 50	053D	GS322C
For 1962		
Model 35	004D	VTS597E
Model 35 Sports	004D	VTS554E
Model 45	893B	VTT375B
Model 50	053D	GS354C
Model 45 ends (Dec)	—	VTT412
Model 50 ends	—	9S372
Model 35 Sport ends (Dec)	—	VTS610A
For 1963		
Model 120S	63ZA101A	28461
For 1964		
Model 35	—	VTS705
Model 45	—	VTT712
Model 100 de luxe ends	63MS101A	28455
Model 120S	64ZA159A	28759
Model 35 'Red Panther' (kickstart) (Apr)	—	W101A
Model 35 'Red Panther' (Siba) (July)	—	WS218A
For 1965		
Model 35 'Red Panther' (kickstart) ends	—	W467A
For 1966		
Model 35 'Red Panther' (Siba)	810B-5134	WS464A
For 1967		
Model 35 'Red Panther' (Siba)	208D-1158	WS530A
Model 120S	267001A	—
For 1968		
Model 35 'Red Panther' (Siba)	208D-1235	WS605A
Model 35 'Red Panther' (Siba) ends	—	WS613A
Model 120S	68ZA101	29305

Panther: colour schemes

1950 *Model 65* Petrol tank Royal Blue with Eggshell Blue panels; mudguards, toolbox Royal Blue, cycle parts black. *Model 65 de luxe, Model 75* Chrome petrol tank, forward panel cream, cycle parts black, wheel rims chrome with black centre, red lined. *Model 100* Chrome-plated petrol tank, cream upper and side panels lined red and black. All cycle parts black. Wheel rims chromed with black centre, red lined. Optional Panther Green for cream portions. *For all* Chrome and red 'escutcheon' tank badge.
1951 As 1950 until May; then *Model 65* as 1950, *Model 65 de luxe and Model 75* as Model 65. *Model 100* Grey Metallic enamel mudguards, toolbox, petrol tank overall, with 3 inch horizontal strip in front of kneegrips, lined red and gold; wheel rims chromed with grey-enamelled centre, cream-lined.
1952 *Model 65, 65 de luxe, 75* Cycle parts black. Polychromatic light blue for toolbox, mudguards, petrol tank overall, with 3 inch horizontal cream strip in front of kneegrips,

lined red and gold; wheel rims chromed with polychromatic light blue centre. *Model 100* As 1951.

1953 All as 1952.

1954 *Model 65* As 1952. *Model 75* As 1952, but petrol tank chromed with blue enamel V-shaped panel, and other colour blue enamel; new slanted capital script red and gold tank badge for 75 but not 65. *Model 100* Chrome petrol tank with cream V-shape panelling and new tank badge as Model 75. All other cycle parts black, mudguards gold-lined, wheel rims chromed with black centre, gold-lined.

1955 *Model 65* As 1954 but petrol tank chromed as Model 75 with colour Mediterranean Blue for V-band. *Model 75* As 1954, but toolboxes, mudguards, V-band on tank, Sherwood Green, with mudguards and tank band gold-lined. *Model 100* As 1954, but with optional alternative of black, gold-lined, for V-band on petrol tank.

1956 *Model 65* Cycle parts black, deep Maroon finish for toolboxes, mudguards, petrol tank, with mudguards and side-panel shape on petrol tank gold-lined. *Model 75* Still Sherwood Green, but petrol tank now with chromed side-panels, gold-lined. *Model 100* As 1955, but petrol tank now with chromed side-panels, gold-lined. *For all* New round red and silver plastic tank badge with 'Panther—England' around raised panther's head in centre.

1957 *Model 35* Finish as 1956 Model 65, but wheel rims silver painted. *Model 65* As 1956 but petrol tank acquires chromed side-panels, gold-lined. *Model 75* As 1956. *Model 100R* As Model 100 1956, but petrol tank all black, with tank side-panel shape gold-lined. *Model 100S* Cycle parts black, toolboxes, mudguards, petrol tank maroon, with mudguards and petrol tank side-panel shape gold-lined. *Model 100 de luxe* As Model 100 1956. *Model 100S and de luxe* Wheel rims all chrome plated.

1958 *Model 35* As 1957. *Model 35 Sports* All Pearl Grey, with chromed tank panels, gold-lined. *Model 65 and 75.* As 1957. *Model 100* As 1957. *For all* (but Model 35) Wheel rims chrome plated.

1959. *Model 35, 35 Sports* As 1958, but Model 35 wheel rims chrome plated. *Model 45* As Model 35 Sports but colour Devil Red. *Model 65 and 75* As 1958. *Model 100* As 1958. *Model 120S* All cycle parts as Model 100 de luxe, but tank colour silver-grey, with chromed side-panels, red-lined.

1960 *Model 35* Petrol tank Italian Red with chromed side-panels, gold-lined, *Model 35 Sports, Model 45* As 1959. *Model 50* As Model 45. *Model 65, '75'* as 1959. *Model 100, Model 120* As 1959.

1961–64 As 1960. *Model 120* Tank colour optional red.

1965 *Model 35, 35ES* All Devil Red, mudguards polished alloy. *Model 120* As 1964.

1966–68 As 1965.

Panther

Publications

The Story of Panther Motorcycles by Barry Jones (Patrick Stephens)
The Book of the Panther [Lightweight] 250 and 350 cc, 1932–58 by W. C. Haycraft, Pitman (o/p)
The Book of the Panther [Heavyweight] 600 cc and 650 cc, 1938–66 by W. C. Haycraft, Pitman (o/p)
A small selection of reproduced factory manuals and illustrated spares lists from Bruce Main-Smith Ltd, PO Box 20, Leatherhead, Surrey (Tel: 0372 [Leatherhead] 375615).

A good selection of high quality reproduced manuals and spares lists is also available from the Owners' Club.

Spares suppliers and specialists

Autocycle, 50 Church Road, Moxley, Wednesbury, West Midlands (Tel: 0902-45528).
A. Gagg & Sons, 106 Alfreton Road, Nottingham, Notts: (Tel. 0602-786288).
For Villiers spares, see SUN (p.185)

Owners' Club

Panther Owners' Club, Membership Secretary, Peter Ryan, 25 Kenilworth Drive, Padgate, Warrington WA1 3JT.

Royal Enfield

The Enfield Cycle Company, Redditch, Worcestershire

Royal Enfield's geographical position was an indicator of its status in our period—within reach of the industry's Birmingham/Coventry epicentre, but not quite there. Always in the picture and frequently innovative, Royal Enfield, while producing a full range of lightweights, sporting singles and big twins, somehow, then and now, have never been quite of the mainstream (though none the worse for that). Low post-war production levels probably contributed: as we shall see, almost the total output for four years in the sixties was just 6,600 machines—which represented about six weeks' production in a good year at Meriden Triumph.

The company sprang from a pair of 19th century bicycle manufacturing concerns which had been housed at Redditch since 1894, a few miles south of the outskirts of Birmingham. It was the 1890s which provided the 'Enfield' company name, adopted for a new amalgamated range of bicycles: this was apparently due to a contract with the Royal Small Arms factory at Enfield in Middlesex to make interchangeable parts for guns. Their umbrella company for a wide range of manufacturing processes was to be The Enfield Cycle Co, but in 1893 they adopted the 'Royal' prefix for the cycle side; together with a new logo, an artillery piece—a field gun. For a company whose slogan was 'Made Like a Gun', bullets could not be far behind.

Motorized vehicle production commenced in 1899 with De Dion-engined tricycles and quadricycles. Motorized bicycles followed in 1901, and in 1903 one of these featured a characteristic design signature of future Royal Enfield powerplants, with the oil-tank being embodied in the engine's crankcase. Following an unsuccessful spell as a car manufacturer, and a final move within Redditch to the Hewell Road site (which ultimately was to cover 24 acres) some corporate manoeuvring saw BSA take over Eadies, one of the original bicycle companies, and Robert Walker Smith left in charge of what remained. (Smith was also a Director of BSA until 1909, when he resigned, probably to avoid any conflict of interest.) The Enfield Company at first concentrated on the manufacture of cycle and motor cycle components such as brakes and hubs (which they were to continue to supply for the industry for the next fifty years) and the frames for Scotts, but soon got back into motor cycle production for themselves. They quickly hit form in 1912 with their renowned Model 180, a 770 cc JAP-engined V-twin outfit, the first of several sturdy side-valve 'V's of varying capacities. The Model 180, as well as being bang up to date in featuring chain-drive and two speeds, initiated a completely new piece of design for Britain, Enfield's famous rubber 'cush-hub' in the rear wheel, to minimize chain snatch. This was a first, and was to feature in all subsequent larger Royal Enfields (later as the 'double-cush', in conjunction with a clutch shock-absorber); and eventually was either sold to or copied by several other marques.

In 1913 there followed another pioneering move with the introduction of the 3 hp 425 cc ioe V-twin; this was the first English production motor cycle to feature a dry sump lubrication system with an automatic geared oil pump, at a time when splash lubrication, and Pilgrim-type pumps squirted by hand, were still very much the norm. The pump fed oil under pressure to the big end bearing through a hollow crankpin, and returned the lubricant from the crankcase to a receptacle beneath the saddle. This container left no doubt whether the system was operating or not, since it was a cylinder made of clear glass!

Made like a gun.

A 350 cc version of this machine enjoyed some success at Brooklands and the TT, and by 1915 production also included a 225 cc two-stroke single, the beginning of the full range of machines for which the company was to be noted. When the First World War intervened, Royal Enfield supplied JAP-engined machine-gun and ambulance sidecar outfits to the Allies, as well as solo twins to the Imperial Russian Army, and bicycles in bulk to our forces. R. W. Smith's three sons all served and all survived, including Major Frank Walker Smith who had been a Royal Flying Corps pilot in France, and was later to take the helm of the company right into the 1960s. The family character of the firm, with the brothers keen road and Trials riders, encouraged innovation and made the Enfield Cycle Co a rewarding place to work. Royal Enfield's post-war Trials ace Johnny Brittain recalled how Frank Smith had appreciated both his own and his father Vic's role as ambassadors for company and country at ISDTs and the like. In contrast with the sometimes autocratic gaffers at AMC, BSA and Triumph, the Trials champion found that 'they were a pioneering little company and I really enjoyed riding for them. We never had a cross word in fifteen years', so much so that when Brittain started his own motor cycle shop in Bloxwich, the factory assisted him. The distinguished development engineer Tony Wilson-Jones also helped in the running of the firm's apprentice training scheme: 35 to 40 apprentices would be operating at one time, and to the end the good name of Redditch meant that every year there were more applicants than places.

Two designers of note came to the factory during the twenties. The first was E. O. 'Ted' Pardoe, who was to lay out both the post-war Bullet and the 500 twin. In 1924 he initiated a 350 side-valve single, a further step in the direction of factory self-sufficiency, since up till then bought-in engines from Vickers and JAP had featured largely in the range. The 350 was followed in 1927 by a 500 sv, which shared bore, stroke and piston with the big V-twin: good commonality and compatibility of parts throughout the range was to be another Enfield feature from then on, sound economic sense for the factory, and since then useful for the owner or restorer seeking replacement parts.

The second significant arrival happened in 1925 with the appointment, at the age of 24, of Tony Wilson-Jones as Head of Development. Wilson-Jones was an amiable, gifted gentleman whose physical resemblance to the late Sir Michael Redgrave reinforced the impression of absent-minded boffin. He was to be a frequent contributor of papers to the Institution of Mechanical Engineers, whose Automobile Division he was to chair in 1958, and as the above indicates, was an

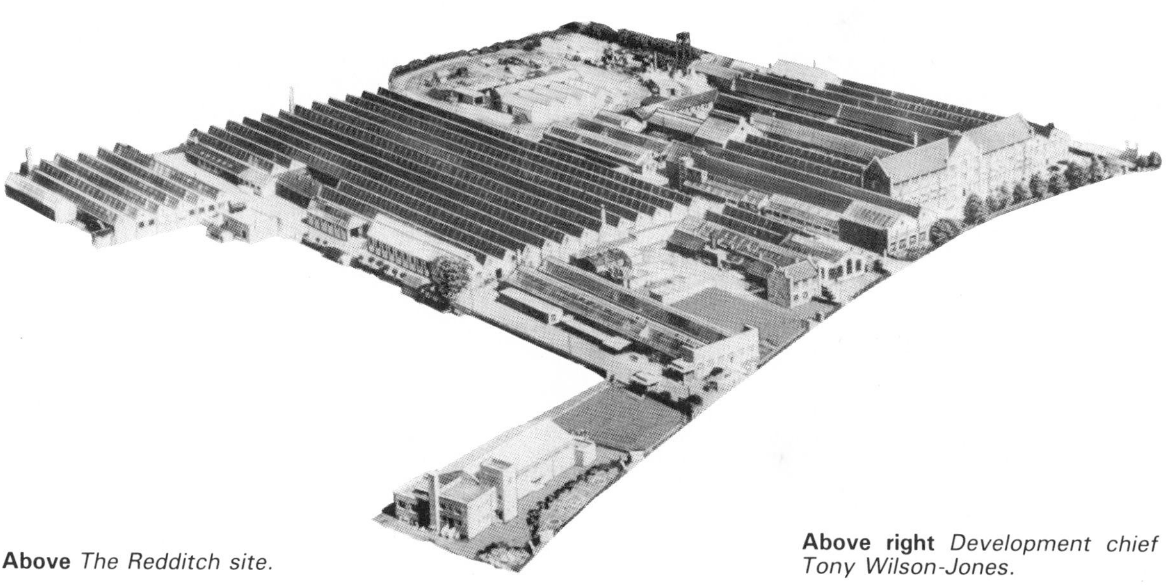

Above *The Redditch site.*

Above right *Development chief Tony Wilson-Jones.*

engineer with a keen interest in theoretical matters, the study of problems in all their aspects rather than merely their solutions in practical terms alone. It was therefore somewhat paradoxical that he should be in charge of production development, rather than working as a pure designer. There is evidence, in the failure over a fifteen-year period to cure the post-war four-strokes' tendency to leak oil, or to develop the big twins with which he was involved in a finally satisfactory manner, that the roadster range suffered as a result of this paradox.

But this aspect should not be over-exaggerated. As we shall see, the small design and development staff worked together closely: Wilson-Jones was himself a competitor in Trials pre-war, and always a keen all-weather motor cyclist, with a consequent sound understanding of the rider's real needs. This applied to several of the designers and workforce, and contributed to the Enfield sports machines' strength and their built-in adaptability to a variety of roles; which together with Trials successes culminating in 37 major trophies at home and 6 Golds in the 1937 ISDT explains their popularity with Clubman competitors from then on. Above all, Wilson-Jones' questing intelligence provided the stimulus for innovation, already seen with the cush-hub and the early use of dry sump lubrication (which were to continue to be features of the marque). Another was the plain big-end bearing with a floating bush, developed by Wilson-Jones and Glacier Metal Company from 1935, and standardized for all but 250 and two-stroke Enfields in 1940.

That such innovations passed quickly into metal was the result of a compact product planning committee. The committee was headed by Major Frank Smith, whose engineering background provided the knowledge for informed discussion, and whose position as both Managing Director following his father's death in 1933, and Chairman from 1935, gave him the power to implement decisions taken. In addition to Ted Pardoe, who would draw out ideas to Tony Wilson-Jones' material specifications, ready for the latter to develop, the committee later included the factory's ex-Trials ace Jack Booker, who rose to the position of General Manager.

In addition to this enthusiastic and knowledgeable core, it was important that the concern proceeded on financially stable lines. In 1930, the year when the Depression hit, they sustained a loss for the first time: but it was of £2,000 only, and the trend was reversed in the following years. To the end Royal Enfield were one of the few British motor cycle companies never to default on the shareholders' dividends. This was partly done by providing ultra-economy models, such as their own two-strokes, often small-capacity to take advantage of road-tax concessions.

For the enthusiast since 1930, a line of 500, 350, and from 1933, 250 cc inclined-engine single cylinder sporting machines had been under development, bearing the name, and in some cases the tank logo, of a speeding bullet. By 1937 for all models the oil, carried low down in a compartment cast on the front of the crankcase, was circulated by another Enfield trademark, two plunger-pumps driven by a worm at the end of the timing-side mainshaft. The singles had been developed continuously, featuring at various times two-port heads, upswept exhausts, and for the 1934 500 another unusual

Father and son. Pre-war ace Vic Brittain (but astride a Norton!) and ***(right)*** *his son and Enfield's ace, John.*

feature for a production roadster, though not a particularly successful one—a four-valve head, modified to three-valve for 1935 and back to four for the 1936 super sports 499 cc Model JF, which like the previous year's Model G 350, now featured a vertical cylinder.

With the coming of war, Royal Enfield were among those companies who supplied military machines to the Allied forces. However, their contribution in this field was not a par with other major military motor cycle manufacturers: compare their total wartime output of around 55,000 machines with BSA's 425,000. One interesting wartime machine was the 125 cc two-stroke Model RE, or the 'Flying Flea' as it was known in an allusion to a brief 1930s' craze for 'an aerial motorcar for every family'. Airborne Troops used it, glider-borne or canister-contained on drops, to increase their mobility. With a certain grim irony, this little weapon's origin, like that of BSA's post-war Bantam, had been the German DKW factory. Before the outbreak of war, DKW's Dutch agents were informed by the German company that they would receive no more of their 98 cc RB machines until they had purged themselves of all members of Jewish descent. Since these were in a majority, the Dutch company with commendable initiative took the German design to Royal Enfield, as a potential alternative supplier. There Ted

Major Frank Smith, (second from left) MD and chairman of Royal Enfield.

Enfield's beautiful 500 twin for 1949.

Pardoe increased its capacity by 25 cc, and with hand-change and a pressed-steel front fork whose movement was controlled with nothing more than rubber bands, put it into production as a civilian utility model from 1939. It would return to this role after the war also, when its use by *The Motor Cycle*'s columnist 'Torrens' for fishing trips provided some welcome publicity. After a redesign for 1951, modified still further from 1953, it continued as Enfield's lightweights, the Ensign and Prrince.

Other military Enfields included some side-valves, 570 cc for the Navy and D/D 250 cc models for training purposes, as well as a few of the earlier type 350 Model G and 500 Model J2S ohv machines. But the bulk of their output were 350s: the side-valve WD/C, and in a large majority, around 29,000 of the ohv Model WD/ CO. The engines of these two models were almost identical apart from the head and barrel, and the cycle parts similar for the C and the early-type CO. Save for a few tele-forked COs in 1941, these were rigid and girder-forked machines, and despite their origins in Trials work, were never very highly regarded by the despatch riders who used them.

However this did not prevent their being bought back in bulk by Enfield from the Ministry of Supply at the end of hostilities, then refurbished, painted black and offered to a transport-hungry public. The renovation took place in one of five works from which the company had pursued its wartime activities. This one was located 90 ft down in a large cave near Upper Westwood, Bradford-upon-Avon, Wiltshire, where art treasures were stored and hush-hush war work had taken place (and MoD contracts on secret matters such as guidance systems were to continue to be fulfilled as late as the 1970s). Diesel-powered generator units as well as marine gearboxes were to continue to be a mainstay of Enfield industrial output after the war.

There were difficulties afflicting the whole industry during the immediate post-war period, due to shortages and restrictions on raw material: Enfield themselves were down to a four-day week for a period early in 1947. But to the stimulus of the same demand for personal transport which sold the ex-WD bikes, Royal Enfield responded in characteristically individual fashion. Tony Wilson-Jones kept them in contention with the other factories by designing telescopic forks which, with minor variations in the extent of their leading spindle, were adopted by the whole range bar the lightweights from 1946; and Ted Pardoe designed a 500 cc parallel twin. In the Enfield way, the twin

Left *Crucial and controversial: the spring-frame 350 Bullet Trials iron for 1950.*

Right *J.V. Brittain and Bullet go for grip.*

was 'modular' in that the dimensions of its cylinders (they were separate, something only the AMC 500 twin would emulate) were the same (64 × 77) as the pre-war 248 cc Model S (itself to be reintroduced in the UK for 1954 as the economy Model S 250 and the 250 Clipper). In addition, the 500s' spring-frame was in common with the new G2 350 Bullet. Otherwise the 500 Twin was an exceptionally good-looking, low output (25 bhp) tourer. It shortly proved itself a good all-rounder in the 1951 ISDT, which was held in Italy and featured conditions and speeds so hectic that it was referred to as the Italian Grand Prix! The Enfield Twin contributed to Britain's victorious Trophy squad as big Jack Stocker's ride and with two other riders similarly mounted collected that year's Maker's Award for Enfield. But the 500 Twin, probably in the absence of a fast sports version, never really took off with the public, and from 1952 was somewhat eclipsed in the Redditch range as much larger capacity twins became available.

Paradoxically the Enfield flagship was to be a smaller, single cylinder machine introduced at the end of 1948, the G2 350 Bullet. Material shortages at first restricted Royal Enfield to the choice of either a new 350 or a new 500 single, not both. But in this early post-war period, the 350 class of single was a live one. 350 singles were familiar to wartime and pre-war riders in a way that the sought-after twins could not yet be (most of the latter were still being exported), and were suitable tools for the most popular sport at the time, Trials. The Bullet was one of the true all-rounders and on the road the 350 Bullet's lower gearing and pleasing manners were to make it very well suited to the conditions of the day, and it was not much slower, marginally more reliable and generally preferred to its 500 successor.

Details of the new Bullet's rugged powerplant, developed by Tony Wilson-Jones over the four-year period prior to its launch, will be found in the appropriate section, but a crucial part of the overall package was the move of the crankcase oil compartment to behind the cylinder from its pre-war position in front, with the Albion gearbox bolted tight into the rear of the oil chamber in a semi-unit arrangement. Thus the engine, with its rigid, square, notably tall crankcase (to permit the cylinder spigot of unusual depth), was sufficiently short-based to keep the wheelbase short also (at 59 in). This permitted the adoption of a swinging-arm frame without any increase in overall machine length from the pre-war rigid machines. The majority of the other factories made do with compromise suspension systems tacked on to existing rigid frames for the next five or six years.

For Enfield it produced a frame so right from the start that it only ever needed adjustment rather than redesign, and was equally good on mud or on tarmac. The latter is a fact sometimes overlooked: as very experienced road tester, journalist and now motor cycle bookseller Bruce Main-Smith remarked while discussing the factory's twins, they 'have been much underestimated. The handling is by no means inferior, and the ride is comfortable. Even the 735 cc Interceptor is not over-engined for the chassis.' On the Bullets the high, short-wheelbase roadster frame provided a distinctly individual feel to the ride; one that perhaps made its contribution to setting the marque apart from the mainstream, and, for what it's worth, on two occasions decided me against buying one.

With the 350 Bullet, several strands of the Enfield story came together; the marque's pre-war record in Trials, Tony Wilson-Jones' own experience in the field, his preoccupation with essentials like handling and his openness to innovation. There had already, in 1939, been a prototype leaf-sprung Enfield on test, but it was the 1946 introduction of the Wilson-Jones-designed telescopic forks with two-way damping (something BSA had to wait over twenty years to acquire) that convinced him of the necessity for a complete new suspension system. Despite, unusually, opposition from the upper echelons within the factory, who wanted to adapt to a plunger system, he took his cue from a paper delivered to the Institute of Automobile Engineers by the brilliant Australian development engineer Phil Irving. The latter had been working pre-war at Velocette on the swinging-arm rear-suspension system for some racers and experimental machines such as the Model O twin and the supercharged 'Roarer'. Irving's system might have featured the typically Velocette patented method of adjustment by sliding the tops of the spring units, but it was not to go into production for the Velocette roadsters until 1953. The 350 Bullet went on the market as a sports roadster, and only lightly modified for Trials use, for 1949.

Apart from Vincents, with their patented frame, and Douglas, with their torsion bar system, only AMC among the major manufacturers could boast pivoted-fork rear suspension in that year, and the latter's system was marred by the quality of their proprietary 'candlestick' and then 'jampot' rear units. Later, Norton were just ahead of the hunt with limited numbers of their peerless Featherbed frames produced for the Dominator twins from 1952. Otherwise, until the all-change year of 1954, Triumph would be stuck with their dodgy optional spring hub, Ariel with the fiddly plunger and Anstey-link system, and BSA with plungers; all were means of continuing production of lightly modified previous rigid frames.

In the field of Trials, where there spring frame was to encounter the most bitter derision and damaging resistance, Enfield's lead was equally clear. Of the other major contenders, Norton never did leave the rigid format, BSA's production mudpluggers got a spring frame only in 1953, AMC's big bangers and Johnny Giles' Triumph twin in 1954, and Ariel singles in 1955. Why then was Enfield's courage in pioneering the system not rewarded by greater British sales success?

This can be explained partly by the fact that Enfield never produced in great volume—only around 9,000 bullets would be made in 13 years—and partly by Enfield's early own-brand suspension units which with only two inches of movement made the first Bullets go through sections looking like 'pogo sticks'. But primarily, sales of sports machines like the Bullet were generated by sporting victories, and these were slow in coming for Enfield in the principal area of interest for British enthusiasts, namely one-day Trials events. As has been indicated by Enfield's pre-war record and Johnny Brittain's remark quoted earlier, the company's MD, Major Frank Smith, had a lively awareness of both the prestige, and (due particularly to the marque's strong markets in Scandinavia and France) the commercial advantage of success in the ISDT, at a time when supplies of restricted raw materials were available only for companies whose products sold well overseas.

Hence the Bullet was formulated specifically with ISDT requirements in mind. That event interspersed its observed feet-up off-road Trials sections with gruelling timed road sections and high speed runs. This called for an engine that would combine the ability to plonk and rev, and a bicycle carrying no great weight penalty which would handle equally well on or off the road. This the 350 Bullet provided, as proved by the fact that in the hands of British riders, and of the Swedish, Danish and Irish teams, Enfield springers took 26 ISDT Golds, as well as the Manufacturers' prize three times between 1948 and 1953. Of its contemporaries in the dual-purpose field, only Triumph's rigid TR 5 Trophy is recalled as respectfully and affectionately.

A large part of the successful equation, however, was the spring frame, and here there were great obstacles to be overcome, even within the factory. While designer Pardoe and developer Wilson-Jones may have been convinced of the theoretical benefits of the system, the works Trials riders at the sharp end were not. According to Don Morley, the only factory rider to share Wilson-Jones' vision was the pre-war ace Jack Booker, still a member of Enfield's post-war squad, but by now also promoted to competitions manager. Booker called in fellow works rider and competition shop foreman Charlie Rogers, and together they converted one of Pardoe's swinging-arm prototypes for Trials use. They then systematically tested it on identical sections against the tried rigid Trials Model G, finding it superior in over 80 per cent of situations. But the rest of the works team remained unconvinced, as would the buying public. Both distrusted the spring frame's apparent absence of grip due to loss of rear wheel contact with terra firma on the rebound. At a time when the crude pre-war knobbly tyres were under an ACU ban and the first purpose-built Trials tyres were not to appear until the 1949 Show, a suspension system that appeared to break the apparently vital direct connection between a rider's power-pulses and the dirt, seemed ludicrous and was derided as such. Johnny Brittain recalled, how other factories' riders 'went on about that spring frame . . . they all felt sorry for me.'

At the beginning of 1947 the Redditch factory riders remained lukewarm, until nineteen-year-old Enfield apprentice Bill Lomas, the future Moto Guzzi road-race champion, won an award on his first event on the springer prototype. During 1948, despite continued managerial resistance, Trials machine production was boldly switched entirely to the rear-sprung Bullet. In February 1948, at the Colmore Trial, Charlie Rogers, George Holdsworth and Jack Plowright put in a surprise appearance on the production prototype springers. They collected only two first-class awards, as well as a lot of mockery. Later in the year Tom Ellis led the field in the prestigious Scottish Six Days until sidelined on the very last day by mechanical failure. Charlie Rogers himself was the first to gain a premier award, at that year's Alan Jefferies Trial. None of it did any good, and even Enfield's own riders lacked faith to the extent that pre-war star Vic Brittain had to come out of retirement to re-form the works team. Resounding success in the 1948 and subsequent ISDTs altered little: the British Trials men believed that the same versatility which did so well there was at odds with the one-day game's requirements. As a result, top names would not sign with Enfield. They were further discouraged by the fact that, at a time when the big names tended to be all-rounders, Enfield could not offer a ride in top-class road racing.

This lack of top riders was crucial. From Trials' emergence between the wars, star riders had won renown and sales for their factories by excelling on good bikes, and also by extracting winning performances from flawed or unsuitable ones. Small Heath riders were doing it then on their unsuitably low and heavy plunger-sprung mounts, while Enfield's clever design stagnated for lack of rider talent. It was a vicious circle: without

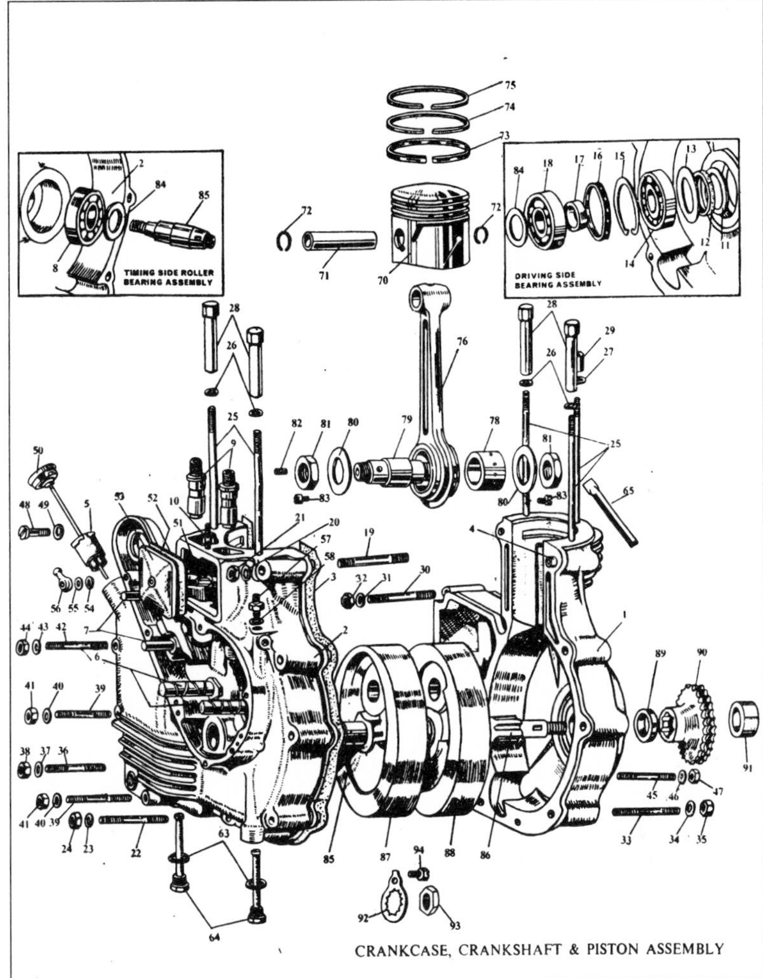

CRANKCASE, CRANKSHAFT & PISTON ASSEMBLY

Rugged powerplant: 350 Bullet engine.

top riders they got no premier victories, and with no victories they lost both sales and the means to attract top riders. The situation was very serious, tantalizingly coming at a time of high demand for motor cycles, while the factory was totally committed to the new and unpopular system.

Things began to be remedied from 1950 when a tall gangling Wolverhampton eighteen-year-old joined his father riding for the Redditch firm. (His lanky build would tell against him in one area; after consistent complaints from his father that the works were providing him with slower machines than the others for the ISDT speed tests, an exasperated Jack Booker laid on a dawn speed run on public roads, which proved him marginally slower on *all* ISDT Bullets—probably as a result of his height.) J. V. 'Johnny' Brittain, still almost a schoolboy, was immediately allocated a Bullet whose *HNP 331* registration would become as famous in its day as Sammy Miller's *GOV 132* did later. In fact Brittain's number would jump from works bike to works bike, but a legend is always good. The state-of-the-art pre-'58 example to which the number finally attached is now owned by top photographer and Enfield historian Don Morley himself.

It took a while for the youngster to hit form, and 1950 was a flat Trials year for Redditch. In 1951 though, Brittain's riding skills began to show through, with participation on a 500 Twin as part of the winning Manufacturer's squad in the ISDT. But it was 1952, the year the production

Trials machine acquired an alloy barrel, that his talent exploded on the public, most notably with his victories in the British Experts and the Scottish Six Day Trials. It may have come a year or two after it should have, but it was a definite turning-point for the Bullet and the company. 'They'd never known anything like it at Enfield's,' Brittain recalled, 'and Major Smith threw a party at the factory.'

From that year on as success continued, the works 350 bikes began to diverge widely from the versions available to the public. In addition to one engine benefit that passed on from the works Trials bikes to the production roadster, (namely new cylinder head castings to allow larger Gold Star-type inlet valves), wider, lighter, all-welded frames of chrome-molybdenum were also adopted by the whole Bullet range for 1956. Though better-handling on the road, they proved less than ideal for the Bullet's multi-purpose role, as the whole 1956 ISDT team, which included Sammy Miller, broke their frames and the hard-riding Rickman brothers, later to be part of the tail-end of the Enfield story, but employed that year in a one-off effort as works scramblers, broke their bikes on every single occasion, which led to their moving on and the 500 Bullet scrambler being withdrawn. Another result of the new frame was the shipping of the old jigs to India, where the 350 began to be manufactured under licence, something which continues to this day and will be dealt with more fully later.

Brittain was to win both British Experts and the Scottish again, as well as the Scott Trial twice, 52 trade-supported Championships and a great many non-Championship events, plus thirteen ISDT Gold Medals, and in 1957 the top domestic accolade, the ACU British Trials Championship Star. The award came as the climax of a long duel with his BSA opposite number, also young, the future world champion scrambler Jeff Smith, who had taken the Star from 1954 to 1956. In the opinion of marque historian Peter Hartley, although Johnny was to continue to ride Enfields for another six years, 1957 represented his peak since, other factors apart, from then on there were the demands of the thriving Royal Enfield agency which he now set up in Bloxwich.

Enfield had its star, and the Bullet gained belated acceptance with the public. Johnny remained modest. 'I didn't win a lot of Trials because I was a super rider,' he said later in an *MCN* interview, 'I think I won a lot of them because I was on a spring frame.' Don Morley too speculates whether the story might have had an even more successful outcome overall if Brittain had been not just a top rider but a maestro like Viney, Miller or

Far left *Johnny Brittain and the Bullet deep in action during the 1956 ISDT in Bavaria. The new frame broke.*

Left *Late days with the Bullet — Pete Fletcher contests the 1962 Scottish.*

Right *US export versions of the Enfield were marketed as 'Indians'.*

Smith. For, in a sense, the success came too late: that ACU Star was won a year after 1956, when, due to Major Smith's decision to concentrate on the 250 class, which will be discussed shortly, the factory had actually stopped offering for sale a production version of the heavyweight Trials Bullet. Thus they missed the immediate commercial advantage to be gained from both the Award and a string of other victories achieved by the team that year.

Then, to try and recoup, a 'works rep' 350 Trials Bullet was offered for 1958, but once again it was a counter-productive move, for to conceal the disparity between the mounts of the works team (Brittain, Peter Fletcher and Peter Stirland), their bikes were called in by the factory, one-off electron cases and all. 'Just when they got the bloody thing right,' fumed Peter Stirland, 'they went and mucked it up. The works bikes were never the same again.' Morley points out, however, that for the average clubman the works replica, despite a badly restricted steering lock and a weight penalty (he confirms a weight of 328 lb with oil) 'was still better steering and easier to ride than most manufacturers' products of the day.'

It was, however, nearly the end of the Bullet's glory days for other reasons too. On the road demand for big singles fell off sharply from 1960 onwards: and off it, Trials themselves were changing, as sections and penalization became stiffer to match the better machines now available, and consequently specialized dirt-bikes, and more particularly quick-response power delivery, exemplified by two-strokes both domestic and Spanish, became the order of the day. By 1961 only Enfield and AMC were offering traditional 'heavyweight' Trials bikes, and for Redditch that was the last year they did so. Ironically, with the single-minded pursuit of the 250 class by Major Smith and his successors, Enfield was potentially equipped with a four-stroke which, like BSA's C15T and Triumph's Tiger Cub, duplicated the two-stroke characteristics of responsiveness and lightness. But the potential was never fulfilled, the 250s remaining in practice indifferent performers on the dirt. With a badly flawed clutch and their unsuitable characteristics never developed out, they never scored well or caught on.

Backtracking a little, another element in the Bullet's comparative commercial obscurity had been, unlike its rival, the Goldie, a lack of road-racing success. The factory ISDT machines were 100 mph motor cycles, though, and after the 500 Bullet had appeared for 1953, the following year saw a number of racing specials, both 350 and 500, produced to order for approved riders, with bigger inlet valves, racing cams, GP

carbs and Lucas Wader mags. There was also the disappointing late 'Big Head' Bullet from 1959. Finally in America from 1955 Royal Enfields were marketed as Indians by the Indian Sales Corps (see 'Indian', Vol 3), until mid-1961 when they were again handled under their own name by independent distributors. The toughness and low-down torque of the 500 Bullet, sold there as the Indian Tomahawk, did well in cross-country sport Stateside, with a sixteen-year-old named Eddie Mulder winning the prestigious Big Bear event, and Elliot Shultz and others carving out an impressive record of flat-track wins. For this market, in addition to the higher performance 700 Constellation twin, the very hot export-only GP 500 Fury version of the 'Big Head' 500 was created specifically to take on the Gold Stars.

Real, highly publicized racetrack success for the Bullet in Europe had to wait until much later, when in 1977 Bedfordshire nurseryman Steve Linsdell came from nowhere on a classic racer built up around a 1950 350 Bullet he had purchased for just £10. Extremely painstaking assembly plus a bigger inlet valve and opened-up port, a skimmed head, own-ground cams, a caged roller big-end bearing to replace that plain floating bush, and a pre-war solid skirt piston to help bump up compression, all were part of a winning formula that regularly saw off ohc Manx 350s and 7Rs. Bill Lomas, harking back to Charlie Rogers' specials lore, also reckoned Linsdell's machine would be up to 40 lb lighter than some of his Velocette opposition. He dominated the pre-1953 350 class in vintage racing, frequently trounced bigger-engined bikes in unlimited events, and in addition went that way himself on a 1953 Meteor-based 700 cc twin (with the same extensively revised crankcase breathing and oiling arrangements as on his 350, about which he was not forthcoming). On the Meteor he won the 1979 Vintage Race of the Year. From 1981 he switched from VMCC events to the Kenning/ Classic Bike series with its less strict regulations on originality, and ran a Seeley-framed 500 Bullet with belt primary drive, a GP Fury head, B50 piston, Weslake rod and shortened barrel, on which he went on to achieve second place, against modern competition, in the 1981 500 cc Newcomers' Manx GP. He lapped the Island at 96.54 mph, a near-incredible feat for a pushrod single, as well as a belated vindication for all those who had recognized the marque's potential.

Here, to interject a last personal note on the Bullet and perhaps on the marque's contradictions, I can only record that on the (village) street in the fifties when I grew up, the image of the marque was a long, long way from the tale of serious-minded innovation, competition endeavours and high production standards told subsequently in the history books. Not to put too fine a point on it, Royal Enfield meant dirt, noise, and oil leaks so bad that even we lads noticed them. The consonance of the words 'Royal' and 'oil' may have been unfortunate, giving rise to composites like 'Oiler', 'Royal Oilfield', 'Oily Enfield' and 'Iron Horses with Oily Feet': but they did have a basis in fact. Thin joint faces, an engine breathing system still inadequate after a redesign for 1950, the poor cylinder head to barrel joints with ineffective gaskets—these were some of the causes, and where they were not eventually developed out by the factory, owners have now come up with cures for most of them. Don Morley in a *Superbike* interview said it was the 500 and the twins rather than the 350 Bullet that leaked and caused the reputation, but while this is probably true comparatively, one notices that he includes some remedies for the 350 in his Trials book!

Remedies were no part of the thinking of our village's Bullet rider. It was an average two-wheel community of the day. There was a jovial labourer who wore a (totally unmerited) red beret and rode an A7 hitched to a double adult chair. There was my expatriate pal on holidays from Eton with a ponderous Jampot AJS 350. Otherwise it was in the days before my best friend among the village boys went into the Navy and graduated to early Bonnevilles ridden to the limit, and I went to university and dithered about on a first Norton twin. Beer was 1s 3d a pint, petrol 4s 9d a gallon, and we the youth were a lane-riding rabble on Villiers power, scooters and plunger DI Bantams. Except for Robbo. Robbo was your actual no-good boyo, son of a local farm girl and a departed black GI, swarthy, greasy, with a perpetual evil leer. What tall, slabsided single did Robbo straddle, the oil-soaked engine at rest fuming gently, infernally, with the smell of hot oil from the puddle underneath it clearly perceptible at twenty paces? Yes, you've guessed it. It didn't seem to do him any harm with the village girls, though.

While the above is just a personal snapshot, it is true that from the mid-fifties Enfield's roadsters, the fastest 250 and the biggest twins with the most chrome, did put them firmly in the undeniably disreputable corner of the black leather jacket and white silk scarf boys. In fact, it was the well-publicized wipe-out rate among big twin-riding rockers which helped push through the 250 limit for learners, which in turn did Crusader and Continental sales no harm at all. But this benefit was hardly calculated, since it was not to become law until 1961, and as mentioned previously, Redditch's concentration on the quarter litre emanated from Major Frank Smith himself and went back to a time before the 250 limit was contemplated.

The pre-war 248 cc Model S had been revived, for export, in 1952, and then marketed in the UK for 1954, both rigid-framed and as the spring-framed 250 Clipper. (The Clipper name, despite the verbal association with the tall ships, invariably indicated economy models for Enfield, often using up end-of-range components, with the price 'clipped' to the minimum.) These 250s, however, were produced to take advantage of one of the many post-war stop/go government economy measures, namely 1953 Budget concessions which to encourage sales reduced the cost of road tax for sidecar combinations under 250 cc.

A completely different 250 of true unit construction had already been put into prototype form as early as 1950, featuring, in common with the eventual Crusader series, the unusual location of the camshaft and pushrods on the left of the cylinder. However, from 1954, Reg Thomas, who had by then taken over from Ted Pardo as chief draughtsman, designed from scratch the 250 that was the basis of the Crusader/ Continental range, with Tony Wilson-Jones developing it until its launch in August 1956.

Above left *Enfield classic racing ace Steve Lindsell with 1950 350 Bullet-based racer, seen here at vintage Mallory, 1978.*

Right *Fruit of a vision: the Enfield Unit 250, in sport 1963 Continental guise.*

'Love it or loathe it'. Albion four-speed gearbox, with unique Enfield neutral finder.

Major Smith had had a vision, correctly as it turned out, that as the fifties continued, the pre-unit heavyweight 350 and 500 single would fade in favour of a unit quarter litre, faster, lighter to handle, easier to work on and more economical to buy, license and insure for the young rider it was aimed at—as well as capable of development. The latter the Crusader/ Continental certainly proved to be. Though experimental versions included a four-valve head design which never materialized and a 200 cc ohc version that never got beyond the prototype stage, the pushrod engine in production form would increase from an initial lowly 13 bhp at 5,750 rpm to an exhilarating 21.5 bhp at 7,500 rpm on the 1964 Continental GT.

For a man in the latter stages of a long career who was still overseeing the development of a good big single, once again this was real forward thinking, both imaginative, and justified by events. Times did change: scooters would have a lot to do with the demise of the Clubs, which dwindled further as sporting mounts became more specialized after 1960. For as well as the 250 learner limit, affluence and changing market patterns meant that where in 1948, the 17–25 year-old category had represented only 33 per cent of riders in the UK, with the lion's share (58 per cent) being the 27–49 year-olds, by 1965, riders aged from sixteen to just twenty years old now represented a substantial 40.3 per cent of owners, with those aged from 20–39 down to 33.9 per cent. It was this which, with all its faults, still made a success of another light unit 250 four-stroke single, BSA's C15, their most profitable model in the sixties. But the C15, like AMC's less happy 'lightweight' 250, was not on the market until 1958. Once again Royal Enfield had got in nearly two years ahead of the opposition.

Once again, however, the vision was only partially fulfilled in reality. At 312 lb dry, the Crusader was over 30 lb heavier than its C15 rival. The short-stroke 250 (its dimensions were the reverse of the Model S 64 × 70) shared the Enfield tradition of breathing problems and oiliness, and they were combined with a barely adequate oil pump. The further major flaw lay in its clutch, despite a redesign for 1960, and its gearbox.

Gearboxes were a problem point with Enfield. The old Albion box on the heavy singles and the twins, with its internals little changed from 1949 to 1970, as Bruce Main-Smith recognized, 'you either love or loathe'. It was one more thing that set the marque apart. The bolted-up box with its exceptionally long high-set pedal belying its unusually short travel, needed firm pressure and a deliberate approach, and even that could fail to avoid a tendency to find neutrals, particularly when changing down. The patented neutral finder fitted on the roadsters was useful if you were locked in gear at the lights, but limited by not working from first, which when worn it could sometimes inadvertently engage. Bolted-up in semi-unit, the box's tall shape made substitution of alternative components very difficult. Bad clutch slip, which will be dealt with in place, would be a feature on most of the twins, especially with the scissors-action device introduced for the 1958–60 Constellation, as well as with singles if their output was raised.

But the heavyweight box was at least massive and quite robust. The 250's was less so, and its own false neutrals were accompanied by a tendency to detach its clutch from the gearbox mainshaft. The later five-speed internals would be even more of a problem. Otherwise the quarter litres were noisy, with both a very raucous exhaust and excessively clattery valve gear, and relatively crude machines with their undamped front forks. Probably they lingered too long at the stage of the more utilitarian Crusader models, but by 1958 the Crusader Sports had hoisted the top speed to around 79 mph, and the Continental models including the GT with its fragile five-speed box were even faster, up in the mid-80s. The latter model was launched in late 1964 with a successful stunt ride from John O'Groats to Land's End by pressmen, interspersed by thrashes round race-tracks on the way by top riders. The speed alone ensured its street credibility, and with only the C15 and AMC derivatives for competition among the Brits, the cherry red and chrome Enfield 250s were the ones for the fast lads when the 250-only hammer came down on learners in 1961. Accordingly they sold quite well, the Crusader Sports keeping up a good average for several years, and just under 1,000 Continental GTs being sold in 1965 alone. But by then it was not enough to reverse overall declining trends. This was despite company publicity emphasizing the 250's capacity for excelling in all areas—on the road, touring as the Airflow Crusader, road-racing (with first-in-class wins at Thruxton 9-hour races), even sheep-herding (with the export Wallaby), and trials. Although it was possible to bore out the engine to 350, the fact was not at first disclosed, so as to maintain promotion of the 250.

The other strand of Enfield's production was the big twin. Once again the factory led the field, this time in sheer engine capacity, in 1952 surpassing the 650 Thunderbird and Golden Flash with their 692 cc Meteor. A little elementary arithmetic reveals that with another touch of the modulars, Enfield had doubled up the 350 Bullet, which shared bore and stroke with this big but soft-tuned parallel twin primarily aimed at the sidecar market (just as the 1959-on 496 cc Meteor Minor was to be a doubled-up Crusader). The 692 cc motor, however, provided the development potential for the most powerful production European road motor cycle engine, after the Vincent and before the Atlas, at a time when the war among the twins was hotting up for the prize of the lucrative American markets. But though the factory saw this clearly, the opportunity was once more substantially lost.

This was true despite the fact that, by the end of the decade, Enfield were offering an additional edge on the opposition, a really desirable accessory for the twins in the shape of the Airflow full fairing (it came for the whole range, but looked and seemed especially appropriate for the big road-burners). It was both exceptionally effective, and handsome, since the other features of the machine, such as an extra large front mudguard and optional pannier equipment, were tailored to suit the lines of the faired bikes, without falling into the impracticality of the quarter-circle panniers often used to complement other radical fairings like the Avon Streamliner or those offered by DMD or Peel.

Early big twin. Meteor 700 on test on a frosty day in 1953.

The Airflow's genesis had been a test project in 1956/57 involving two magazines, the blue 'un (*Motor Cycle*), and *British Plastics*. As the bike journalist involved, Vic Willoughby, explains in his excellent book *Exotic Motorcycles—A Tester's Privilege*, up to that time weather protection had never paid commercially, due to its lack of appeal with the youth market. But by that year the fully-enclosing shells of 'dustbin' fairings were becoming popular even with that flighty market sector, due to their association with the faired racers of Guzzi, NSU, MV, etc. Thus the glamour of increased speeds from streamlining was allied to the solid benefits of better fuel consumption figures and crash

Left *Vic Willoughby rides out on the 'dreamliner' Bullet early in 1957.*

Below right *Practical and good-looking, Enfield's Airflow fairing with matching mudguard and luggage. Seen here on a 250.*

Below far right *A five-ton lorry runs over an Airflow to prove the fairing's strength.*

protection for the rider, as well as protection from the elements, which Willoughby, as a 30,000-mile-a-year tester in all weathers, had appreciated ever since Philip Vincent had given him a glimpse of it in 1955 with his faired Series D Black Knight swan song.

To explore the benefits of a total enclosing fairing, Royal Enfield were persuaded to provide a five-year-old factory hack 350 Bullet, around which Lawrie Watts, the *Motor Cycle*'s talented technical artist, drew out a futuristic shell design. This was 'the Dreamliner—tomorrow's roadster today.' Translated into glass-fibre by Richard Woods from *British Plastics*, the very full-skirted fairing was a striking but not ungraceful sight, with its frog-eyed twin headlamps, rocket launcher-like cooling ducts at foot level, and swirling two-tone pin-striped paint job on the panelling encompassing both front and rear wheels. Belying appearances, handling was unaffected, and on testing, other benefits were found to be substantial and real. The model's top speed was boosted by 10 mph, and petrol consumption cut by between 25 per cent at lower speeds around 40 mph, and up to 35 per cent above that (partly provided by not having to leave top gear on gradients) so that Willoughby could undertake a 400-mile round trip cruising at 70–75 mph and still achieve a 90 mph average, all this in autumn clad in just mac and gloves. The Dreamliner's flowing curves had a purpose, since not being slab-sided it was less buffeted about by side-winds.

Royal Enfield were delighted with the exercise and its attendant publicity, and set about using the Dreamliner as a springboard for their own enclosure. There was just one snag: at the end of 1957 racing's governing body, the FIM, banned dustbin fairings on racers. This was to stop amateurs getting blown off the road in high-sided home-brewed fairings, but as Willoughby observes, the ban had the effect of ending aerodynamic research which had led to the good-looking and efficient fairings on machines such as Guzzi's singles, and might ultimately have had a spin-off benefit for roadsters.

A total enclosure would probably have been too radical a step for Enfield, despite the stylistic leaning to machine enclosure at the time, following Triumph's elegant lead with the Twenty-one 3TA, by Ariel with the Leader, Norton with the Jubilee, and several of the Villiers-powered two-strokes. At Redditch they contented themselves with the Airflow, their excellent version of the dolphin fairings which replaced the 'dustbins' on the racetrack. First offered for the 500 twins in July 1958, and displayed at the 1958 Show on the Constellation, from then on the Airflow and its attendant very large sprung front mudguard was available for the whole range (including the lightweight Prince and Ensign III) except for the works rep Trials 350, and later the leading-link 250s.

Enfield had tried to provide a rigid, rattle-free unit that did not inhibit maintenance, enlarge the turning circle or create backdraughts. The Airflow was constructed of two main fibreglass sections bonded together (as was the sprung mudguard). The larger section formed the main front nose and legshields, with the second making up an instrument fascia and cubby-hole bulkhead, into which the main nose-support fixing was bonded. This bolted to an extension which ran forward from the headstock and was supplemented by lower fixings, located beneath the cooling air ducts in the moulding. The fixings were effected by half-tube sections bonded into the mouldings, which married with extended supports bolted to the front engine plates. The two parts were clamped together with a jubilee clip on each side.

Only 18 lb was added to the machine's weight despite the fairing weighing 33 lb, the difference being made up by equipment discarded when it was fitted: the headlamp 'casquette', for instance, was replaced by a diminutive alloy fork crown with the speedometer blanked off by the Royal Enfield logo (conveniently provided in the shape of an Ensign tank badge), with the speedometer itself mounted in the fairing's bulkhead to the right, with matching ammeter and light-switch on the left.

At first Redditch produced these fairings themselves, but from late 1958 the Airflow was being made by Bristol Aircraft Ltd, whose wind-tunnel had assisted its development. It was joined for 1963 by a smaller version, the Sportsflow, for the unit 250 models. Both fairings were quite reasonably priced: for 1963 the Airflow added £30 to a machine's price, and the Sportsflow £18 18s. The designers had done a really good job, as even when seen today, the lines of the Airflow and the big mudguard chime particularly well with the bulky twin engine, suggesting solidity without clumsiness—and being offered in the machine colours augmented the designed-as-a-whole look. They also managed to more or less suit the unfortunate restyled rear mudguards on the 700s for 1961.

Claimed Airflow plus-points were a 5–8 per cent increase in speed and 20 per cent

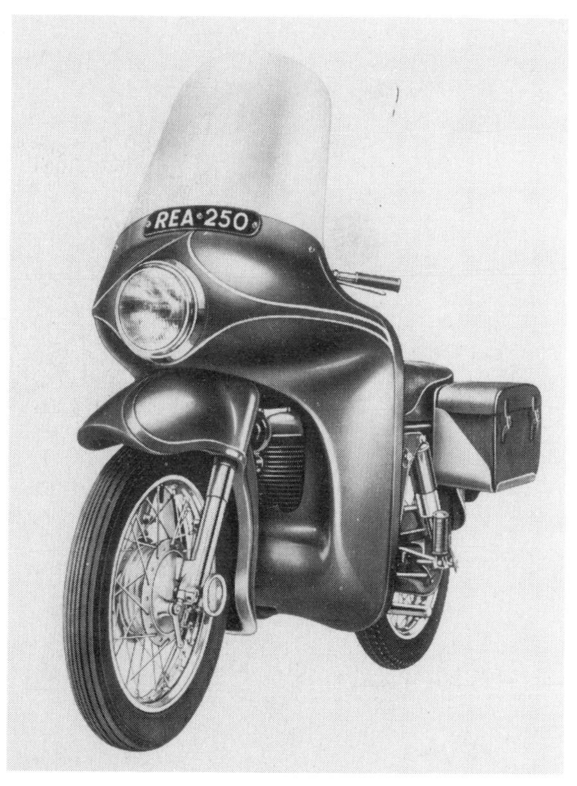

improvement in petrol consumption. Whether this creditable effort helped the company will have to remain debatable. Year-round riders know that fairings make absolute sense, but sense doesn't always predominate in the 16 to 20-year old bracket, and by 1960 the really sensible folk were buying now-affordable cars. As a 20-year-old myself around that time, I would not have considered a faired machine. If pressed, I would have cited the intimidating bulk, the increase in engine noise which was said to result, and the thing's vulnerability in a slip or spill. (The latter point would have conveniently ignored a 1958 photograph in *Motor Cycling* of a 5-ton lorry at Bristol Aircraft backing on top of an Airflow, with no apparent ill effect: a good fairing might get scraped in a crunch, but really did protect the rider). But the truth was that already I had persuaded the university film society to beat the ban on its general release and show Marlon Brando in *The Wild One* ('What you rebelling against, Johnny?' 'What've you got?'), and from then on you could leave fairings to the Black Rats, as Metropolitan motor cycle patrol men in their long dark DR macs were unkindly known, for ignoring the rain outside, my head was filled with dusty backroads, studded leather saddlebags and cowhorn handlebars.

For it was certainly the era, from the mid-fifties on, of the Rocker Follies, and as mentioned, for the US market and the black leather boys, the factories were vying with each other to produce the biggest, fastest, rortiest roadster twin. The arena for this seminal 'Battle of the Twins' was not the familiar ISDT, which Britain never won again after 1953, nor the TT, dominated by specialist racing machinery since pre-war days, nor yet the Clubman TT where BSA Gold Star supremacy brought the series effectively to an end by 1956. It was the emerging long-distance production races which rapidly became an index to the state of the art, closely observed by speed-merchants among the public.

The principle had been inaugurated in 1955 with the Thruxton 9-hour event (the Thruxton 500-miler from 1958); and from 1956, when the Super Meteor, a more sporting version of the soft Meteor, emerged in response to US demand, Enfield had an invaluable man involved with these races. This was Syd Lawton, a canny Southampton dealer who was to become the doyen of the events. In the early sixties he provided valuable assistance for Doug Hele in the development of the Norton 650SS, as well as victory publicity that built its reputation in Britain. But as a recent *Classic Racer* interview made clear, for the first five years it was Royal Enfield's big twins to which Lawton devoted his considerable talents.

The basic tool, Super Meteors soon modified to Constellation spec, he rated highly. At their heart Tony Wilson-Jones had broken ground in 1947 for the 500 Twin by specifying Mechanite 18 ton/in^2 nodular iron (for the 1958 Constellation this would increase to spheroidal graphite iron of 40/45 ton/in^2), for a crankshaft modified during prototype development from built-up construction to a single substantial cast shaft running on two bearings with split ends. This specification was maintained for the bigger twins as well as for the 1958-on short-stroke Meteor Minor 500, which though well-rated, came at a time when the 500 class of twin was being eclipsed in the market place by either bigger or smaller machines. The 692 cc motors highlighted what had always been the 500 twins' weak point, lack of rigidity due to the separate cylinder layout, which together with the engine being a stressed member led to the crankcases eventually shuffling out of shape. The increased capacity also led to increased vibration.

Jack Stocker entered a 692 cc Meteor in the 1952 ISDT (a capacity record for that event which has never subsequently been surpassed.) According to Don Morley, the ride for his Gold that year was truly heroic, involving lashing a broken front fork leg together with a spare rear chain and completing that day's trial one-handed, as he held the fork together, but still unpenalized. In the speed sections of the event vibration on the Meteor was so fierce that five pairs of handlebars broke, and Stocker was numb up to the shoulder for a week afterwards.

Enfield sought to counter this tendency by balancing the twins' crankshafts dynamically as well as statically, and to greater factors; but in contrast to the exceptionally smooth singles, the big twins, though no worse than other parallel twins of the day, and better than most in the mid-range, became known for vibration at the high speeds which their capacity encouraged. They also shared the singles' lubrication and crankcase breathing system, and its discontents. From now on the twins, even after a breathing system revision for 1960, reinforced the marque's reputation for oiliness, as the lack of rigidity combined with minimal joint faces after boring out to the big capacity, and poor sealing arrangements, to result in frequent blown head gaskets. They were also known for running hot if high speeds were maintained. At first this was due to inadequate finning (remedied for 1958), but it also came from the more fundamental feature of the oil compartment's position in the crankcase. The same thing that had been a marque advantage in winter as it warmed the oil rapidly due to proximity with the hot engine-room, became a disadvantage on the bigger and busier twins. Clutch problems continued and even increased after the 1958 redesign on the Constellation.

Nevertheless the vital statistic for Syd Lawton was there: around 51 bhp for the Constellation (at a time when Triumph's top 650, the new T120, was only putting out 46), a top speed around 112 mph in standard form, allied to exceptional low-speed torque and flexibility, with magneto ignition for the relevant sports models, in a frame whose qualities have been noted, and with better than average brakes for the day. While their massive looks suggested excess weight, in fact at around 405 lb dry they were little heavier than the other factories' large twins (with the exception of Triumph's 20 lb lighter T120).

Lawton began his involvement modestly in 1956, by entering the new-for-that-year Super Meteor; it failed to finish, after one of the riders slipped up with the reverse-direction rear-set gearchange fitted for the event, changing the wrong way and bending the valves as the revs went through the ceiling. Lawton, however, had seen the potential, and the company, via Jack Booker, was keen to offer support. Roger Shuttleworth, the foreman in the engine department, built up a special Super Meteor engine for the 1957 event. This fitted W and S valve springs, state-of-the-art Gold Star alloy valve caps and collets, and nimonic BSA valves cut down to fit. (Not coincidentally the cylinder head of the 350 Bullet—'half a Meteor'—had already benefited from a redesign for 1956 from works experience with the ISDT singles. On test the race Super Meteor with the new head returned 118.7 mph, a real advantage at a time when the best T110s were doing 110 mph and Gold Stars, though quicker flat out, lacked the big Enfield twins' acceleration.

The recast head permitted gas-flowed, opened-out inlet ports, the previous head having complicated the use of the same shorter Gold Star inlet valves, springs, caps and collets as were now being featured on the racing twin.) While not strictly within the Production format regulations, these internal changes on the race Super Meteor, with the components Enfield-manufactured, would be adopted for the Constellation which was to be produced for export that year and released in the UK for April 1958.

The 1957 race was both vindication and frustration. Enfield riders Derek Powell and Brian Newman led from the start, but unknown to all concerned, the steel tank on their Meteor, which had been a tight fit over the frame, had been 'assisted' into place by a thump on the sorbo rubber pad on top, where riders rested their chin while getting right down to it. Unfortunately this had dented the tank under the rubber, which was the spot where it split during the race, just where it could spray fuel into the riders' faces. They still finished third, though, and the bike 'ran like a train'.

So 1958 saw a still more serious assault, with Lawton securing the services of top rider Bob McIntyre, whom he teamed with the previous year's Derek Powell and mounted on the tweaked Super Meteor. This was significant, as the new Constellation had been released in the UK in April 1958, and Lawton's other pair, Brian Newman and Ken James, were mounted on it, as well as three other teams of Enfield riders. But while using Constellation parts internally, Lawton says he knew that the Constellation, the fruit of Tony Wilson-Jones' development, 'wasn't as fast on acceleration because of (its) siamezed exhausts.' He strengthened the Meteor's front forks by quietly substituting Norton fork tubes, for 'Bob Mac' had a reputation as a hard, punishing rider.

In the race McIntyre led from the start while still, says Lawton, riding within the bike's limits. Then lightning struck twice, in the form of another split tank. They were prepared with a substitute this time, but along with a later incident involving changing

Bob McIntyre (inset), a hard rider who had no luck production racing Enfield twins. Seen here at Thruxton 1958.

the plugs and magneto arm while trying to trace a misfire (in fact caused by swarf in the carb probably taken in during the tank change) the fracture cost the leading pair 3½ minutes to their principal rivals, Mike Hailwood and Dan Shorey on a Triumph T110. McIntyre's all-out riding clawed back the lead at the rate of three seconds a lap, but the race ended too early for him, with Hailwood's Triumph leading him by half a minute to win.

Despite Newman and James coming third and all but one of the remaining Constellations finishing, the result was a bad blow for the Redditch twins' street credibility. Journalist Dave Minton, a clubman and road rider at the time, recalled how the Sports version of the Constellation, launched for 1959 'was met with understandable public derision' as a result: a reaction that was reinforced by that year's race when McIntyre, riding for Lawton again, once more led off, but after experiencing bad clutch problems, overdid it and retired after dropping the model coming through the chicane.

The pattern of early lead followed by premature retirement seemed to back up street impressions of a twin that was unreliable if driven fast for long. *Motor Cycling*'s Bernal Osborne had sung the 1958 Constellation's praises over a series of ton-plus road runs in Belgium, followed by a dash to the ferry of 65 miles in 47 minutes, a very respectable standing start average of 82.8 mph; but he'd had to admit that he was 'a trifle oil-spattered', as during the run one of the rocker oil-feed pipes parted company with the union.

Matters did not improve. McIntyre, teamed with Alan Rutherford, again rode for Lawton in 1960, this time after a full-distance pre-race test session at Oulton Park. After the previous year's trouble with the clutch, Enfield had experimentally substituted on the race bike the redesigned clutch featured on the Constellation and 500 Meteor Minor, which was face-operated, with a shaft worked by a ball and ramp mechanism outboard of the clutch to the left. But the test session revealed that on the race bike the arm was subject to much high-speed vibration, and the clutch failed on the last lap, with the brass trunnion from the operating arm coming off, as well as the nipple detaching from the cable's end. The Enfield men said they would fix this by substituting a steel trunnion.

This they did, and in the race Bob Mac raced into a two lap lead, of which the less experienced Rutherford lost only half a lap, partly due to a split exhaust bracket.

Burn-up. A serious street racer (Check the leathers) winds on a 1959 Constellation.

A fine fifties period shot during the national rally, evoking quieter days — at least until the Constellation outfit fires up.

McIntyre was still a clear leader in the third hour when the clutch failed, as a cable broke at a point where solder had gone up past the nipple and made it brittle. He signalled the pits and was circulating for a clutchless lap before coming in, when the steel trunnion jammed the chain and locked the engine up solid. With no clutch working to disengage it, McIntyre was flung off at high speed on Club Corner, only escaping serious injury by good luck. 'It was little things like that going wrong,' observed Lawton with masterly understatement, 'which made racing production bikes such a challenge.' (I've heard it put other ways. In the sixties I briefly indulged in sport-parachuting at Thruxton, and remember two of our instructors, regular Para NCOs and veterans of Aden and Suez, judiciously warning me to have nothing to do with the motor cycle racing on the airfield, which they regarded, to paraphrase, as seriously crazy.)

The end of the tale came in 1961. The production clutch was redesigned for that year, with lift now provided by a pushrod through the mainshaft. But meanwhile, according to Lawton, Wilson-Jones 'took it into his head to fit new big-end bolts which were supposedly stronger,' to the engine, also fitting new con-rods. Lawton says that he distrusted these changes and had to be persuaded by Jack Booker not to shift Bob Mac and that year's co-rider to a Triumph. In the race only McIntyre actually rode, as soon after the start he was leading the pack up the hill at 115 mph when a big end bolt sheared, sending the con-rod through the sump and the rider down the road. That was the end of the effort: it had hurt Enfield badly, and even allowing for a big lump of the now familiar ill luck, was as frustrating in its way as the lost years with the Bullet. Lawton would still call the big Redditch twin 'a wonderful unit, strong and dependable, with the potential to be the best British vertical twin', but, 'though I gave (the factory) a list of 30 different points that needed attention, very few of them were acted on—it was as if some people at the factory thought I was treading on their toes.' If this sounds like fairly thinly-veiled criticism of Wilson-Jones in his capacity as development engineer, events did seem to bear out the judgement.

In April 1962, time began to run out for Royal Enfield with the death, at the age of 73, of Major Frank Smith. In British motor cycle companies the passing of the original family of pioneers often signalled the beginning of the end, and in this instance that point came at the start of the lean decade of the sixties which was quickly tightening its grip on the industry. Falling profits had not been arrested by the 250s or aided by the reported mismanagement by AMC of the Indian Sales Corp in the United States, where the market for their big twins might conceivably have provided the lifeline for them as it did for Triumph. So in the spirit of financial prudence already noted, in November 1962 the Enfield board accepted one of a number of takeover bids for the company, and became part of the E. and H.P. Smith Ltd Group.

This was by no means the end for the company as motor cycle manufacturers, however. The Smith Group (apparently no relation to the previous proprietors), owned interests which included companies involved with machine tools, static electrical equipment, electronic components and the packaging and medicine industries, as well as the gearbox producers Albion, and Alpha Bearings, renowned for their motorcycle bottom ends. They also included the necessary enthusiasm for motor cycling in the shape of Leo Davenport, a director of E. and H. P. Smith, as well as a strong enthusiast and ex-racer who doubled his role as joint MD of Enfield with that of competition manager. Retaining his position, his fellow MD and the Chairman of the reconstituted design committee was a 100 per cent Enfield man, the one-time sales manager in the fifties, Major Victor Mountford, who could be relied upon to look after Redditch's best interests. The committee now also included the works manager Gilbert Baker and designer Reg Thomas in addition to Wilson-Jones and Jack Booker; and in the opinion of Booker, the motor cycle side was pursued less vigorously. Booker, now development manager, and Wilson-Jones as consultant engineer, had to take on work for the whole range of powered products for the newly-constituted Enfield Industrial Engines, meaning both marine and industrial diesel work.

There was certainly no appearance of slackening in the 1963 range of bikes, which was trimmed of the big four-stroke singles for which demand had faded, as well as of the last of the old two-stroke Prince models, but introduced the 730 Interceptor and the hot five-speed Continental, as well as the ill-fated unit 350. But as is the way with new brooms in a company, a number of projects already under development were throttled or ground to a halt. In some cases this was legitimate, as perhaps with the five-speed 75 cc two-stroke single; its monocoque frame, housing the fuel tank, reportedly was rejected by dealers invited to inspect it, on the grounds of lack of eye-appeal. A Crusader with electric start via a Siba Dynastart would also probably not have set the market on fire. The supply of 692 cc engines to Berkeley Cars died of its own accord after some Super Meteor powerplants had been fitted to the 1959–on B95, QB95 and Q95 lightweight sports cars, and the 1960 B105 equipped with the Constellation engine, when Berkeley folded after the failure of a proposed merger with Bond. But one project did sound hopeful, namely a 175 cc ohc wet-sump engine which had already been mounted in a modified five-speed Enfield chassis. (The prototype is now on display at Bristol Enfield specialist L and D Motors).

This too was shelved. In their place Davenport's aim was immediately to restore, via the ubiquitous 250 class, the marque's name in scrambling and road-racing. To this

Enfield hired Geoff Duke to promote and develop their GP5 250 racer and other models.

end, in his capacity as competition manager, he brought in some very big names to assist with the enterprise. For a start Geoff Duke, whose racing charisma was useful in late 1964 in promoting the Continental GT which he had also helped to develop. Duke was also to run a race team including top names John Hartle and Percy Tait to contest the 250 class, thus continuing the theme of a model range that, with the addition for 1964 of the Villiers-powered Turbo Twin, was to include no less than nine variants of the quarter-litre capacity. 250 cc racing had not yet been swamped by Oriental machinery, and at clubman level, while the wealthy minority dominated on Aermacchis and a few Bultacos, the rest offered a market opportunity which Cotton and Greeves were taking up with powerplants progressively developed from the humble Villiers two-stroke single. The prototype Enfield scrambler of '63 and racer of '64 also relied on the Villiers Starmaker. But for development at the beginning of 1964 (to join Charlie Rogers) Davenport again hired the best, in the shape of Hermann Meier, the legendary two-stroke wizard from Bremen. Meier had recently tweaked the basic Ariel Arrow sufficiently for it to achieve seventh place in that year's lightweight TT, behind only a works Morini, MVs, and Hondas.

Meier began converting the basic Starmaker. Not unnaturally, given the group connection, the fruits of his labours, the GP5, featured an Albion five-speed gearbox and barrel-cam clutch as used on the rival Greeves Silverstone, and on Davenport's instructions, an Alpha bottom end with its pressed-in crankshaft and crankpins, which Meier reportedly found a handicap even after he had modified it. His engine altered the square Starmaker's 68 × 68 dimensions to a longer-stroke 66 × 72 dictated by the Alpha crank. His skill was displayed in the top-hat shaped combustion chamber, and the use of a barrel with four transfer ports, a notion only seen till then on the Walter Kadden three-port MZ racers, and not to feature on the all-conquering Yamahas for another three years. Power was up, from the Starmaker's maximum of 31 bhp at 7,500, to 34 bhp at 8,200 rpm for the GP5.

A trick feature of the cycle parts was the five-gallon fuel capacity, achieved by a three-gallon tank and a further two gallons carried in an underseat compartment. The GP5

The GP5 250 racer came just too late.

chassis was also excellent and interesting, being based on 1958 prototypes built by Reynolds which could accommodate the NSU Renmax as well as the Duke Nortons. The leading-link front forks housed first Woodhead-Monroe dampers, and then extra long Girling gas-oil units (which unfortunately could not be modified for tuning), inside large-diameter 531 tubes. In conjunction with a fabricated steering head, this made for an extremely rigid assembly, providing good handling reportedly marred only by intense susceptibility to surface conditions, with good brakes to match. The same engine powered the all-white 250MX scrambler, which went on sale in November 1964. The GP5 was racing by 1965, and with Tait timed at 132 mph, was faster than either the Silverstone or Cotton's Telstar.

But both racer and scrambler came just too late. As indicated, this new direction had involved a lot of money, reputedly £150,000 to develop the GP5, and if Greeves, Cotton and DMW were slower, they were at least producing and selling machines while Enfield were still at the prototype stage. Then, just when the effort was coming together, outside events intervened in the shape of the death, in November 1964, of Enfield's joint-MD, Major Vic Mountford.

This left a void soon filled by other voices

Geoff Duke posed on a Villiers-engined Enfield, the 1964 250 Turbo Twin. Keep smiling, Geoff — bike and Redditch company only have two years to run.

from E. and H. P. Smith, for whom the combination of Davenport/Duke's free spending on the GP5 and Continental GT projects, combined with the poor state of the industry as a whole, would provide ample excuse to dismember the old enterprise on cost-effective grounds. Development work ceased on the GP5 project after only around twenty production machines had been completed (these differed subtly from the Meier works bike ridden by Percy Tait and now owned by Burton Bike Bits' Mick Page): though the racer was still listed for sale as late as 1967.

As early as 1965 there was press gossip to the effect that Redditch was in trouble. This was a fact: between the start of 1963 and mid-'66, excluding the big twins, only 6,600 motor cycles would be sold. For 1966 the removal from the home market of the Interceptor (now being built at the Bradford-upon-Avon Westwood works) left the UK range at just three 250s. Behind the scenes a four-valve version of the pushrod 250, scheduled for production in 1968, was dropped. All this was explained by the removal of the entire remaining motor cycle production to the Westwood works in June 1966, the year that saw the fall of AMC. Large-scale redundancies resulted, and Interceptor frames were made from then on by Velocette at Hall Green. The last of the 250s was withdrawn from the market by January 1967.

Rationalization was spoken of to justify the move, but the true explanation was that the parent company was indulging in a little liquidization of assets. The old Redditch works was shortly sold to the local development corporation, and now forms part of an industrial estate. Bob Currie has stated that the Redditch site value brought the parent company considerably more than they paid for Royal Enfield originally. The company as a motor cycle enterprise still had a few more years to go, however. Complicated behind-the-scenes moves resulted in the announcement in March 1967 that the Enfield Cycle Company's share capital had been taken over for £82,500 by the newly-formed Norton-Villiers group, who were fresh from digesting the remains of AMC. It really was complicated, because Norton-Villiers' parent group, Manganese Bronze Holdings, already owned a 30 per cent interest in Enfield India Ltd, the subsidiary who in Madras and elsewhere were quietly producing versions of the pre-1956 350 Bullet at a rate of 1,000 a month for military, police and civilian use, as well as Villiers-powered models.

Dissolution continued apace. Tony Wilson-Jones' work on projects such as balanced-engine designs using planetary-type gear mechanisms to produce straight-line motion of the con-rod in otherwise conventional piston engines, as well as his published papers on stationary engines, had attracted the attention of a Greek shipping magnate. The latter had already taken over the Redditch-based Enfield Industrial Engines, where Jack Booker was MD and Wilson-Jones Chairman, before the 1967 Norton-Villiers announcement. But the new bosses' proposal to move the works to the Isle of Wight finally led Wilson-Jones to retire from the company he had joined over forty years previously. He passed away early in the eighties.

Another thing the deal with Norton-Villiers had not included was the motor cycle spares side of the business, and by April 1967 the sale of this had been completed, to the last of the independents, Velocette, who were

Strange fruit of the Norton-Villiers stake in both the Royal Enfield name and Enfield India. This Indian-built Villiers-engined machine was a 1973 tryout that didn't take.

themselves in terminally bad order financially. Details of this operation are available from Dr Joseph Kelly's thesis on Velocette, and provide an interesting example of the hidden assets that are lost when a firm like Royal Enfield ceases production. The apparently not very constructive step of the spares takeover proved advantageous for Velocette, who survived the next four years until their own liquidation entirely as a result of it.

When Velocette themselves went down early in 1971, the spares and rights, along with the Royal Enfield name, and shortly also the Interceptor tooling and spares, joined the remains of Scott and Vincent as the property of the Aerco concern of industrialist and enthusiast Matt Holder, who died in 1981. As a sidelight it can be mentioned that Leo Davenport had wanted to join the Velocette board to help raise the £100,000 necessary for that company's survival, but was rejected by the chairman who feared his getting control and that E. and H. P. Smith were bidding for Velocette until shortly before its liquidation.

Meanwhile Royal Enfields continued to be produced at Westwood where there were actually two works, the 'cave', where the twins' engines were machined before transfer to a second plant down by the river for finishing. The bikes were made under the name of yet another subsidiary company, Enfield Precision Engineers, which were also still owned by the Smith group, not Norton-Villiers. Although initially the latter had a contract assigning them distribution rights for the Interceptors in the US, these rights shortly reverted to Enfield Precision. This was reportedly due to the fact that Enfield Precision's parent company E. and H. P. Smith had put in an offer for the Villiers concern at the same time as Dennis Poore of the future Norton-Villiers was bidding for it. Poore had been irritated, and therefore relations between the two companies were not good. From then on Enfield Precision used P. Mitchell and Co, a Birmingham import-export agency, to arrange distribution deals both abroad and with the big South London dealers Elite Motors. Mitchells, at one time the biggest motor cycle distributors in the world, were then also the export agents for Velocette. It was this reversion of rights which led in September 1967 to the Interceptor, in 1A form, being announced as returning to the home market—though their two-gallon tanks and high bars betrayed their intended Stateside destination. In March 1968 it was admitted that while a few Interceptors might be available for home sales on an ex-works basis, the absence of a UK dealer network would keep things restricted. This proved to be the case, and few of the 1A and Series IIs became available here.

This was a pity, because under MD Harry Nightingale, (who was also MD of Alpha Bearings) the remains of the Enfield team [at Westwood] were far from idle, and in October 1968 came the last and reputedly best Enfield twin, the 736 cc Series II Interceptor, substantially redesigned by Reg Thomas, with a wet-sump lubrication system, Norton 8 in front brake and Roadholder forks, a revised clutch, and capacitor ignition. Still a tall bike (31½ in seat height) with its massive engine putting out around the same 51 bhp and 110+ top speeds as its predecessors, this Enfield however was oil-tight, notably smooth below 90 mph and with shattering mid-range acceleration. The only hangover from the past was the love-or-loathe gearbox which still required a patient approach.

Left *Glorious swansong. Series 2 750 Interceptor from Enfield precision for 1969.*

Right *Enfield India 350: a hybrid.*

These are rare and sought-after machines now, because sadly the company would not continue the unequal struggle for long. Norton-Villiers declined to help with further production, saying they were too busy with the popular Commando. This meant that the large sum already invested by Enfield Precision in the development of an 800 cc version of the twin was wasted. Marque historian Peter Hartley writes that £1 million had been spent tooling up for the 800, for which 400 advance orders had been received from the USA. At least one complete bike was rigorously road-tested by development engineer Richard Stevens, including trips abroad and runs at spring meetings, as well as a MIRA session where it clocked 128 mph. The prototype machine and a spare engine are now, appropriately enough, the property of the marque's leading Classic racer, Steve Linsdell.

As mentioned, Enfield Precision did not go into receivership, but simply ceased trading to concentrate on MoD contracts which they had secured. It seems that only around 1,300 Series 2 engines were built by the three-man team at Westwood before production ceased in June 1970. Already there had been one side-event involving these motors. In 1968 the flamboyant American publisher and entrepreneur Floyd Clymer, already Royal Enfield's distributor west of the Mississippi, had approached Enfield's agents P. Mitchell and Co about buying engines for a range of motor cycles he was intending to market in the USA under the Indian name. Originally he had meant to use Norton engines but this had been vetoed by Norton-Villiers' hard-nosed American distributor, Joe Berliner.

Clymer settled for Velocette Venom 500 single cylinder motors and 600 or so Series 2 Interceptor engines. The cycle parts were provided by Leo Tartanni of Bologna, the present boss of Italjet. Ian Abrahams of the Rickman Enfield register visually compared one of the Indian Enfield 750s with the later Rickman Interceptor, and found the Italian frames to be of lightweight narrow-gauge tubing, the headstock fairly narrow, the forks of spindly appearance and the main frame lacking the Rickman's secondary bracing. They had reportedly stood up well to exhaustive testing in Italy, however, and styling was impressive in the Western American mode, with high, cross-braced handlebars, skimpy mudguarding and short seat, and a finish catalogued as black with light blue panelling. The first batch was marketed in 1969 and the elderly but still optimistic Clymer foresaw 'A NEW BOOM IS ON THE WAY!... New jobs for returning servicemen will enable them to buy and satisfy a built-up desire to own some make of bike...' But he never saw it happen, as he passed away in January 1970.

This left export agents Mitchells with several hundred engines, no frames (since Velocette went down at that time) and no marketing organization. Casting around, they lit on the Rickman brothers, the same pair who had destruction-tested Royal Enfield's scramblers for the 1956 season. Now established as premier frame-builders, Don and Derek were already producing competition bikes, cafe racers and police machines with Triumph, BSA and Matchless engines, under the generic title of Metisse ('mongrel'). Mitchells commissioned them to build seven Interceptor-engined bikes as demonstrators, with the Rickman nickel-plated, all-welded duplex frame adapted to suit, Ceriani front forks, Lockheed disc brakes front and rear, and a weight loss of over 60 lb from the standard Interceptor 2, largely from the use of a fibreglass tank, seat unit, battery box and mudguards.

According to Abrahams the response to the prototypes was not overwhelming, but Mitchells managed to set up a distribution deal with the big South London dealers Elite Motors of Tooting, and commissioned Rickmans to produce further machines. 130 were built between April 1970 and January 1972, and interestingly, though Rickman aspired to build complete bikes, this was in fact to be one of their largest roadster production runs: 26 were shipped direct to Chariot Motorcycles in Canada, where, as in the States, an extra $600 got you a spare Series 2 engine! After that, although Elite were reportedly keen for further supplies, the engine manufacturing rights had gone to Matt Holder, and no more were built. The Rickman Interceptors are rare, desirable, and a nice swansong for what was, at the time they stopped trading, the oldest established make of motor cycle in Great Britain. Today Enfield Precision is in the hands of a Norwegian engineer who uses it as an investment company.

More of a postscript was the continuing saga of the Enfield India 350s produced by labour-intensive methods at the Tiruvot-Tiyur factory outside Madras. The original dies have long ago worn out and been replaced, and the 350 single adapted to local requirements by the use of components such as a tiny 1 in piston-valve Villiers carburettor, and the availability of accessories such as a sari-guard. By the 1980s a fan-cooled 325 cc conversion for diesel power, claiming to return around 250 mpg, was being offered by Sooray Tractors, while Pradeep P. Dani of Poona produces versions also substituting a 325 cc Greeves Lombardini diesel industrial

engine, which has the added advantage of being convertible back to a pump by bolting on a pulley for driving irrigation machinery!

At one stage in the early seventies Norton-Villiers gave some thought to importing the Madras product as well as a Villiers-engined 175 cc machine also built under licence in India, but rejected the idea on the grounds of quality and performance. By 1977 they had divested themselves of their part-interest in the company. But by then the effective demise of the British industry had set the Classic movement in motion, and in February of that year the enterprising Slater Bros concern imported the first Enfield India 350 'for the more mature type of rider'.

It sounded a nice idea at the time, and details will be found at the end of the Bullet section, but here it can be said that these living, breathing antiques, well finished but badly under-braked, came over as desperately slow for the traffic conditions prevailing by then: a top speed of just under 70 mph might be acceptable in one's old G3L or B31, which could be had for around £300 in those days, but scarcely in the consistently over-priced Bullet (£695 at first, rising to £968 by 1982 and £1,300 by 1984). This was allied to a low resale price, because the bike had never really taken with the enthusiast public (in a rash moment I once proposed to Bullet-fancier Royce Creasey that we should ride a brace of these machines back to their country of origin, but his only response was that in his view we should round up a mob

One of several under-rated models from Redditch: the clean lines of a 1960 250 Crusader Sports.

of riders and drive them *all* back). In addition there was the need to spend around £200 on top of the asking price for British components to provide a satisfactory machine.

The high price was not the fault of profit-hungry importers, but rather of somewhat high-handed Indian business methods. The commercial practices of the sub-continent were one of the things the importers had to learn to live with, along with 80-90 machines damaged in transit, then the interruption of supplies in the winter of 1977/8 due to a strike, followed by a suspension of imports while production resumed at around 1,500 a month, which was only enough to handle domestic orders. Then there was a tidal wave, and the resulting damage meant imports only resumed in January 1979, with about 250 Bullets having been sold here by mid-1980.

When Slater Bros contracted to one brother in November 1981, the Enfield agency was taken over by Derek Chapman at Evesham Motorcycles, just sixteen miles from Redditch. Mr Chapman, an enthusiast, put the 'Royal' back on his goods in 1984, by purchasing the name back from the Holder estate, and even managed to re-export twenty Bullets to Germany. More ambitiously he also planned a radically different 500 version, liaising with the recently redundant Ken Sprayson, Reynold's frame wizard, to design and build a chassis of 531, and intending to employ the GP 500 Fury cylinder head. A prototype was constructed, but at the time of writing (1986) the project, which was to have been undertaken jointly with the Indian factory, was vetoed by the latter in 1985 and sadly appears to have foundered. It won't be the first time—in 1979 a Welsh enthusiast, Jim Norris of Newton Powys, having built up a Series 2 Interceptor for himself and discovered most of the tooling intact, presumably at Matt Holder's Aerco, proposed a limited production run, but the idea never came to fruition.

The story of Royal Enfield is in some ways a puzzling one, with a certain sense of unfulfilled promise, or at the very least a resolutely unfashionable image. In recent years the marque has stubbornly resisted a move among writers like Tim Holmes, Royce Creasey and Don Morley to elevate some of their products to Classic status, and Enfield prices continue to keep them among the best bargains on the old bike scene. They were never market leaders, and it is easy to blame that fact on their deficiencies. But no marque, and especially no British motor cycle in the fifties and sixties, was without faults, and those of the Enfields were rarely fundamental. Their good qualities (comfort, handling, finish and for the most part, reliability) were mostly invisible from outside, where what was chiefly apparent was noise and oiliness. They were forgiving of neglect, and robust: Dave Minton tells of a Series 2 owner whose broken crankshaft did no other damage; *Classic Bike*'s Tim Holmes got to Germany and back on a Series I with shot main bearings; and *Bike* magazine featured a well-used Rickman Interceptor which made the long run overland from England to Australia with no problems. The undoubted Royal Enfield weak point was the gearbox. In contrast, say, to Velocette's complex clutch which at least is highly praised when it is working well, the Albion box seems genuinely to be just something that you live with, its only virtue being longevity.

It was other factors (and one of them may have been luck, or the lack of it) that kept the Redditch bikes outside the post-war popular pantheon of AMC-Norton-BSA-Triumph, or the more exclusive coteries such as Vincent and Velocette. Its probable true classmates are Ariel and Greeves. All the above explains why, to the understandable irritation of their owners, *Classic Motorcycle*'s man at the auctions, Mike Worthington-Williams, can only confirm that Royal Enfields rarely fetch high prices. That very fact may have something to do with another observation, this time from alternative biking person Royce Creasey, to the effect that all the Enfield owners he'd ever met were nice people. Well, he never met that Robbo: but it does seem a happier note on which to leave the marque.

Royal Enfield: The Model G 350, Model J2 500, Model S 250/Series I Clipper (250), and 1956 Model G De Luxe 350 Clipper

The rigid-framed iron-engined Model G 350 single was Royal Enfield's first and basic post-war offering for the home market, principally differing from the pre-war machines and the wartime WD/CO 350 in fitting telescopic front forks to the old diamond-pattern cradle frame; these forks had been announced in November 1945.

The Model J 500 single very closely resembled the G. While a similar design to the 350, the J was completely different in detail, with a heavier frame, larger crankcase, and different gearbox fitting, rear hub and stand, among much else. It was not to be available on the home market until 1950, by which time it had changed (for 1949) to the J2 format. This involved a twin-port cylinder head and twin exhaust systems, something only Panther offered on a big single in post-war days. The particular exhaust note it provided was relished by enthusiasts. Though Royal Enfield silencers tended to be loud, this exhaust note was crisp and positive rather than noisy.

The 350 and 500 shared a common stroke at (70 × 90) and (84 × 90) respectively. These single cylinder engines were to be joined by the Clipper, a very similar 250, for 1954. Though rigid 250 machines with that (64 × 77) powerplant, the S and SF, had been in production since 1951, though again they had been for export only. The Clipper's 250 motor was to be mounted in a version of the older Bullet chassis.

The easiest external clue to this series of singles is the oil compartment jutting out in front of the cylinders, topped with a filler cap incorporating its own dipstick. Like all post-war four-stroke Enfields they carried the oil in the crankcase (but in a dry sump arrangement). Later machines had their oil case behind the cylinder, but in these early engines the three or four pints were carried in a compartment surrounding the flywheel housing, in front, behind and below.

The lubricant was circulated by the patent Enfield double-action pump, located towards the base of the timing cover, with a rectangular plate at either end, and driven by

Simple single: 1950 J2, mostly a sidecar hack.

a worm on the end of the crankshaft. Beneath the pump compartment lay the characteristic circular bulge containing the felt pad filter element, which was removable by undoing a one-armed wing-nut over its large end cover and drawing it out, together with its various washers and a pressure relief spring. The advantage of the double-action pump was that every stroke of its oscillating and plunger action was a working one. The pump to the rear of the timing cover was the delivery one, taking oil to the big-end bearing and rear cylinder wall. The one at the front, being a pump of slightly larger capacity, was the scavenge, collecting oil from the flywheel housing sump and returning it to the reservoir. (The idler pinions also fulfilled a secondary function as a kind of oil pump, returning the oil from down the pushrod tunnels to the reservoir.)

The only external oil-line ran from the top of the front end of the timing chest, where a spring-loaded ball-valve fitted to the oil return passage allowed a portion of the returning oil to be forced up a pipe, to lubricate the rocker gear under pressure. The oil compartment vented through the cap at the front, and at the rear on the 500 via a shallow S-shaped groove in one side of the joint face between the two halves of the crankcase, which could be blocked by too much jointing compound during a rebuild. The 350 Model G vented at the rear immediately behind the magdyno.

The bolted-up crankshafts on these models ran on a double-row roller race on the drive side and a single-row roller race on the timing side. The rollers were manufactured and built up by Enfield themselves by selective assembly. Con-rods were of RR 56 aluminium alloy, with the big ends consisting of a pressed and ground hardened steel sleeve running in the unique Enfield way, on a plain floating steel bush. For the 500 this was faced with white metal on both sides. According to writer Roy Bacon, the Model G 350 used a special alloy bush not needing to be white metal coated. Prior to this use in motor cycles, the plain floating bush had principally been seen in radial aircraft engines. The system worked well, and like the bottom end often gave a service life in excess of 50,000 miles. If the white metal of the floating bush did run, it was due to lack of oil: the bush contained evenly-spaced holes and an internal circumferential groove for oil distribution. The white metal coat could be renewed by rebore specialists and the floating bushes could be obtained as spare parts, but not the hardened steel ring, as in the event of failure a replacement con-rod with the race already fitted and ground had to be used.

The alloy pistons were ground oval and tapered, and for 1950 gave lowly compression ratios of 6.5:1 for the 350 and 5.75:1 for the J2 (though a higher compression piston was available for the latter). The valve gear was driven by part of a train of six gears which ended by also driving the 60 watt Magdyno on its mounting stacked behind the cylinder. The separate cams operated directly on the flat-faced tappets working in an oil bath. Adjustment was made in the way customary to Enfields: behind a plate at the base of the cylinder's right side, secured with a one-armed wing-nut, with clearance being taken up by screw adjusters at the base of the pushrods in their cast-in tunnel. Also housed behind this tappet cover was a decompressor fork, which operated on the base of the exhaust pushrod.

The head was secured to the barrel by four nuts and sealed with a copper head gasket. Post-war, in the interests of an oil-tight joint around the pushrod tunnel, a tubular ferrule screwed into the head around the pushrods, so that oil was conveyed across the joint by running through this tube, with thick hallite washers surrounding the tubes to stop oil working down the threads. At the top end of the pushrods the rockers occupied a single lower split housing and two separate top halves, with the rocker assembly positioned beneath a symmetrical alloy cover on top, secured by a single large nut. The rockers were forged in one, and the valves ran in pressed-in guides, with duplex springs and hardened end caps. An exhaust valve lifter was fitted.

On the drive side, behind a pressed-steel cover secured by a single central bolt and remarkably oil-tight for its type, primary drive was by a single strand ½ in chain. Adjustment to it was effected by swinging the gearbox about its pivot bolt. Located separately and well behind the case, this four-speed Albion gearbox was unusual in several respects: the length of its gearchange pedal, the massiveness of its internals, and the fact that the moving gears were all shifted as one by one fork, unlike the more

Powerplant of the 1954 Model S 250, a rigid machine for that year only. Note prominent forward oil compartment.

conventional arrangement of splines on the shafts and dogs on the gears. The two centre gears on the mainshaft were cut on one piece of steel, and splined to the shaft; the two corresponding mainshaft gears, though separate, were forced to slide together though rotating at different speeds. They engaged a series of dogs on the layshaft to give the required sequence of changes. It was claimed that this system 'made it quite impossible to engage two gears at once, no matter how much wear had taken place.' In practice, the combination of the system, and its components' bulk and consequent inertia, meant that overchanging and false neutrals resulted, unless a highly deliberate approach was adopted: this was a problem that would worsen with Enfield machines of higher output.

In the opinion of *Classic Bike*'s Richard Dames-Longworth, it also made 'gearchanging impossible while there is the slightest power being fed into the gearbox'. He found, too, a big gap between third and top on the 1952 Model G he tested, something shared with the Bullets. A more benign feature was the patented Enfield neutral finder, which worked via a shorter pedal pivoting on the gearbox and was operated by the rider's heel pressing the lever down to an adjustable eccentric mounted stop. It operated from second, third or fourth gears, and could be useful if a rider was stuck in gear in traffic or at the lights.

The clutch was a three-spring device with cork inserts, and contained for the 350 Model G, but not the 500 J2, one element of the Enfield's forgiving transmission, the clutch cush rubber. The other element sat in the hub of the rear wheel, the famous cush drive shock absorber, with six rubber blocks sandwiched between three vanes. As well as reducing chain wear, the cush hub was an important part of Enfield's comfort package, and again worked well, so long as an occasional check was made for backlash due to worn rubber blocks; when the driving member was held rigid, more than an inch of movement at the wheel rim indicated time to renew the rubbers. Wheels were 19 in and brakes 6 in SLS, front and rear, the latter being rod-operated. The rear wheel by 1950 was semi-quickly detachable, with an ingeniously 'split' spindle so that the rear inner tube could be entirely withdrawn without the rear wheel having to be removed. If it did, the mudguard was qd.

Front forks were the Enfield telescopics, running on substantial adjustable head bearings. They featured very long internal springs, fixed at both ends to work on rebound as well as compression. These springs were fastened at their bottom end to a long tapered stud. The stud was anchored to the lower fork end, and its minimum diameter was in the middle. There it passed through a port formed in a bronze ring screwed to the bottom of the upper fixed tube. Oil carried in the bottom end of the lower tube was forced through this orifice as fork movement occurred, hence controlling the degree of damping.

The light alloy fork end carrying the front wheel spindle was offset forward, to reduce the inertia effect on the parts, and at first screwed on to the lower fork tube. But difficulties in keeping the threaded joint oil-tight, and failures of the thread (which was alloy into steel) led to this lower fork end on the rigid machines being cast integrally with the sliding member for 1951, when forks for the iron-engined singles became the same as those for the Bullet, with the same 1½ inch spindle lead. A novel feature of Enfield forks was that their leading spindle configuration meant that if the lower sliders were simply reversed, a crude version of sidecar trail was achieved; though Bruce Main-Smith confirms gently that 'this trail reduction does not bring all expected benefits once a chair is fitted.'

However, alternative sidecar versions of the fork for the G and J2 were offered, with heavier springs but also different yokes giving a smaller amount of trail and thus lighter steering. The earliest version of the fork top yoke was known as the ball-head clip, located on the top of the steering stem and the tops of the two fork legs. Sidecar forks were distinguished by a different ball-head clip, and by V-shaped steering crown bridges pushing the legs further forward from the steering stem and giving less trail: on the solo forks the front end of the bridge was practically straight. Another feature of the period was the deeply valanced front mudguard, hung on a pressing fixed to the lower fork yoke, and not featuring stays. However, when a steering damper was fitted, as it usually would be for sidecar use, this type of mudguard could not be employed, and was replaced by one fixed to the lower fork tubes and the wheel spindle lugs by three stays. The Enfield forks, as we shall see, despite their two-way damping were slightly less than ideal, but for 1946 represented a big step forward from girders.

The diamond-shaped rigid cradle frame featured very substantial single top and down tubes, a single saddle tube and duplex upper chain stays. All main tubes were of chrome molybdenum, with brazed joints. A saddle, Amal carb with oil wetted air cleaner, simple headlamp-mounted ammeter and light switch and fork top-mounted Smiths Chronometric speedometer completed the package. Finish, from 1951 a sober black with gold lining, emphasized the model's utility role. With an output of 15 bhp at 5,500 rpm for the G, and 21 bhp at 4,750 rpm for the J2, these sloggers were built for durability rather than speed, with the J2 very much meant for sidecars. The price reflected this: of British rigid ohv 350 singles in 1951, only BSA's volume production put their B31 about £2 10s below the Model G's £166 2s 3d, which undercut both the Ariel NH and Matchless G3L at £172 10s, and Norton's Model 18 at a whopping £201 17s 9d.

A test in mid-1951 of a J2 and chair found it well suited to the role, with exceptional low-speed torque and transmission smoothness meaning that top gear could be used for anything over 20 mph, including climbing hills in traffic queues. The engine could not be overdriven, was easy to start, and idled well. Minus points included a small oil leak, a noisy engine (piston slap) and exhaust (at everything but low throttle openings), and a vibration period from 35 to 45. However, in general these models had a reputation for exceptional smoothness among big singles; a correspondent in the REOC magazine, *The Gun* recalled 'an uncanny stillness' through the handlebars, tank and footrests on a J2 at 70 mph on sidecar gearing. For that reason the same gentleman judged that you could 'forgive the front forks' which were 'imperceptibly below average' but gave quite nice handling 'until they fell apart'. Don Morley too confirms that the Enfield forks did not work very well (though he is referring to off-road), which he blames on their weight, and on the internal mainsprings being too closely wound, consequently becoming coil-bound. This he

Model G 350.

Model J2 in harness.

says can be remedied by substitution of smaller gauge, more open section springs (he mentions those from the BMW R100 RS, while Royce Creasey recommends trimming Norton Roadholder, though not Commando, springs to suit). Otherwise, Morley rates them a good design.

As bottom of the range models, the rigid 350 and 500 were little developed. For 1950, the J2 debut year in the UK, both followed the Bullet in adopting a Lucas 'long-type' dynamo, and the rear end was tidied up, with the mudguard simplified, a single central lifting loop replacing the previous one on either side, and for the G a single toolbox on the right side replaced the previous three, while for the J a box was fitted on either side. For 1951 there were modifications to the oiling system, and they joined the rest of the range in fitting the front mudguard with three stays on each side, which moved with the wheel, and abandoning the guard fixed to the fork yoke. They also adopted the Bullet's fork ends, which were less bulbous in appearance than their predecessors. The J2, when provided at some extra expense in sidecar trim, as well as a steering damper, appropriate gearing and heavier springs, in place of the ball-head clip now featured a new top yoke cast in alloy to carry the speedometer, and a new forged bottom yoke giving the appropriate trail.

For 1952 the Model G also adopted this cast alloy fork top yoke, while for 1953 both went with the rest of the range in adopting front brake cam spindles modified to be allowed to float, as well as the chrome-plated, red and gold, winged Royal Enfield motif on the tank (a version of this badge featured on the first Indian Enfields imported to Britain, but was met with such obloquy that it was hastily replaced by transfers!). Roy Bacon also mentions that there was an uncatalogued swinging-arm frame Model J produced during this year, presumably employing a version of the same frame as the Bullets and twins: though the rigid J2 certainly continued to be produced for some years.

The Model G 350 however, survived no longer, squeezed out by the more expensive Bullet and a brace of 250 cc newcomers for 1954, the rigid Model S, and the Clipper 250. The latter was offered at the same price as the Model G (fallen by now to £162), but for that included a modified version of the Bullet's swinging-arm frame. As with the Bullet's open diamond, the engine was an integral part of the frame, with the front down tube bolted to the top

Left *1955 250 Clipper.*

Below right *Misty morning, and a 1956 350 Clipper.*

front corner of the crankcase. The top tube split into two loops which swept back to hold the tops of the Newton damper units, and on the Clipper from there continued on under the gearbox. From them pressings braced the swinging arm pivot and the gearbox plates, which were also attached to the single saddle tube.

As mentioned, the Model S had been in production for two years previously for export only, and the 250s were introduced in the UK to take advantage of road tax concessions. The 'S' only lasted for that year, but the Clipper 250 was to be quite a popular model, featuring a version of the Bullet's casquette headlamp (but minus its twin pilot lights) and optional Vynide-covered dual-seat. The motor was simply a scaled-down Model G, with the same iron engine, 6.5:1 compression ratio, separate gearbox, and oil filler at the front of the crankcase. A significant difference from its predecessors, however, was the use of a/c electrics, with a crankshaft-mounted alternator, a rectifier and coil ignition. The contact breakers were accessibly mounted behind the cylinder, where the magdyno had been. Alternator electrics were perceived (correctly) by riders at that time primarily as an economy measure. The stator for the Miller alternator was mounted either in the back half of the primary chaincase, or for an RM13 Lucas alternative which coexisted with the Miller for a while before replacing it for 1955, in the outer half of the chaincase, enlarged to take it. In the latter arrangement, concentricity between stator and rotor was ensured by means of a spigot on the engine shaft locating in a bush in the outer half of the case. With this system an ignition warning light was visible through a small red window in the ammeter.

Another difference from the 350 and 500 was a lighter version of the gearbox, with internals similar to than employed on the larger Villiers engines of the time. There was consequently a different cable run to the rear of it, and no neutral finder.

'A full size motor cycle' at 330 lb, the Clipper was a shade under-powered at just 11 bhp at 5,500 rpm. A *Motor Cycling* test for 1954 managed a top speed of just over 60 but found it could cruise at 55–60 on long runs. They also liked the brakes (29 ft from 30 mph, despite front brake shudder when applied hard), found the a/c electrics reliable in the wet, and they appreciated the economy aspects: the 3½ gallon tank gave a range of over 300 miles, since an overall average of 95 mpg was recorded, though less welcome economies included the absence of a prop-stand or lifting handle.

For 1955 there were no changes to the J2, as with the 500 Bullet there to fulfil the sidecar role if necessary, this was its last year in production. The Clipper 250 had its gearbox end cover cleaned up to enclose the clutch lever and lower the gear pedal pivot so that it was concentric with the kickstarter. Inside, the gear ratios were made wider. On the bicycle the existing twin tool boxes, one in each rear frame loop, were supplemented by an oval air-clearer box as opposed to the previous year's square one, which also meant the deletion of the previously long inlet manifold, as the carburettor could now bolt directly on to the rear of the black cylinder barrel. This in turn had been permitted by the tidying up of the contact breaker mounting, which was now smoothly curved rather than juttingly triangular.

Further changes in this department followed in 1956 with the adoption of an Amal Monobloc carburettor, as well as the movement of the ignition switch from its position with the ammeter and headlamp/light switch on the casquette, to the front of the right-hand toolbox. The quarter litre bike was also joined by a 350 Clipper, its origin indicated by its early title of 'Model G De Luxe'; both models quietly emphasized the role of the Clippers in using up end of range components. For they soldiered on with the old, lower Bullet frame, with its saddle and its easy-to-spot rear mudguard stays passing outside the Armstrong rear suspension units, while for 1956 the Bullet range had gone to the new taller and lighter all-welded frame. Visually distinguished by a green finish rather than the maroon prevailing on the rest of the range (and much of the rest of the industry), the Clipper 350 featured the old 15 bhp Model G engine and gearbox, hence the latter's Magdyno, and hence the old type Amal 276 carburettor and no oval battery and air cleaner box as there was no room to fit them. Other differences for the 350 included the Bullet-type casquette with twin pilot lights, as well as 3.25 × 18 in tyres and wheels, against the 250's 3.00 × 19 in.

That was really that for the old iron-engined range: the Clipper 250 continued unaltered for 1957, but, overshadowed by the newly-arrived Crusader 250, was quietly dropped at the end of that year. There would be a Series 2 Clipper 250 for 1958, but that was an economy Crusader and will be found dealt with in the unit single section. Likewise there would be a Series 2 Clipper 350 for 1958, but again these were completely revised, being all Bullet bar the iron head, and more properly dealt with in the Bullet section.

The iron-engined Enfields were well-liked at the time and today are rated as economical, reliable yet distinctly Redditch transportation, and have not yet been 'discovered' in the same way as the rigid BSA B31 and the rigid Norton and Velocette singles. Weak points include the forks, as mentioned, though when intact they worked well enough. The single-sided 6 in brakes fitted all round were judged satisfactory at the rear but less so at the front.

While fuel economy was excellent, and even today, well-worn, a 350 will return around 70 to the gallon, oil consumption (and loss) was always a feature, the factory admitting realistically that while a new, correctly run-in model would use about a pint of oil about every 500–600 miles, this figure dropped to 200–250 on a worn engine, due both to leakage at the joints as well as inevitable loss in cylinder bore lubrication when oil worked down the valve guides and past the piston and rings to be burnt. One minor source of gush was admitted by Tony Wilson-Jones when he explained in 1955 that the Bullets featured a decompressor rather than the iron engines' valve lifters, due to the fact that sealing the spindle on the latter from oil leakage had proved extremely difficult.

Balancing that, there was the quite lively performance for both the 350 and 500, due to comparatively light flywheels (in big single terms), and to the alloy con-rod which also made its contribution to these models' notably smooth running. Looks were not a particular plus point—the correspondent in *The Gun* recalled that the police once wanted to check the frame number of his 1952 J2 because the style of the model seemed so much older. The Albion gearbox has already

1956 350 Clipper, popular iron-engined cooking model.

been discussed, and the 250 was saddled in its earlier versions with the Miller electrics, usually something to be avoided, in addition to its comparatively heavy cycle parts. But the Model G and J2, while not a particularly common sight, today surely represent the same good, understressed and economical transport as they did the first time around.

Royal Enfield: The Model G/J2/ Model S/Series I Clipper 250/Model G De Luxe 350 Clipper—dates and specifications

Production dates
Model G—1946-53
J2—1949-55
Model S—1954
Series I Clipper 250—1954-57
Model G De Luxe/350 Clipper—1956-57

Specifications
Model G/Model G De Luxe 350 Clipper
Capacity, bore and stroke—346 cc (70 × 90)
Type—ohv single
Ignition—magneto
Weight—Model G (1951) 370 lb; 350 Clipper (1956) 362 lb

J2
Capacity, bore and stroke—499 cc (84 × 90)
Type—ohv single
Ignition—magneto
Weight—(1951) 395 lb

Model S/Series I Clipper 250
Capacity, bore and stroke—248 cc (64 × 77)
Type—ohv single
Ignition—coil
Weight—Clipper (1956) 330 lb

Royal Enfield: Model G/J2/Series I 250 Clipper/Model G De Luxe 350 Clipper—annual development and modification

1950

For Model G/J2
1 Rear mudguard support simplified. Single central lifting handle replaced two on either side. For G, one tool-box on right side, for J, one on either side, replaced previous three smaller boxes.
2 Lucas long-type dynamos fitted.

1951

For Model G/J2
1 Modification to oiling system, with components of the oil filter and timing pinion assembly simplified.
2 Sprung front mudguard replaced by one with three stays on each side which moved with the wheel.

3 Forged fork ends now welded rather than screwed to their sliders. Forks as Bullet.
For J2
4 If provided in sidecar trim, 'ball-head' clip fork top yoke now features new yoke cast in alloy to carry speedometer, plus new, forged bottom yoke giving appropriate trail.

1952
For Model G
1 Cast alloy fork top yoke as for J2, 1951.
For J2
2 Spring prop-stand fitted.

1953
For Model G/J2
1 Floating brake cam spindles for front brake.
2 Chromed petrol tanks replaced by enamelled, with new 'wing' Royal Enfield pressed metal tank badges.

1955
For Clipper 250
1 Gearbox end cover cleaned up to enclose the clutch lever and lower gear pedal pivot so that it was concentric with kickstarter.
2 Oval air cleaner box replaces previous square one.
3 Long inlet manifold deleted, carburettor now bolts directly to rear of cylinder.
4 Contact breaker mounting housing tidied.
5 Miller alternator progressively replaced by Lucas RM13 with stator mounted in outer half of an enlarged primary chaincase.

1956
For Clipper 250
1 Amal Monobloc carburettor adopted.
2 Ignition switch moves from casquette to front of right-hand toolbox.

Royal Enfield: The 350 Bullet, 500 Bullet, and 1958–62 350 Clipper/350 Clipper De Luxe

The Bullet was in many ways Royal Enfield's crowning achievement in the post-war period, and some of the reasons for this have been discussed in the marque history section. Here we will confine ourselves principally to what the roadster Bullet was, how it developed, and as a postscript, how to get the best out of one today.

There were not that many post-war roadsters conceived from new and built as a whole, rather than evolving by versions of old engines being fitted in new frames, or vice versa. The Bullet powerplant might have had features in common with the pre- and post-war iron engines, but it was individual enough to merit the description 'new', and it was slotted into a new and unusual frame. Its character too was distinct; as Don Morley puts it succinctly, 'it would plonk *and* rev,' pull and go. Among British springer roadster singles this side of the Gold Star, only Velocette could say the same.

It was also assisted by the fact that it was originally conceived as a 350 and thus did not have to haul around a 500's cycle parts. This meant that despite an appearance of weight from the massy engine, it was at least 30 lb lighter than the AMC 350 springer, and some 60 lb lighter than BSA's swinging-arm B31 when it came for 1956.

The 350 Bullet for 1949 may have shared its cylinder dimensions with the Model G (and acknowledged this with a G2 prefix), but it was the fruit of four years of Wilson-Jones' development work. Unlike the pre-unit Model G, the Bullet's gearbox was bolted-up

1949, first spring-frame Bullet.

to the rear of the crankcase, shortening the unit length. The crankcase was completely different, with the oil for compactness carried behind, not at the front of the case. Its cams were set significantly higher and its head was of alloy and of an entirely new design, with the external clue being the polished alloy caps enclosing each valve assembly. Internally the iron engine's narrow angle valves were replaced by ones set at 90° in the hemispherical alloy head, with cast-in inserts for their seats and for the spark plug. Further down, the distinguishing feature of the cylinder, which for the production roadster was of cast iron, was its deep spigoting, about three inches, into the crankcase which was finned around the neck.

The head was held down by five long studs in the crankcase, together with case-to-barrel fixing between the pushrods, and a similar stud above, in the top of the tappet chamber, gave a further fixing point between cylinder and barrel. (The latter was an easy one to forget when dismantling, and in that instance applying force could break the crankcase at the point where the stud was attached.) A substantial headsteady was an important factor in minimizing the effect of engine vibration on the rider.

Utterly distinctive. Close-up on the Bullet engine-room for 1950.

The crankshaft was built up, with the mainshaft keyed into flywheels of polished steel and held by a nut. It ran at first on a phosphor-bronze bush on the timing-side and a pair of ball-races on the drive side, where, like a Vincent, the crankcase was ribbed internally for strength and rigidity. The shaft was connected, by a big-end featuring the famous white-metalled floating bush (see p.82), to a light alloy (RR56) con-rod and a Lo-Ex alloy piston, giving a compression ratio for the roadster of 6.5:1, suited to the low-octane rationed Pool fuel that still prevailed in '49. The lightness of the rod and piston was a major contribution to the Bullet's notably smooth running.

Primary drive, again in contrast to the Model G's single strand chain, was by ⅜ in duplex chain, behind a handsome alloy cover with a round rubber sealing strip secured by a single central nut. While this was as vulnerable to overtightening and subsequent distortion as such arrangements can be, it did not necessarily happen that way (the single central bolt case on my 750 Commando stayed oil-tight for eight years), and the Bullet's was a good deal more effective than the pressed steel covers of several contemporaries. Enfield specialist Jack Gray has found that leakage from the joint can be caused by the groove for the rubber sealing ring being deeper at one point, and that a piece of soft string soaked in jointing compound and laid in the deep section can cure the trouble. A minor flaw was the lack of a drain plug. Since the gearbox was attached by four bolts to the hindside wall of the case, requiring fixed sprocket centres, primary chain adjustment was by slipper tensioner; once worn, this could pull out of the case, and classic racer Steve Linsdell (see p.64) was not alone in preferring adjustment by shimming the gearbox away from the engine. The rear chain was ⅝ in, and featured quick and handy adjustment by a snail-cam type arrangement on each side of the wheel spindle.

On the timing side, as with the iron motors, both camshaft and magdyno drive were by a train of gears. The magdyno for the roadster Bullet, stacked up on its platform behind the engine, above the oil filler neck and tight in to the rear cylinder fins, had led to a change in the shape of the top of the timing cover from the G, with a bulge cast in to allow the fitting of an auto-advance to the magneto drive pinion if desired. But the bottom half of the case resembled the iron engine's, with the circular bulge containing the felt pad oil filter element at its base. There were also detail alterations to the timing pinion and the oil pump worm, which were each initially machined as part of the mainshaft. Otherwise the layout resembled the G, with flat-footed tappets running in an oil-bath behind the familiar inspection plate, though due to the depth of spigoting of the cylinder, this plate with its single wing-nut was now attached to the crankcase, rather than the cylinder base as on the G. The tappets worked in pressed-in guides, to operate, within the cast-in tunnels, alloy pushrods with hardened ends and screw adjusters which were reached behind the plate.

The lubrication system too consisted of the customary twin double-acting oscillating plunger pumps, circulating oil through internal drillings and abetted by the timing gears, which due to the engine running at negative crankcase pressure acted as a further scavenge. There were the same benefits to the system of fast initial circulation of oil to minimize wear, and fast engine warm-up in cold weather, and the same drawbacks: proneness to obstruction by jointing compound (forcing oil down immediately after reassembly was the answer to that) or by fragments of engine; to leaks; and in combination with the proximity of the four-pint oil compartment to the crankcase, to running hot. The system's breather worked through the drive side mainshaft, which on these early models contained a non-return disc valve; it discharged not into the crankcase, but via an extension of the engine sprocket nut into a recess in the chaincase cover and thence via a drilled passage down through the cover wall into open air.

The exception to the all-internal oilways was once again the feed pipe to the rocker gear, which ran up from beside the front of the tappet inspection plate to a T-junction at the top of the cylinders, where each line ran to a union which supplied the inlet and exhaust rocker spindles. The rockers were steel blocks and cast iron, and though polished as standard, wear rate could be high. The valves themselves, with hardened caps, worked in pressed-in phosphor bronze guides. A final feature of the head, which was spigoted to the barrel, was its copper-asbestos gasket. This was designed both to seal the outer lip of the pushrod tunnels, and it was thicker there, as well as to act as a conventional inner head gasket. In the experience of writer and Bullet-owner Royce Creasey, it leaked at the former location and at the latter blew under hard use, especially after it had dropped with age. Creasey thinks that the connection had been originally designed as a gasketless ground joint as on the alloy engine Bullets of 1939, and points out that a further disadvantage of the copper-asbestos gaskets was their tendency to inhibit heat transfer from the head and valve seats to the barrel, so that in addition to a further cause of hot running, exhaust valves burning out were not unknown. However, leaving the inevitable potential weak points aside, the 350 Bullet was fundamentally a fine sturdy engine with a great deal of development potential.

The Albion gearbox, as mentioned, dispensed with the G's conventional mounting plates, being bolted directly to the rear of the crankcase. The general arrangement of operation was as described for the iron-engined singles. The internals were equally massive, and the ratios were notably low, with fourth at 5.67, third 7.37, second 10.2 and first 15.8:1; in Royce Creasey's opinion, early Bullets were 'grossly undergeared' for today's roads, and this remained unchanged until 1959. As with the iron engine, there was a big jump between third and fourth. The long, high-set gear pedal with its short travel, the need for a deliberate approach and firm pressure, and the propensity for producing neutrals once worn, were all as great as on the rigid singles, as was the patented heel-operated neutral finder (fitted on roadster Bullets only). But the stress on the box from later higher-output twins was missing, and once the Albion's character was accepted, it was unlikely that an owner would have to dismantle it in the course of a Bullet's working life. Something Don Morley has found liable to wear, though this was with the stress on competition engines, was the final drive-shaft bearing. The three-plate clutch was now operated by a quick-thread worm rather than Enfield's customary long lever: it incorporated a cush drive, and was six-spring, not three-spring as previously, with the extra three located inside the clutch cap by three small collars riveted inside the

350 Bullet and factory tester on the pave at MIRA.

cap. The clutch lever was fastened to the outside of the gearbox outer cover.

The swinging-arm frame which housed this semi-unit engine was constructed of weldless chrome-molybdenum steel tubes, with the engine forming an integral part of the chassis. It was attached to the single top and down tubes by the headsteady, by a small cross-tube bolting at the front to the top of the engine plates, and by a cross bolt at the rear passing through the bottom of the gearbox shell. The swinging-arm pivoted on plain bronze bushes. Clamping its mounting in place was an unusual (Creasey: 'illogical') miniature triangulated layout braced against the gearbox plate; but it worked well enough.

Nineteen inch wheels, cush rear hub, 6 in brakes front and rear, the internals of the Enfield telescopic fork, the sprung front mudguard, the headlamp and square box air-cleaner were all as on the Model G. However, the fork design differed in detail initially, with a greater (1½ in) lead to the spindle, and different headlamp brackets (though from 1951 onwards the Model G and J2 would share this fork). Initially too there were plated domes on the top of each fork leg, but from 1950 for the Bullet there was a new design of fork head incorporating an alloy facia panel housing the speedometer. Other distinctive features were the much-loved, sporty (and loud) upswept exhaust and silencer system with its drooping water-excluding tail pipe, and the rear mudguard. The latter was fully detachable after loosening the four nuts that secured both the two distinctive long stays which ran back from the frame outside the rear units, and the curved stay to which they were welded and to which the mudguard was attached. It ran round the line of the guard to the sub-frame. In conjunction with the two-piece rear spindle, this was one of Enfield's typically rider-friendly features in the event of a puncture. The rear units in these early days incorporated both a filler plug at the top and a level plug at the bottom.

The finish of the 350 Bullet and of its spring-frame was both handsome and distinctive. Their shapely chromed tanks, at 3¼ gallons half a gallon larger than the iron-head singles, were panelled in frosted silver, with dark blue and red coach-lining. The fine alloy castings and the heavy chrome on their fork sliding members, rear spring boxes and saddle springs as well as more conventional parts, set off the lustrous silver-grey finish of the rest of the cycle parts including the frame and chainguard.

A 1950 *Motor Cycle* road test immediately fastened on the essentials of this 'enthusiast's mount' (it had, after all, initially been catalogued as 'designed for the Clubman who wishes to take part in competitive events'). They wrote of 'handling qualities second to none' from the spring frame, and an engine that pulled well from very low revs (from 15–16 mph in top, with correct use of the manual ignition control), allied with smoothness and comfort. It proved to be both a 'get-in-top-and-stay-there' motor cycle which also could not be overdriven, with a distinct power step at higher revs; changing up from second at 48 mph and third at 65 was recommended, top speed of this low-tuned 18 bhp version being 73 mph. No fault was found with the gearchange (though the clutch was judged rather heavy in operation) which suggests that the box's problems are at least amplified with wear. Careful attention to the throttle setting (fractionally open) was necessary for a successful starting technique. Mechanical noise, and after 600 miles, 'a slght oil leak at the cylinder head' plus seepage from the oil filler cap were noted, and a braking figure of 32½ ft from 30 mph was not over-impressive. It was a fair summary of the Bullet's strengths and weaknesses towards the start of its career.

For 1950, as well as the introduction of the polished alloy speedometer facia panel already mentioned, the forged fork ends were now welded not screwed to their sliders, and the sprung front mudguard became of deep section in place of the previous side valances. A Lucas 'long-type' dynamo was fitted, and the silencer, though still upswept, was altered to a more cylindrical shape.

For 1951, perhaps in response to competition stresses, the roadster Bullet's timing side plain phosphor bronze bush was supplemented by a single-row caged roller race, located inboard of it. The oil pump worm, which had previously been integral with the timing side shaft became, as on the iron engines, detachable; the timing pinion, also previously integral, was now keyed on to the mainshaft by this oil pump worm, which was internally threaded. On the cycle side, the front mudguard was now mounted on three stays per side, and moved with the wheel.

There were further progressive attempts through 1951 and 1952 to tackle some of the problems associated with the internal-oilway lubrication system. Previously, on the return stroke of the double-acting pump, oil had been delivered through the oilways in the crankcase to the tappets and guides, with surplus oil at this point passing through a spring-loaded ball-valve behind the tappets, to be fed to the annulus between the cylinder spigot and the crankcase neck. From there, oil holes through the cylinder gave an oil feed direct to the piston skirt.

In the first modification, all oil from both feed and return strokes of the double-acting pump was fed to the big-end bearing instead. This was done by plugging the left-hand hole on the joint face between the crankcase and the timing cover, the hole that conveyed oil to the tappets and the cylinder annulus. The oil from the return stroke of the delivery pump was now forced through an oil passage in the pump disc itself, into the oilway to the oil filter and big-end bearing. The piston received enough extra oil by splash from the big-end feed to compensate for the loss of direct feed. In a modification for 1951, the oil passages to the tappets and cylinder annulus were no longer drilled, so the by-pass oil passage in the pump disc was no longer required.

Then for most 1952 and all subsequent 350s, and all 500s, the oil return was further modified slightly. Previously, after the oil collected in the sump was passed up to the rockers by the external oil pipe, any surplus oil was blown off into the timing-gear housing. Now an extra oilway was drilled through the crankcase behind the tappets, with a hexagon-headed by-pass valve fitted in the forward end of the pasage. (It should be mentioned that this pressure relief valve was non-adjustable, and if the spring in it weakened so that it was permanently open, the rockers would be starved of oil.) Surplus oil blown off from the rocker supply flowed through this passage to join the main oil return pipe and emerge into the main oil compartment through a short pipe. The end of this pipe could be seen when the oil filler cap was removed, so that the flow of return oil could be checked visually. These modifications were certainly completed for 1953. On the cycle side for 1952, dual-seats became available as an optional extra for the first time.

1953 was a major change year, with the introduction to the UK, after a year of export only, of the 500 Bullet, and the uprating of the 350 to some of its specifications. The 350's engine sprocket became a splined fit onto the drive side mainshaft instead of a taper and key. Since the previous sprocket nut had had a disc valve in it and acted as the engine breather, this indicated a revision of the crankcase breathing arrangements. The previous arrangement, with the engine breathing through the mainshaft, had been found to lead to sticking clutch plates when the oil fumes leaked into the chaincase, and build-up of crankcase pressure had not helped the oil-leak situation. Now a separate disc-type breather with a banjo union was fitted to the left-hand side of the crankcase, with oil mist led away to the rear chain. In further lubrication revisions, the oil return pipe assembly and plug in the crankcase base now incorporated an oil non-return valve where the plug had been. On the 500, these arrangements also featured, and the drive-side shaft was also splined for the sprocket, but was a parallel press fit from the inside of

Left *1953 and the first 500 Bullet.*

Below right *Well-used 1953 500 Bullet — note the state of the exhaust.*

the flywheel, with a locating key and a flange at the inner end.

The change in the 350's engine sprocket location led to a minor change in the arrangement of the drive-side bearings. Previously the two ball journals had fitted a spacer between the outer or fixed parts only. Now there was a spacing tube between the sprocket and the outer main, and a large bore cork washer ran on this instead of on the axle; the outer bearing was now located by a circlip, the spacer between the fixed races stayed in place, and on all models there was a thrust washer between the inner main and the flywheel. As Jack Gray points out, from then on tightening the sprocket nut drew the flywheel assembly hard against the drive side bearings, locating it rigidly, and there was no end float.

The 500 Bullet was very similar in layout and general appearance to the 350, but its alloy head sported larger valves, and the inlet tract had been increased to take a 1⅛ in carburettor. Valve seats and valve faces were radiused to produce a 10 per cent increase in efficiency, and a longer inlet-valve opening period was used. In answer to works scrambles experience of bottom-end whip on the 350's built-up crank, the 500's crankshaft was wider and heavier, with, as we have seen, flywheels keyed into the tapered mainshaft, and their spacing increased to permit the use of a heavier white-metal coating on the hardened steel eye big-end bearing. The 500's drive side main bearings were one ball and one roller bearing, and on the timing side a double-row roller bearing.

The crankcase assembly was of different dimensions, with finning around the base of the oil compartment where the 350 had none, and a less pronounced upward angle where the shorter timing cover rose to the magneto. Though there was no finned collar at the exhaust to barrel joint, the cylinder was bulkier and more massively finned, bulking outwards directly from the crankcase rather than tapering up like the 350. Don Morley wrote that all but 1 lb of the bigger Bullet's 20 lb extra weight, at a claimed 370 lb dry, was located at the top end (head, barrel and piston), and together with harsher engine characteristics, affected at least off-road handling adversely; though this location of weight is hard to reconcile with the heavier crank and its 24½ lb flywheels. These were fitted to the Trials (but not the roadster) 350 Bullets, and interestingly Morley says that on the 500 they lacked sufficient overall diameter to really plonk. Conversely on the street the 500 was known for breathtaking torque and excellent acceleration, but the stigma of harshness remained, and many contemporary riders preferred the flexible and quite adequately quick 350. A further deterrent was price. With the 500 Bullet costing £204, only AMC's offerings and the MSS Velo (of British springer 500 ohv singles in 1955) were more expensive.

Further distinguishing features of the 1953 500 from the 350 were the absence of the upswept exhaust pipe and silencer with its drooping water-excluding tail-pipe, the presence of the unpopular underslung pilot light on the headlamp as adopted by the twins, together with a new number plate with Lucas stop-tail light and red reflector, the stop light switch being housed in the nearside tool box. On the near-identical chassis, a 7 in rear brake, a stiffened-up rear fork with a 3.50 × 19 in (against the 350's 3.25 × 19 in) rear tyre, together with sidecar mounting points, indicated that the big Bullet was being groomed to supplant the J2 in the role of sidecar dray. In that capacity it could be supplied, at extra cost, with sidecar gearing, a steering damper, a front fork with reduced trail but a 3 in spindle lead, plus stronger springs for the front fork and for the rear units. For the latter, at some stage during this, their last year, the Enfield dampers no longer fitted their leak-prone drain plug.

Both 350 and 500 adopted floating cam spindles on their front brakes; since both retained a 6 in SLS brake, any improvement was welcome. In this arrangement, the operating cam and lever were mounted on a plate secured to the hub by two bolts. The bolt holes were slotted to allow movement, with spring washers fitted so that the bolt need not be fully tightened. The intention was to provide some compensation for wear on the leading shoe, and hence the bite that conventional set-ups lost with wear. If not overtightened, it worked quite effectively.

The 500 Bullet certainly delivered, with an output of 25 bhp and in a 1953 *Motor Cycle* test, a top speed of 78 mph. There was no power step as with the 350, and no need to rev through the gears, with 'beefy' acceleration available from low revs in top as in all the other gears. They liked the handling, the 'effortless, loping gait', and the smoothness at speeds below 60 and above 65 mph, the polished crankcase castings and the all-over polychromatic bronze finish. The beautiful Enfield chrome tanks had gone for a while thanks to the current nickel shortage, which also imposed zinc-plated wheel rims that year. There arrived instead the winged metal tank badge, echoed by a winged motif on the tool and battery boxes, as well as knee-grips stamped with 'Enfield'. Suspension was found a bit harsh, though this improved with the carriage of a passenger. One niggle was that, though the footrests were adjustable, the right-hand one could not be moved upwards and backwards due to its closeness to the gearbox; this led to discomfort on long runs, and in conjunction with the high position of the gear pedal pivot, meant that the foot had to leave the rest to change gear. There was a first mention of the clutch's tendency to slip under prolonged heavy use. Brakes were still only 6 in at the front, but after reversing the shoes (since on the test hack the floating cam had reached the limit of its travel) stopping distance from 30 mph was 29½ ft.

For 1954, for both 350 and 500, Armstrong rear units replaced Enfield's own, and though these were not adjustable for load, they provided more movement and superior performance. The 350's forks adopted the one-piece cast aluminium fork-sliders as on the 500 and the twins; and in an unpopular move, lost its sporty upswept silencer, adopting a conventional item with tail-pipe as on the 500. Cosmetically the big change for both models was the adoption of the 'casquette' headlamp, a one-piece fork head cast in aluminium (in line with Tony Wilson-Jones' preoccupation with lightness around the steering head, in the interests of good handling). It incorporated the instruments, light switch and lights, including pilot lights high up on each side which protruded hyperthalmically from the casquette and were thus distractingly visible to the rider. Vertical adjustment of the main beam was achieved by pivoting the whole assembly. Two further criticisms were that the holes in the casquette through which the control cables passed could also let in water, and that routing the cables in this way could make them stiff to operate. While not approaching the elegance of Triumph's trend-setting macelle, the casquette's chunky looks went well with the solid appearance of the

range. For the 500 Bullet, brazed-on malleable lugs replaced the bracing-tubes and welded-in steel gusset plates that had previously constituted the stiffened-up rear fork, and an alloy centre stand was fitted.

In mid-1954, the Bullets (in common with the twins) had their gearbox end-covers tidied up, and the previous criticism of the position of the gear-pedal in relation to the right footrest was met by the pedal and the kick-start crank being positioned on a co-axial shaft, which allowed the pedal to be placed lower. The former worm-gear operation of the clutch pushrod, which had involved a lever mounted on a shaft in which was cut a quick-thread worm, was superseded by an orthodox clutch fulcrum lever which was fully enclosed within the end cover. All this was from gearboxes 39654 (350 Bullet), 40211 (500 Bullet with 21-tooth gearbox sprocket for solo) and 40212 (500 with 18-tooth sprocket for sidecar).

1955 saw some welcome additions. The Bullets acquired dual-seats as standard, had their frames modified in the area of the rear fork pivot, and followed the Meteor's lead since 1953 in acquiring dual 6 in front brakes, mounted back to back in the front hub. This notion, with its obvious nod in the Vincent direction, had been used by works riders like Jack Stocker and Bill Lomas on their specials for some time, and got 'full marks' from *Motor Cycling*'s Bernal Osborne during a 1955 test, where used on their own the dual front brakes pulled a 500 Bullet up in 40 ft from 30 mph. The test machine, which was emphasized as being in standard trim including air cleaner, now returned a top speed of 85.6 mph, as well as a commendable 75–80 mpg overall. In service the dual brakes were good but not exceptional, a lot of braking energy being absorbed by the two cables and the cable's whiffle-tree or beam compensating mechanism, which further cluttered up already full handlebars.

For both Bullets as well as the twins, there was a new air cleaner with a smaller oval container. Internally, to take advantage of premium fuel, new pistons raised the compression ratio on the 350 to 7.5:1, and its output to 19.5 bhp. Contributing to this and to the 500's higher top speed was the fact that they both featured redesigned cams, with quietening ramps. The 350 followed the previous year's 500 in fitting a cast alloy centre stand (replacing the previous tubular item). Neither were very highly rated, being awkward to operate and flimsy when worn. The spiked side-stand too could be trouble: it was pivot-fitted into a lug on the frame and sometimes turned in this, dropping the bike. Finally, from March 1955, for that year the 500 Bullet joined the twins in adopting a full-width hub for a rear wheel now quickly-detachable, though retaining the cush drive.

For 1956 the real golden era for roadster Bullets arrived, with the 350s strengthened and with boosted performance, and the introduction of the lighter, higher, and better-handling all-welded frames (from engine no 38101 for the 350, and 14194 for the 500). Once again this frame was of chrome molybdenum, with no cradle beneath the engine, which was still a stressed member. While this frame proved a mite fragile off-road as stated earlier, on the tarmac it was

Thoroughly revised after 1956, this 350 Bullet is 1957 Model.

1956 500 Bullet featured new, taller all-welded frame.

adequately sturdy and provided superior road-holding to its predecessor. Compatability was still good: according to Don Morley the Bullet main frame will accept all engines from 1948 on. The new frame was wider across the swinging arm, to permit a wider section rear tyre and bigger sprocket for the competition variants. A version of this open-diamond frame was also adopted by the 700 cc Super Meteor of that year, and the 500 twin the next.

On the 1956 machines, the absence on the frame of a seat tube was exploited to incorporate a large pressed-steel box between the gearbox and dual-seat, each of its side-panels attached by a one-armed tommy-bar nut. This displaced both the previous year's oval air cleaner box and the former tool-boxes in the frame loops, since it contained the battery, Vokes air cleaner and tool kit. With 19 in wheels still, and the new frame, the Bullet's seat height rose to 31 in, and overall appearance changed from the more flowing lines of the old frame to a chunkier, slab-sided look.

The 350 acquired the full-width hub and though this was optional now for both, the qd wheel (which also meant a different rear chainguard), but retained its 6 in rear brake. The 350's gearing altered, with a larger 46-tooth rear sprocket as on the 500 replacing the previous 38-tooth standard, and the gearbox sprocket going up from the previous fifteen to eighteen teeth.

There was change, too, in the electrics, with the magdyno replaced by a Lucas SR1 magneto for ignition which meant the end of manual ignition control; and the dynamo functions taken over by a Lucas 6 volt 70 watt crankshaft-mounted alternator. This new feature was housed in a revised primary chaincase, with a rectifier prominent beneath the nose of the petrol tank. In the view of some, with magneto reliability, this represents the best of both worlds. The increased space thus gained behind the cylinder allowed the use of an Amal Monobloc carb for the Bullets. Other detail changes included a boxed-in rear light and number plate, a new and comfortable dual-seat, slimmer and uptilted at the rear, where it was attached by a tubular loop; on the tank, a revised mounting system, a new plastic badge, different shape gold pin-striping on a finish now maroon as standard, and plain kneegrips. Handsome chrome panels were fitted to the tanks, despite the sales literature not recording this. The horn button and dip-switch were combined, and a folding kickstart fitted as standard. All this represented the 'smoothening' process then sweeping the industry; but from the timing side the lines of the tall gearbox and square crankcase remained intransigently themselves.

The 350's engine was strengthened and brought into line with the 500 in several ways. Externally, the oil compartment sump acquired finning, and for both machines a small oval 'Royal Enfield' plate supplanted the words which had previously been stamped into the crankcase casting. Inside, the 350's flywheels became spaced further apart, and the nuts securing them changed from the previous ¾ Whitworth size to a slghtly smaller and slimmer 11/16 Whitworth type. As on the 500 the engine sprocket became a parallel press fit from the inside of the flywheel, with a locating key and flange at the inner end (on both models the outer end now of course carried an extension for the alternator rotor). The width of the big-end bearing increased from ¾ in to the 500's 1 in. Main bearings became inner roller (now a non-lipped component) plus outer ball on the driveside, with a double row roller now on the timing side, again as on the 500. The timing side's plain out-rigger bearing stayed in place, its function mainly being to act as a seal to stop oil draining from the timing cover into the crankcase. It had a worm groove to assist this, and Jack Gray mentions that replacements sold now do not have this groove. (He also says that the pre-'56 single row cages for rollers are scarce, but that there is a modified cage for the double row which takes 10¼ × ½ in rollers or 20¼ × ¼ in). Con-rod and piston remained different on 350 and 500. A further visual clue to all this was the change in shape of the 350's oil pump cover plates from rectangular to oval/elliptical, as on the 500 from the start, with retaining screws down from six to four; this indicated uprated oil pumps within, with the spindle and the disc it drove now of the same large diameter as the 500. All this represented a near unburstable bottom end.

Already, in June 1955, a new cylinder head for the 350 had been introduced. The inlet valve size was enlarged to 1 9/16 in as on that year's 'double-Bullet', the Super Meteor, with gas-flowing at the port, and valve lift improved by radiusing the valve seat into the port and blending the throat of the valve into its port. This head redesign had its origin in 350 competition experience. On both 350 and 500, the size of the tappet feet was increased, to reduce noise and wear, and the tappets themselves changed from a two-piece assembly to a one-piece: the earlier arrangement is replaceable with the later as these are only slightly longer, but may need the diameter of the base reduced to operate on early cams. The previous stub-fit of the exhaust pipe became a push-fit.

With the new frame, developed engine, magneto ignition and dual brakes, these are consequently the most tuneable, best-handling, reliable and strongest of the 350 Bullets. They were also quick, with a top speed closer to 85 than 80 mph in standard form, and potential for considerably more. Royce Creasey was seeing a regular ton-plus on his tweaked road bike—and it wasn't until 50,000 high-speed miles had passed that the alloy con-rod let go ('. . . it never leaked any oil until the rod went, then it leaked it all—engine, gearbox, primary chaincase—in about one fifth of a second. . .').

1957 saw the launch of the Crusader 250, and there was little change for the Bullets. The qd rear wheel became standard for both Bullets, the circular pattern air filter fitted previously was replaced by a larger D-shaped filter, and chrome side-panels, detachable and with matching kneegrips, were catalogued for the petrol tanks. 1958 was the year of the Constellation and Meteor Minor, but with the rest of the range the Bullets acquired a new pattern of Burgess silencer, with no tail pipe; with polychromatic finishes of Burgundy, with Wedgwood Blue or Silver Grey options, and the comfortable dual-seats with their saddle portions now picked out in white piping—this seemed about as smooth as the old girls would get. A new type of Armstrong rear unit, though still not adjustable, was fitted. As on the new Constellation, the gearbox sleeve gear was modified from a plain steel to a bushed component.

By contrast, also for 1958, they were joined by a 350 Clipper. It will be recalled that an iron-engined version of this machine, in the pre-'56 frame, had been available for 1957. Now it featured the new frame with its large central battery box and twin rear loops, though the older style rear units were fitted and the old petrol tank, with the winged metal badges and kneegrips to suit. These features, as well as its Terry's saddle (though a dual-seat was an optional extra), silencer with tail pipe, 6 in front brake (though in a full-width hub as on the Crusader and with Crusader-type undamped front forks, but with longer stanchions) and a black finish, all indicated its cut-price role in using up end-of-range components. But the engine was pure Bullet, up to the level of its black-painted iron cylinder head. A further economy measure was the absence of the SR1 magneto: ignition as well as lights were

The second big restyling: 350 Bullet for 1960, with small wheels, chrome tank.

taken care of for the 350 Clipper by a crankshaft-mounted 60 watt alternator, with the stator spigoted to the crankcase and an ignition switch mounted in the right-side tool box. As with the Bullets, a Monobloc carb was fitted. The 350 Clipper, though not common, and despite the cut-price electrics, is well-considered by Club owners today as a cheap and reliable hack.

1959 was another major change year for the Bullets, and little of it was for the better. In a further effort to modernize the big bangers, a 'lower, sportier' look was aimed at by the use for the 350 of 17 in wheels front and rear, with the front forks similar to those on the Meteor Minor, with separate tapped-in bushes, screw-on seal holders, spindle lead reduced to ½ in, and a change in mudguard mounting. It adopted a 7 in SLS front brake in a full-width hub, while at its rear now came the 7 in stopper from the 500: these new front brakes were not very satisfactory items. The 350's seat height was down to 29½ in, and its gearing was raised to 5.2, 7.0, 9.5 and for first, 14.3:1, though the big jump between top and third still remained.

For both 350 and 500 the restyling was dominated by large, square, all-chromed petrol tanks (the 4¼ gallon as fitted on the Constellation for the 500 but with the bottom cut out to clear the cylinder head, and the 3¾ gallon job from that year's Crusader Sports for the 350). They featured the same winged shield badges as previously but new knee grips, and a painted panel on the top only. Together with all-chromed mudguards, this certainly transformed the singles' appearance, though the 350's 17 in wheels are generally judged to give less precise steering, being floppy at low speeds without really feeling solid when travelling fast.

The 350 Clipper's wheels remained at 19 in, and in fact the only change to it in this, its last year, was the adoption of the dual-seat as standard. The 500's rear tyre section diminished to 3.25 × 19. All the singles, along with the rest of the roadsters, were available with the Airflow fairing (for details of which see p.69), as well as another sensible development, full enclosure of the rear chain by upper and lower runs of pressed steel. Drawbacks to the Airflow included increased engine noise, and bothers such as variable tickover due to the necessary re-routing of cables. The centre stand was also redesigned, but remained unsatisfactory.

For the Bullets the sporting impulse for 1959 went beyond the chrome, however. For the 350 there were higher lift cams, a large bore (1$^{1}/_{16}$ in) Monobloc, and a raise in compression from 7.25 to 7.75:1. On the exhaust side there was a modified sweep to the pipe and a new, longer silencer, still with no tail-pipe. Output went up to 20 bhp.

The 500 entered its final phase with the 'big head' version, with output raised from 25 bhp at 5,250 rpm to 27 bhp at 5,750. This was an effort to get on terms with the ton-plus Velocette and Gold Star 500s of the day, but it failed to deliver; the recorded top speed on test was only just over 90 though this was into a 5 mph breeze, and the factory had estimated 'approximate maximum speed' at 95–100 mph. There was also the compensating factor noted in a *Motor*

Cycling test for 1960, that the low-geared 'big head' 500 was tractable enough for town work and returned a 74 mpg overall average fuel consumption. But they did gently suggest a version 'stripped for speed work'.

The reason one never emerged, according to a *Classic Bike* article on the 'big head', was that the factory had found out via competition experience that the built-up crankshaft and alloy con-rod could not cope with any further power. They increased the size of the inlet valve from 1¾ to 1$^{31}/_{32}$ in—there had been scrambles and export valves of those dimensions previously, but the layout of the new head meant that they had been much shorter, and used different springs, collects and collars. However, on the 'big head', which fitted a larger (1$^{3}/_{16}$ in) Monobloc, the inlet tract, now downdraught and inclined to the right-hand side of the machine at an angle of 18° from the longitudinal centre line, did not emulate the 1½ in tract on the previous racing variant of the engine. Instead it was sleeved down to 1$^{3}/_{16}$ in, which effectively throttled the extra urge of the redesigned alloy cylinder head. (Only the GP Fury 1960 export version of the 'big head' dared to go out with an unrestricted 1½ in inlet port, which together with 9.5:1 compression ratio, scrambler cams and higher gearing put out 34 bhp at 5,900 rpm and achieved 104 mph on test. The Fury had some success on the flat-tracks, but for that work tuners would usually fit steel Gold Star or JS con-rods, plus different pistons and home-ground cams.) This head featured better-supported bushed rockers, operating on shafts fixed between the walls of the new cast-in rocker boxes. A pair of small inspection caps, each fastened by a single nut, replaced the previous domes retained by four studs each, and the finning on the head was deeper and of a revised pattern. With the new design, the head could not be removed with the engine in the frame without first removing the head studs, so these now had squares machined on their top end to enable them to be removed first.

Higher lift cams, and a compression ratio increased from 6.5 to 7.3:1, plus two-rate valve springs and hardened valve stem tips,

Above Motorcycling's *Bernal Osborne checks out the 1960 'Big Head' 500 Bullet. He was a little disappointed.*

Left *1960 two-tone 350 Clipper, mostly Bullet, and in its last year.*

Above right *Tappet adjustment on a 1960 Bullet: it was always very accessible.*

all played their part. But they had to be offset against an overall weight increase catalogued at 5 lb but in fact probably rather more. With big singles on the wane, the 'big head' was not a success: few were made, and in the opinion of Jack Gray, the production costs of tooling up for the new head can hardly have been covered. Today it is a different story, the late 500s being one of the few Redditch models that fetch high prices (on occasion reportedly in excess of £1,500) and classic racing experience has demonstrated thoroughly that for track use at least, they can be made to hold together and to fly.

1960 saw continued rationalization along the previous year's lines. The 350 Clipper was dropped, being replaced by the 350 Clipper De Luxe, which was now simply a cheaper version of the 350 Bullet. It featured the latter's alloy head, qd rear wheel, 17 in wheels, full width hubs, 7 in rear brake with 42-tooth sprocket (though still 6 in front), raised gearing and 3¾ gallon tank, though this and the mudguards were painted not chromed. But since compression remained at 6.25:1, claimed output stayed low, 17 bhp at 5,500 rpm.

The 350 Bullets' output rose that year to 21 bhp, with a further change to the valve gear—one that can be retro-fitted to any 1956 and later 350. Up till late 1959 the valves had had tapered collets with steel top and bottom plates for the valve springs, and stem caps were fitted. For 1960 they altered to semi-circular grooves, with larger collets. As with the 500, valve ends were hardened: smaller valve springs gave better control. The springs used dural collars at the top and steel collars at the bottom.

As the Clipper became more like the Bullet, the converse obtained with both 350 and 500 adopting full a/c electrics, with a crankshaft-mounted Lucas RM 15 alternator, and contacts mounted behind the cylinder in a distributor unit assembly in the same position as the discarded magneto, and driven by the timing gear in the same way. The pre-unit singles' clutch, perhaps to help cope with the raised outputs, now used Neolangite-bonded plates. In a welcome move, the 500 reverted to the dual front brake. Cosmetically, in common with the twin range, there was a revised casquette, with the parking lights on either side of it finally mounted further apart. It housed the

speedometer, with the ammeter and lightswitch side by side behind it. Its alloy casting now ran back over the fork legs and encircled the steering head as well as the damper knob, if one was fitted. Petrol tank mountings on the 350's 3¾ gallon tank were also modified, still with a transverse bolt at the front, but at the rear now with a spring clip which snapped around a sleeve on the top tube.

By 1961, demand for old-style singles was falling off dramatically and the Bullets ran on largely unchanged in their twilight years. In common with the twins and the Crusaders, there was a new silencer for the 350 and 500 Bullets (but not the 350 Clipper De Luxe, which continued with the silencer before last, complete with tail pipe). The new item was in three parts, which meant it could be dismantled for cleaning, and featured a polished, cast aluminium tail-piece decorated by a distinctive narrow fin on its upper face: exhaust gases were discharged downwards, through a longitudinal slot in the underside of the cast tail. For that year also, the traditional bronze-bushed pivots for the swinging-arm were replaced by bonded-rubber components. In a further detail mod the 500 Bullet's 4¼ gallon tank also changed its rear mounting, the tank tunnel at the back now being supported by a profiled rubber block carried in a clip welded to the frame top tube with a loose clamping strap pulling the tank into place against the block.

For 1962 the 350 Bullet, but again not the 350 Clipper De Luxe, suffered some prime British Mickey Mouse styling in the shape of a restyled rear mudguard and seat, introduced the previous year for the Constellation and Super Meteor and now featured on the Crusader, Crusader Sports and Super 5. This consisted of steel pressings which blended with the lines of the dual-seat, the latter now having black sides and a grey and white checked top. The unattractive pressings shrouded the sub-frame, and the ones on either side concealed the upper mountings of the rear suspension units. A lifting handle was provided each side, passing through rubber grommets in the mudguard pressing. In the UK the Bullets were now spent, though for the 350 there was a posthumous change, listed in parts books from then on, of the sleeve nuts on the rocker covers which altered from the slotted to the hexagon-headed type. The name lived on briefly in the New 350 Bullet for 1963, which was an ill-fated attempt to produce a 350 version of the unit 250, and will be found dealt with in that section.

The story did continue with the Madras 350, which was first imported in 1977. 'The Enfield 350' was the correct name for these machines as the 'Royal' had not yet been bought back from Matt Holder by the importers, and the 'Bullet' name had been re-registered by British Leyland for their own use. By then the original machinery shipped to India had long since worn out, and the Enfield 350, with many of its thread forms changed from the original to metric, and a speedometer measured in kilometres per hour, represented a hybrid creation, as well as being a mixture of good and bad. Its frame, though welded, featured toolboxes in its loops plus the square airbox, and the casquette: this was basically the 1949–55 design, with the rear mudguard stays passing outside the non-adjustable made-under-licence Armstrong dampers. The chromed deeply-valanced mudguards, though, were something like the early Crusader, though the front one was a different diameter and shape, featuring two stays each side against the Crusader's one. The carburettor was a tiny 1 in piston-valve Villiers model, clip-fitted to an adaptor bolted on the cylinder head flange, and returned anything between 65 and 80 mpg. The 6 volt electrics were by alternator, distributor and coil: the absence of any fuses in the system led to an electrical fire on one test bike. There was a change to the alloy casting housing the drive shaft from the gear to the points cam and its auto-advance, which were all now contained under a small cover. Winkers were initially fitted to the models sent here, but these were phased out late in 1981. In the engine, which featured an iron cylinder head, compression reverted to 6.5:1, in view of the fuel available in the sub-continent, and the main bearings were twin ball races.

The ride is smooth, with the heavy flywheels and light con-rod in place. Finish has been praised, including the quality of the chrome panels fitted until 1981 on the 3¼ gallon petrol tank (when transfers also replaced the metal tank badges), and of the chromed mudguards. Comfort is good from

Enfield India.

A sought-after model today: the 1960 'Big Head' 500 Bullet.

the thickly padded dual-seat with its chromed grab rail, and the exhaust note from the old-style silencer with tail-pipe is a delight. The gearbox is the later type, with the pedal concentric with the kickstarter, and evoked less comment on neutrals and jumping out of gear than might have been expected, another indication that wear may be a major part of its problems. Likewise oil tightness on test bikes has been near perfect. Performance, never sparkling, with a top speed down to 70 mph and best cruising speed 50 mph, is badly affected by the weight of a passenger and by hills of any description, and handling, while reasonable, is not helped by the Dunlop Universals made under licence and fitted as original equipment. The 6 in brakes front and rear, with a stopping distance of 38½ ft from 30 mph, excited the tester's liveliest comments. Even British Ferodo replacement linings, and a switch to full-width hubs and the qd rear wheel for 1980, brought no improvement, and the brakes were once described as poor stoppers but great laxatives. One reason may be the absence of the floating bush in their backplates. A small improvement to the cycle parts has been the substitution of a welded tubular centre stand for the original awkward and unreliable cast alloy one.

For a reasonable roadster for European conditions, the tyres, carburettor, rear chain, tank seals, clutch pushrod and adjuster nut, brakes, coils, plug, ignition and light switch should be, immediately or progressively, replaced with British components. There was also trouble with snapping of the rockers, which had changed from forgings to castings: but this failure of Indian metallurgy seems to have been confined to an early (1978) batch of bikes. Dave Messent, the man who rode his Rickman Enfield from England to Australia, in 1981 toured India two-up on a new-bought Enfield 350. In *Bike* magazine he described how he found the bike in delivery trim poorly fettled and even allowing for his assessment that 1 km in India had a punishment value of at least 3 km in Europe, the fork seals had blown and the brake linings were worn down to the rivets by 5,500 km. With his 15,000-km tour complete, the bike needed a new big end, one main bearing and a camshaft bush. But it had never seriously let him down, and little after-sales trouble has been reported from dealers who have sold them here. Perhaps the expectations which the high price aroused, as well as the heavy right hand of the press, have obscured a basically decent, though dated, plodder.

In the UK the Indian bike is also welcomed as a source of new spares for the Bullet. The shift to metric main bearings rules these items out along with parts such as the drive-side shafts. The steering head races are also different but floating bushes (though not the crankpins) are a usable replacement, as are engine plates, the bottom gearbox plates, the as-original 38-tooth rear wheel sprockets, the cush-drive components and fork seals. Even the brake shoes will fit the dual front brake, as well as the Crusader's rear.

Today any Bullet, and especially any 1956–58 350 Bullet, represents a desirable and economic buy in the big single line. Owners find them robust and forgiving of neglect, but recognize that modification is necessary if they are to be rendered oil-tight, and if they wish to exploit the tuning potential. Royce Creasey in *Classic Bike* has detailed several modifications on both scores, but his casual approach (born of the engineering ability to make necessary adjustments himself) has concealed some pitfalls. For the 350s, in the go-faster department, he recommended the use of a 250 Crusader exhaust pipe, but a correspondent told me that this does not fit the Bullet 'unless you know a good pipe-bender', as the angle of the pipe into the cylinder head and its position in relation to the right-hand footrest have to be altered to stand a chance of it fitting.

Royce also suggested the use of a steel Velocette con-rod to replace the Bullet's more fragile alloy rod; but neglected to mention that the difference in weight means a great deal of material has to come off the crankshaft to get it in balance again. More fundamental is the way that hotting up in one area reveals weaknesses in another. Owners Club member Julian Swingler fitted scrambles cams and a 9:1 compression piston in his late 350, but the three-plate clutch developed terrible slip after the step-up in power, and was never satisfactory even after re-covering the bonded segments. All new parts and careful assembly were the answer. So tweaking a Bullet is something to be approached, if it is to be done all, with careful thought.

On the matter of oil-tightness, both Royce and Don Morley advocate improving the head-to-barrel joint. Royce's suggestion is fairly radical, aiming to get the inner ring to fit perfectly and the outer to have a minute clearance. First one must machine off the existing spigots, then lap in both faces with grinding paste to get 100 per cent contact on both halves of the inner spigot, and a rougher finish on the outer faces: then the outer face only is carefully sealed with modern RTV jointing compound. The result, according to Creasey, is the gasketless joint that may well have been the designer's original intention, and as side bonuses, a slight rise in compression, cleaner carburation, and better heat dissipation, with consequently less chance of burning out the exhaust valve, which, as mentioned, the hot-running Bullets were prone to do. The practice was originated by Velocette: it worked well for them, and has done for some Owners' Club members who have tried it for their Bullets.

Less extreme solutions are suggested by Don Morley: starting with careful attention to evenly torquing down the erratically spaced cylinder bolts, by regularly slipping the rocker boxes off and retorquing the four through-bolts as well as the permanently visible outer studs. He also advised use of either a well-annealed solid copper gasket, or one made of modern materials. More permanently, he says that the cylinder head spigot recess can be filled with modern silicon jointing compound. A further final point from Creasey concerned something present in all Enfields bar the Interceptor II, due to the use of over-fine threads in alloy. This was the tendency of the threads of the holding-down studs to become fouled with alloy from the head, which makes removal difficult. Royce advocates running the appropriate drill down the holes to prevent it happening next time.

For engine breathing and lubrication, although some experts question the need for extra breathers, Morley suggests that the early flap valve, if fitted, should be dispensed with, and replaced by the later self-sealing rubber tube breather outlet pipe on the nearside at the bottom of the barrel fins, which Royce agrees works well. Both think that depressurizing the oil compartment is a good step, and fairly simply done. Royce advocates drilling a hole through the filler cap, Aralditing a piece of metal pipe in it, and attaching to the pipe flexible tubing, which is then led away to hang clear of the rear wheel. Morley favours brazing a copper breather pipe into the oil compartment's filler neck, well below the cap. Replacing the original fracture-prone metal oil pipes to the rockers with suitable plastic piping is also advisable.

For improving the easily-stressed clutch and imprecise gearbox, Royce advises replacing any clutch parts that look rough, especially distorted plates, and oiling and careful routing of the cable. On his own Bullet he removed all the clutch plates and replaced them with one pair less of Norton Navigator plates, which were thicker and longer-lasting. Morley's modification here is to cut the clutch pushrod in half, harden the two ends and insert a central ball bearing—this lightens the action and prevents the shaft, which is over-long, from bowing, and binding inside the mainshaft. The springs of the three-plate clutches, unusually, were not adjustable, and can be of slightly different lengths and hence pressures: personal selective assembly is called for, says Morley, by careful matching and by selection of the lightest springs, shimming out those of unequal length. For the gearbox, Royce points out that gear selection is both adjustable and accessible, and that careful adjustment of the selector and of the spring pressure on the selector fork can make cleaner changes possible, if not smooth ones.

In the cycle department, as mentioned previously, Creasey endorses Morley in advising substitution of the springs in the somewhat flimsy front fork and adds the use of gearbox oil to improve their damping. Some people have gone further and followed Enfield's own lead with the late Interceptors, by substituting a Norton Roadholder front end complete with 8 in front wheel, as well as Girlings at the rear. The frame's weakest spot was at the rear, and Royce advises stiffening this up by welding a ¼ in plate, approximately 4 in long, across the two frame tubes that go under the rear of the engine. Engine to frame fixing can also be improved by the use of the alloy block fitted at the rear of the Interceptor's gearbox, which is compatible for the Bullets.

To improve the action of the dual front brakes, he suggests grinding their rectangular operating cams into smooth ovals. Front forks with a spindle lead of aproximately 1½ in (ie, the ones actually fitted to solo Bullets prior to 1959) seemed to work best for them, as do 19 in wheels shod with Avon tyres. On gearing Royce, as we have seen, considers the 350 Bullets undergeared for today, which contributes to wear and to their running hot. He suggests that on 17 in wheels they should pull the highest (21-tooth) gearbox sprocket; he says they will do so on 19 in wheels also, but for general use including around town, a sprocket one tooth down is probably more advisable.

As far as engine reliability goes, the white metal big end, the valve guides, and eventual cracking of the piston are all points to watch, but Royce thrashed his hotted-up Bullet for 50,000 miles before the big end let go. Today a roller-bearing conversion is available, as an exchange item at around £70, from Gander and Gray.

The latter, with L and D in Bristol as well as several other excellent outlets, are all prime sources for Enfield spares, which are fairly plentiful though starting to dry up, with some basic 500 items such as pistons already hard to come by. (Pattern 350 pistons can be had, but they are in metric sizes, so a matching rebore to suit is necessary.) The 500 spares situation is one more reason, unless the competition bug has bitten you, to opt for the pleasanter and less stressed 350, with its 80 mph top end for 1956-on examples, and overall mpg in the seventies. The 1958 cut-off, incidentally, should not really be a hard and fast one, as it's easy enough to substitute 19 in wheels

1961 350 Bullet.

and even a magneto, and if not, alternators despite a certain vulnerability in the main work well, are cheaper and easier to fettle and find parts for, and make starting easier than with a magneto. Oil leaks, the gearbox, only reasonable brakes and forks have to be set against a rugged engine, good handling, acceleration and smoothness, and the fact that a 350 Bullet can still be found today (1986) for around £400. With all that, who's counting oil leaks?

Royal Enfield: The 350 Bullet, 500 Bullet, and 1958-62 350 Clippers—dates and specifications

Production dates

350 G2 Bullet—1949-62
500 JS Bullet—1953-62
350 Clipper—1958-59
350 Clipper De Luxe—1960-62

Specifications

350 Bullet

Capacity, bore and stroke—346 cc (70 × 90)
Type—ohv single
Ignition—(1949-59) magneto; (1960-62) coil
Weight—(1950) 350 lb; (1962) 365 lb

500 Bullet

Capacity, bore and stroke—499 cc (84 × 90)
Type—ohv single
Ignition—(1949-59) magneto; (1960-62) coil
Weight—(1953) 379 lb; (1962) 375 lb

350 Clipper/350 Clipper De Luxe (1958-62)

Capacity, bore and stroke—346 cc (70 × 90)
Type—ohv single
Ignition—coil
Weight—(1958) 362 lb; (1962) 365 lb

Royal Enfield: The 350 Bullet/500 Bullet/1958-62 350 Clippers—annual development and modifications

1950

For 350 Bullet

1 Polished alloy speedometer facia panel fitted.
2 Forged fork ends now welded (not screwed) to their sliders.
3 Sprung front mudguard became of deep section in place of previous valances.
4 Lucas 'long-type' dynamo adopted.
5 Upswept silencer of more cylindrical shape.

1951

For 350 Bullet

1 Previous plain timing side bearing bush supplemented by single-row caged roller race located inboard of it.
2 Oil pump worm, previously integral with timing side shaft, became detachable. Timing pinion, also previously integral, now keyed onto mainshaft by this internally threaded oil pump worm.
3 Front mudguard mounted by three stays each side, and now moved with the wheel.

During 1951

4 Oil feed, previously to big end on pump's delivery stroke and to piston skirt on return stroke, now to big end on both strokes (for details see text).

1952

For 350 Bullet

1 Dual-seats available as optional extra.
2 Further modification to oiling system; return system modified with an extra oilway drilled through the crankcase behind the tappets (for details see text).
3 Modified prop-stand with over-centre return spring fitted, as on J2 500.

1953

For 350 Bullet

1 Engine modified in line with new-for-UK 500 Bullet. Engine sprocket now a splined fit onto drive side mainshaft, not a taper and key. Since previous sprocket nut had disc valve in it to act as engine breather, now a separate disc-type breather with a banjo union was fitted to left-hand side of crankcase, with oil mist led away to rear chain.
2 Drive side main bearings previously fitted a spacer between outer, fixed ports only. Now a spacing tube fitted between sprocket and outer main, with a large bore cork washer running on this instead of on axle. Outer bearing now located by a circlip, and thrust washer fitted between inner main and flywheel.

For 500 and 350 Bullets

3 Rear suspension units no longer fit drain plug at base.
4 Front brake adopts floating cam spindles.
5 Winged, chrome-plated and painted tank

badge, fitted on tanks no longer chromed but enamelled.
For 500 Bullet
6 Headlamp with underslung pilot light.
7 New number plate with Lucas stop-tail light and red reflector; stop-light switch housed in nearside tool box.
8 7 in rear brake.

1954
For 500 and 350 Bullets
1 Armstrong rear suspension units replace Enfield's own.
2 First 'casquette' headlamp, with twin pilot lights mounted high up.
For 500 Bullet
3 On stiffened-up rear fork, previous bracing tubes and welded-in steel gusset plates replaced by brazed-on malleable lugs.
4 Alloy centre stand fitted.
For 350 Bullet
5 One-piece cast aluminium front fork sliders adopted (as on 500 and Twins).
6 Silencer parallel to ground adopted.

Mid-1954
For 500 and 350 Bullets
7 From gearboxes Nos 39654 (350) and 40211/40212 (500), gearbox end-cover tidied, with gear pedal and kickstart crank now positioned on a co-axial shaft. Previous worm-gear operation of clutch pushrod replaced by clutch fulcrum lever enclosed within end cover.

1955
For 500 and 350 Bullets
1 Dual-seat now standard.
2 6 in dual front brakes fitted, with whiffle-tree beam compensating mechanism at handlebars.
3 New air cleaner within oval container.
4 Redesigned cams with quietening ramps.
5 Frame modified in area of rear fork pivot.
For 500 Bullet
6 From March, full-width rear wheel hub and qd wheel (as on Twins), with revised rear chainguard to suit.
For 350 Bullet
7 Alloy centre stand fitted.
8 New pistons raise compression from 6.5:1 to 7.25:1.

From June 1955
9 Revised cylinder head with inlet valve size increased to $1^{9}/_{16}$th in, port gas-flowed, valve seat radiused into port, throat of valve blended into port. Previous stub fitting of exhaust pipe to cylinder changed to push fit.

1956
For 500 and 350 Bullets
1 From engines Nos 38101 (350) 14194 (500), new lighter, higher, all-welded frame; wider across swinging arm.
2 Large pressed steel box with detachable side-panels contains Vokes air cleaner, battery, tools.
3 Lucas SRI magneto and 70 watt crankshaft-mounted alternator in revised primary chaincase replace previous magdyno.
4 Amal Monobloc carburettor fitted.
5 Boxed-in rear number plate.
6 New dual-seat, slimmer and uptilted at rear, attached there by a tubular loop.
7 Plastic circular winged tank badges and new-shaped knee grips, now plain; and revised petrol tank mounting. Screw-on chromed side-panels on tank.
8 Combined horn button and dipswitch.
9 Folding kickstart as standard.
10 Full-width hub qd rear wheel, previously standard for 500, now optional for both. Revised rear chainguard to suit.
11 Small oval 'Royal Enfield' plate on timing side crankcase casting replaces previous stamped-in 'Royal Enfield'.
2 Size of tappet feet increased and tappets change from two-piece to one-piece assembly (interchangeable with previous).
For 500 Bullet
13 Improved 7 in rear brake.
For 350 Bullet
14 Engine bottom end brought into line with 500 (for details see text). Oil pump cover plate changes from rectangular to oval, oil compartment sump now finned, engine 1 in wider.
15 Gearing altered, with 46-tooth rear sprocket replacing previous 38-tooth, and 18-tooth gearbox sprocket replacing previous 15-tooth.

1957
For 500 and 350 Bullets
1 Qd rear wheel now standard.
2 Previous circular pattern air filter replaced by larger D-shaped item.

1958
For 500 and 350 Bullets
1 New pattern Burgess silencer, with no tail pipe.
2 Saddle portions of dual-seat now picked out in white piping.
3 New type Armstrong rear unit (still not adjustable).
4 Gearbox sleeve gear modified from a plain steel to a bushed component.

1959
For 350 Bullets
1 New front forks as on Meteor Minor, separate tapped-in bushes, screw-on seal holders, spindle lead reduced from 1½ in to ½ in, and altered mudguard mounting.
2 7 in SLS front brake.
For 500 and 350 Bullets
3 All-chromed mudguards front and rear.
4 New, squarer, all-chromed petrol tanks (4¼ gallon for 500 as on Constellation, 3¾ gallon for 350 as on Crusader Sports) with painted panel on top only, and revised knee-grips.
5 Rear chain enclosure with top and bottom runs, and Airflow fairing with matching mudguard, both available as optional extras.
6 Redesigned centre stand and engine plates.
For 500 Bullet
7 Revised 'big head' cylinder head, with $1^{31}/_{32}$ in inlet valve, downdraught inlet tract inclined to right-hand side of machine, sparking plug on left, cast-in rocker boxes with better-supported bushed rockers operating on shafts between their walls, deeper finning, smaller inspection caps fastened by single nut each (for details see text). Monobloc's size increased to $1^{3}/_{16}$ in.
8 Higher-lift cams, two-rate valve springs, hardened valve stem tips.
9 Compression ratio raised from 6.5:1 to 7.3:1.
10 Rear tyre now 3.25 × 19 in.
For 350 Bullet
11 17 in wheels front and rear, reduced seat height from 31 to 29½ in.
12 7 in rear brake (as on 500).
13 Gearing raised to 14.3:1, 9.5:1, 7.0:1, and (top) 5.2:1.
14 Higher-lift cams.
15 Monobloc's size increased to $1^{1}/_{16}$th in.
16 Compression raised from 7.25 to 7.75:1.
17 Modified sweep to exhaust pipe.
18 New, longer silencer.
For 350 Clipper
19 Dual-seat adopted as standard.

1960
For 500 and 350 Bullets
1 Coil ignition adopted, with crankshaft-mounted Lucas RM15 alternator, contacts mounted behind cylinder in distributor unit, ignition switch on right side of tool box.
2 Neolangite-bonded plates fitted in clutch.
3 Revised casquette, wider-set pilot lights.
For 350 Bullet
4 Previous valve springs with tapered collets and steel top and bottom plates, and stem caps, altered to semi-circular grooves and larger collets, with smaller valve springs using dual collars at top, steel collars at bottom. Valve ends hardened as on 500. (Interchangeable with 1956-on previous.)
5 3¾ gallon tank fixing modified at rear to a spring clip which snapped around sleeve on top tube.
For 500 Bullet
6 6 in dual front brakes readopted.

1961
For 500 and 350 Bullets
1 New three-piece silencer with tail fin.
2 Previous bronze-bushed pivots for swinging arm replaced by bonded-rubber components.
For 500 Bullet
3 4¼ gallon petrol tank's rear fixing modified as 350s for previous year.

1962
For 350 Bullet
1 Restyled rear mudguard and seat (as on 1961 Constellation, Super Meteor, 1962 Crusader, Crusader Sports, Super 5).
2 (retrospectively, in later parts books) Sleeve nuts on rocker covers altered from slotted to hexagon-headed type.

Royal Enfield: the Crusader, 250 Clipper Series II, Crusader Sports, Crusader Super 5, New 350 Bullet, Turbo Twin, Continental, Olympic, Continental GT and Turbo Twin Sports

The unit 250 was central to Royal Enfield's design philosophy and production for ten years. As discussed in the marque history section, it was the direct inspiration of Enfield's chief, Major Frank Walker Smith, and Reg Thomas' design fulfilled all his employer's parameters, up to and including

Light, compact, and with much potential: Enfield 250 Crusader for 1957.

development potential for what could fairly be called the ultimate British post-war pushrod-engine 250, the Continental GT.

The beginnings of the series were more sensibly cautious, coming in August 1956 in the shape of the soft-tuned, low-output (13 bhp) Crusader. In Light Surf Green finish with a chrome-panelled tank, 'the advanced 250 with the SMOOTH look' came with a fully enclosed rear chain and valanced mudguards, and was offered with optional legshields and tailored panniers (and shortly with the Airflow fairing), as if to emphasize a touring role.

The short-stroke unit engine, oversquare at 70 × 64.5, was very distinct externally from its pre-unit forbears. Uncluttered by the Bullet's magydno, magneto or the points housing that would follow in its place, without even a projecting oil filler neck, the power egg shape of the crankcase was amplified by a matching winged 'RE' motif on either side.

The layout was traditionally Enfield to the extent that the three pints of engine and primary transmission oil were housed in a chamber to the rear of the crankshaft. But inside the engine was distinctly different, and unconventional, reflecting Thomas' and Tony Wilson-Jones' ideas during the years of development. From the bottom up, though the single strand primary drive and rear chains were positioned conventionally (for British) on the left, at the other end of the crankshaft the alternator was housed on the *right*. It sat, together with the clutch lever, gearbox selector mechanism and the points, behind a separate outer cover, which (like the winged motif it bore) was symmetrical with the primary chain cover on the left side. Wilson-Jones had taken advantage of the team's clean sheet of paper for the unit 250, for he considered that the primary chaincase with its oil bath, where an alternator normally ended up when an existing design was adapted for it, was not the ideal situation.

Another striking feature of the design was that, to facilitate the re-positioning of the alternator, the timing gear, as well as the primary drive, was located on the left. The slipper-tensioned double-row timing chain (unusually located outboard of the primary chain), the camshaft directly over the crankshaft, the unusual cam-followers with curved instead of flat-base tappets, plus the pushrods in a barely discernible cast-in tunnel in the barrel, which like the head was of iron—all were on the left. Not for decades had a British single deviated from the 'pushrods on the right' rule.

A third unconventional feature was to be found in the gearbox, which while built in unit with the engine, was housed in a separate chamber with its own oil supply. Unusually again, the lightweight Albion internals were laid on their face, so that the layshaft sat behind the mainshaft, instead of traditionally below it. This permitted the unit's neat shape, as well as optimum placement for the gear pedal (this was no longer concentric with the kickstart, as on the revised heavyweight box). Otherwise the gearbox internals were similar to those for the rest of the range (though not nearly so bulky), with the moving gears all shifted as one by one fork. The box could cause some problems, which will be dealt with later. One can be mentioned now; this lighter box, while it did feature a gear indicator, did not include the neutral finder—somewhat ironically, as neutral could often be virtually impossible to re-engage.

The heart of the motor was imaginatively different for a lightweight, in the best way, with a one-piece crankshaft of Meehanite cast iron. The shaft was carried on massive bearings, a roller on the timing side and a ball-race on the drive side. Again this bearing arrangement was the reverse of the norm, but considered acceptable in view of the ball bearing's very large dimensions and its lateral location, as it had its outer race fixed in the case and its inner race clamped securely against a shoulder on the shaft, by the same nut which retained the primary drive and timing sprockets. (Some consider that this nut and the connection it provided could have been more substantial; it sometimes came undone, causing the timing to slip, because it could not be tightened really hard due to the hollow stud.) The two substantial flywheels on their stubby mainshafts noticeably overlapped the crankpin journals, to form an impressively rigid assembly. Con-

Enfield Unit 250. Note unorthodox placing of pushrods.

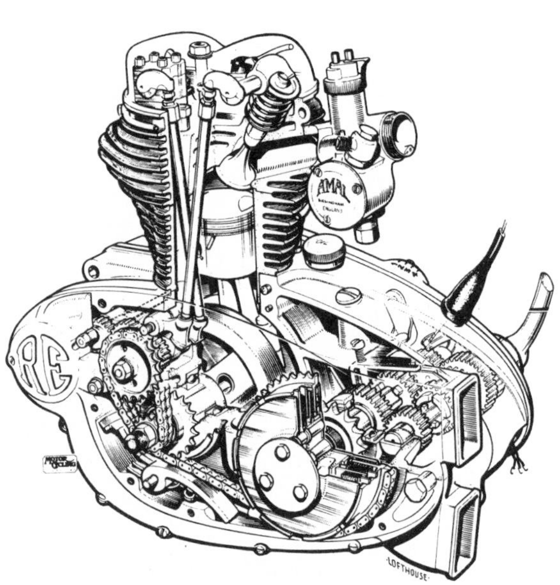

rods were of RR56 light alloy, and ran on big ends which, due to the big ball bearings and one-piece crank, finally abandoned the Enfield white metal floating bush, in favour of steel split-shell bearings. Here was a sound basis for later tuning of the powerplant. The crankshaft had a balance factor of 75 per cent which together with the light con-rods made for smooth running.

On the left end of the crankshaft, where the alternator would have been, the double sprocket for the duplex timing chain was cleverly retained on the mainshaft both by a tongue that married with the shaft, and by a hollow stud screwed onto the shaft. This hollow stud went through a seal in the chaincase cover to a recess supplied with oil to feed to the big end, via the hollow crankpin and an alloy tube pressed into it.

The lubrication system with its typically Enfield crankcase oil compartment also still featured twin oscillating-plunger pumps and a cylindrical felt oil filter. In this instance the two plungers lay side by side on a cover plate at the front end of the engine, again on the left-hand side. They were operated, via gear-drive from the camshaft, by the eccentric pin on the end of a shaft running across the front of the crankcase; this shaft also drove the cam for the coil ignition system. Another difference was that for the first time the scavenge plunger was larger than the delivery one, where previously Enfield had been unique in having feed and delivery pumps of the same size. One result of the change was that the feed pump plunger with its smaller diameter tended to wear more rapidly than the return plunger. The pump was barely adequate, which was a major flaw: if its oil pressure dropped for any reason, the big ends failed.

The cylindrical felt filter was relocated, not as before inserted horizontally at the right-hand base of the crankcase, but now slotted vertically into the case's left-hand top side behind the cylinder, and topped with a hexagon-headed nut. There was potential for a serious problem associated with the filter, which had a separate brass carrier at the bottom, and rested on a felt washer, a steel washer and then a spring. If the spring was omitted then the brass carrier could block an oil-discharge hole at the bottom of the chamber, deprive the engine of lubricant and knock out the big end. This early version of the filter had its top connected to a spring-loaded pressure-control valve, which was screwed into the top of the crankcase and discharged into the oil tank. It would be deleted by 1958, and as we shall see, the absence of a pressure-relief valve for some years would contribute to another traditional Enfield characteristic, namely oiliness. However the reason it was to be deleted was that if it stuck open, it allowed oil back into the tank in such large quantities that it deprived the engine of lubricant.

The lubrication system otherwise was similar to the pre-unit singles in featuring only one external line, namely the pipe running up from the right rear of the barrel to the cylinder head to lubricate, via two banjo units, the rocker spindles. Oil draining from there went to the timing chest, in which a weir level took care of lubrication for the cams and their followers and gear train, the surplus going over the weir to supply the primary chaincase and its slipper-tensioned single-strand chain. A second weir permitted the overflow from there to return to the sump for scavenge collection. The oil compartment itself vented into the chaincase. Via a further connection from there into the crankcase, breathing to the atmosphere was by means of an outlet union on the front of the crankcase ahead of the barrel.

Compression with the initial iron head was 7.3:1. To achieve this the height of the combustion chamber had to be kept low, so the valve's included angle was a low 65°. The valve springs were duplex. The rockers operated in separate split pedestals: they were housed beneath a single alloy rocker cover, retained by a single shouldered nut. The inlet port was slightly inclined, and tapered from ⅞ in diameter at the Monobloc carburettor's flange to 1¼ in at the valve throat. The port was located directly to the rear of the cylinder, a compromise position sacrificing some swirl of the charge but dictated by two factors—the wish to run the exhaust pipe conventionally on the right, together with the position of the short-reach spark plug on the right of the head, due to the pushrods etc, being on the left.

The engine unit weighed 98 lb and was mounted in a frame similar to the other Enfields, an open diamond arrangement with the power unit as a stressed member at its base. The front fork, with alloy sliders, was a new design, with much less forward offset of the wheel spindle than on the usual Enfield job. It was also relatively crude internally, having no oil damping or bushes, and no drain plug or grease nipples. What oil there was inside was for lubrication only. At least this prevented blown oil seals! The fork was topped by a version of the casquette headlamp, with its unpopular twin pilot lights which riders knew could be dangerously mistaken by other drivers or pedestrians for a car's lights in the distance. The casquette housed the speedometer, old-fashioned light switch and ammeter.

One of the most innovative features of the cycle parts was the use of 17 in wheels, giving a low seat height for the dual-seat which was fitted as standard. Initial publicity, showing a pony-tailed teenage girl astride a Crusader, emphasized the unisex benefits of this and of the relatively low dry weight of 312 lb, and later the hotter versions would be a favourite mount for girl rockers. However, racing versions of the machine would usually substitute 18 in wheels, which were felt to handle better.

Brakes were 6 in sls front and rear in full-width hubs, with the rear one featuring the Enfield cush-drive on a qd wheel. The rear suspension units, unlike the pre-unit's Armstrongs, were the superior Girlings, featuring three-position load adjustment. The rear chain was adjusted by a convenient snail-cam arrangement, and was totally enclosed by a good-looking design of upper and lower runs plus flexible 'bellows' where the chain entered the primary case. The mudguards, as mentioned, were the big fully-valanced touring type, and by loosening the two bolts at the top of the rear suspension units, the whole rear subframe, mudguard and dual-seat could be lifted clear of the machine: obviously the price of this convenience was permanent vigilance about the tightness of the two bolts. Another point to watch was the single screw which held each entire front fork leg in place. The swinging-arm was unbushed, and hence liable to wear and subsequent play, if not greased regularly via the grease nipples provided.

An under-seat box contained the Vokes 'micro-vee' aircleaner, battery, coil and tools, and the rectifier was suspended beneath it. The box had lids on either side—the left one housing the ignition switch—and these initially were retained by a single knurled nut apiece. This was replaced for 1958, though

they appear to have remained as an alternative for the Clipper II, by the traditional one-armed wing nut. In practice the lids were found to be awkward to fit. The petrol tank held 3 gallons, and was decorated with the new-for-'56 plastic-winged shield tank badges, and detachable chrome side-panels whose shape married with that of the kneegrips behind them. All controls were adjustable, and comfort from the dual-seat good. The Crusader was a tidy package, but in looks as in specification it was very much a scaled-down 'proper motor cycle' rather than a sporting lightweight. The price too was not super-competitive; at a time when around £170 would buy you a 250 two-stroke like the James Commodore, the Crusader at £198 8s was significantly dearer.

Real comparison would have to wait for the arrival of the BSA unit 250, the C15, at the end of 1958 and by then (since March 1958 in fact) the Crusader range had been expanded for the first time to include the Series II 250 Clipper. True to Enfield form, the Clipper name again heralded a cut-price version of one of their range, which at an initial £179 19s 6d was in the ring with the BSA, whose volume production runs got its price down to £172.

The new Clipper had the same basic engine, frame and forks as the Crusader, but a saddle not a dual-seat, an unenclosed rear chain, the engine castings unbuffed and an unvalanced front mudguard. The rear units were non-adjustable, the rear wheel fitted a single-sided rear brake on a non qd hub, and finish was black enamel with gold lining on a tank without chrome panels: even pillion footrests were extra. Both the 250 Clipper and the Crusader's compression ratios had risen to 8:1 by then, and output to 14 bhp. Otherwise changes for the '58 Crusader were minimal, with the adoption, like most of the range, of the new Burgess silencer with no tail-pipe, as well as minor alterations to the gearchange mechanism and the lubrication system with the deletion of the pressure-control valve by the oil filter.

Early in 1958 the Crusader had become available with the Airflow fairing. (There was also a Police version, the RE 250 Airflow Clipper, with 7.5:1 compression and a ⅞ in diameter inlet tract.) The Airflow added around 20 lb to the Crusader's dry weight. Though a smaller version was used than that for the rest of the four-strokes, its appearance did not suit the lower, slighter-built single as well as it did the range's twins: the bulkiness of the fairing and its enlarged front mudguard visually overbalanced it forward. Improved cruising speeds, weathershielding without interfering with maintenance, and mpg improved from 92 at 50 mph on the unfaired machine to 99 on the faired, were some of the compensations for this.

Motor Cycling tested a Crusader in February 1958. The economy and docility aspects were emphasized, rather than the top speed which was just 70 mph. High gearing (top gear was 5.8:1) meant that it took a long time to reach that figure, after

Far left *1958 Crusader 250 on test.*

Left *New for 1958, the budget 250 Clipper.*

Right *1958 Crusader 250.*

quite brisk acceleration up to around 55 mph. During the course of exploring that acceleration, the test bike developed clutch slip which required adjustment. The clutch was the three-spring design (very early 1956/7 clutches had featured six springs). With two friction plates at this stage, it was to be something of a liability, although when working was light and pleasant enough in operation. The springs, unfortunately, were not individually adjustable for tension. On the plus side, starting, with the coil ignition, was found to be easy, the excellence of Enfield handling and steering undiminished, and there was smooth fast cruising and good pick-up from low speeds, both aided by the cush hub.

In service, the Crusader was to be dogged by somewhat familiar Enfield faults, mainly stemming from the lubrication system. A 1965 *Motor Cycle* Reader's Report, though its subject was the later Sports versions, spelt out the most visible effects: 'appalling' oil leaks principally from the cylinder base and head joints, and the rocker box. The base joint leaks were abetted by the Enfield habit of over-fine thread forms in alloy, in this case the crankcase stud holes. 'The sale of jointing compound must have trebled' was one disgruntled comment. Internally, the condition of the oil feed rubber and oil seal in the primary chaincase outer cover was crucial. In the opinion of journalist Bob Currie, one culprit was the lack of an oil-pressure relief valve in the system. This meant that the engine, especially when cold, ran at quite a high oil pressure. Though it fell when the engine warmed up, if any of the gaskets were unsound, they would blow during this initial period. Crankcase joints too were far from oiltight, and a further source of gush was the owner's tendency to overfill the gearbox: the level screw was located, rather inconspicuously, halfway up the middle of the right-hand crankcase cover. One improvement on the pre-unit singles was in oiltightness at the no-neck filler cap, though the riders found it inconvenient to use, and some machines went out with the caps' integral dipstick lacking high/low markings.

In addition, the 6 in front brake was not good. The comparative crudeness of the unit 250, already mentioned in relation to the front forks and the unbushed swinging-arm, also extended to considerable valve gear rattle, and to the absence of a cush-drive in the clutch. Testers found the gearbox required firm pressure, especially to get into first, and as the riders reported, frequently found false neutrals. They had no complaints about the clutch though, which Don Morley pinpoints as the unit bikes' Achilles heel in competition terms. He says that the tiny key holding the clutch onto the gearbox mainshaft had a bad habit of shearing and throwing the clutch itself off, and diagnoses Loctite as the cure today. He also mentions gearbox pinions 'shedding their teeth like dandruff'. As we have seen, early tests do mention the two-plate clutch getting out of adjustment, and it would be modified for 1960.

Left *Hop-up: the powerful 1959 Crusader Sports, perhaps the best of them all.*

Below right *1959 Crusader Sports on the road.*

1959 saw the start of the hotting-up process, with the Crusader Sports. Claimed output was boosted to 17 bhp at 6,250 rpm and a top speed two miles short of 80 mph was achieved on a *Motor Cycling* test of this 'fastest standard roadster of its size yet tested', which was also faster than most traditional 350 singles. The essential point had been made for the younger audience.

The power hop was achieved principally by the use of sports cams with quicker lift and a greater degree of overlap; by the use of a new crankshaft, with the previous dural sleeve removed and replaced by two Allen type screws, and a reduction of flywheel weight (this became common to the rest of the 250 range by 1960); and by the use of an alloy cylinder head (also adopted by the standard Crusader, and distinguishable externally by the fact that its metal was not painted black like the iron engines'). Compression rose slightly to 8.5:1. Fed by a larger (15/16 in) choke Monobloc 376/216 carburettor, the head incorporated austenitic iron valve seats, phosphor-bronze valve guides less fragile than their predecessors, a larger ($1^{9}/_{16}$ in) inlet valve, with hardened tips for both inlet and exhaust valves. This meant that, on this and all later engines other than the Clipper and standard Crusader (which maintained valves of the previous size), no hardened valve stem-end caps were fitted, and the top valve-spring collar was secured to the valve stem by a split collet which had a narrow internal projection fitting into a corresponding groove in the valve stem. The bottom collar remained steel, but top collars were alloy. Inlet and exhaust valves were not interchangeable, having different size stems and being made of different grade steel. The length of the new and subsequent engines' duplex valve springs was 1½ in for the inner and $1^{11}/_{16}$ in for the outer, against $2^{1}/_{32}$ in for both inner and outer for the standard Crusader and Clipper. (However, caution should be observed on this, as at various points in the workshop manual, the length for the iron head's outer springs is also referred to as either $2^{1}/_{16}$th in or $2^{3}/_{32}$ in, while the alloy head outer springs' length becomes 1¾ in!) Valve clearances for the Sports were down from the standard's .004 inlet and .006 exhaust to .002 and .004 respectively. With the hotter cams, difficult starting became a frequent problem. Exact ignition timing and carburation, with the needle in the centre notch, plus keeping the throttle completely closed, were the secrets here. Engine breathing now replaced the previous crude piece of neoprene pipe with flattened end emerging from the breather point on the front of the crankcases between the front engine plates, with a flanged breather body and metal pipe, attached to the right-hand crankcase by three screws.

On the cycle side, the Sports Crusader's footrests were higher and further back than standard, the exhaust pipe had a sharper rearward sweep and led into a revised version of the tail-pipeless silencer shared by the Crusader. The noise from this was reckoned 'deep and quiet' by the Green 'un, but 'too pronounced' and 'liable to give offence' by *Motor Cycle* the following year: both remarked on valve chatter. The rear chain was exposed and liable to particularly rapid wear.

Perhaps the most welcome addition of all

sat between the front forks in a full-width hub. This was the 7 × 1½ in front brake, which in conjunction with a claimed dry weight of 305 lb was noticeably more effective than its 6 in predecessor, though in the rain it could let in water. The Crusader Sports now stopped in 28½ ft from 30 mph, and the result of the tweaked engine was cracking acceleration, allied to taut handling which was marred only by skittishness while cornering at high speed, due to some back-end whip. Yet the performance was not achieved at the expense of tractability, or economy (well over 90 mpg was still average). It was an impressive package, and the Crusader Sports would be a steady seller for Redditch from then on.

Visually its biggest impact came from the combination of the dual-seat, uptilted at the rear but comfortable with it, plus chromed mudguards, and the chromed slab-sided 3¾ gallon petrol tank, all of which gave the 250s very much the appearance of a junior 700 Constellation. In addition there were dropped handlebars, but the *Motor Cycle* test felt that the crouch they induced put too much weight on the wrists and arms, at all speeds;

and they also commented on something endorsed by the later 'Rider's Report', that in order to prevent the rider's thumbs being trapped between tank and bars, the steering lock had been restricted so much that turning in even medium-width roads was awkward.

At the other end of the scale, 1959 saw the economy Clipper edging into line with the Crusader, being offered now with pillion footrests and a dual-seat as standard, as well as chrome panels on the petrol tank. The compression of its iron engine was reduced slightly to 7.5:1.

1960 saw an attempt on the unit 250 engines to get to grips with the distortion which caused the leaking rocker box covers, at the same time as strengthening the rockers and improving their geometry. The rocker assembly changed; from being one-piece stampings carried in split cast-iron bearings, they became a spindle with a plate arm at each end retained by nuts, spring-loaded and now carried in a single alloy body, which was secured to the head by two small studs at each end and a larger one in the middle. This resulted in longer rocker bearings and the improved geometry. Also, on the earlier alloy heads, in addition to the five head-securing nuts, there had been a single counter-sunk Allen screw located between the two sleeve nuts on the pushrod side of the engine; now there were two Allen screws, located in the pushrod tunnel, presumably to try and improve the head to barrel joint. Finally in April 1960 all the 250s had their crankshafts modified with oil passage plugs in the flywheels replacing a previous sleeve.

There was also a redesign in the slip-prone clutch, with all models adopting an extra pair of friction-insert and plain plates. The two Crusaders got their casquettes restyled. The gearing on the Crusader Sports was altered—now it was brought in line with the Crusader and Clipper II—and a *Motor Cycle* test that year found the 8.29:1 ratio for third ideal for overtaking as well as for main-road gradients. The Sports' front mudguard stays were also modified, now being tubular, and looping over the blade for extra support.

1961 saw little development. The Crusader Sports compression was raised to 8.75:1. Apart from the 250 and 350 Clippers and the Meteor Minor, all the other four-strokes including the Crusaders fitted a new three-part silencer, torpedo-shaped, with a narrow

fin decorating its upper face. The bottom run of both the Crusader and Crusader Sports' exhaust pipes were shortened to suit the longer silencer. Both the standard Crusader and the Clipper adopted the same slab-sided 3¾ gallon fuel tank as the Sports, but enamelled not chromed.

The Crusader Sports had sold steadily, but with the 250 cc learner limit in force, 1962 saw the next evolutionary step with the Crusader Super-5, or 'Fiver' as it was soon nicknamed. The first British production machine to be manufactured with a five-speed gearbox as standard, this was another Enfield coup. However, it was scuppered by the combination of another unusual feature, its leading-link front forks, and the gremlins lurking in the five-speed box, which had been packed into an internally modified version of the four-speed shell with a modified gearchange mechanism. (This means that only 1962 and later four-speed boxes can be converted to five-speed, whereas any five-speed can be re-converted to four—indeed the later five-speed Continental GT had a kit to so convert it.) While the four-speed box, if imprecise, had at least been traditionally robust, the extra cog, without extra space to fit it in, meant that it was necessary to thin down all the gears, which added fragility and further selector trouble.

By contrast there was nothing at all wrong with the Armstrong leading link fork with its two-way damped units, except customer resistance. It provided good steering and stable braking, and the chrome tank and Marina grey finish offset with red striping here and there was not unattractive. The leading link fork sat beneath a casquette without sidelights, and between them there was an unfortunately large floating front mudguard, echoing the unattractive pressed steel deep rear guard of the type introduced on the big twins the previous year, as well as a dual-seat with black sides and a chequered grey-and-white top. None of this in the least attracted the lads who were already patronizing E and S Motors and Deeprose Bros in Catford for cafe racer go-faster bits like modified front brake plates, six-spring clutch conversions and even Wal Phillips fuel injectors, for their Crusaders. Road tests of the Super 5 in both weeklies confirmed 83–84 mph top speeds, still reasonable economy, and excellent handling; but according to Dr Kelly's thesis figures, in all only 114 were sold.

Enfield had really wrong-footed, because the Super-5's internals featured the 250's latest developments. There was a second oil filter, a nylon-gauze item locating on the left side inside the crankcase which would be adopted by the other 250s for 1963. This was shaped like an elongated thimble and could be inserted either way up. The open end was supposed to go into the chamber, but if the thing was fitted upside down with the blind end downward, it could block the oilway. Compression was 9.75:1, achieved by a domed piston and requiring 100 octane petrol. The Monobloc choke size was up to $1^{1}/_{16}$ in. There was a new connecting rod, still of RR56 alloy, but with the big-end cap now retained by two Allen screws, in contrast to the previous arrangement with pegged bolts whose lower ends had been secured by castle nuts and split pins. The new screws were a close fit to hold the alignment, and screwed into self-locking helicoil thread inserts in the rod. This type was used on the 250s from then on.

The five-speed Albion gearbox itself had three pairs of gears which as before moved together along the shafts to engage with driving dogs in turn. Its top ratio of 6.02:1 was only slightly higher than that of the four-speed Crusader Sports, and the closeness of top to the 7.52:1 fourth gear and 9.57:1 third was good for economy as well as high average speeds. During 1962 the five-speed box became an option for the Crusader Sports. For that year also, both Crusaders got the new rear mudguard and dual-seat, while all got new-type Lucas horns and alternators, and in January a steering-head lock became available for all except the Clipper.

1963 saw the factory regrouping fast after the previous year's stylistic errors of judgement. The Super 5 was still offered, but in a more conventional black and polychromatic Blaze red or Gold finish. Compression was brought into line with all the 250s, which standardized for that year at 9:1. The cover of the leading link itself was de-emphasized in silver not black paint, and a smaller unsprung front mudguard fitted, in chrome, as was the bulky rear one. It was nevertheless quietly faded out, being available to special order only later in the year.

But more successfully, the five-speed unit was now the basis of a junior rocker's special, 'Super styled for NEW Moderns', the 'two-five-zero' Continental. One substantial change to the cycle parts, introduced for this machine but applying to all the 250s, was that the front fork stanchions were thickened, with the springs reduced in diameter to compensate, though the alloy fork sliders were unaltered. Otherwise, while basically a Crusader Sports, with an air scoop on its 7 in front brake, chequered sticky tape on the upper forks, a detached chrome headlamp shell supported from beneath on brackets and carrying the ammeter, an alloy dash panel carrying matching rev-counter and speedometer, dropped bars with ball-ended control levers, a chrome 3¼ gallon kidney-shaped racing style tank, skimpy chromed mudguards, and dampers with exposed chromed springs, this was 'The Business', and 535 of them sold in their first year (the final total would be 1,029). The price tag was £202, £7 more than the Crusader Sports, but comparing very

Above far left *An ill-fated model that deserved better: a 1963 Super-5, with leading link fork.*

Above left *Getting to the points with a 1961 Crusader Sports.*

Right *Tailored for the youth: the 1963 Continental, chequered sticky-tape an' all.*

favourably with BSA's slower and less flamboyant sports 250, the C15 SS80, at £210.

Internally, the Continental's valve clearances, like the Super-5's the previous year, were zero for the inlet and .002 for the exhaust. In common with all the 250s, the new model featured bonded rubber swinging arm bushes where before these had been unbushed. A combination of the new management's presence and the industry's crisis was making itself felt, and there were further changes to the 250 range. The standard Crusader, long overshadowed by the Sports, was dropped, its role being taken over by the Clipper, which adopted the alloy head.

The heavyweight singles also went, so to supplement the 250s a 350 version of the unit single, the New Bullet, was introduced. It had the same universal bore of 70 mm as the 250s (and the Meteor Minor 500 and the Constellation), but its stroke was lengthened to 90 mm, the barrel being longer, with an extra fin. This conversion also involved an extra drive side plain bronze main bearing outside the 250's ball-race; and a new crankshaft which was built up, not one-piece as on the 250s, with flywheels and engine shafts being integral castings. Both the 350's steel crankpin and its white-metal floating bush big-end were near identical to the old pre-unit Bullet.

There the resemblance ended, however, because the New Bullet's engine was another famous failure for Redditch. With a claimed output of 22.5 bhp, although the four-speed gearbox was strengthened, it was to prove the 350's fatally weak point. According to Don Morley the competition variants, at least, would shed gear pinion teeth, or even shear their gearbox mainshafts, and the much lighter flywheels restricted their low down pulling power. Morley writes that most of the New Bullet roadsters sold were recalled under guarantee, and that after their owners had accepted payment in compensation, the 350s were converted back to 250s: not too difficult to do, with the common bore, and since their cycle parts were those of that year's Crusader Sports, which had reverted to a conventional chromed rear mudguard. Though the New Bullet continued to be catalogued for 1964 and 1965, a total of only 252 were sold all together.

A more useful development for 1963 was the introduction of the Sportsflow fairing for any of the unit singles. As mentioned, the Airflow option was always on the bulky side for the quarter litre crew, and this was now remedied by a good-looking dolphin-type fairing with its own screen, and a slot in the lower right-hand panel through which the exhaust could exit. Costing a reasonable £18 8s, the Sportsflow was used in conjunction with the machine's regular front mudguard and came in colours to match the bike, or in

Left *New 350 Bullet for 1964. Not a good idea.*

Right *Sportsflow fairing, seen here on a 1965 Continental, suited the 250s.*

Far right *Villiers 2T-engined Turbo Twin for 1965.*

white. Slightly later the Speedflow, a race-styled fairing with a transparent nose cone and racer's windshield was offered. One of these was fitted to Gander and Gray's 'Gannet' 250 racer and today they can still be obtained from Sprint Manufacturing.

1964 saw Enfield struggling with an uncompromising market downturn by pushing the economy button in an unexpected way, with a Villiers-engined model costing just £195. The 4T 250 twin cylinder motor was housed in Clipper cycle parts, including that machine's front forks and execrable 6 in front brake, though topping the fork was not the traditional casquette but a separate headlamp mounted on conventional enamelled brackets, with a new design of fork crown, incorporating the handlebar mountings and routing for the cables. Despite the 8.75:1 cr 4T unit's reputation as a harsher and more seizure-prone motor than its 2T predecessor, much play was made of the 'turbine-like smoothness' of this machine, and this in fact proved to be the case, with a *Motorcycle Mechanics* test awarding 9 out of 10 for engine smoothness.

The impression was aided by the use of a pair of Villiers' own silencers which had improved internal baffling for that year. Despite a crankcase logo giving slightly more prominence to the word 'Enfield' than to 'Villiers', other Villiers gear included the S25 carburettor with its somewhat superfluous choke plunger and its rectangular air filter (from which the felt element could occasionally be sucked into the inlet tract), and the customary ignition switch set in the right-hand side of the crankcase.

Comfort was good on the Turbo Twin, as was handling—*Motorcycle Mechanics* even judged it superior to the four-stroke 250s due to the pilot's lower centre of gravity. Useful acceleration, effortless 65 mph cruising plus a maximum speed around 75 mph, and fuel consumption of about 75 mpg overall, were all satisfactory characteristics. However, the centre stand was prone to grounding on corners, especially with two up, and economy-inspired drawbacks included the lack of a stop-light (on some but not all of them), of a side-stand, of a petrol tap with a reserve supply, of adjustment for load on the Armstrong rear units, of kneepads (again only on some models) to stop the paintwork rubbing away, and of an adequate toolkit. But all in all it was and is one of the better Villiers-engined options and 992 were to be sold, of both versions.

Possibly bearing the Super 5/Continental episode in mind, the initial Turbo Twin was quickly followed in March 1964 by a Sports version, though at an increased price of just £9, the differences were cosmetic only, with chromed mudguards, dropped handlebars, and chromed panels on the petrol tank in a sort of 'dead comma' shape outlined in thick inner and thin outer gold lining. The petrol tank itself was a new design for all the 250s

and the New Bullet for 1964. It was slim, long and deep, though still with the customary rim at the front, and capacity was down slightly (for all but the Continental) from 3¾ to 3½ gallons.

For the Continental the hand of economy was also evident this year, as it bifurcated into a standard and a de luxe model, the latter featuring at extra cost the flyscreen, rev-counter and chromed mudguards which had been standard the previous year, as well as gold-lined chrome panels on its tank like the Turbo Twin Sports. Something similar happened with the Crusader Sports, as for that year only it too was offered in a standard version with painted guards and tank, or de luxe, chromed as previously. On the Continental, as on the Clipper and Crusader Sports, the urge to get rid of stocks of the unpopular leading link forks was evident, as these were now offered as optional alternatives to tele forks. Finally for all the 250s and the New 350 Bullet there was a new silencer, rather tacky and Japanese-looking with seams top and bottom, but claiming to meet the requirements of forthcoming legislation without affecting performance much.

At the end of 1964, in a blaze of advance publicity, came the ultimate version of the 250, the Continental GT. This bike evolved very much in the light of the Super 5 experience, and also because others more in touch with the street were already making money, which Redditch badly needed, by selling things for the 250s that cadet rockers wanted. Since 1963 Deeprose Bros of Catford had offered Continental-type conversions for Crusaders, including engine performance aids, swept-back exhausts, rear-sets, separate headlamp shells and 3 or 5 gallon fibreglass petrol tanks (as had Gander and Gray with their 'Gannet' range of accessories). Redditch now took the imaginative leap-frog of turning the Continental over to selected dealers and to their own apprentices (among whom were numbered riders of the calibre of future Trials ace Mick 'Bonky' Bowers), to find out what The Youth was really after. Then Reg Thomas designed their suggestions into a satisfactory whole.

The result was an exceptionally sleek and good-looking sportster, which as Bob Currie has pointed out, did also actually serve a useful purpose since bodged home-brewed versions of the clip-ons and rear-set brake linkages featured on it had been known to cause accidents by failing under stress. The styling was dominated by the long, low, fire-engine red fibreglass 3½ gallon petrol tank, with 'Royal Enfield' in bold white lettering on its sides, and a butterfly-catch racing-type filler cap, with a wreathed 'Continental GT' transfer behind it.

Equally eye-catching were the big perforated dummy cooling rims of polished alloy on the front wheel with its 7 in stopper with air-scoop, the abbreviated black plastic gaiters on the front forks, the exceptionally handsome alloy fork top panel housing the recessed matching speedo and rev-counter. The clip-on handlebars, featuring chromed ball-end levers and light grey rubber grips, disappeared with their grey cables beneath the panel from the rider's eye view. The discreet flyscreen also married neatly with the panel as well as with the chrome separate headlamp shell, which as before carried the ammeter, though for the rider this was obscured by the screen. With the graceful bend in the swept-back exhaust pipe where it cleared the crankcase, the cylindrical silencer (with no seams!), the racing-style rear hump to the dual-seat with its black sides, white piping and light top, the big clear plastic breather tube running racer-style from left rear crankcase to the rear mudguard where it crossed over to exit on the right, the big bell-mouth on the carb and the exposed chrome springs of the rear dampers—the factory had got it very right. The only things that looked like afterthoughts were the way the electrics—battery, rectifier, coil and ignition switch—clustered exposed, save for a vestigial cover plate, beneath the nose of the seat; and the choice of polychromatic silver as the colour for the frame and upper forks. For 1966 both would be remedied, with a black frame and upper forks setting off the skimpy red mudguards and red rear chainguard, and an equally skimpy red fibreglass cover to contain the coil and ignition switch and shield the top of the white Lucas MLZ9E 6 volt battery. Interestingly, from the start the GT's front wheel also changed from the 3.25 × 17 in customary on the 250s, to 3.00 × 18 in.

The GT's engine too had been breathed on, as John 'Moon-eyes' Cooper's averages of over 70 mph round Silverstone on the publicity launch suggested. The latter wheeze involved journalists in relays riding a GT from John O'Groats to Land's End in 24 hours (in November), with stops for Cooper, and Enfield employee and GT developer Geoff Duke, to bang in quick laps at Oulton and Silverstone (Duke was inhibited by an icy track at the former). It was a good scheme, with the journalists' involvement ensuring proper coverage, and the fact that the 250 completed the trip faultlessly (bar a slight misfire pre-Silverstone due to the ignition switch housing coming loose), in 22 hours and 20 minutes, spoke for itself. Bruce Main-Smith, *Motor Cycling*'s man at the time, recalled 'an extraordinarily noisy exhaust, sublimely good handling, excellent brakes and a peppy engine. It was fast—about 82 mph with the rider crouched—and accelerated well.' Interestingly, he adds that 'despite the stopwatch proof that the fifth gear was not really necessary for outright acceleration, in actuality the extra cog was more than a mere sales aid. It did indeed add to both the enjoyment and the usefulness of the ohv single for spirited riding.'

Engine mods had included an opened-out inlet port, a 1⅛ in Monobloc (though initially this had been 1$^{1}/_{16}$ like the standard Continental), 9.5:1 compression and lightened valves, which resulted in a claimed output of 21 bhp at 7,500 rpm, for 1966. The performance again was not at the expense of tractability; a highly approving *Motor Cycle* road test in 1966 called the GT 'sweet-natured and accommodating', noted a stopping distance of 28½ ft from 30 mph, and a fuel consumption of 64 mpg even at a steady 70 mph.

They also noted that the unit stayed perfectly oil-tight. That big breather pipe to the rear wheel was not just for show; the engine breathing had been revised considerably. As on the 250s since mid-1959, at the right-hand front side on top of the crankcase, a flanged union was secured by three screws. Inside it there were three overlapping circular recesses, with the middle one leading to an outlet pipe and the other two leading to the crankcase. These latter two contained a thin steel disc each, and a thin steel base plate with two small diameter vent holes was fitted beneath the flange body. But on the GT the outlet pipe from the middle recess was led over into the cam housing on the top left side of the crankcase. From there a large bore pipe led into the oil tank behind the cylinder barrel, and vented via the big breather pipe into the atmosphere. It was a distinct improvement.

Back on test, *Motor Cycle* conceded that

Magnificent 1965 Continental GT.

the clip-ons and rear-set riding position imposed strain in town traffic, but they found that this cleared on the open road, and confirmed that the rear-set brake and gearchange pedals married nicely with the rear-set footrests (the right one folding to allow clear use of the kickstart), and could be worked from the crouch with no awkward wiggling of the ankles. In praising the way the mchine 'flowed through the bends without a waver', they suggested that the suspension as well as the engine had come in for some tuning; springing seemed a little on the soft side, but with 'impeccable damping which allowed the machine to float over the ripples'. (Author Roy Bacon described it rather differently—a hard rear end and light front one which made the bike 'leap about over bumps like a racer'.) There were inevitably some negative points. Riders were to find that despite the continued presence of the cush hub, rear chain wear was very rapid, sometimes as little as two months, and the model would be known for bad deterioration of the gearbox outer sprocket, which sat in a kind of cavity that filled up with road dirt. But in summing up, *Motor Cycle* called the GT 'undoubtedly the finest two-fifty Royal Enfield have ever made', a conclusion with which it is hard to quarrel.

The punters thought so too. Despite a comparatively high price (£275 in 1966, when £283 would get you a 500 cc Triumph 5TA), 988 were sold in 1965, and a total of 1,702 before production ceased in January 1967. This made the GT by far their fastest selling 250 model of the decade. The GT, and variants on it, had some success on the race track. Race school proprietor Chas Mortimer, for instance, had one of his first professional rides on a Gander and Gray-entered GT in the Thruxton 500-miler of 1967, finishing fifth in class with his partner, having averaged over 70 mph for six hours and G and G's ultimate development, the Gannet racer, would also be quite successful. It will be no surprise to see the GT, like the Bullet before it, scoring again in Classic racing when the 25-year rule allows it.

Stooping from the comparatively sublime GT to the somewhat ridiculous predicament of Redditch still trying to off-load their stock of leading link forks (and at least one Turbo Twin had been sold with them), there was another 'new' model for 1965, the Olympic, which was essentially a Clipper but with the early Super 5's front end (drop bars, casquette with no sidelights, mudguard supported from the wheel hub, and the link cover in black). The old pressed steel rear covering was in place, but inducements to buy included the 7 in front brake as on the Super 5, a petrol tank with chrome panels like the Crusader Sports, Turbo Twin Sports and Continental, and a price tag of £224. Only 105 were shifted, but every little helped, for with the Olympic it was not just the leading link fork that had to go; this was also the last of the Crusader variants. The standard Continental that year got the GT's front fork dust-excluding gaiters.

1966 saw the end of the road for Redditch, and the unit range had contracted to the Continental GT with the changes described above, the Turbo Twin Sports and the perennial favourite, the Crusader Sports. The series came to an end that year with the demise of Redditch, the Crusader ceasing in June, the two-stroke in October, and the GT as mentioned, in January 1967. Late export versions of it were offered with a raised and braced motocross handlebar in place of the flyscreen, this version being known in the States as the '250 cc TT Road Racer'.

Today, though no longer learner-legal, the 250s make a sparky alternative to other British quarter-litre four-strokes. The GT and the Sports Crusaders are the most desirable, though the former's high state of tune make it one for knowledgeable enthusiasts only, and the latter is probably the best choice all round; and any 250 engine can be brought up to their spec. Engine spares and the Lucas electrical components are reasonably plentiful, and the commonality with the 'doubled-up' Meteor Minor 500 twin should be borne in mind. However, cycle parts are said to be very thin on the ground (Russell Motors in Clapham once dumped tons of them due to lack of demand), though the Continental GT seems well served in this respect by Burton Bike Bits. There are some improvements available today (modern jointing compound may be one of the most relevant!). These include Gander and Gray's conversion for worn examples of the unbushed fork legs, with the legs bored and bushes inserted. Fitting a Concentric carburettor is said to facilitate achieving tickover on the sports engines.

The looks (as well as the noise) of the sporting variants will still turn heads, but the presence of *any* of them will interest an enthusiast, as the Enfield unit 250 is a rare sight on the road today, in contrast to the ubiquitous C15. Possibly their performance and a young target audience usually led to a good thrashing until they wore out and were discarded. They were never machines for the mechanically unsympathetic. That 1965 Rider's Report liked the built-in ease of access for cleaning and servicing (the complete engine and gearbox except for the crankshaft and con-rod could be dismantled without removing the unit from the frame), but confirmed that they were reliable only if carefully maintained. This incuded regularly greasing the gearchange unit, and checking the engine oil *daily*. There is, too, some evidence of declining standards after the takeover at Redditch affecting the machines; chrome finish on the Sports' petrol tank was said to be poor, with factory spares service 'slow and unhelpful', and only 65 per cent of the owners in the Report had felt that they would buy another Enfield.

A more fundamental factor in their

Above far left *Second leading-link fork model, the 1965 Olympic.*

Above left *1966, and last Crusader Sports.*

Right *Coffee bar cowboy (note the spotlight switches) has ridden this slightly modified Crusader into the coffee bar. Ah, youth.*

comparative rarity were annual production runs barely in three figures for many of the variants, while Small Heath in the 1950s were regularly churning out 250, and sometimes 350, quarter litre singles a week. Enfield's unit 250 cc was far from a flawless design, but it was certainly faster and better-handling than a C15.

Royal Enfield: the Crusader, 250 Clipper Series II, Crusader Sports, Crusader Super 5, New 350 Bullet, Turbo Twin, Continental, Olympic, Continental GT and Turbo Twin Sports— production dates and specifications

Production Dates

Crusader—1956–62
250 Clipper Series II—1958–65
Crusader Sports—1959–66
Crusader Super 5—1962–63
New 350 Bullet—1963–65
Continental—1963–65
Turbo Twin—1964–65
Turbo Twin Sports—1964–66
Olympic—1965
Continental GT—1965–66

Specifications

Crusader/250 Clipper Series II/Crusader Sports/Crusader Super 5/Continental/ Olympic/Continental GT

Capacity, bore and stroke—248 cc (70 × 64.5 mm)
Type—ohv single
Ignition—coil
Weight—Crusader (1957) 312 lb, Clipper II (1960) 305 lb, Crusader Sports (1963) 305 lb, Super 5 (1962) 310 lb, Continental (1963) 308 lb, Olympic (1965) 305 lb, Continental GT (1965) 300 lb

Turbo Twin/Turbo Twin Sports

Capacity, bore and stroke—249 cc (50 × 63.5mm)
Type—Two-stroke twin
Ignition—Flywheel magneto
Weight—Turbo Twin (1964) 298 lb, Turbo Twin Sports (1966) 298 lb

New 350 Bullet

Capacity, bore and stroke—346 cc (70 × 90 mm)
Type—ohv single
Ignition—coil
Weight—(1963) 310 lb

Royal Enfield: Unit 250 and 350 singles, and 250 two-stroke twins— annual development and modifications

1958

For Crusader

1 Spring-loaded pressure control valve previously connected to top of oil filter, now deleted.
2 Knurled nuts retaining tool-box lids replaced by one-armed wing-nuts.
3 Compression ratio raised from 7.3:1 to 8:1.
4 New Burgess silencer with no tail-pipe.
5 Minor alteration to gear change mechanism, with gear operator anchor pin pivot, previously one pin screwed in from top, replaced by two piece assembly with bottom anchor pin screwed in from a drilling in the bottom of the casing.

1959

For Crusader

1 Alloy cylinder head as on that year's Crusader Sports adopted, but maintaining valves and valve springs of previous size (for details see text).
2 Revised silencer as on Crusader Sports.

For 250 Clipper II

3 Dual-seat and pillion footrests now fitted as standard.
4 Compression reduced from 8:1 to 7.5:1.
5 Petrol tank now fits chromed side-panels, as Crusader.

For all 250s

6 Airflow fairing available as option.

From June

7 Engine breathing revised, with flanged union secured by three screws; union containing three discs and fastened to crankcase top front right (for details see text).

1960

For all 250s

1 Clutch, previously four-plate, acquires an extra pair of friction-insert and plain plates.
2 Gearing altered to 6.1, 8.3, 11.1, 18.0:1 (first).

For Crusader, Crusader Sports

3 Restyled casquettes with side-lights mounted on either side further apart than previously.
4 Rocker assembly modified (for details see text), and single countersunk Allen screw between two nuts on pushrod side replaced

by two Allen screws located in pushrod tunnel.
For Crusader Sports
5 Front mudguard stays become tubular, and loop over blade for extra support.
For Crusader, Clipper II
6 Crusader Sports crankshaft adopted.
For all 250s
7 From April crankshaft modified, now with oil passage plugs replacing previous sleeve.

1961
For Crusader Sports
1 Compression raised to 8.75:1.
For Crusader, Clipper II
2 Same 3¾ petrol tank as Crusader Sports fitted, but painted not chromed.
For Crusader, Crusader Sports
3 New three-part silencer with tail-fin.
4 Bottom run of exhaust pipe shortened to suit longer silencer.

1962
For Crusader Sports, Crusader, Clipper II
1 Gearing altered to 6.14, 7.8, 11.05, 18.0:1 (first).
2 New con-rod with big end retained by Allen screws, as on Super 5 (for details see text).
3 Lucas Type 8H horn replaces previous Type HF 1849; Lucas type RM18 alternator replaces previous Type RM13; and Lucas MLZ9E battery replaces previous PUZ7E.
4 Gearbox shell modified internally to take five-speed internals if desired, and change mechanism modified, with gear change stop plate now slotted and previous stop pegs deleted.
For Crusader Sports, Crusader, Super 5
5 (From January) Steering head locks available.
For Crusader Sports, Crusader
6 New large pressed-steel rear cover/mudguard, as on Super 5.
7 New dual-seat with black sides, white piping, grey and white chequered top.
For Crusader Sports
8 (Mid-year) Five-speed gearbox as on Super 5 (6.02, 7.52, 9.57, 12.82, 17.4 [first]) offered as optional extra.

1963
For all 250s and New Bullet 350
1 Bonded rubber swinging-arm bushes now fitted.
2 Sportsflow fairing option becomes available, and shortly afterwards, Speedflow.
For all 250s
3 Front fork stanchions thickened up, with springs reduced in diameter to compensate.
4 Extra oil filter fitted (as on 1962 Super 5), nylon-gauze, locating on left side inside crankcase.
5 Compression standardized at 9:1.
For Sports Crusader
6 New absorption-type silencer.
For Super 5
7 Leading link cover now silver not black.
8 Smaller unsprung front mudguard replaces previous large sprung item. Both front and rear mudguards now chrome.
For Clipper II
9 Alloy cylinder head, as on previous Crusader, adopted.
10 One-armed wing nuts subsituted for knurled nuts securing toolbox lid.
For Crusader Sports
11 Conventional chrome rear mudguard replaces previous pressed steel rear cover.

1964
For all 250s and New Bullet 350
1 New 3½ gallon petrol tank, for Turbo Twin Sports, Continental De Luxe, Crusader Sports De Luxe, with gold-lined chrome panels.
2 New silencer with seams top and bottom.
For Crusader Sports, Continental, Clipper II
3 Leading link fork as on previous Super 5 offered as optional alternative.
For standard Crusader Sports, standard Continental
4 Painted mudguards replace previous chrome. Standard Continental, no rev-counter or flyscreen.
For Crusader Sports
5 Carburettor main jet reduced from 140 to 130.
For Clipper II
6 Carburettor main jet reduced from 120 to 95.
For Continental
7 Carburettor main jet reduced from 180 to 170.

1965
For Continental
1 Dust-excluding plastic bellows, as on new Continental GT.

1966
For Continental GT
1 Frame and fork top now black not silver.
2 Fibreglass cover over coil and ignition switch.

Royal Enfield: The 500 Twin, 700 Meteor, Super Meteor, Constellation, Meteor Minor, Interceptor and Interceptor Series II twins

Royal Enfield's twins are one of the great 'sleepers' of the post-war British industry. Undoubtedly flawed, yet flawed in ways that are mostly remediable, they have suffered both unfair neglect and, for the last of them, the Interceptor Series II, slightly excessive canonization due to rarity value.

The background and sporting achievements for the twins are covered in the marque history section, so here we will begin with the announcement of the 500 Twin in November 1948. Enfield management had concluded, correctly, that if the company was to stay competitive in the post-war world, a parallel twin cylinder machine was a necessity. To minimize the outlay involved, the cycle parts were those that had already been initiated for the roadster 350 Bullet and Ted Pardoe's engine design also continued the usual Enfield policy of good commonality with the rest of the range.

In other respects it was a markedly original layout, however, featuring separate (and interchangeable) cast-iron cylinders, each with its own alloy head and integral rocker box. As well as engine cooling, the kind of advantage this arrangement could provide was ably demonstrated in the 1951 ISDT, when works team member Stan Holmes blew a head gasket on one cylinder of his twin during the final speed test, but was able to finish successfully on one cylinder. Major servicing could be simplified and cheapened, but the downside was the lack of the rigidity a monobloc cylinder casting provides for a unit. This could lead to eventual shuffling of the crankcase mouths, and consequent oil leaks and distortion.

Good-looking 1950 500 Twin.

A further contributory factor to engine distortion and vibration was the way the engine and gearbox formed a stressed member of the frame, and eventually worked loose within it. As we shall see, the last twins would remedy this by a firmer supplementary fixing method, and this can be applied retrospectively to all the twins as well as the Bullets.

Other features distinguishing the first 500 Twin from the rest of the range, and from most other twins at the time, included electrics by coil and a car-type distributor mounted behind the cylinder. Camshaft drive was by chain, tensioned by a jockey sprocket carried on a movable quadrant. This was a design originally laid out by Tony Wilson-Jones in the 1930s, and cunningly, the quadrant plate was reversible, to give maximum adjustment. According to Bruce Main-Smith, the chain drive so flummoxed some Enfield owners that trouble with the timing chain due to lack of attention used to be a point to watch for, as some assumed that gear drive was used, as on the singles! Externally, both the swinging-arm frame with its high-fronted line, and the handsome silver-grey and chrome finish, distinguished the Twin in the best possible way from the black or maroon-coloured rigid or plunger-sprung crowd.

But there were many more points in common with the rest of the range. The cylinder dimensions at 64 × 77 mm were those of the pre-war Model S single (which would be revived in the UK for 1954). The oil compartment was positioned like the Bullet's to the base and rear of the crankcase. The Albion gearbox was (as usual) bolted to the rear of the case, with internals similar to the singles from 1949 to '62. The box itself was the same as the Bullets and the future twins from 1956 to '62. The same cylindrical felt and gauze oil filter was used, only not, as on the pre-unit singles, inserted along the length of the engine beneath the housing of the same double acting twin plunger-type oil pumps; but for the 500 Twin, stuck into the bottom of the crankcase from the side, beneath the familiar oil filler neck. The filter also differed in being on the return, not the

Royal Enfield's 500 Twin engine.

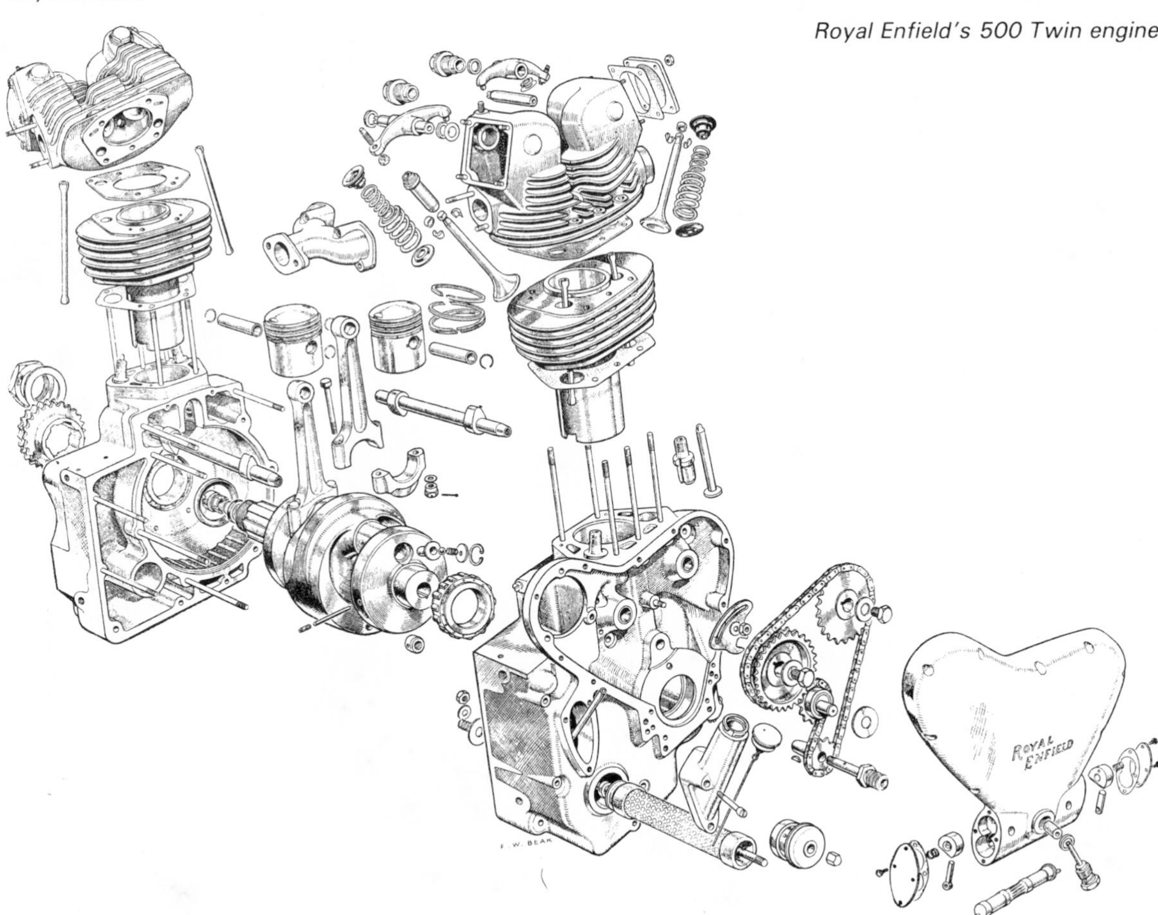

delivery side of the system.

The cylinders, as on the Bullet, were spigotted a full three inches into the squarish crankcase, making for a tall but compact and shapely unit. The camshafts sat high; there were two of them, fore and aft of the cylinders in the Triumph manner, with the short light alloy pushrods located at the outer ends of each shaft, the intention being optimum cooling.

Cooling of the unit as a whole would be a problem, the causes being firstly the same quickly-heated oil as the singles suffered from, due to its crankcase location. Oil capacity was also relatively low—compare this marque's 4 pints with a BSA's 5½ pints—and head and barrel finning less than adequate. The latter would be remedied on later models, but the problem of hot oil would not, despite an increase in circulation rate, until the advent of oil coolers. The lubrication system, with almost all its oilways internal and its inadequate breathing arrangements, is generally agreed to be the twins' major weak spot, and a prime source of oil-leaks.

The heart of the 500 Twin and the basis of its fundamental reliability was the one-piece crankshaft and central flywheel assembly of 18 ton/in^2 alloy iron. The shaft, which also incorporated small outer flywheels, was dynamically balanced from the start, making for a smooth-running engine which gave more speed for the same power. There had been early experiments with a built-up crank running on three main bearings. AMC, the other marque to adopt separate heads and barrels for their twins, would take that direction; no discernible benefit ensued for them. Redditch found the built-up crank flimsy, the bearings difficult to align, and the plain centre bearing needing so much clearance that it ceased to be a useful support. In production, just two main bearings, each virtually of the same diameter, were employed. They reversed convention in utilizing a single-row ball bearing on the drive side, where stresses made a roller more usual, and a roller on the timing side; however, these mains were rarely to give trouble in service.

Oil feed to the big ends was via the crankshaft. The crankpins were drilled out, and then sealed at either end with steel discs held in place by circlips. A reservoir for oil was thus formed within, to ensure that the big ends never had a dry start. Split, plain big ends were used, with their caps attached in the Enfield way by fitted bolts secured by nuts and split pins. As with Triumphs, they ran directly on the shaft, and again in service were found perfectly satisfactory, with a working life of up to 50,000 miles. The gudgeon pins too ran directly in the rods, again without problems.

On the timing side oil went from the pump through a large hollow feed plug, with a big hexagon bolt head at its top end protruding from the timing chest cover in a way characteristic of Enfields. The feed plug connected to the hollow crankshaft via internal drillings and a long centre-drilled spindle running through the timing sprocket. This spindle also drove the oil pump via a worm located on it. Centrifugal force as well as pressure carried the oil to the big ends, with the drive side crankpin's sealing disc incorporating a ball-valve for pressure relief. The drive side mainshaft, also bored out, was fitted with a crankcase oil breather clack valve.

On these early engines there were no external oil lines whatsoever, a rather vulnerable arrangement which clearly made it essential that the oilways between inner and outer cases should never be obscured by gaskets or dirt, and that oil seals should be well maintained. A further hazard for the restorer today is that the oiling system would change several times over the years, and timing covers in particular would not always be interchangeable.

The cast-iron barrels were slightly spigotted up into the bulbous light alloy heads, with the slightly domed pistons giving a compression ratio of 6.5:1. Beneath distinctive humped plates, each fastened by four corner bolts, the rockers ran on spindles supported by the body of the casting for rigidity, with screw adjusters secured by locknuts. Valve springs were duplex: clearances were tight, with the setting correct when the inlet rocker could not be moved endways on its spindle, while the exhaust rocker could just be moved. A single Amal carburettor fed the barrels via a U-shaped manifold.

The unusual electrics consisted of a dynamo mounted behind the cylinders: this was driven from an additional small row of teeth on the inlet cam drive sprocket. The dynamo was of a special type (Lucas C35SD/O H12/O) with skew gears to operate the distributor unit which sat upright on top of it, directing current to the spark plugs from the coil. The coil itself lived in a black electrical control box, matching the black battery strap-mounted on the left, and located to the right behind the distributor. The rectangular box also housed the ignition switches and the dial of the ammeter, which naturally made the latter instrument unreadable to the mounted rider. It left the headlamp bare, with the single speedometer mounted initially on a bracket in front of the handlebars, like the Bullet's.

Like the Bullet, too, the primary chaincase cover was fastened by a single bolt and was effectively oil-tight unless distorted by over-tightening, and behind it, primary drive was also by duplex chain. The Albion gearbox with its neutral finder, and the six-spring clutch operated at this stage by quick-thread worm, were the same too. Cycle parts as mentioned were identical to the roadster Bullet (see p.92), including the cush hub, the front fork with its long springs and spindle offset forward 1½ in, the fully valanced front mudguard attached to the frame, the handsome chrome 3¼ gallon petrol tank with its cream panels coach-lined in red, the twin toolboxes, Terry's saddle, Enfield rear suspension units and 19 in wheels with their single-sided 6 in front brakes. The front one in particular was to prove less than adequate (a very poor 38 ft from 30 mph) for stopping a machine whose dry weight at this stage was 400 lb.

There was mention of that front stopper in a *Motor Cycle* test very late in 1950: it was only by then that the Twins were becoming available generally in the UK, the first ones having gone for export. But the test gave every other essential feature full marks. In the age of the sprung hub and the Jampot, the spring frame provided a very real advantage both in terms of handling (marred only by footrests which grounded too easily), and of comfort, all of which with a notably smooth engine contributed to high average cruising speeds. A further factor in this was a relative absence of noise pollution, for unlike the singles, the 500 Twin was found quiet mechanically, aside from the whirr and rustle of all-chain drive, and achieved a 'good standard of exhaust silencing', unless revving hard in third. 75 mph was available in that gear, and good acceleration a further plus point, with top speeds around the 85 mph mark.

On the negative side there was mention of oil seepage at the cylinder head during high speed testing, and leaks there were to be a feature of the 500 Twin while there were no external oil lines. Centre and side stands were awkward and ineffective. In service the bolt holes attaching the engine to the rear engine plates would prove liable to wear oval due to inadequate engine-to-frame fixing, something that would continue with all the twins until the Interceptor. (Today identical substitute engine plates for the 500 Twin are available in the shape of those off the current Enfield India 350.) Cylinder head-steadies could break and play develop in the swinging arm due to worn thrust washers or bushes. But in its essentials, Enfield's 500 Twin was a good and reliable example of that breed.

It was to sell only moderately, however, for a number of reasons. The main one, with its 25 bhp and the 85 mhp top speed, was probably lack of charisma. Despite following industry policy and dutifully entering twins for both the 1951 and 1953 ISDTs, where they acquitted themselves excellently, there were to be no other sporting associations such as 500 twins like Triumph with the Grand Prix, or Norton with their race-bred Featherbed frame, could claim. Perhaps more importantly, there was no attempt to provide the illusion of such associations with a Sports version, as Matchless did with their Super Clubman, Ariel with the KH Red Hunter or BSA with the A7 Shooting Star. Royal Enfield, perhaps too honest for their own good, simply continued to provide the basic and perfectly adequate item: they didn't even bother to give it a name. In a *Motor Cycle* profile on the engine when it appeared, Tony Wilson-Jones had spoken of plans for a later specification including electrics via a base-mounted magneto, high compression pistons and high-lift cams. That this never came about for the 500 can probably be explained by the fact that Royal Enfield was a small company and from then on was concentrating all their its efforts on the Bullet, until the mid-50s by which time a readier tool for sports development lay to hand in the shape of the 700 twins.

1952 500 Twin. Worthy, but not a big seller.

This is not to say that the 500 Twin suffered from total neglect. For 1950 the changes, mostly shared by the Bullet, were minor; a fork-top alloy facia casting to hold the speedometer, mudguards of deep section replacing those with valances, and the lower fork end now cast integrally with the sliding member, in place of the previous screw-in type, which had had a tendency to leak oil and to work loose. On the Twin, the combined switches on the electrical control box were moved from the outside panel to the front. For 1951 there was evidence of factory commitment in the shape of proper patterns for the bottom half, the Twin's crankcases were now die-cast, which brought the overall dry weight down to a respectable 390 lb. As on the Bullet, the front mudguard was now mounted on three stays per side, and moved with the wheel.

For 1952 due to the Korean War situation, tanks lost their chrome but dual-seats became an optional extra. The twins' restless electrics went on the move again, with the ignition light and headlamp switch mounted in the headlamp along with the finally readable ammeter. The inlet manifold was given a slightly greater rearward extension,

First big 'un. 1953 Meteor 700, with Enfield Dual-seat and pannier set.

and a larger more accessible air cleaner was mounted in the black box; while the ignition coil was mounted on the front portion of the rear mudguard and the ignition switch put inside the right-hand toolbox with the key projecting. Other than that, an assault was made on the leak-prone cylinder head joint, with internal pressure relieved by the rocker boxes being lubricated via external pipes for the first time by oil feed from bosses just above the rear of the cylinder base. On the same theme of oil-tightness, two additional grub-screws were fitted for increasing the pressure between the crankcase halves in the area of the cylinder joint faces. The drive side case also gained a pair of screws on the outside which allowed access to the grub-screws via drillings. The breather outlet on the chaincase also gained a banjo unit.

1953 saw the big leap forward for Enfield, to a capacity class larger than anything British and current, outside a Square Four or a Vincent twin. In the face of the 650s from Triumph and BSA, Redditch went one better with the 692 cc Meteor. This capacity was achieved by cylinder dimensions of 70 × 90, which it did not take folk long to realize were those of the 350 Bullet: this meant that future tuning for the Bullet's head would pass directly to the big twin. The crankcases, however, allowing for the different cylinder mouth dimensions, were those of the 500 Twin, so production economy was served in two directions. The cylinder dimensions were those of a prototype pre-war V-twin primarily intended for sidecar work, and that was the area the new big twin was initially aimed at (many of the opposition's Golden Flashes and Thunderbirds were in harness also).

The format was identical to the 500, with the separate alloy heads and deeply spigoted cast-iron barrels, one-piece crank and exactly the same massive main bearings. One difference was that the con-rods, while still of RR56 light alloy, had big ends now with shell bearings with white metal liners. Another was that the Meteor's pushrods were solid steel. The clutch fitted an extra driving plate (the '53 ISDT 500 Twins were to do this too) making five in all, and for the big 'un the primary chaincase had a slight dome to provide the necessary clearance. The only other external clue to the larger capacity was that the fins were larger and that there were an extra three protruding on the cylinder head (one more than on the 350 Bullet). This first big twin produced 36 bhp at 6,000 rpm, with the same low compression at 6.5:1 as the 500 Twin. Both now achieved this with low expansion silicon alloy split-skirt pistons. (It may be worth mentioning here that ace Enfield racer Steve Linsdell used Triumph pistons in his '53 Meteor-based racer, for their solid skirts.)

The cycle parts came in for some useful upgrading to cope with the extra power, the 405 lb dry weight and the probable prospect of pulling a chair. The Meteor petrol tank was 4 gallons against the 500's 3½ gallons, the rear brake was enlarged from 6 to 7 in diameter, the rear tyre was 3.50 not 3.25 in, the mudguards were deeply valanced and (as for the 500) there was an optional dual-seat in Vynide matching the 700's attractive polychromatic beech finish. While the frame was initially identical to the 500, a new cast alloy centre stand was fitted, though unfortunately it was little better than its predecessor. The Meteor's rear fork was also stiffened up, as on the new 500 Bullet.

At the front there was a real advance with the first appearance of the dual 6 in front brake, with twin cables balanced by a beam (or more quaintly, a 'whiffle tree compensator') on the handlebars, and the full-width hub employing two separate cast aluminium brake drums mounted back to back, each incorporating a spoke-flange and with cast-in chromidium iron inserts to provide the braking surface. Each brake also incorporated something adopted by the conventional front stoppers for the Bullets and the 500 Twin that year, namely floating cam spindles (see p.95 for details). If care was taken to balance the duo brakes correctly (and not just at the beam, which provided only a limited range of adjustment), if the correct linings were fitted and the spindles kept floating, these were good brakes, bringing a '56 692 cc machine to a halt in 29½ ft from 30 mph. The front fork's cast-aluminium sliders were fitted with integral brake-plate anchor slots, and at the rear the Enfield dampers lost their drain plug.

On test as a solo the Meteor was judged tractable and smooth, with top gear providing speeds from 20 mph to its rather underwhelming top speed of 94 mph. If the sidecar option was selected from new, for the small extra expense of £2 4s 9d the machine was supplied with gearing lowered from (4.47, 5.8, 8.05, and 12.4:1) to (5.03, 6.53, 9.05 and 13.95:1). A steering damper was fitted, and sidecar forks with different crowns to alter the trail and stronger springs both there and in the rear units. As mentioned in the singles section, alternative trail more suited to sidecar work could be achieved simply by reversing the solo fork's lower sliders, but with a chair fitted, this did not prove very satisfactory. In sidecar trim the Meteor was judged very satisfactory, with all day 60 mph cruising on tap.

For the 1953 500 Twin, the cylinder heads, like the crankcases, became die-cast, with the special iron valve inserts, previously cast in, now shrunk in. The induction manifold was altered from a V to a Y shape, all in line with the Meteor. The same was true of a further modification to the oiling system, which adapted to an arrangement found on the 700. The crankcase breathing, previously through the hollow drive-side shaft, past a disc-valve and into the primary chaincase, was supplemented by a breather on the left hand top of the crankcase. Two small disc valves were carried on the breather body, and when refitting the body it was important to see that the little discs were not trapped and that jointing compound did not get on the disc valves or their seatings.

Both twins, with the rest of the four-stroke range, adopted the new Enfield chrome and painted winged tank badge. The twins also joined the 500 Bullet in adopting a new number plate, with a Lucas stop-tail light and red reflector, the stop-light switch being housed in the nearside toolbox. At the front there was a new Lucas headlamp with an underslung pilot lamp.

1954 saw a major styling change, namely the first version of the 'Casquette Fork Head'. This one-piece aluminium fork head casting incorporated the lights and instruments, with a facia panel sweeping to the rear providing a recess for the handlebar mounting. Headlamp adjustment, which was limited to a rather restricted alteration in vertical angle only, was made by pivoting the whole assembly. Twin pilot lights were fitted, on these early versions high up and irritatingly visible to the rider. The casquette had the effect visually of further raising the front of the bikes, complementing the lines of the angled shock absorbers, tall engines and long forks; though for the American export version of the 700 (though not the 500 machines) with their 'real Western type handlebars', a separate headlamp was fitted.

One practical result of the casquette was that for the 700 it was no longer easy to change the fork trail for sidecar work by fitting different crowns. From then on, bikes for that purpose were offered with different and longer bottom tubes and lugs, giving reduced trail but 3 in as opposed to 1½ in solo spindle lead. In service they provided a very stiff ride at the front. There was also a frame change, as on the 500 Bullet, for the Meteor, with brazed-on malleable lugs replacing the bracing tubes and welded-in

700's stablemate, restyled and modified 1953 500 Twin.

steel gusset plates that still carried the pivoted rear fork for the 500 Twin. Internally the Meteor's steel pushrods became of alloy, while externally it alone featured the oval air cleaner box which the rest of the range would adopt the following year. For both the twins the rear suspension units fitted were now Armstrongs, a distinct improvement, and small winged transfers decorated the frame-loop toolboxes.

That year the 500's electrics went through a first turn. In a move that was claimed to be based on experience in the '53 ISDT, where the twins involved had employed magdynos, that item was now offered as an optional alternative to the dynamo and distributor set-up, and mounted where the dynamo would have been. To ensure that the magneto ran at half engine speed, the size of the second of the two sprockets attached to the inlet camshaft was halved, with dynamo speed recovered by gearing up between it and the magneto. Claimed power for the 500 rose fractionally to 26 bhp at 6,000 rpm.

1955 was a year of consolidation, with both 500 and 700 adopting the magdyno and dual-seat as standard, and the 500 getting the 6 in dual front brake. From March both twins acquired a qd rear wheel as an option. As on the Bullets, a neater gearbox end cover was fitted, with the footchange pedal and the kickstart now mounted on a coaxial shaft. The former worm-gear operation of the clutch thrust-rod was superseded by an orthodox clutch fulcrum lever, fully enclosed within the end cover. Also as on the Bullets,

the cams were redesigned with new quietening ramps, and the frame modified in the area of the rear fork pivot. The 700's head-steady was redesigned. For the rest of the cycle parts, on the 500 the black air cleaner box gave way to the oval type.

More significantly, there was the first sign of tuning for the Meteor, a model which was more often than not advertised with Enfield's own-brand pannier equipment in position, to emphasize its touring role. Now, like the 350 Bullet, compression was raised to 7.5:1, and claimed output was up to 39 bhp at 6,000 rpm.

In truth the biggest parallel twin could not stay on the sidelines much longer, though the factory may almost have wished that it could. Their previous experience with its vibration when pushed hard during the ISDT has been recounted earlier: they were perhaps the first to learn the lesson that awaited Norton with the Atlas and Triumph with the 750 Bonneville, on the subject of oversize parallel twins. But in America the next stage, the Super Meteor, had been previewed for 1955 as the Indian Tomahawk, with an Indian's head front fender light, the 'Royal Enfield' tactfully omitted from its timing cover, and a Steward and Warner speedo in place of the Smith's Chronometric which conditions Stateside tested to early destruction with monotonous regularity. The Bullets and twins were building up a small but faithful following there—one reason for Redditch to go ahead with the faster big twin in the UK for 1956.

The 1956 Super Meteor tackled several of the problems associated with the twins, with varying degrees of success. To improve cooling, the finning of the head and barrel was much increased. Oil circulation was doubled, by changing the oil-pump driving worm from a single-start to a two-start thread; also the felt oil filter was now situated not on the return line, but between the feed pump and the big-ends, as on the singles. To improve oil-tightness, the deeply-spigoted location of the heads on the barrels was replaced by the use of two hollow dowels for each joint, surrounding the outer head-retaining bolts. This permitted an increase in the width of the cylinder-head gasket at the points adjacent to the pushrod tunnels, and enabled the previously angled tunnels to be straightened. These measures were not to prove fully successful in sealing

Below left *1955 Meteor 700.*

Right *1956, uprated 700, the Super Meteor.*

the head/barrel joint.

To strengthen the already robust bottom end against the coming increases in output, crankpin diameter was increased—and to compensate for the increase in weight this entailed, the previously circular crankshaft outer webs were cut away adjacent to each crankpin. Hollow alloy pushrods with hardened ends replaced the previous solid ones. In line with development work already done on the racer and scrambler Bullets, the 700's inlet valve head size was increased to $1^{9}/_{16}$ in. They were gas flowed at the port, and valve lift was improved by radiusing the valve seat into the port and blending the throat of the valve into its port. Compression was still 7.5:1 and claimed output up to 40 bhp at 5,500 rpm, and overall gearing raised from the Meteor's by some 3 per cent (at 4.33, 5.63, 7.87 and 12.05:1).

This engine was now slotted in cycle parts which, like the Bullets', were significantly uprated. There was a new, all-welded frame, still an open diamond, but braced between the tank rail and downtube, and lacking a seat tube. This permitted the replacement of the old twin toolboxes, air filter box and battery by a large pressed-steel box, with a lid on each side retained by a one-armed wing nut, containing all these items. The space behind the engine which this provided permitted the use of an Amal Monobloc carburettor. The 700's electrics changed, now retaining the existing magneto half of the previous magdyno for ignition, but coping with other functions by a crankshaft-mounted 6 volt 70 watt Lucas RM 14 alternator, with the system's rectifier hung beneath the nose of the tank.

A quickly detachable rear wheel, now with a full-width light alloy hub, was still an optional extra. The new frame's dual-seat was supported by a rail at the back. Along with the Bullets and the 500 Twin, there was a revised petrol tank mounting, a new combined horn button and dipswitch, a boxed-in rear mudguard and a folding kickstart. Tank decoration was revised, with the new plastic tank badges and (for the Super Meteor) plain knee grips; the 'Royal Enfield' previously stamped on the timing chest was replaced by a small metal plate (perhaps more easily detachable when Enfields became American Indians), and finish became maroon, with double gold lining on the tank. The Super Meteor was a compact, powerful-looking machine.

Although the sidecar options were available, the Super Meteor was clearly more in contention as a serious solo roadburner, and in May 1956 *Motor Cycling*'s Bernal Osborne took one on an extended test, using a model still running in to cover the Scottish Six Days Trial. With panniers and a windscreen, he found it a relaxed long-legged tourer, clocking 70 mph at under 4,000 rpm. Comfort, handling and braking were well up to par and the gearbox perfectly satisfactory, while to the continuing niggles of clicking valve gear and the centre and prop-up spiked side-stand were added the facts that the new toolbox lids could not be closed properly and more seriously, starting was difficult, due to a combination of weak pilot-jet adjustment and low kickstart gearing. But with road speeds in the mid-90s, a top speed of 101 mph and yet an average of 70 mpg on a run from Edinburgh to the Midlands (55 mpg being the overall figure), this was clearly a good under-stressed all-rounder. A curiously low-speed vibration period, between 55 and 60 mph in top was mentioned, but not as serious interference to 'the pleasantly flexible performance. . . from traffic-crawl speeds to the 80s and 90s'. In sidecar trim the extra power yielded top speeds in the 70s as well as welcome acceleration. Bearing in mind that it was the Super Meteor which Syd Lawton would specifically favour as the basis of his production racing efforts, I should say the big twins from these years deserve serious consideration.

In fact 1956 to '58 was something of a golden age for Enfield four-strokes. The 500 Twin for 1956 was improved in several ways in addition to the detail changes already noted, the principal one being the fitting of the 700's 7 in rear brake, with the full-width qd rear wheel still as an optional extra. Internally the engine's compression was raised to 7.25:1, with power now up to 27 bhp at 6,000 rpm. It was not until 1957 that the 500 adopted the new all-weelded frame as on the 700 and the Bullets the previous year, with the same Monobloc and central box. These are the models most rated by the knowledgeable, with the indefinable charm of a soft yet lively engine intact within superior cycle parts.

For both 1957 twins the air cleaner within the box altered from a circular to a D-shape. The arrangement to the rear of the dual-seat was standardized, with a rear mudguard mounting similar to the new Crusader's which was said to give a more swept-back look. The mounting was no longer connected to the back of the seat by a tubular loop, as it had been for the 700 the previous year and still was for the Bullets, and it had a neat horizontal loop on either side, serving as both bracing strut for the mudguard, and lifting handle. The 500's gearing was lowered slightly, and its electrics also changed for the second and last time. An alternator was now fitted, as on the 700, but ignition was by coil, with a distributor unit once again fitted behind the cylinder where the magdyno had been: this time, in the interests of space-saving, it lay horizontal and was driven by chain from the camshaft.

For 1957 also, both the Super Meteor and 500 Twin fitted the good qd rear wheel, with its cush-hub in place, as standard; and chrome side-panels on the petrol tanks, where the 500 came into line with plain knee grips.

1958 was a major change year for the twins, but not until mid-season. Initially alterations were largely superficial. Along with most of the range, there was the adoption of a new Burgess silencer with no tail pipe; the saddle portion of the dual-seat was picked out in white piping; and polychromatic paint jobs were provided. The Super Meteor standardized with the 500 Twin in terms of electrics, abandoning the magneto in favour of coil ignition and the chain-driven horizontal distributor.

This might have given a clue that it was soon no longer to be top of the range and in April 1958 a new 700 twin, the Constellation, and a new 500, the Meteor Minor were announced. The reasons for this shift of emphasis were a typically Enfield mixture of development and expediency. They did indeed want to exploit the 700's potential as the largest capacity twin now on the market, as well as offering a sportier 500 to match the Crusader. But the bottom line was that the dies for the castings of the older machines' crankcases, which it will be remembered were in common apart from cylinder mouth dimensions, were worn to the point where renewal was due. So the opportunity was taken to redevelop both power plants.

The Constellation had been available as an export model the previous year. While maintaining the previous engine's dimensions, it was substantially altered internally. The camshafts were positioned higher, by designing the cylinders to be sunk lower in the crankcase. As well as shortening the pushrods, which were lightened further by

construction from light-alloy tubing (now with induction hardened steel ends), this move was claimed to reduce the chance of valve clearance altering with engine temperature. Finning on the head and barrel was also greatly increased. New racing-type cams (ie, with no quietening ramps), gave higher lift and longer opening dwell. A useful built-in feature was that the camshafts were mounted in detachable bearing housings. After removing the timing cover and camshaft sprockets, undoing three screws allowed the camshaft bearing housings to be removed and the camshafts to be withdrawn, and if desired, swapped for others for different purposes, all without having to split the crankcases.

Tony Wilson-Jones had specified that to cope with the increased output, the crankshaft should now be of 40/45 ton/in^2 spheroidal graphite nodular iron, and all but a few of the very early engines' cranks were dynamically balanced. The crankpin diameter was now increased to a hefty 1⅞ in, dimensions which as Tim Holmes pointed out, Triumph would only equal at the end of the 1970s! As on the previous big twins, the H-section light alloy con-rods were fitted with shell-type big end bearings, with the detachable bearing caps bolted to the rods by high tensile socket screws secured by cotter pins. From very early on (eng no SMSA 6964), the drive side bearing's felt washer which had been fitted on the Super Meteor, located in the steel housing at the back of the chaincase behind the engine sprocket, was replaced by a neoprene oil seal.

The crankshaft-mounted alternator remained, but ignition was by a Lucas K2F magneto with manual control. The valves had benefited from work first done on competition Bullets and then on production racing twins (see p.71), with the head modified to take Enfield parts modelled on Gold Star components. Dual valve springs were based on W and S items; exhaust valves were of En 54 austenitic steel with the stems Stellite-faced, with inlet valves of En 52 silicon-chromium steel, and alloy caps and collets were fitted. All this let the engine rev higher in safety. Despite Syd Lawton's demonstration of the superiority of the simpler Amal Monobloc carb, the first Constellations came supplied with a big 1^3/16 in TT9 racing instrument, which did have the desired magnetic effect in the market place. Gearing was lowered from the Super Meteor, at 4.44, 5.77, 7.99 and 12.35:1. Higher compression pistons gave a ratio of 8.5:1. The output and performance figures were quite striking; a claimed 51 bhp at 6,250 rpm, flying quarters under 8 seconds, with top speeds at one MIRA test of 116 mph, best one ways of 115 mph by Bernal Osborne on the open roads of Belgium and a 112 mph average achieved on a subsequent road test.

The other major area of redesign had been the clutch. There had evidently already been problems with the Super Meteor in that area: its instruction book for 1956/7 carried a stuck-in insert printed in bold red, warning that 'It is important to keep the end of the clutch pushrod and the ball in the end of the adjuster screw well greased.' So Wilson-Jones and Reg Thomas, faced with the

Left *1957 500 Twin, now with electrics by coil and distributor.*

Right *1958 Super Meteor.*

problems of handling the increased output without increasing spring strength to wrist-straining levels, had gone back to scratch.

The result was the so-called 'scissors clutch', due to two levers, one fixed and one moving, which met at a pivot point like scissors. They were housed on the opposite side to normal for a clutch mechanism, within the primary chaincase, though the clutch itself was normally located on the gearbox mainshaft. Between the levers were four ¼ in diameter steel balls, seated on indentations in the clutch and in the levers. Rotary movement from the cable to the moving lever made the balls ride up the ramp sides and out of their indentations, and hence moved the lever sideways to the left as well as forward. The sideways movement drew the inner pressure plate away from the friction plate, by means of the central bolt: this further compressed the six clutch springs held by the outer plate, and released the friction plates. Both plates rotated with the clutch. The outer friction plates used a cork/plastics compound friction material, while the inner plate and sprocket rings were of a moulded material. The combination was intended to avoid slip with the moulded stuff, and overheating from the cork compound alone. A clutch shock absorber with cush rubbers was incorporated. The whole clutch was statically balanced to prevent the heavy unit vibrating. There was an extra plugged aperture in the primary chaincase, to adjust the scissors through. In the gearbox, there was one modification, with the sleevegear now fitted with a bushed sleeve.

The Constellation's frame, fork, brakes and tyres were similar to the Super Meteor's, but it fitted heavy chrome mudguards and a new 4½ gallon tank. The tank was squarish and deep, handsomely finished in polychromatic Burgundy, with the plastic badges, and plain grips in recesses for the rider's knees. The rear number plate was sportily angled and not boxed in. The butterfly knob steering damper was fitted behind another prestige item (now very difficult to find)—a Smith's 150 mph speedometer. The timing case was drilled and carried a small plate (behind which lay the drive) from the front camshaft sprocket, for an optional rev-counter. The exhaust system was siamezed to a single silencer with no tail-pipe, carried on the right; while this was a handsome and weight-saving system, it will be recalled that Syd Lawton considered that it marginally cut acceleration. The Super Meteor would also adopt this system for 1959.

The other newcomer, the 496 cc Meteor Minor, displaced the old 500 Twin which was dropped at the end of 1958. It was initially offered in two versions, a stingy standard and a better equipped De Luxe. A pretty bike which was billed as 'a 500 that handles like a 250', it was conceived very much in line with the new Crusader, with oversquare cylinder dimensions identical to the latter at 70 × 64.5. This was an almost exact short-stroke reverse of the old Twin's 64 × 77, which also brought the pistons of both twins and the unit 250s into line.

The Meteor Minor's iron barrels and alloy heads were of similar design to the Constellation, with the same heavy external

finning. Close inspection of the barrels would reveal a ½ in base below the finning of the 700. The Meteor Minor's crankshaft was a one-piece casting of Mehanite nodular iron, with the big ends now similar to the larger twins in featuring split shells. The shape of the timing cover altered, with a lip around its rim and, like the big twins and the Bullets, the familiar cylindrical oil filter now lying in line beneath the oil pump and inserted from the front. The Constellation's scissors clutch was fitted, but though valves were larger than the older 500, the state of tune was less sporting than the big newcomer, with 8:1 compression and cams that incorporated quietening ramps; the engine's claimed output was 30 bhp at 6,250 rpm. Electrics were by alternator and coil ignition, with the auto-advance unit and distributor mounted in a tiny wedge-shaped pressing to the rear of the cylinders, and an ignition switch in the left side of the tool-battery box.

This motor was fitted into a frame that was described in *The Motor Cycle* at the time as 'the lightweight frame first seen on the Crusader', though Don Morley thinks that it was in fact 'the rare and desirable all-welded lightweight Clipper frame' (the Bullet-based 350 Clipper rather than the 250 Clipper II, as he goes on to say), 'which is of the same dimensions as the 350 or 500 Bullet, but almost ⅓ lighter.' The matter was clarified for me by REOC Crusader specialist Jim Chalk: though the works had fitted a prototype Meteor Minor engine into the Crusader frame, it proved too tight a squeeze, and the 500's production chassis was indeed a suitably modified version of the '56 all-welded Bullet frame, as also found on the 700 Twins. It had two mounting lugs at the front against the singles' one, and a bifurcated headsteady. The 500 did, however, fit a new two-way damped front fork, with a bottom tube with no spindle lead. It also fitted (in the De Luxe version) the 250's enclosed rear chain, Girling suspension units (though in the twin's case these were three-position adjustable) and 3.25 × 17 in rear wheels, an instant identifier that provided a commendably low seat height at 29 in. Catalogued weight was 388 lb, but Roy Bacon put the true dry weight at 370 lb, some 20 lb lighter than its predecessor.

The standard machine, £25 cheaper than the £274 9s De Luxe, had a saddle, a non-valanced front mudguard, an exposed rear chain, no air filter for its Monobloc, the 6 in sls front brake, a plain painted tank, black finish overall, a non qd rear wheel, and no propstand, pillion footrests or stop-light; when Redditch economized, they really economized. The De Luxe had a dual-seat, the rear chain enclosure with its upper and lower runs as on the Crusader, an air filter within the central pressing, the Crusader's efficient 7 in front brake (both fitted a 7 in rear brake), the qd rear wheel, chrome tank panels, a choice of polychromatic paint finishes, plus the other three items the standard didn't. Both had siamezed exhaust systems as on the big twin. All were offered during that year and from then on with the Airflow fairing option, for a description of which see p.69.

The Constellation was on the home market in numbers for 1959, in the version known as 'the fast one' because of its relatively

Above left *The new 700 for 1958 — Constellation.*

Left *Chunky good looks of the Constellation.*

Right *Compact 500 in single's chassis. The 1958 Meteor Minor, seen here in 'standard' form.*

Enfield detailing: the casquette, seen here on 1958 Super Meteor.

high compression, that prominent racing carb (though during that year it was replaced by a single Monobloc 389), and the fact that subsequent road tests of later versions never quite equalled those early mesmerically high but essentially irrelevant top speeds. Very quickly and very generally it became known among riders as a model that would not sustain for long the high speeds its specification invited, without major trouble. A straw pole of the surviving hard-riding '50s rockers of my acquaintance produced a unanimous retrospective verdict that if the Connie was ridden as hard as the standards of the Ace and the Busy Bee cafes required, it was very quickly sidelined. This was in contrast to Triumph, who had had a 112 mph motorcycle since 1954 in the T110, so that the fast boys were by now learning how to make them stay together as well as rev to the limit. The Constellation's reputation was partly due to Enfield's unfortunate track record in production racing, but it was also based on fact.

A correspondent to *Classic Bike*, though recalling a 1961 model, touches on most of the main points. After an inauspicious start, with his exhaust valves sticking open and trashing the main bearings in two days, he went on to experience much trouble with blowing head gaskets. In traffic he discovered that the scissors action clutch was incapable of any slipping: all clearance would instantly disappear, leaving him with no means of disconnecting the drive. The engine and gearbox leaked oil like sieves: burn-ups would leave the machine soaked in oil and the sump virtually empty. The clutch bolts would undo and hit the outer chaincase, and the primary chain slipper tensioner mounting bolt pulled out of the alloy of the inner chaincase. Yet strangely enough he still remembered the machine with affection, much of which was due to its chunky looks—the sheer size that 'exuded power and desirability'.

A more detailed retrospective was provided, also in *Classic Bike*, by Roger Woods, evidently the kind of enthusiast who would take the pains that the Connie's foibles and high state of tune absolutely required. He and a friend had both run second-hand '59 Constellations in the early sixties. He confirmed a trait noted earlier in the Super Meteor, namely difficult starting, stemming from the kickstart's gearing, and aggravated by the higher compression as well as by the absence of a throttle stop on the TT9, which meant that the cable stretched with the heavy slide on the end of it and altered the starting characteristics. The TT9 also leaked and flooded easily.

The problems with head-to-barrel joint leaks were confirmed, and one source identified the 'rather delicate' one-way valved breather already described, which was located on the crankcase left side just below the barrel, as a source of trouble: it would easily stick closed and cause a pressure build-up in the crankcase. To aid the other half of the system, in place of the existing small-bore vent-pipe fitted to the top of the primary chaincase, a simple large-bore pipe from there to the atmosphere, led to the mudguard, was the traditional and reasonably effective remedy; some riders also drilled through the timing case into the oil chamber and installed another big breather pipe from there too.

A further problem, unique to my knowledge, arose from this fact that the primary chaincase formed the reservoir into which part of the breathing system discharged. In a phrase reminiscent of the Big Bang theory of the start of the universe, Constellations blew up. Not in the normal biking sense of sending a rod through the sump (though they could do that too): according to Woods, the early Constellations actually exploded, due to ignition of the volatile gases in the chaincase by a spark, either from the primary chain running on its hardened steel slipper tensioner, or from the alternator. Woods had known three instances of it happening; his own just blew out the rubber seal, but another blew out the centrally located chaincase cover so that it could never be sealed again.

A contributory factor to the explosions, in some cases, was one solution to the problems of the scissors clutch; the use in the chaincase of a very light oil, compounded of half SAE 20 and half paraffin. In conjunction with keeping the oil level lower than recommended, this was fairly effective in reducing clutch slip. The use of sidecar-strength clutch springs made the pull uncomfortably hard, and still did not entirely eliminate the slip. The Albion gearbox, on the other hand, with its very short pedal travel and the need for heavy foot pressure, Woods appreciated for its robustness, and claimed that it could be made to engage positively if the gear selectors were carefully centred. Oil seepage from the box's drive-side bearing could be cured, he found, by putting some soft grease in with the oil.

The handling could feature some pitching on fast bumpy bends, which Woods pinpointed to a combination of two factors. The first was the uncertain rebound damping in the Armstrong rear units with their knurled adjusting rings; though, unusually, he preferred the way that the weaker of their two internal springs would soak up minor bumps to the performance of the Girlings that followed them. The second was the comparative weakness of the Enfield telescopic front forks. With the owner standing astride the front wheel, the bars could be wiggled well off centre even with the pinch-bolts done up dead tight, and Woods believed that the heavy mudguard had a vital double function as a fork brace. The footrests were too far forward, making for a stressed, stretched-out, Commando-like riding position at high speed. Ground clearance was limited by the centre stand stops on both sides, but these could be bent out of the way, and on the right even the silencer could be realigned for real scratchers. The front brake was not quite as good as it looked, but in general the handling

Gleaming 1960 Constellation hitched to Watsonian chair.

faults were never alarming, and compensated for by 'spectacular' mid-range acceleration. Exiting a roundabout, for instance, the Connie would blow off any Triumph, though going for speed by revving through the gears produced excruciating vibration, and quickly overstressed the long alloy con-rods. But there was no need for it; the real street top speed of 106–110 mph could be run up to from 40 in top gear, and was as fast as almost any Triumph at the time.

As for the Constellation's baby brother, while some would regret the passing of the soft 500 Twin, an archetypically fifties piece of machinery, it's notable that many also remember the Meteor Minor with respect, as an underrated bike. Bruce Main-Smith called its 500 unit a good one, and the later Meteor Minor engines are the only Enfields Don Morley considered the class equal of the 350 Bullet. A 1958 road test of the De Luxe version had some niggles; footrests a few inches too far forward for speed work, top edges of the seat pan that dug into the thighs, some clutch slip, and some weaving on fast bumpy bends. But these were compensated for by easy starting, light, precise steering, good 7 in brakes all round that were now completely rain-proof, and smoothness from the double-cush drive. The lack of vibration below 60–65 made that the ideal cruising speed, while top speed was 89 mph. Other sources suggest that the penalty for the small wheels and forward footrests was a machine that grounded too easily when cornered hard. But the engine was durable: 50,000 miles before major attention being needed was normal.

1960 saw the introduction of a rortier variant of the 500, the Meteor Minor Sports, while the economy standard model was quietly dropped during 1959. The Sports was tuned similarly to the Constellation, with quick-lift cams giving more overlap on the valve timing, pistons said to give a higher compression ratio though this was still catalogued at 8:1, and stronger two-rate valve springs with light alloy top collars. The result was an extra 3 hp (33 bhp at 6,500), and the Sports looked the part, with chromed mudguards and chromed square petrol tank styled like the Constellation's, and its capacity increased from the previous 3 to 3¾ gallons. The rear tyre size was increased slightly to 3.50 × 17 in. Estimated top speed was hoisted into the mid-90s. The clutch for both was modified, with the operating lever balls enlarged and the operating lever pin fitted with an appropriate washer.

But the factory's main efforts for 1960 were being aimed at the trouble-prone Constellation. The high level of vibration at speed was the first subject for attention; the balance factor for the statically and dynamically balanced crankshafts was increased from 50 to 75 per cent, and in the interest of this their flywheels were changed to bobweights, which reduced the dead weight of the shaft by 2 lb to 24 lb approximately. Lighter pistons were also used, with the bottom piston ring groove modified to contain two separate oil control rings; the compression ratio was reduced to 8:1. The Super Meteor also adopted the new crankshaft and pistons.

The previous year's single Amal went, too, in favour of a first for Enfields, twin Monobloc carbs, which brought their own problems in terms of the constant adjustment of the twin-pull cables needed to avoid rough running. Each Monobloc was mounted on a short splayed inlet stub, with the right-hand one nevertheless having its float chamber cut and blanked off, it being supplied from the left via flexible piping joining the two main jet holders. The centre toolbox pressing was also modified, with two ears on the lids to shroud the intakes, and depressions in the boxes to clear the carbs; there had been no aircleaner as standard for the Constellation since early in 1958. The ignition timing was changed from 0.375 to 0.437.

Two further areas were tackled, and these changes applied to all the twins. Again to counter vibration, there was a new and more substantial cylinder headsteady, which became a torque stay from the head back to a lug now featured on the underside of the frame top tube. Secondly, to try and help engine breathing, a flap valve was again embodied into the drive side end of the crankshaft, now discharging through a special drilled bolt securing the alternator rotor on the end of the shaft, which contained in a recess in its head a pen-steel disc which breathed into the primary chaincase. On the top of the case, the previous neoprene pipe discharging directly

Left *1960 Super Meteor.*

Above right *1963 Constellation, with rear enclosure.*

into the atmosphere from the breather body was replaced by an external metal pipe, which led oil from there via the oil tank to the rear chain. Also where the previous crankcase breather mechanism had been screwed on to the outside left of the crankcase, there was now a drain pipe leading from the base of the cylinder block on the left, conveying excess oil from the camshaft tunnels and cylinder walls to the oil container; the drain connected to annular cavities at the base of the cylinder. A magnet was fitted into the main oil filter. All these measures were helpful and showed that Redditch was willing, but as the 1961 rider's experiences already recounted suggests, they did not really solve any of the problems.

On the cosmetic front, for all the twins for 1960 there was a redesign of the casquette, with the sidelights further apart than previously. The Super Meteor and Meteor Minor had revised rear tank mountings, while the Constellation's tank was now catalogued at 4¼ gallons capacity. Friction plates in the clutch became Neolangite-bonded. The Meteor Minor's exhaust system and brake pedal were revised, and its silencers gained tail pipes. Finally, on all four twins, the run of the siamezed exhaust pipes was modified, with an offset eliminated at a point where the horizontal run of the pipe entered the forward end of the silencer. The Super Meteor, which incidentally was retained principally to fulfil the sidecar role, in solo form had its gearing brought into line with the Constellation at 4.44, 5.37, 7.99 and 12.35:1. These ratios were fairly wide, but the big engine's wide spread of power offset the gaps.

For 1961, Enfield mutely recognized the inadequacy of the scissors clutch, which was replaced by a conventional design with a star-shaped outer plate and the clutch lifted by a pushrod through the mainshaft. It fitted an extra pair of plates, making six pressure plates and five friction plates including the sprocket, which was soon to be lined on both sides with friction material. It was not to signal the end of clutch problems, however, with slip continuing to be the most frequent one, though now this would normally be due to faulty assembly or adjustment, rather than design. Checking for distorted plates, or springs weakened by heat, was desirable. On assembly, the two driven steel plates which were dished had to be fitted so that the dished portion fitted inside the clutch, and the clutch centre had to move freely in and out as the clutch was operated. The six springs were still not adjustable, and careful matching for spring length was necessary, with adjustment by selective assembly or by insertion of thin washers under the spring tension bolts.

For the 1961 Constellation and Super Meteor, petrol tanks were standardized, with both now the 4¼ gallon item. This had adopted a modified rear mounting for the previous year, with the tank tunnel at the back now supported by a profiled rubber block carried in a clip welded to the frame top tube, and a loose clamping strap pulling the tank into place against the block. For the Super Meteor the tank was painted not chromed.

Both twins also appeared with a belated and unfortunate nod to the fashion for rear enclosure that had swept the industry, in the shape of a new deeper enclosure in place of a conventional rear mudguard. Initially the mudguard section of this was of moulded fibreglass, but by January 1961 it had changed to a steel pressing. The enclosure blended with the lines of a new dual-seat, and shrouded the rear sub-frame, with the ugly pressed steel panels at each side concealing the upper mountings of the rear suspension units, and a chromed lifting handle on each side passing through rubber grommets in the mudguard section. At least there was no sacrifice of practicality, as the complete assembly, seat and sub-frame were quickly detachable, being secured by two clips at the front, and by slotted lugs to the suspension unit tops.

The Constellation now came with 'ace'-type dropped sports handlebars. Both big machines adopted the new three-part torpedo-shaped silencer, which could be dismantled for cleaning, with a polished, cast-aluminium tail-piece decorated on its upper face by a narrow fin, and with exhaust gases discharging downwards through a longitudinal slot in the underside of the cast tail.

The 1961 500s, Sports and De Luxe, both acquired the restyled casquette, and standardized with the Sports' 3¾ gallon tank, in appearance similar to the Constellation, and with dimensions in common with the 250s. With interest in the 500 class waning, the 500 Sports, still a single carb model though retaining its sports cam etc,in other respects became a utility model. The timing cover, primary chaincase and gearbox end covers were no longer polished, but had a vapour-blast satin finish and the rear wheel was no longer qd. The De Luxe model by contrast adopted the new three-part silencer.

Early in 1962, for the Constellation and Super Meteor the pivoted fork bearings were changed from bronze to Silentbloc bushes. Shortly afterwards, from engine no SC 11034, the Constellation's gearbox mainshaft, its ballrace and the ballrace oil thrower cap were altered. (The gearbox mainshaft would continue to be something of a weak spot for the big twins; the only major trouble long-distance rider Dave Messent experienced with his Rickman Enfield, in the 50,000 miles prior to his overland trip to Australia, was a broken gearbox shaft.) At the same time the primary chain tensioner as well as the stator fixing assembly were also modified, possibly in response to those 'big bangs'.

For 1962 there was little development, with the factory concentrating on the 250s, and a new big twin in the offing. The 500s adopted the Silentbloc bush swinging arm bearings, and the Meteor Minor Sports was offered with the dual 6 in front brake. From January, steering head locks became available for the Super Meteor and the Constellation. With the day of the sidecar largely gone, it proved to be the Super Meteor's last year.

1963 saw the advent of the Interceptor 750; Enfield, still with a faithful following in the US, weren't about to be upstaged by Norton's Atlas. The Interceptor's capacity was actually 736 cc, achieved by fractionally boring out from 60 to 71 mm, and slight stroke lengthening from 90 to 93 mm. Even this was cutting things fine, and it meant that with the limited meat available, cylinder to head sealing was not now by gasket, but by a wedge-shaped Cross sealing ring. In appearance it somewhat resembled a piston ring, but with a triangular profile and a flat top; the sloping side fitted into the top of the bore and the upper face mated with the cylinder head. The pushrod tunnels were sealed by washers of special heat and oil resistant rubber, bonded to metal and fitting in recesses in the cylinder head.

This indicates a commendable attempt to improve oil tightness and tackle the big twins' other problems; though once again not fully successful, it did involve some improvements, which can be retrospectively fitted to the 700s. The Interceptor engine broadly resembled the Constellation, and was

Airflow fairing suited the twins. It's seen here on a 1958 Meteor Minor 500.

mounted in scarcely modified Connie cycle parts. One major plus point was that it was more securely mounted, since it will be recalled that movement of the twin's engine and gearbox in the open frame, with vibration and oval holes in the engine plates resulting, had been a problem from the start. The Interceptor rear engine plates were more substantial than their predecessors, and at the lower rear of the gearbox there was now a large alloy block attaching to the frame just below the fork pivot, and acting as a bracket retaining the box; this can be used with any of the twins.

Internally for the Interceptor there was a new nodular iron crankshaft running in redesigned crankcase castings. The big ends were still secured by high tensile socket screws, only these were no longer fastened with a cotter pin, but screwed into inserts in the connecting rod, and were drilled for wiring, though there is no evidence that the factory ever did this. The alloy heads were redesigned, with the pair of 1³/16 in Monoblocs now flange-mounted on parallel, not splayed, induction stubs, and head to barrel bolt size increased from ⁵/16 to ⅜ in.

The oil system was revised. As before, after lubricating the rockers, oil flowed down the pushrod tunnels into the cam tunnels to lubricate the cams and tappets. But the previous small holes from the inlet cam tunnel through the cylinder walls to lubricate the piston skirt, as well as the holes from the inlet and exhaust cam tunnels into the timing chest, were deleted, so that the camshaft tunnels were now sealed from the bore of the crankcase mouth. Oil from the inlet cam tunnel was returned direct to the oil tank through a drilled passage, and oil from the exhaust cam tunnel now simply overflowed into the timing chest, before draining to the sump. The sump itself was enlarged, and both sides of the return pump now drew from it, where before, one side had pumped back the big-end oil and the other the valve gear oil from the timing chest.

The crankcases also featured ready-tapped feed and return points for fitting a purpose-built oil cooler, which the factory had also been offering for some time past for the Constellation, especially if the latter was to be raced. In the company's somewhat confused situation from now on, however, not all Interceptor cases would be so drilled.

Electrics remained as on the Constellation

New big twin, 750 Interceptor. This model is for 1965.

up till now—but for 1963 the Connie adopted coil ignition. For the Interceptor the drive to the K2F magneto was now by duplex chain. Standard compression remained at 8:1, with a claimed output of 52.5 bhp at 6,000 rpm. In addition, low compression 7.25:1 pistons were available, and these were also fitted as standard to the Constellation, which took over the Super Meteor's sidecar role to the extent that it could be had in solo trim only to special order. Its gearing was therefore lowered (to 4.33, 5.63, 7.87 and 12.05:1), a single carburettor was fitted, both tyres became 3.50 × 19 in, and sidecar forks, stiffened damping, tougher clutch springs and a steering damper were part of the package. This would be its last year. There was also 8.5:1 compression on the Interceptor for the American export model, and the variation was achieved by the use of two compression plates, with one in place to give the 8:1 UK ratio, and two giving 7.5:1. It should be noted that when *Classic Bike*'s Tim Holmes removed both plates from his '63 Interceptor, however, a terrible banging ensued and a neat hole was scribed in the tops of the pistons, where the crown had been hitting the Cross ring.

These differences can lead to some fine old confusion, with permutations of the two plates and two different pistons giving six possible variations. There is also worse complication attending camshaft differences, as a justifiably bemused Tim Holmes discovered. 'Enfield's arrangements for opening and closing the valves', he wrote, 'were many, varied and almost impossible to understand . . . [there were] several types of cam, all with alternative keyways, sprockets and timing.' (Three principal variants, standard, sports, and super-sports, marked A, were offered for the Interceptor at this time.)

But that wasn't all of it; Holmes talked to ex-factory workers, and reported that 'it seems the cam-shaping machine was so old and worn-out that it had constantly to be re-set. The chances of finding two cams with identical profiles are remote indeed. . . the best [or only] way of sorting out the valve timing is to try every permutation and see which works best.' To richen the mixture a little further, in addition to the factory's own racing cams, batches of hot cams from America were also imported during the sixties. All this should clearly be borne in mind by those contemplating purchase of a well-worn Enfield twin.

The new engine was mounted in a frame and cycle parts similar to the Constellation's, though reverting to bronze bushes for the swinging arm, and also happily lacking the latter's rear mudguard pressings: the Interceptor fitted a chromed mudguard, and apparently for the first 85 machines, the old up-tilted dual-seat with white piping, before changing to a broader-based shape similar to the later Constellations. A new and more effective prop-stand was offered as an optional extra, positioned further forward than previously.

With the use of a 21-tooth gearbox sprocket as opposed to the previous solo Constellation's 20-tooth, gearing on the Interceptor was notably high (at 4.22, 5.72, 7.8 and 11.75:1). It was as well that the engine's flexibility and torque gave speeds in top from 25 mph all the way up to the claimed 115 mph maximum (112 was still probably more accurate), as there was a particularly big jump between third and fourth gears.

The Interceptor's other stable companion for 1963 was the half litre bike, now renamed simply the 500 Sports Twin; the De Luxe variant had already been dropped. It reverted to the 7 in front brake, was offered with the option of twin exhausts, and with the Constellation, was discontinued at the end of the year.

With the company in increasing disarray, from then until the end of 1965, there was little development for the Interceptor, and what there was often came unannounced, in mid-year. In mid-1963, for instance, the alternators changed from Lucas RM15 to RM19 models. At this time also, Monoblocs with float chambers for the right as well as the left hand became available.

Other examples of change during this period show the men at Westwood pegging away at the Twins' perennial problem. The clutch was modified: it will be recalled that the driving plates included the clutch sprocket itself with its ring of friction material (initially riveted on, later bonded). The sprocket had been located on the clutch centre drum by an anti-friction bearing which had consisted of 54 balls, but this changed to a ring of low-friction material. Then there were the four loose friction plates splined to the clutch outer drum. Previously, in line with the pattern of mixed inserts initiated for the Constellation, the two plates nearest to the sprocket had keystone-shaped inserts of friction material, and the two outer plates had bonded-on segments of J17 synthetic-cork based material: this changed, with all driving plates using bonded-on facings of J17. Finally the Interceptor's clutch springs had from the start been provided with adjusting screws, for three arms only of the

Right *Late 1965 750 Interceptor.*

Below left *Last 500, 1963 'Sports Twin'.*

clutch pressure plate; the springs fitted were alternately weak and strong, and it was imperative that the weak springs should be fitted behind the adjusting screws. A test late in 1962 had found that this development allowed the clutch to be slipped normally in traffic.

Internally, a steel washer fitted to the timing-side outer roller race was replaced by a more effective steel and rubber oil seal. After pressing the outer race home until it nipped the seal, the latter then had to be secured by making four equally spaced centre-punch marks in the surrounding case, so as to spread the aluminium over the radiused edge of the race; if this was neglected, the seal would pop out and be mashed up by the bevel gears of the oil pump, breaking oil feed to the big ends. Another modification concerned the oil seal behind the engine sprocket which had been secured by a garter spring, backed up by a steel washer. It now incorporated a second, thinner steel washer, lying between the thick washer and the edge of the outer race of the drive side main ball bearing.

Further changes included a minor alteration to the primary chaincase outer cover from engine no YA 15411 at the very end of 1963: a different oil filler neck extension and fitting pins with an altered oil filler cap and dipstick, from engine no YB 16319 in the latter half of 1965 and an end to the useful detachable camshaft bearing housings which came at engine no YB 16573, right at the end of the first Interceptor production run, in late 1965.

Previously, for 1964, the Interceptor had bifurcated in a familiar way into De Luxe and standard versions. The former offered a similar finish to the previous year, and 12 volt electrics, with a Zener diode hung under the toolbox, and two 6 volt smaller MKZE-2 batteries wired in series. It was easier to add a second battery and a piece of wire than to retool the case for a big 12 volt battery. The standard was offered cheaper, with 6 volt electrics and painted mudguards and petrol tank. There was also a sidecar version for what was left of that market, with low compression, forks with altered trail, lower gearing (4.43, 6.75, 9.07, and 13.70:1), and heavy duty suspension. All the Interceptors still featured magneto ignition, but the K2F magneto was of different specification, including the points, for in the interests of easier starting auto advance now replaced its manual ignition control.

For 1965 the standard Interceptor was dropped, and the domestic model, increasingly overshadowed by export production, came with the 12 volt electrics and—goodbye the casquette—a separate headlamp, though this lacked the quickly detachable snap-connectors of the US model. The latter, known as the TT Interceptor, fitted separate exhausts, a smaller tank with chrome panels, and 3.50 × 19 in front with 4.00 × 18 in rear wheels. From that source for the UK model, however, came the handsome alloy instrument facia panel into which the fork legs screwed as they had with the casquette; the panel had room for a matching rev-counter next to the Smith's 120 mph speedo.

The American raised handlebars with appropriately long cables were also available, and a more significant move was the standardization of the long wheelbase frame demanded by the cousins and provided for the export Interceptors from the start, with benefits of both increased stability, a rangier feel to the ride, and provision for that fat rear tyre. At 57 in against the previous 54 in wheelbase, this was achieved by the use of an extended swinging arm, cross-braced for strength just to the rear of the pivot point, and once again pivoting on Silentbloc bushes. There was therefore no alteration to the frame loop, except for longer rear damper upper mounting brackets, so that springing geometry was unaltered for the three-position Girling units which now replaced the previous Armstrongs.

The UK model continued with the previous shrouded front forks, while the US version had its upper tubes stylishly protected by gaiters. The Interceptor's fork legs had consisted of two main alternative types of steel tubing, one of 12 or 14 gauge chrome molybdenum alloy steel, the other of 8 gauge carbon steel. The latter had the same outside diameter and was at least as strong as the former, but owing to the different thicknesses of the walls, different springs and other internal fittings were used with them. The 8 gauge type were never used for US export machines or for sidecar forks. The special fork ends with reduced trail for sidecar work, incidentally, were no longer available for 1965.

As the year drew to a close and Redditch foundered, there followed a hiatus, with the big twin withdrawn from the UK market, all production going for export. Apparently about 1,800 Interceptors had been built in all, and they were impressive machines, booming red and chrome monsters which provided, as a 1965 *Motorcycle Mechanics* test would point out, 'a confident edge over almost anything it was liable to meet' on the street in those days, with more torque at low speeds than an Atlas, and the ability to see off a stock Bonneville. But sadly the reliability record still failed to match the performance; these Interceptors leaked oil when pushed, and crankshaft breakages were not unknown.

The *Motorcycle Mechanics* testers noted a 32 in seat height and an impression of size. They found the dual front brake disappointing, needing a great deal of muscle to get anything like a respectable braking effect. Starting too was tricky, with plenty of kickback, and they couldn't come to terms with that irreducible element, the Albion gearbox, finding its movements stiff and clunky, and the chances of missing a cog ever present. But they loved the bike, with its flexibility and 'great fistfuls of power available', its ton-plus ability without feeling as stretched as a 650 would, the smoothness from the double cush drive, and sweet and precise handling.

There was then silence for a year on the Interceptor front for the UK, broken only by a description of the latest Road Sports and Road Scrambler versions for 1967—but these were for export only. Then in September 1967, when the dust had settled on the Enfield upheavals and acquisitions, and the Interceptors were identified as made at Westwood by Enfield Precision (though the frames were now quietly being built by Velocette), these new variants, named as the Interceptor 1A, were offered again on the home market.

The IA's appearance was now firmly

1967 American spec Interceptor 1A in road scrambler trim.

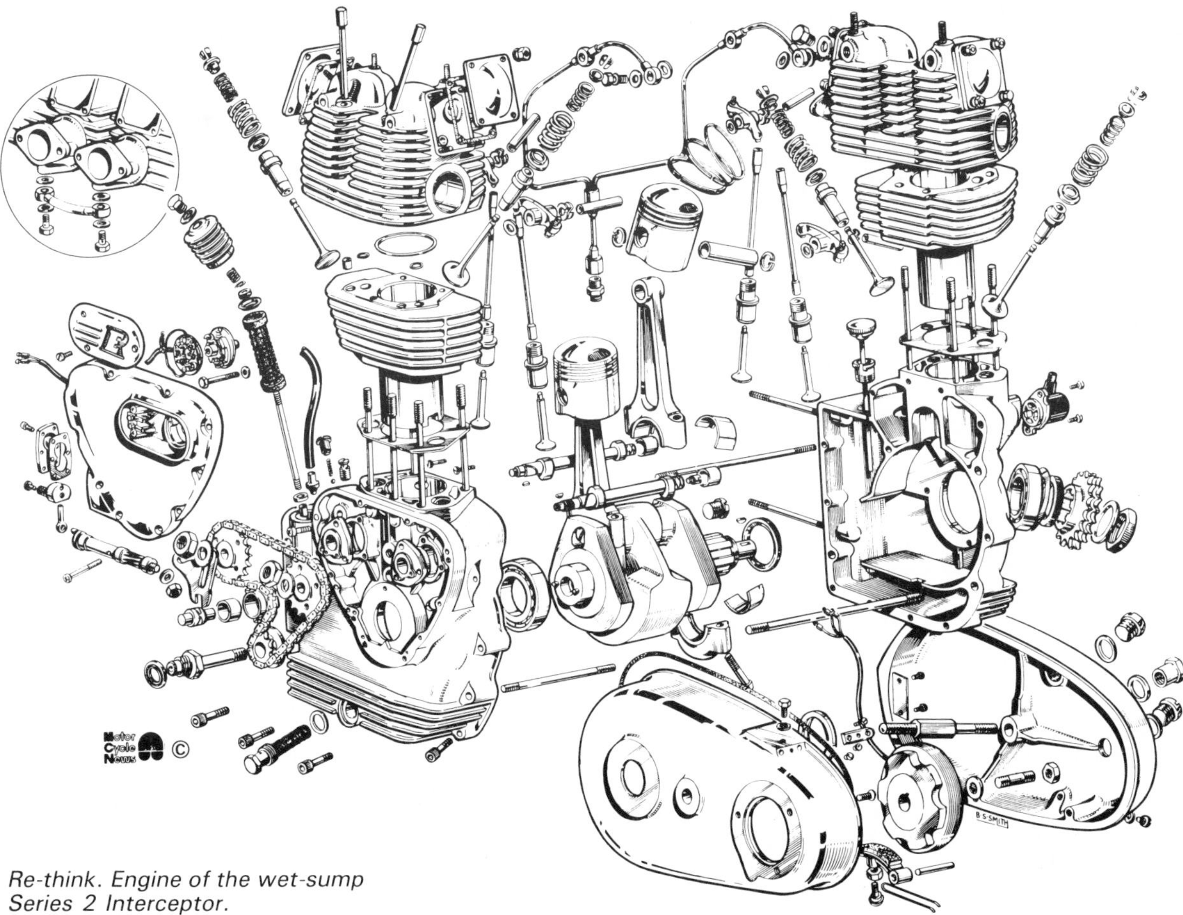

Re-think. Engine of the wet-sump Series 2 Interceptor.

export-oriented, with tiny 2¼ gallon tanks (blue painted with chrome panels, knee-grips and badges for the Road Sports, but all chromed with 'Royal Enfield' transfers for the Road Scrambler), and wide, cross-braced handlebars. The front brake had reverted to the 7 in one, but was decorated with big perforated spun-alloy 'bacon slicers', dummy cooling discs clamped to the front hub in the manner of the Continental GT. Front forks were gaitered like the previous export model, and of the heavier duty pattern, though the bottom tubes and lugs remained the same. The headlamp shell, now chromed but still containing the ammeter, as well as a toggle switch for the headlight, sat in front of a new alloy fork crown, to which the 125 mph speedo and matching 8,000 rpm rev-counter were bolted on a bracket. A steering damper was still fitted. Exhausts were twin, flat on the Road Sports and handsomely upswept on the Road Scrambler. The rear chainguard was now in two portions, and chromed. The seat was the same for both, a short sports item with a speed hump at its tail. The rear number plate was bent up at a rakish angle to match that of the suspension units, which for the Road Sports retained their shrouds, though these were now chromed, while the Road Scrambler sported fully exposed chromed springs. The wheels were as for the previous American model, 3.50 × 19 front and 4.00 × 18 in rear.

The carburettors had changed to 30 mm Amal Concentrics with open bell mouths. The battery/toolbox pressing which had previously held the aircleaner had been dispensed with. This left the 12 volt battery exposed, and under the seat behind the battery back plate were located the two coils which, with the magneto also gone, now provided the ignition. In that position also was the spring-

mounted capacitor, so these street scramblers could be run with the battery removed and the lights detached. The points lived in a circular housing where the magneto had been, and the ignition/lightswitch was mounted on the right panel of the vestigial battery back plate, in front of the system's Zener diode in its large finned heat sink. The rear light was the type with a pointed dome. All this was Lucas' latest and best, as found on that year's Atlas and Commando. (On some examples of the IA, but not those in the publicity photos, the engine was further modified with a large bore nylon pipe taken from the top of the crankcase oil compartment, to finally effectively de-pressurize this in the interest of oil tightness.)

These beauties may not have been the height of practicality for British conditions, but they did look magnificently lean and purposeful, with their dry weight down to 414 lb, a very useful figure for a 750. Compression had standardized at the upper 8.5:1 ratio. About 1,000 IAs were built, but as their numbering suggested, they were an interim model, and late in 1968, what was to be the final development was unveiled in the shape of the Interceptor Series II. With one major exception the cycle parts were those of the IA, but the engine had finally been radically redesigned. One principal area for this was the clutch. The previously milled slots around the clutch centre were replaced with splines, as on the Norton Commando clutch. L and D's Jeff Lewis says that whatever the theoretical benefits, in practice the drums were soft and didn't last as well as the previous ones, though these clutches were marginally less affected by oil. The other was the lubrication system. Here Enfield, the firm that long ago had pioneered dry sump lubrication for motor cycles, in a last burst of innovation switched to a car-type wet sump system.

The oil, still four pints of it, was carried in a very large finned sump, and circulated at four times the previous rate through a two-stage pressure system, with oil going at 60 psi to the big ends and 15 psi to the rockers, by a new bigger oil pump. The pump sat behind a cover attached by six Allen bolts to the rear of the new timing cover. This timing cover was triangular, featured wider joint faces, and was smoother-looking than previously without in any way seeming bland. Behind it the camshafts, which were redesigned high performance items, were again quickly removable, with the detachable timing side camshaft bearing housing secured by three screws. On the other side, the Series II's primary chaincase acquired an extra hole to permit strobing up.

To the timing cover's front end was screwed a rectangular cover, decorated with a new 'RE' motif, with the encircling 'R' and three bars behind it picked out in red. This rectangular cover housed the contact breakers, which were operated by a cam on the end of the exhaust camshaft. In the space behind the cylinders where points had previously been, there was the oil filler cap, flush to the casting as on the Continental GT; this was at first fitted with an adaptor for its collar, but the adaptor was deleted at engine No IBI333. There was also the pipe for the rocker oil feed, the spring-and-ball-bearing rocker oil release valve and oil pressure relief valve, and the futuristic chromed and finned circular tower, topped by a hexagonal bolt head, of the same tubular felt mesh oil filter that had previously lived in the sump. A thick black nylon breather tube ran from the top of the crankcase casting behind the cylinder, to the rear wheel. The same finned light alloy oil cooler, but with its internals modified to suit the new lubrication circuit, was at first optional: when fitted, it was coupled by armoured piping to the oil filter tower behind the cylinder. All these measures achieved their intention, as all agree that the Series II Enfields were finally and famously oiltight, and Reg Thomas managed this with good production economy in not disturbing the drive side or the top end.

The one major change to the cycle parts was the adoption of a Norton front end, with the renowned Roadholder front fork, a chrome front mudguard which replaced the previous middle stay with a bracket, and an 8 in front brake. The latter may have been only SLS, but was generally conceded to have been the best of its type produced in Britain, and the fork also allows the substitution of a TLS Commando brake. The cable featured a switch activating the rear brake light. The fork was gaitered, and topped by a speedo and rev counter in chromed cases, with the rev-counter drive taken from the exhaust camshaft via the left front of the crankcase.

The battery was no longer exposed, being shrouded by a simple battery cover secured by a single wing nut. The carburettors were still Amal Concentrics with bell mouths though some would feel that Monoblocs suited the engine better, and that the Concentrics contributed to the fact that the Series II was no faster than its predecessors. The claimed output varied from 52 bhp at 6,500 to 56 at 6,750 rpm, but top speed with standard gearing remained around 110 mph. Certainly when the machine was first tested in 1968, a slight hesitancy was noted at the lower end of the power band before both instruments came on song. The exhausts and silencers were similar in appearance, though differing in detail, to the upswept versions on the IA Road Scrambler, while the rear units opted for the sensible Road Sports route with the chromed shrouds in place. Side reflectors were fitted, in line with US legal requirements, and optional extras included a fibreglass toolbox to fit over the rear mudguard, an engine undershield, and a large capacity air filter in an oval housing (the element being taken from a Ford Transit) which bridged the carburettors' intake mouths.

For 1969 there were some internal modifications. The machine was normally offered with the raised and braced handlebars and the chromed 2¼ gallon tank, decorated from the start with a new name transfer, the 'Royal' in red script and the

Above far left *Impressive Series 2 Lump.*

Above left *1970 Series 2 Interceptor under test by Bob Currie.*

Right *1970 Series 2 in English trim.*

Tasty and exclusive, one of just 137 Rickman Enfields produced.

'Enfield' in black capitals on a white background. But during this year there was a UK option, with the 4¼ gallon tank, painted and decorated with an S-shaped gold stripe, the old plastic badges and plain kneegrips, and a conventional handlebar. The air cleaner, bash plate and now a chromed grab-rail at the rear of the dual-seat, were all optional extras.

A *Motor Cycle* road test that year found the bike with its long-stroke motor to be tall, but not uncomfortably so for the rider, since the seat tapered at the front, and both it and the tank were a sensible width. Once aboard there was no undue feeling of bulk, despite the Series II's weight having risen to 425 lb. The handling, with the Norton front end and the low centre of balance from the sump, was excellent, and unaffected by the fat 4.00 × 18 in rear wheel, which contributed to a comfortable ride. Torque was tremendous, though the standing quarter figure of 14.4 seconds did not rival Norton's Commando (13.7 in early incarnations, and later dropping to the 12s.) The range of power was still good, though again an irritating unevenness was noted at minimum throttle openings, despite the fact that tickover was reliable and acceleration from there very quick.

In view of the Series II's general reputation for exemplary smoothness, it is interesting to note that the statically and dynamically balanced crank was only felt to produce results that were 'reasonably smooth', with a short vibration period setting in after 90. The gearing at 4.44, 6.05, 8.19 and 12.4 still retained the very noticeable jump between third and top. Another minus point was fuel economy which had fallen sharply, the big bike returning 43 mpg to the gallon at 60 mph and only 35 mpg at 70. (The 1969 price of £455, on the other hand, was competitive with a Fastback Commando at £466.) Braking was excellent for the type, with a 28 ft stopping distance from 30 mph.

Top speed was 112 mph overall, with a best one-way of 119, but top speed was never the point. With the material to hand Enfield had tried to build in torque and reliability. Up to the 90 mph speed achieved at around 5,000 rpm, the 750 was a tireless all-day cruiser, but if higher speeds were held for long then something would break, up to and including the crankshaft. But with that limitation the Series II was a strong and reliable motor, as evidenced by Dave Messent's 12,000 overland trip to Australia with only minimal adjustments, on a bike already with 50,000 miles on the clock.

For 1970, the air cleaner, oil cooler, bash plate and grab-rail were offered as standard fittings and from engine No IB2002 the crankcase differed from the one used up to that point. On 3 July at engine no IB2200 production at Westwood ceased, with the fully developed 800 cc prototype expiring at that point also. Three men had been responsible for the Series II's engine building, at the rate of around 25 a week, though only 546 Series II Interceptors were sold in 1969, with a further 600 or so of the engines going for Floyd Clymer's Indians. Construction proceeded along selective assembly lines, with each man ensuring that every group of parts fitted perfectly, out of the entire stock to hand—this had been no small factor in the Series II's reliability. The last act was still to come in the shape of the Rickman Enfield, though the first prototype had already been shown early in 1970 at the Sporting Show. The background story will be found in the marque history section: here we will simply give a brief description of the 137 bikes that were built.

The Series II engine was fitted in a version of the Rickman brothers' frame, though with a wider loop than previous models, and also not their customary oil-bearing chassis. The frame was built of 1¼ in diameter Reynolds 531 tubing, all bronze-welded, with duplex tubes throughout, and nickle-plated. The very strong front fork was Rickmans' own, derived from their motocross fork, with stanchions of thin gauge 42 mm steel and forged alloy yokes; they were ungaitered. Wheels were 4.10 × 18 in front and rear, with Dunlop K81 tyres fitted on Borrani alloy rims. Lockheed disc brakes, 10 in front and 9 in rear (the latter as used on the Triumph Herald car) were fitted, both on the right and both with gold-anodized hubs.

Rickmans' distinctive and good quality glassfibre ware in a choice of four colours was present in the shape of the front mudguard, the three-gallon tank, peculiar in being wider at the rear than at the front, but not unhandsome, and the one-piece seat/rear mudguard unit whose low horizontal lines chimed well with those of the tank. A wrong note was provided by the rather naff-looking white side panels. That much was cafe-racer styling, and the use of larger (32 mm) Concentrics, with an option of hotter sports cams, seemed to emphasize performance. The handlebars were high, wide and totally impractical at speed, though in a further twist, *Classic Bike*'s Peter Watson found that flat bars, fitted in Alf Hagon alloy clamps by Rickman Enfield enthusiast Alan Abrahams, transmitted a lot more vibration over 70 mph than the standard set-up with each bar clamped to a fork stanchion. Another odd feature was the way that the footrests, their position still too far forward but dictated by the intractable gearbox, were welded to the (necessarily well-anchored) exhaust pipes. This however was intelligently done, the pegs themselves being slotted into tubes butt-welded to the pipes, with an Allen bolt pinching the pegs into position: if the machine took a tumble the pegs could hopefully swivel in their mounting tubes, rather than damaging themselves and the pipe.

Expensive at £685 in 1971, when £670 would buy a Trident, the Rickman Enfield weighed in at just 365 lb, and all who tried one enthused about the peerless handling and the brakes (though the latter were not very effective in the rain). But an *MCN* tester was disappointed in the engine—'vibration is this machine's worst enemy' he declared, after the horn snapped and the headlamp came loose. The riding position and rather thin seat did not aid rider comfort. *MCS* found it quick to 90 mph, then flatter to 105 mph. Detail finish was good, with all the alloy surfaces polished, an abundance of aircraft-type locking nuts, big bore bolts and hefty brace plates, with metal shields on cables near exhaust pipes, and the crankcase breather fed neatly into the frame tubes.

The gearbox remained the Achilles heel: Peter Watson commented in exasperation, 'What a rotten thing to fit to an otherwise sporting motor cycle'. Some forerunners to the Rickman Enfield had been two teams of Welshmen riding Rickman-framed Series II Interceptors in the 1970 Bol d'Or at Montlhéry (won that year by Paul Smart on a Trident). One pair were lying seventh, in the

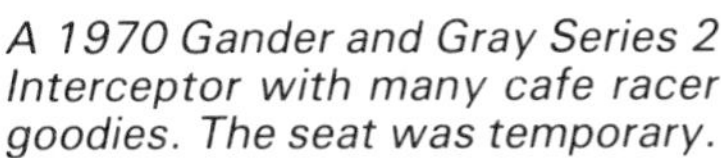

A 1970 Gander and Gray Series 2 Interceptor with many cafe racer goodies. The seat was temporary.

ninth hour, when they were put out by the box seizing. The pre-Constellation early steel sleevegear had occasionally seized if the oil level dropped at all; but they were using the later modified sleevegear with the bushed sleeve. This worked well until it got hot, but then the bush turned in the sleeve until the oil holes no longer lined up; and then it too would seize, which is what had happened. The second Welsh team stripped all the teeth from their close ratio box. The Albion gearbox was a definite limitation to the upper end of the motor's over-50 bhp performance.

It was the one really non-negotiable flaw, because from the start the 500s had charm, and both the 700 and 750 twins a lot of potential. Today the use of an oil cooler, the Interceptor's alloy block behind the gearbox, the Series II clutch and even a Norton front end, can bring any of them close to Series II efficiency. Electronic ignition will have its usual smoothening effect on any large capacity twin, and the use of one or more breather pipes, perhaps fabricated from car brake hose and possibly supplemented by external oil lines, will take some pressure off the overworked internal oilways, as classic racer Steve Linsdell proved with his '53 Meteor-based 700—though he was running on short circuits where the oil didn't have time to overheat. Linsdell also adjusted his primary chain by shimming the gearbox away from the case, a good way to avoid the use of the unreliable primary chain tensioner of which the delicate thread-form, an Enfield vice, made it too likely to pull out of the alloy of the case.

If one can overcome the hurdle of unfamiliarity, the big 'uns can make a robust and reliable fast tourer for someone with some mechanical ability and sympathy, with the '56, to '58 Super Meteor, or any Series II-engined bike, being particularly desirable starting points. The spares situation and interchangeability is good. On the other hand there's always the Enfield luck to contend with: the only Rickman Interceptor it has been my privilege to inspect, was promptly knocked over by a car when its keeper came into my house for a cup of tea, and having survived that, seized on its way home!

But I'll leave with a happier recollection. Very early on Sunday mornings, north of San Francisco in Marin County, speed-minded folk on two wheels have gathered for years at a gas station at Mill Valley, for an unofficial fast run over the foothills and north along the coast cliff road to the railroad station at Point Reyes. It's a tight, exhilarating route, and they don't hang about. When I attended, one misty morning in 1982, there was only one British bike there. It was an immaculate Interceptor Series II, with its chrome tank, tall build and rakish lines making it an outstanding machine even in some fairly distinguished and exotic company. The rider was friendly and relaxed in the Californian manner, but the way he ripped off, exhaust crackling, into the first uphill hairpins was clear evidence that for him the surefootedness and torquey motor of the Enfield made it far from merely ornamental. And that's what it's all about.

Royal Enfield: The 500, 700 and 750 Twins—Dates and specifications

Production Dates

500 Twin—1949–58
700 Meteor—1953–55
Super Meteor—1955–62
Constellation—1958–63
Meteor Minor—1958–63
Interceptor—1963–68
Interceptor Series II—1968–70

Specification

500 Twin

Capacity, bore and stroke—495 cc (64 × 77 mm)
Type—ohv twin
Ignition—(1949–54) Coil; (1954 [optional], 1955–56) Magdyno; (1957–58) Coil.
Weight—(1950) 400 lb; (1953) 390 lb

700 Meteor

Capacity, bore and stoke—692 cc (70 × 90 mm)
Type—ohv twin
Ignition—(1953–54) Coil; (1955) Magdyno
Weight—(1955) 405 lb

Super Meteor

As Meteor except
Ignition—(1955–57) Magneto; (1958–62) Coil
Weight—(1956) 410 lb

Constellation

As Meteor except
Ignition—(1958–62) Magneto; (1963) Coil
Weight—(1958) 403 lb; (1963) 410 lb

Meteor Minor

Capacity, bore and stroke—496 cc (70 × 64.5 mm)
Type—ohv twin

Ignition—coil
Weight—(1958) 370 lb

Interceptor
Capacity, bore and stroke—736 cc (71 × 93)
Type—ohv twin
Ignition—(1963–67) Magneto; (1968) Coil
Weight—(1963) 410 lb; (1968) 414 lb

Interceptor Series II
As Interceptor except
Ignition—Coil
Weight—426 lb

Royal Enfield: 500, 700 and 750 Twins—annual development and modifications

1950
For 500 Twin
1 Polished alloy speedometer facia panel fitted.
2 Forged fork ends now welded (not screwed) to their sliders.
3 Sprung front mudguard became of deep section in place of previous valances.
4 Combined switches moved on to front of electrical control box.

1951
For 500 Twin
1 Crankcases now die-cast.
2 Front mudguard mounted by three stays each side, and now moved with wheel.

1952
For 500 Twin
1 Ignition light, headlamp switch and ammeter now mounted in headlamp.
2 Dual-seats available as optional extra.
3 External oil feed lines to rocker boxes.
4 Two additional grub-screws fitted to increase pressure between crankcase halves at cylinder joint faces, and two screws on driveside exterior for access to the latter grub-screws via drillings.
5 Aircleaner box enlarged.

1953
For 500 Twin
1 Silicon alloy split-skirt pistons fitted.
2 Cylinder heads die-cast, with previously cast-in special iron mounting.
3 Induction manifolds change from U to Y shape.
4 Rear suspension units lose their drain plugs.
5 Crankcase disc-valve breather body fitted on left-hand top of crankcase below left-hand cylinder.
6 Winged, chrome-plated and painted tank badge, fitted on tanks no longer chromed but enamelled.
7 Headlamp with underslung pilot light.
8 New number-plate with Lucas stop-tail light and red reflector, and stop-light switch housed in nearside tool-box.
9 Front brake adopts floating cam spindle.

1954
For 700 Meteor, 500 Twin
1 Casquette fork head incorporating instruments and twin pilot lights mounted high up.
2 Armstrong rear suspension units replace Enfield's own.
For 700 Meteor
3 Sidecar forks with different bottom tubes and lugs, as opposed to previous different fork crowns.
4 On rear fork, previous bracing tubes and welded-in steel gusset plates replaced by brazed-on malleable lugs.
5 Oval air cleaner box.
6 Pushrods now of alloy.
7 Small winged transfers for frame-loop tool boxes.
8 Front mudguard stay becomes tubular, doubles as front stand.
For 500 Twin
9 Magdyno offered as optional extra.

1955
For 700 Meteor, 500 Twin
1 Magdyno adopted as standard.
2 Dualseat now standard.
3 Gearbox end-cover tidied, with gear pedal and kickstart crank now positioned on a co-axial shaft. Previous worm-gear operation of clutch pushrod replaced by clutch fulcrum lever enclosed within end cover.
4 Redesigned cams with new quietening ramps.
5 Frames modified in area of rear fork pivot (From March 1955).
6 Q.d. rear wheel offered as option.
For 700 Meteor
7 Compression raised to 7.5:1.
8 Headsteady redesigned.
For 500 Twin
9 Oval air-cleaner box adopted.
10 6 inch dual front brake.

1956

For 500 Twin

1 7 inch rear brake.
2 Optional q.d. rear wheel now with full-width alloy hub.
3 Compression raised to 7.25:1.
4 Folding kickstart fitted.
5 Boxed-in rear number plate.
6 Combined horn button and dipswitch.
7 Small oval 'Royal Enfield' plate on timing side cover replaces previous stamped-in 'Royal Enfield'.
8 Plastic circular winged tank badges and revised petrol tank mounting.

1957

For Super Meteor and 500 Twin

1 Full-width alloy qd rear wheel as standard.
2 Air-cleaner altered from circular to D-shape.
3 Chrome side-panels fitted to petrol tanks, with appropriate plain kneegrips for 500 Twins.

For Super Meteor

4 New rear mudguard mounting, no longer connected to back of dual-seat by a tubular loop, with neater horizontal bracing strut/lifting handle loop on either side.
5 Improved magneto.

For 500 Twin

6 Coil electrics readopted, with horizontal chain-driven distributor.
7 All-welded frame, with pressed steel central battery toolbox, alloy centre-stand and Monobloc carburettor.
8 Gearing lowered from (5.0, 6.5, 9.0, 13.9:1) to (5.2, 6.7, 9.4, 14.3:1).

1958

For Super Meteor and 500 Twin

1 New Burgess silencer with no tail pipe.
2 Saddle portions of dual-seat picked out in white piping.

For Super Meteor

3 Coil electrics adopted as on 500 Twin.

1959

For Super Meteor

1 Siamezed exhaust system adopted.

For Constellation

2 Carburettor becomes a single Monobloc 389.

1960

For Constellation, Super Meteor and Meteor Minor De Luxe and Sports

1 Cylinder headsteady became a torque stay from the head back to a lug now featured on the underside of the frame top tube.
2 Crankcase breather flap valve embodied in drive side of crankshaft, discharging through a special drilled bolt securing alternator to end of shaft; bolt contained in its head a pen-steel disc, breathing into primary chaincase. Latter's breather body replaced previous plain neoprene pipe discharging into atmosphere with metal pipe leading oil via oil compartment to rear chain. Where previous breather mechanism had been screwed on to outside left of crankcase, now a drain pipe conveyed excess oil from camshaft tunnels and cylinder walls to oil container, with drain connected to annular cavities at base of cylinder. Magnet fitted in main oil filter.
3 Offset eliminated at point where horizontal run of pipe enters forward end of silencer.
4 New-style casquette side-lights mounted further apart than previously.
5 Friction plates in clutch become Neolangite bonded.

For Constellation and Super Meteor

6 Balance factor for crankshafts increased from 50% to 75%, flywheels changed to bobweights, dead weight reduced to 24 lb approx; lighter pistons used, with bottom piston ring groove modified to contain two separate oil control rings. Constellation's compression ratio reduced to 8:1.

For Constellation

7 Twin Amal Monoblocs fitted, each mounted on short splayed inlet stub. Central toolbox pressing now with two ears to shroud the intakes and depressions in the boxes to clear the carbs.
8 Ignition timing changed from 0.375 to 0.437.
9 Rear tank mounting now a clamping strap pulling tank down on to sponge rubber sheeting.

For Super Meteor and Meteor Minors

10 Rear tank mounting now a spring clip which snapped around a rubber sleeve on the top tube.

For Meteor Minors

11 Clutch operating lever balls enlarged and operating lever pin fitted with appropriate washer.
12 Exhaust system and brake pedal revised, and silencers gained tail pipes.

For Super Meteor

13 Gearing becomes as Constellation (4.44, 5.37, 7.99, 12.35:1).

1961

For Constellation and Super Meteor

1 New clutch with star-shaped outer plate, conventional pushrod, and six pressure, five friction plates including sprocket.
2 New Lucas MLZ 95 battery.
3 New deeper rear mudguard enclosure, upper section of fibreglass but from January 1961 of pressed steel as are side section panels.
4 New three-part dismantlable torpedo-shaped silencer with tail fin.
5 Early 1961, pivoted fork bearings changed from bronze to Silentbloc bushes.
6 Early 1961, primary chain tensioner and stator fixing assembly modified.

For Constellation

7 'Ace' dropped handlebars adopted.
8 Early 1961, from engine No SC 11034, gearbox mainshaft, its ballrace and the ballrace oil thrower cap modified.

For Super Meteor

9 Constellation's 4¼ gallon tank adopted, but enamelled not chromed.

For Meteor Minors

10 Modified casquette as Constellation etc, for 1960.
11 De Luxe model adopts Sports' 3¾ gallon tank.
12 Sports rear wheel no longer qd.
13 Sports timing cover/primary chaincase/gearbox end cover no longer polished but had vapour-blast satin finish.
14 De Luxe model adopts new silencer as for Constellation, etc.

1962

For Constellation and Super Meteor

1 From January, steering head locks available.

For Meteor Minors

2 Silentbloc swinging arm bushes adopted.
3 Sports offered with dual 6 in front brake.

1963

For Constellation

1 Coil electrics adopted.
2 Sidecar trim as standard; 7.25:1 cr pistons, lower gearing (4.33, 5.63, 7.87 and 12.05:1), single carburettor, both tyres 3.50 × 19 in, sidecar forks, stiffened damping, tougher clutch springs, steering damper. Available in solo trim to special order only.

For Meteor Minor (now '500 Sports Twin')

3 7 in front brake readopted.
4 Optional twin exhaust system.

For Interceptor, during 1963

5 3 adjustable clutch springs fitted.
6 Clutch sprocket's anti-friction bearing changes from 54 balls to a ring of low friction material.
7 Clutch's two inner driving plates change from inserts of friction material to bonded-on facings of J17 synthetic cork-based material, as on two outer driving plates.
8 Mid-year, alternators change from Lucas RM15 to RM19.
9 Mid-year, Monoblocs with float chambers for right as well as left become available.
10 Steel washer previously fitted to timing-side outer roller race replaced by more effective steel and rubber oil seal.
11 Garter spring securing oil-seal behind engine sprocket had its steel washer supplemented by a second, thinner steel washer.
12 Late 1963, from engine No YA 15411, minor alteration to primary chaincase outer cover.

1964

For Interceptor

1 De Luxe variant offered; 12 volt electrics via 2 × 6 volt MKZE-2 batteries in series and Zener Diode. Trim as previous Interceptor. Standard model with painted tank and mudguards.
2 Magneto ignition via modified K2F magneto (42369B) incorporating automatic advance (LU 540 44111), so manual control goes and contacts different.

1965

For Interceptor

1 12-volt electrics as standard.
2 Separate headlamp shell.
3 Alloy instrument facia panel.
4 Long-wheelbase (57 in) frame by adoption of lengthened and cross-braced swinging arm, and lengthened upper mounting brackets for rear units, which with this frame become Girlings.
5 Optional high cross-braced handlbars.
6 Late year, from engine No YB 16319, altered oil filler neck extension and fitting pins, with an altered oil filler cap and dipstick.
7 Late year, from engine No YB 16573, deletion of detachable camshaft bearing housing.

1967
For Interceptor
1 Late year, Interceptor IA available again in UK, for details see text.

1968
For Interceptor
1 Late year, Interceptor Series II supersedes IA, for details see text.

1969
For Interceptor Series II
1 From engine No IB1333, adaptor on oil filler collar deleted.
2 UK option with painted 4¼ gallon tank with badges and kneegrips, plus conventional handlebar, offered.

1970
For Interceptor Series II
1 Previously optional air cleaner, oil cooler, bash plate and grab rail now standard.
2 From engine No IB2002, crankcase altered.

Royal Enfield: engine and frame numbers

(It is regretted that particularly the early stages of these lists are very incomplete. It should be noted that all works experimental engines were prefixed 'EX'. Enfield numbering is also to some extent random and inconsistent, but there is a safety net. The RE Owners Club dating officer holds ledgers which enable him to provide an owner with the date of despatch of any machine, if he is supplied with the engine and frame number. Contact the dating officer via the Club.)

	Engine	Frame
1952		
Meteor 700 Twin	101	101
1953		
500 Bullet	12501	12501
1954		
Model S	101	101
1955		
250 Clipper	2601	2601
1956		
350 Clipper	37601	37601
350 Bullet	38101	38101
500 Bullet	14194	14194
Super Meteor 700 Twin	3151	3151

	Engine	Frame
1957		
Crusader 250	6220	6220
1958		
Crusader 250	7000	7000
(Feb 1958) Crusader Airflow	8820	8820
(Mar 1958) Series II 250 Clipper	10270	10270
350 Clipper	42201	42201
350 Bullet	41725	41725
500 Bullet	14600	14600
500 Twin	5676	5676
(Mar 1958) 500 Twin Ends	5725	5725
(Apr 1958) Meteor Minor Standard	5426	5426
(Apr 1958) Meteor Minor De Luxe	5426	5426
Super Meteor 700	SMQA 4614	5551
(Apr 1958) Constellation	7001	7001
1959		
Series II 250 Clipper	10632	10632
Crusader	9150	9150
Crusader Sports 250	11270	11270
350 Clipper	42709	42709
(Aug 1959) 350 Clipper Ends	43200	43200
350 Bullet	43301	43301
500 'Big head' Bullet	15771	15771
Meteor Minor Standard	5500	5500
(Aug 1959) Meteor Minor Standard Ends	6304	6304
Meteor Minor De Luxe	5976	5976
Super Meteor	5760	5760
Constellation	7203	7203
1960		
Series II 250 Clipper	12020	12020
Crusader	9550	9550
Crusader Sports	12570	12570
350 Clipper De Luxe	45896	45896
350 Bullet	44055	44055
500 Bullet	15800	15800
Meteor Minor De Luxe	6350	6350
Meteor Minor Sports	6376	6376
Super Meteor	8451	8451
Constellation	9301	9301
1961		
Series II 250 Clipper	12401	12401
Crusader 250	14571	14571

	Engine	Frame
Crusader Sports	16875	16875
350 Clipper De Luxe	46001	46001
350 Bullet	45525	45525
500 Bullet	16275	16275
Meteor Minor De Luxe	6675	6675
Meteor Minor Sports	6675	6675
Super Meteor	8790	8790
Constellation	10001	10001
1962		
Series II 250 Clipper	—	19650
Crusader 250	—	19650
Crusader Sports	—	19650
Crusader Super 5	—	19650
350 Clipper	—	53050
350 Bullet	—	53050
500 Bullet	—	16500
Meteor Minor Sports, De Luxe	—	—
Super Meteor	—	11550
Constellation	—	11550
1963		
Series II 250 Clipper	—	21750
Crusader Sports	—	21750
Crusader Super 5	—	21750
(Aug 1963) Crusader Super 5 Ends	13941	20475
Continental	—	21830
(Jan 1963) New 350 Bullet	—	53306
Meteor Minor Sports/ 500 Sports Twin	—	6725
(Aug 1963) Meteor Minor Sports/500 Sports Twin Ends	35596	6845
Constellation (sidecar model)	—	11625
(Aug 1963) Constellation (sidecar model) Ends	11205	11615
Interceptor	SMYA15001	11182
1964		
Series II 250 Clipper	14151	23390
Crusader Sports Standard	14007	—
Crusader Sports De Luxe	14007	22089
Continental Standard	14048	23083
Continental De Luxe	14048	23083
Turbo Twin	701E-151	68538
Turbo Twin Sports	—	—
New Bullet 350	167	57049

	Engine	Frame
Interceptor Standard	15444	11293
Interceptor De Luxe	15444	11293
1965		
Series II 250 Clipper	—	—
(Dec 1965) Series II 250 Clipper Ends	17118	71973
Crusader Sports	—	—
Continental De Luxe/ Continental Standard	—	—
(Aug 1965) Continental Ends	1340	68389
Olympic	15325	69738
(Aug 1965) Olympic Ends	16596	71872
Continental GT	15539	69896
New Bullet 350	—	—
(Aug 1965) New Bullet 350 Ends	329	71612
Interceptor	—	—
(Dec 1965) Interceptor Ends	16581	69869
1966		
Crusader Sports	—	—
(Jun 1966) Crusader Sports Ends	18046	72393
Turbo Twin Sports	—	—
(Oct 1966) Turbo Twin Sports Ends	2053	71771
Continental GT	—	—
1967		
(Jan 1967) Continental GT Ends	18485	73135
1968		
Interceptor IA	500	500
(Oct 1968) Interceptor IA Ends	999	999
1969		
Interceptor Series II	IB-1000	F-1000
1970		
(Jul 1970) Interceptor Series II Ends	IB-2200	F-2200
Rickman Enfield Interceptor Series II prototypes	—	R651 R652 R797 R810 R811 R979

	Engine	Frame
(Apr 1970) Rickman Enfield Interceptor Series II Production		R1001
1972		
(Jan 1972) Rickman Enfield Interceptor Series II production ends		R1130

Royal Enfield: colour schemes

These finishes are the catalogued ones. In practice there may be variations.

1950 *Singles* Model G, J2, black cycle parts, chromed wheel rims and chromed petrol tank, panelled in frosted silver with dark blue outer and red inner lining. 350 Bullet, cycle parts (including rear chain guard) lustrous silver grey; chromed wheel rims and rear spring boxes. Tank finish as Model G. Black headlamp, air cleaner box. *Twins* 500 Twin as 350 Bullet.

1951 *Singles* Model G/J2, all cycle parts black enamel, including petrol tank, which features double gold lining and a chrome tank-top strip. Chromed wheel rims. 350 Bullet as 1950. *Twins* 500 Twin as 1950.

1952 *Singles* Model G/J2, as 1951 but with polished chain case and facia panel. 350 Bullet as 1951 but now also lustrous silver grey where chrome had been on petrol tank. Polished crankcase, timing cover, primary chain cover, and facia panel. *Twins* 500 Twin, as 350 Bullet.

1953 *Singles* Model G, J2, as 1952, but gold lining and previous painted name on petrol tank displaced by new winged tank badge in chrome, red and gold. 350 Bullet, as 1952 with finish now described as 'silver grey polychromatic', but tank panel and lining replaced by badge as on Model G etc. 500 Bullet as 350 Bullet but Copper Beech polychromatic in place of silver grey, and wheel rims bright zinc plated. *Twins* 500 Twin as 350 Bullet. Meteor 700, as 500 Bullet but with optional matching dual-seat, and chrome-plated wheel rims.

1954 *Singles* Model S, Model G, J2 as 1953. 250 Clipper, olive green cycle parts including headlamp casquette. Tank with winged badges, chromed wheel rims. 350 and 500 Bullet, as 1953, but headlamp casquette (though not air cleaner box) in cycle part's colour. 500 Bullet's wheel rims now chrome-plated. *Twins* 500 Twin as 350 Bullet. Meteor 700 as 500 Bullet.

1955 *Singles* J2, as 1954. 250 Clipper, as 1954, but with deep maroon or silver-grey alternatives, and all with new double gold lining on tank (thick upper, thin lower) continuous lines creating both top and side panels. 350 Bullet, as 1954, but deep maroon or olive green alternatives, and tank lining as 250 Clipper. 500 Bullet as 1954 but colour now deep maroon, with olive green or polychromatic silver grey alternatives, and tank lining as 250 Clipper. *Twins* 500 Twin as 350 Bullet, 700 Twin as 500 Bullet.

1956 *Singles* 250 Clipper, as 1955. Model G De Luxe/350 Clipper, as 250 Clipper but finish olive green. 350 Bullet, as 1955 but sole finish deep maroon, and double gold tank lining now outlines tank panel only, with new winged plastic badge at its centre. 500 Bullet as 350 Bullet. *Twins* 500 Twin, Super Meteor, both as 350 Bullet.

1957 *Singles* Crusader, light surf green for all but boxed-in rear number plate, and chrome panels on petrol tank. Clipper as 1956, but 350 and 500 Bullets new catalogued with chrome panels on petrol tank. *Twins* As 1956 but with chrome panels on petrol tank.

1958 *Singles* Crusader as 1957, but black as standard, with options of tank, mudguards, toolbox lids and chainguard in polychromatic Burgundy, polychromatic Wedgwood Blue or polychromatic silver grey, rest in black. Series II Clipper 250, black with tank gold-lined (thin outer, thick inner, following shape where chrome panels would have been back to knee-grips), plastic badges. 350 Clipper as 1956 (old-style gold lining, winged metal badge) but colour black. 350 and 500 Bullets, as Crusader. *Twins* 500 Twin, Meteor Minor, Super Meteor, as Crusader. Meteor Minor standard black, chrome side panels. Constellation, Polychromatic Burgundy toolbox lids rear chainguard and top panel on chromed petrol tank. Chrome mudguards, rest black.

1959 *Singles* Crusader, as 1958, but in polychromatic burgundy, or peacock blue. Crusader Sports, colours as Crusader for tank, top panel, toolbox covers, rear chainguards, but finish chrome tank and mudguards, rest black (as 1958 Constellation). Series II 250 Clipper, as Crusader but colour cherry red. 350 Clipper as 1958 but colour cherry red. 350 Bullet and 500 Bullet as Crusader Sports. *Twins* Meteor Minor standard, as 1958, but colour black with cherry red for coloured parts as Crusader Sports. Meteor Minor De Luxe as Crusader. Super Meteor as Crusader. Constellation as Crusader Sports.

1960 *Singles* 350 Clipper, as 1959, but plastic badges and two-tone finish of mist grey for mudguards and tank top, black for lower tank (divided by thin gold line) and for rest. Crusader, Crusader Sports, Series II Clipper, 350 and 500 Bullets, as 1959. *Twins* Meteor Minor De Luxe as 1959. Meteor Minor Sports, as 1959 Crusader Sports. Super Meteor and Constellation, as 1959.

1961 *Singles* 350 Clipper, Crusader, Crusader Sports, 350 and 500 Bullets, as 1960. Series II 250 Clipper as 350 Clipper. *Twins* Meteor Minor De Luxe as 1960. Meteor Minor Sports, as 350 Clipper. Super Meteor and Constellation, as 1960, with enlarged rear mudguard in machine colour.

1962 *Singles* Crusader, Series II 250 Clipper, 350 Clipper, new two-tone finish with mudguards and upper portion of petrol tank in Burgundy, lower half of tank (divided by two thin and one thick gold lines) and toolbox covers in cream, rest black. Crusader Sports, 350 and 500 Bullets as 1961, with enlarged rear mudguard in machine colour. Super 5, Marina grey for all cycle parts bar black fork link covers, engine plates and rear number plate mounting, and chrome sides of petrol tank. Red pinstripe around enlarged rear mudguard, tank top panel, and down outer side of front forks and centre line of front mudguard. Mid-year, fork link covers changed to grey, frame to black. *Twins* Meteor Minor De Luxe and Super Meteor, as Crusader etc. Meteor Minor Sports, as Constellation but rear mudguard chromed. Constellation as 1961 but with black for rearside pressings.

1963 *Singles* Series II Clipper 250 as 1962, but upper colour Flame. Crusader Sports as 1962, but colours polychromatic Blaze or Gold. Super 5, New Bullet, as Crusader Sports. Continental, as Crusader Sports but with checker tape on upper fork yokes. *Twins* 500 Sports twin, as Constellation, but in Gold, with polychromatic Blaze option. Constellation, as 1962 but two-tone tank with cream where chrome was, and colour in Flame. Interceptor, chrome tank and mudguards, polychromatic Blaze or Gold tank top panel, toolbox covers, rear chainguard, rest black.

1964 *Singles* Series II Clipper 250 as 1963, New Bullet and Turbo Twin as Series II Clipper 250. Crusader Sports and Continental as 1963 but alternative colour Hi-fi Blue. Turbo Twin Sports, chromed mudguards and chromed petrol tank sides in new shape, outlined in thick outer, thin inner gold lining, colour Flame as Turbo Twin standard. *Twins* Interceptor standard, as 1963 Interceptor but with polychromatic silver mudguards and tank side panels in place of chrome. Interceptor De Luxe, as 1963, with colour option polychromatic blue.

1965 *Singles* Series II 250 Clipper, as 1964. Turbo Twin, tank Flame sides, cream top, divided by gold lining, flame mudguards rear chainguard and toolbox covers. Turbo Twin Sports as 1964. Continental was 1964, but petrol tank with chrome as Turbo Twin Sports, colour White as standard, polychromatic Blaze, Hi-fi Blue as options. Crusader Sports, as 1964, but tank's chrome as on Turbo Twin Sports. Olympic, tank as Turbo Twin Sports but with top painted silver, as was front fork and side panels; polychromatic Blaze or Hi-fi Blue for tank bottom and enlarged rear mudguard. New Bullet as 1964 but colours Cambridge Blue (upper) and White. Continental GT, red tank, mudguards, battery cover piece; frame, upper forks, silver. *Twins* Interceptor as 1964 but colour option of polychromatic Blaze or Hi-fi Blue.

1966 *Singles* Crusader Sports, as 1965, but gold-lined chrome panelling on tank now as for Turbo Twin Sports. Turbo Twin Sports as 1965, but toolbox covers now black. Continental GT as 1965 but all bar tank/mudguards/battery cover piece now black.

1967 *Twins* Interceptor Road Sports, all black bar polished alloy fork heads, chrome headlamp, mudguards, rear suspension unit shrouds, and tank panel with winged plastic badge, on blue painted petrol tank. Road Scrambler as Road Sports but petrol tank all-chrome with red transfers, and chromed springs of rear suspension units exposed.

1968 *Twins* As 1967.

1969 Interceptor Series II as Interceptor Road Sports, but instrument housings now polished alloy not black, and tank chromed with tank transfer 'Royal' in red script, 'Enfield', in black capitals. 'RE' motif on

crankcase picked out in red. Alternative UK 4 gallon tank in red, with plastic badge.
1970 As 1969. Rickman Interceptor Series II, frame bright nickel plated. Headlamp chrome, instrument housings black. Fibreglass tank/seat unit and mudguards, in orange, red, bright blue or green. Side-panels white.

Some approximate modern colour equivalents
Polychromatic Burgundy—Rolls Royce Regal Red or Honda Candy Ruby Red (MCP PY6 or Holts MB1-H35).
Polychromatic Silver-grey—Toyota Flowline Windsor Grey (1662).
Polychromatic Green—Chrysler/Talbot Glade Green Metallic (132).
Polychromatic Grey—BMW Baikal Metallic (042).
Polychromatic Copper Beech—Opel Costa Rica Metallic Brown (420LL).
Polychromatic Peacock Blue—Chrysler/Talbot Blue Palmador (8372/PLX).
Polychromatic Hi-fi Blue—Yamaha Candy Blue (MCP PY14, or Holts MB1-Y8).
Wedgwood Blue—BS2660 7/084 Wedgwood Blue.
Peacock Blue—BS381E 102 Peacock Blue.
Blue (Rickman)—Ford Electric/Monza Blue (U).
Flamboyant Blaze—BL Blaze (16/EMA).
Orange (Rickman)—Ford Vista Orange/Phoenix Orange (V5, V6).
Cherry Red—BL (Triumph) Cherry (22).
Maroon—BL Embassy Maroon (RD21).
Deep Maroon—Volvo Maroon/Wine Red (103).
Red (Rickman & Continental GT)—BL (Triumph) Signal Red (32).
Marina Grey—BL Marine Grey (—).
Blue Grey—Mercedes Blue Grey (+ touch of black) (DB166).
Mist Grey—BL Mist Grey (GR23).
Black—BMW Black (086).
Olive Green—BS381C 220 Olive Green.
Surf Green—Fiat Brilliant Green (374).
Flame Red (Turbo Twin)—Rouge Persan (1346).
These matches are courtesy of the REOC's, Paul Narramore; they are listed with the car maker's serial number, or (for a few) with the British Standard paint colour number, or Holts or MCP number.

Royal Enfield

Publications

The Story of Royal Enfield Motor Cycles by Peter Hartley (Patrick Stephens Ltd).
Royal Enfield—The Postwar Models by Roy Bacon (Osprey).
The Book of the Royal Enfield Singles (1946–62) by W. C. Haycraft (Pitmans) o/p.
The Second Book of the Royal Enfield (Singles, 1958–66) by W. C. Haycraft (Pitmans) o/p.
Royal Enfield Motor Cycles by C. A. E. Booker (C. Arthur Pearson) o/p.
Reproduction factory manuals for Constellation, Series I and Series II Interceptor from L & D Motors (address below).

A good selection of reproduced factory manuals, illustrated spares lists and catalogues from Bruce Main-Smith Ltd, PO Box 20, Leatherhead, Surrey, (Tel: [Leatherhead] 0372 375615)

Spares suppliers and specialists

Gander and Gray, PO Box 58, Romford, Essex (Tel: [Romford] 07008 61383). Mail order, or callers by appointment only.
L & D Motors, Bath Road, Brislington, Bristol (Tel: [Bristol] 0272 770223)
Burton Bike Bits, 152 Princess Street, Burton-on-Trent, Staffs. (Tel: [Burton-on-Trent] 0283 34130)
Bill Thomas Motorcycles, 80A Barnsley Road, Wombwell, S. Yorks. (Tel: [Barnsley] 0226 752309). Staff include Ken Heeley and Tony Lynch, REOC Committee men.
Evesham Motorcycles, Unit 2, Hampton House Industrial Estate, School Road, Hampton, Evesham, Worcs. (Tel: [Evesham] 0386 2937). Importers of Enfield India 350.
Alan Hitchcock's Motorcycles, Long Close, Glasshouse Lane, Hockley Heath, W. Midlands B94 6PZ. Postal only.
Kidderminster Motorcycles, 60–61 Blackwell Street, Kidderminster, Worcs. (Tel: [Kidderminster] 0562 66679).
Roy Bevitt. Moulds to produce Sportsflow fairings. Contact via REOC.
Bob Joyner, Wolverhampton Road, Worley, W. Midlands (Tel: [Birmingham] 021 552 2962),.
Hi-Ton Engineering Ltd, Grange Road, Selly Oak, Birmingham. (Tel: [Birmingham] 021 472 3041). Some Albion gearbox spares.

Owners' CLub

Membership Secretary—Pete Miller, 35 Eisele Close, Bulwell, Nottingham NG6 7BH.

Scott

Scott-Aerco Jigs and Tools Ltd, 2 St Mary's Row, Birmingham 4

Alfred Angas Scott was a Yorkshire designer and engineer of genius who was responsible for a machine that was very different from any other, both in its designer's day and subsequently. Scott owners tend to be different also, having been described with some hyperbole as 'a clan. . . a devoted band of admirers to whom the four stroke cycle is a heresy and the ownership of any other make of machine unthinkable.'

To them the author must apologize, as this section must necessarily be brief. In 1950, the year when our period begins, the original Scott works at Shipley closed down, and the number of machines produced by the new owner of the name from then until 1978 was only around 270. So, though no disrespect is intended, the 'yowling two-stroke' must remain marginal to this work. The same must also apply to the Scott's heir and derivative, the 700S Silk, as although no one can question the enthusiasm and perseverance of its progenitor, George Silk, or the fact that he produced what was in many respects a fine motor cycle, only 140 were made between 1975 and the end of 1979 when production considerations brought the project to a halt.

Alfred Scott's engine was initially developed by him for use in his motor boat and on bicycles, with the first motor cycle built in 1908. The engine was an inclined 180° parallel twin two-stroke. It was water-cooled, initially for the heads only but soon extending to the barrels also and featuring a beautiful and distinctive honeycomb radiator with a cylindrical header tank.

The compact 333 cc engine broke new ground, as a three-port crankcase compression design with deflector pistons. It was also really unusual in having a single large central flywheel running in air between the separate crankcases. This meant a crankshaft with single overhung crankpins set 180° apart on two short shafts, spigoted to the central wheel, in each of the small cases. This provided a comparatively high compression ratio and good gas-charging. It was also a smooth, flexible engine.

But innovation was heaped on innovation, with the machine featuring all-chain drive. This was itself a novelty then, but here doubly novel in coming from the centre, on two chains running from sprockets on each side of the central flywheel, to the expanding-clutch type gear. This two-speed was operated by foot-pedal, another first, as well as the first ever kickstart, and sliding front forks with internal springs in a central unit, the first forerunners of telescopics.

Furthermore the chassis was also completely original, with a wide duplex frame whose straight tubes were carefully triangulated along scientific lines. Most strikingly, the frame was open, like a lady's bicycle, with a barrel-shaped fuel tank attached to the saddle tube. It may have looked curious, but after some early teething troubles, with the engine well down in the frame, the light machine's low centre of gravity assured it stable and secure handling.

It is not hard to see why this revolutionary conveyance, so very different from the heavy, slogging, macho four-stroke singles and V-twins of the day, attracted at first cynicism and then outright resistance. After a Scott had cleaned up at its first major hill-climb, the other manufacturers forced the ACU to handicap water-cooled two-strokes (of which the Scott was the only one) with a capacity formula of 1 to 1.32. This naturally increased the clannish attitude of those who believed in the design, while Scotts continued to win proudly despite the odds.

Alfred Scott had introduced rotary induction valves for 1911, with a cylindrical

Left *The 'Proper Scott' — a 1912 two-speed model.*

Left *1935 Flying Squirrel.*

Below *1949 596cc Flying Squirrel.*

valve that controlled the transfer phase as well as the inlet; and when the handicap was lifted in 1912, a Scott won the TT then and in the following year. 1914 saw the origin, as a glorified works outing, of 'the greatest of all Trials', the Scott Trial in the Yorkshire Dales behind the Saltaire, Shipley factory; a competition against the clock of such deliberate difficulty that aces were made there, and commentators would report with satisfaction how 'the standard of course frightfulness was well maintained'. 1914 also saw Alfred Scott's final redesign, with drip-lubrication adopted, gear-drive for the rotary valves, and the engine put in unit with an eccentrically-mounted gearbox.

After that the designer's talents took him in other directions, such as an in-line beam engine for aircraft, and the Scott Sociable, a three-wheeler once unkindly described as looking 'like a tiny car that had had a very nasty accident', or at the time as 'the Crab', or 'the Mouth Expander', due to the facial expressions it induced in people seeing it for the first time. Scott was still working on this when he died in 1923, at the age of 48. In 1914, however, he had felt that he had gone as far as he could with the motor cycle; and the rightness of his basic formula is underlined by the current long predominance of water-cooled two-stroke twins on the racetrack. Certainly many felt subsequently that there has never been a 'proper Scott' since the open-framed two-speeder.

What replaced it was the Squirrel series, beginning auspiciously in 1922 with a third place in the TT by their top rider Harry Langman. Scotts were popular in the later twenties, with their purple finish tanks, polished nickel-plated radiators, and red cylinder barrels, the characteristic rattle of their clutch plates when withdrawn, and the exhaust note that rose dramatically under hard acceleration from a quiet burble to the legendary high-pitched yowl (though this music was only heard in its pure form on the racers). While never the fastest in a straight line (few would ever top 80 mph), such was their charm that the ace rider Noel Mavrogordato could say at the 1931 Manx Grand Prix 'I would rather lose on a Scott' [than win on a Norton] and proceeded to do the former; and their fine handling and acceleration kept them competitive. But they would never again be at the forefront technically.

Allegiance to the marque, while equalling that afforded to Bugatti cars, like them required plenty of money, as Scotts were always sought-after and expensive. Production was low, reliance on small runs from outside suppliers kept costs up (and quality sometimes dubious) and the firm's financial difficulties were fairly continuous, with the Receiver in residence more than once.

Ownership was also, as marque historian Jeff Clew put it, 'a test of enthusiasm', for as Titch Allen wrote, 'no other machine provided the owner with so many little chores on which to practise his skills and try his patience', and continuous regular attention was absolutely necessary. While the engine itself remained simple and efficient, this was not true of ancillaries like the chain-driven engine-speed magneto, and above all of the Pilgrim duplex total-loss oil pump which replaced the drip-feed lubrication. These were temperamental, and as Allen says, you could adjust their chains to a nicety and their two sight-feed oil pumps until you were cross-eyed, and might or might not be rewarded.

It was said to require a three-year apprenticeship to get on terms with a Scott. One *MCS* correspondent with a post-war model found that in those three years and 30,000 miles, he used five pairs of pistons, two cylinder blocks, one crank, countless big-ends and dozens of plugs, for which Scotts had a great appetite. But he was sufficiently hooked to persevere until all the major problems were overcome, except that of the overhung crankshaft; the rising power output had put this component at risk, and this would remain so until later development.

The engines went to 498 cc and 596 cc (the latter initially intended for sidecar use) in 1925, and went long-stroke in 1928 with dimensions that would remain until the end. Tuned Flying Squirrel versions in 1926 offered the unique but elegant wedge-shaped elongated petrol tank used by the TT machines, which ended the true open-frame layout. First principles began to be lost sight of; the frames were still low and triangulated, but inevitably power increases meant that they had to be heavier ('the Firth Bridge kind of construction', as George Silk would put it) as were the braced front forks. Overall weight began to rise, and with full-width hubs and further frame changes would

Left *Always competitive, this stripped 1952 J.C. Scott special has a purposeful look.*

Below right *The 'Birmingham' Scott takes to the road.*

top 400 lbs kerbside after the war, nearly twice that of the two speeder; while the bigger engine's output remained on the low side, at 30 bhp at 5000 rpm.

Factory output fell sharply after 1930 with the Depression, and never really recovered. The last significant engine development was when the cylinder heads became detachable in 1934. No motor cycles were made during the war, and only around 600 after it. Heavy, under-powered and extremely expensive at £252 (plus an extra fiver for a speedo) for the 596 cc in 1950, when £194 would buy you a Triumph 650 Thunderbird, the Shipley Scott's days were numbered. They had adopted Dowty air forks for 1947, and for 1949, coil ignition, which eliminated the troublesome chain-driven magneto. But in mid-1950 the Saltaire company went into voluntary liquidation and in December it was announced that the name had changed hands and that Scott production would be moving to 2 St Mary's Row, Birmingham, home of the Aerco Jigs and Tools company, whose boss was Matt Holder.

Holder was a silversmith by trade, and a long-time Scott fanatic, who even before the war had produced a number of Scott-engined specials. He had made his money in the war, and latterly by lending money to local councils. While an undoubted eccentric, in whose company a person could end up asking themselves whether it was him or them that were mad, he was in fact a clever man. He was also a hoarder, who drove around in a Morris Minor but had Alvises tucked away: after his death in 1981, caches of Scott and other components turned up in attics and lock-ups all over Birmingham.

Finally, though it should not be forgotten that even with limited resources he did manage to get Scotts back into low volume production, it must be said that he was something of a procrastinator. The machines could be built to customer's specifications—but a good deal of patience was then normally necessary on the part of the customer; and more than one hopeful scheme, such as that for the 350 racer, foundered on the gap between what Holder promised and what he delivered. Also, though his workforce never much exceeded double figures, motor cycle manufacture had to take place in addition to his metal-work enterprises (imitation coachwork, bugles etc) as well as ownership of Ward's Guns. Furthermore, he progressively accumulated the tooling for the Royal Enfield and Velocette concerns as they went under, and later that of Vincent; and with each new enthusiasm, previous schemes, including Scott production, would languish, in favour of a run of Mk VIII cylinder heads or Venom silencers. Yet he strongly resented offers from others to produce anything for which he held the rights.

So it was on a somewhat erratic basis that Scotts continued to be made. A final idiosyncracy was Holder's method of ensuring that the two-strokes only went to suitable owners; though there may be an element of myth to the story, according to Brian Wooley, who collaborated with him at one point, he would not sell a Scott to someone who had not owned one before!

Though the machines continued to be catalogued from 1950 onwards, the few that were sold were rigid models from the stock of complete bikes which Holder had acquired with the spares, name and tooling (a package said to have cost him about £10,000). He had apparently intended continuing production at the Shipley works, but when the latter had been taken over by Hepworth and Grandage, the piston makers, for work in connection with the Korean War, he had perforce to use the converted eighteenth century dwelling in St. Mary's Row. It took time both to move everything there, and to obtain the necessary craftsmen, who included Harry Longman as development engineer, as well as Holder's partner Bill Read. Over the next years five prototypes were constructed, trying out various ideas, until in June 1956 the 'Birmingham' or 'Red' Scotts (the latter because of their optional Maroon finish) were announced as in production.

Those Flying Squirrels had a new swinging-arm frame, big brakes, a new tank shape and, like the last Shipley Scotts, the internals of their Dowty forks converted to springs. A rigid version was available, £23 cheaper than the Springer. Though previously a 498 cc version had been spoken of, they were initially available only as 596 cc, and almost every one built from then on was to be of that capacity. Holder largely left the engine alone, and the only other major change was to electrics by crankshaft-mounted alternator for 1958. Production was erratic and when it happened, rushed, not only for the reasons outlined above, but because, according to a source once close to him, Holder would hurry through bulk production of, say, 100 gearboxes, and then stop, having frightened himself with the expense. The production situation was further complicated in that by then the Scott concern had two official depots, Geoff Milnes at 74 Dewsbury Road in Leeds (where Harry Langman now also worked) and Murphy Motors at 54 Common Road in Sutton, Surrey; and some machines were also built up on both these premises.

There were other diversions in the form of a projected new model, the 500 Swift, announced in 1958; this was on the same general lines as the other Scott twins, but extensively redesigned internally, including the use of flat top pistons, and the three port system going over to loop scavenging with side transfer ports. Six prototype Swifts were built, but there the project stopped.

Then in 1963 a prototype 344 cc road bike, castings for which had come from Shipley, was built up by Holder and Bill Read with the aid of Bantam components to become the basis of an air-cooled road racer. Top tuner Hermann Meier was initially enthusiastic and involved for a while, but the man mainly responsible for the engine's development was Brian Wooley, who now works for *Classic Bike* magazine. Wooley secured the services of Brian Bulmer to do the cycle parts and Barry Scully as his rider, and the bike became very quick, and had great potential. But limited resources and the procrastination factor took their toll—items like pistons were promised but took a long time to materialize—and after Wooley pulled out in mid-1965, this project too foundered, as did a 498 cc roadster developed from it and described in prototype form in 1969. During that year Aerco moved from an interim location at Carver Street to 558 Bromford Lane, Birmingham 8, where production trickled on, very much to special order only. In 1971, south-west London car and bike restoration specialist Mike Berry planned his own limited production of 'new' Scotts, but the scheme was halted through lack of components, probably due to Holder's jealous attitude to his charges.

The last Birmingham Scott was built in 1978 (though spares continued to be produced spasmodically after that) and Holder would tell the story of it amusingly at his own expense. It seems that he was pursued persistently by an old party of about 70, who with a catch in his throat and tears in his eyes would tell how he had desperately wanted a Scott all his life. At length Holder reluctantly agreed to build one for him: the price by then had risen to £1,500, and the old man's querulous tone now changed to moans about the cost, which Holder eventually dropped a little. Imagine his feelings when shortly after the bike had been delivered to the customer, Holder saw it for sale in *Motor Sport* as 'the last Scott'—for £2,500!

Scott: The 596 cc Flying Squirrel

The paradox of the large post-war Scott roadsters was that despite being a two-stroke twin, and despite the marque's previous reputation in sprints and road-racing, these were comparatively low-revving engines (a 5,000 rpm limit being laughable in today's terms) with good torque and a smooth, relaxed feel about them. Their real suitability was for backroads touring.

The factory had adopted the Dowty Oleomatic air-sprung front fork for 1947, described in the Panther section (see p.40). They also fitted, in addition to an 8 in rear brake, 6 in dual front brakes in full-width hubs operating through a self-compensating balance box, though these proved disappointing in action. Then for 1949, as well as a roll-on stand and a qd rear mudguard, coil ignition was adopted, eliminating at least one of the mass of chains whirling around in the engine, as well as the engine-speed magneto which had tended to have a short life. The ½ in primary chain between the two crankcases was also now better enclosed, by means of shields and light alloy castings. Starting and slow running were improved, and on the right side in the space where the magdyno had been, a 5 pint oil tank was fitted, as well as an air cleaner for the downdraught Amal carburettor. The dynamo side of things was now taken care of by a new Lucas MC45 'pancake' 6 volt 70 watt dynamo bolted direct to the left-hand crankcase door, taking its drive from the left end of the crankshaft. (These doors in the crankcases were a Scott feature, giving instant access to the wide roller bearings fitted throughout).

The 'Red' 596cc Flying Squirrel.

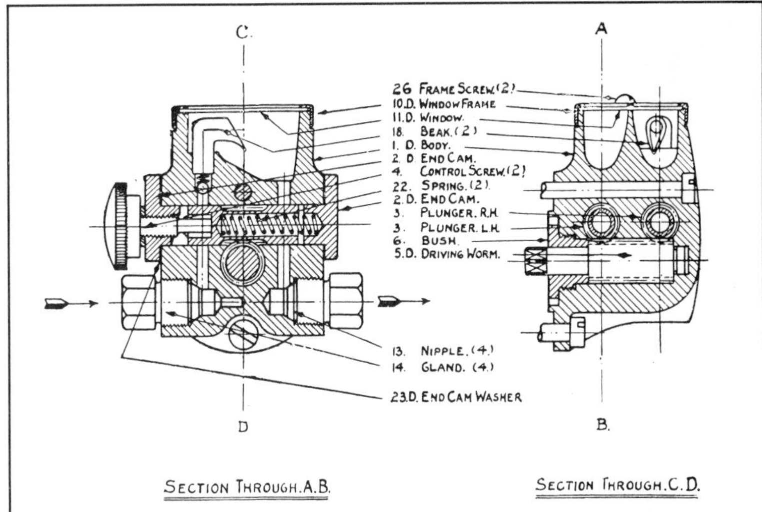

The Pilgrim oil pump, source of much discontent.

On the outside of the right-hand door sat the Pilgrim twin sight-feed oil pump. This had been driven by the right-hand end of the crankshaft, but now a short skew gear was interposed between the driving dog of the crank and the pump, to drive a car-type distributor, incorporating automatic advance and retard, and mounted vertically to the rear of the cylinder on the outside of the crankcase casting.

The Pilgrim pump was undoubtedly the Scott's weakest point. It was said to require resetting by hand before entering and leaving a town; 'two spits and a drip' was the traditional formula, or something like eight to ten drops a minute at tickover. Especially when pulling away in town, Scotts tended to lay smoke anti-socially (though modern oils can improve this, straight SAE 40 being favourite—the Scott does not use self-mixing two-stroke oils). The smoking was augmented by another design feature, a well at the base of each crank chamber, holding enough lubricant to get a rider some five miles if the main oil supply dried up or failed, but meaning that according to some, bumpy going can agitate this reserve oil and cause temporary over-oiling and more smoking; though not all Scott owners agree that this is so.

The 1950 machines got wider D-shaped mudguards with heavier stays, and a 7 in Lucas headlamp which incorporated the lightswitch and ammeter but not the speedometer. The Dowty forks had been altered internally to oil-damped springs giving about 6 in of movement. Only the Flying Squirrel in its rigid frame was offered, with the engine's compression 6.9:1, and the ratios of the three-speed gearbox (which in a four-speed world seemed a little dated) 4.2, 5.5 and 8.9:1; both sidecar and wide gear ratios were alternative options. Capacity of the wedge shaped petrol tank was 3½ gallons, and tyre and wheel sizes 3.25 × 19 in front and 3.50 × 19 in rear. The exhaust was siamezed and led to an uptilted conventional silencer with tail-pipe. A saddle was fitted, and finish was black. Claimed weight was 376 lb dry, average petrol consumption around 65 mpg, output still 30 bhp at 5,000 rpm, and top speed 75–80 mph. Then came liquidation and limbo until 1956.

The Birmingham Scotts came with the same engine, gear ratios and all, in an all-welded swinging-arm duplex cradle frame. This had no triangulation and no straight tubes, but still carried the engine's weight down low, and provided good handling. A comfortable Lycett stepped dual seat with mattress-type internal springing was provided, as was a new 3¾ gallon petrol tank, more conventionally shaped but still distinctively angled forward. Overall, vintage expert Titch Allen felt that Aerco had made a good job of the restyling as 'it still had the unique look of the Scott', and satisfied enthusiasts without upsetting traditionalists too much. There was a weight penalty

Miller headlamp fitted on Birmingham Scott.

though, with dry weight for the springer up to 395 lb. Curiously the rigid version offered of this new frame weighed even more, at 406 lb.

Details included mudguards and side-panels from BSA, and a Miller headlamp shell now incorporating the Smith's speedometer. At the front the same modified Scott forks were fitted, while the rear units were initially Armstrong but later could be Girlings. The brakes had been improved front and rear, with the dual front brakes now of 7 in diameter and with the previous compensator box replaced by a simple handlebar device to ensure an even pull; while the 8 in rear brake's width was increased to 1⅜ in. These were powerful and effective stoppers.

The oil compartment now stretched all the way across the frame and was increased in capacity by a pint to ¾ gallon. The crankcase and cylinder head were now die-cast, with a claimed increase in water capacity due to improved passages, and hence better cooling. There was a new forged steel centre-stand. The price still sorted out the wheat from the chaff; £298 for the spring-frame version, when a 650 Triumph T110 was £265.

The only subsequent major development came for 1958, with the adoption of a crankshaft-mounted alternator, which was of larger diameter than the dynamo, but, mounted in the same place, on the left-hand end of the crankshaft, in a protuberant housing attached by three nuts and bearing the Scott name. In conjunction with the brake pedal, this left insufficient room on the footrest for a large boot, and the rider's foot had to stick out at a 45° angle.

On the road the springer Flying Squirrel was undoubtedly heavy and somewhat underpowered, a trait emphasized by the three-speed gearbox. Though changes were smooth enough, there was a big gap between first and second and a rather high top gear; and since the engine had to be wound up to really go, this reduced the already limited performance, as well as encouraging a reluctance to use the massive gear pedal. The customary harmless Scott foible of rattling plates when the clutch was withdrawn stayed in place, and the way the engine hunted when stationary was also distinctive. Starting was easy with the carburettor flooded and the throttle held open. Modern NGK BFES plugs help cut down the Scott appetite for them.

The Flying Squirrel cruised well and tirelessly up to 65 mph, and liked long journeys on the open road rather than stop-go motoring and towns. Brakes were first class and the dead-steady chassis allowed almost any bend to be taken in top as fast as the machine would go, with the centre stand grounding easily. The Burgess glasswool lined silencer gave a pleasant, organ-pipe type of note, until the temptation became unbearable and the power-step that lay on the far side of 70 mph was explored: the sudden howl that ensued was part and parcel of the Scott magic, but such treatment did engine life no good at all. The maximum catastrophe centred around that overstressed crank: the journal is too small, and if abused is prone to fatigue, crack and finally shear.

Today the clan is intact in the shape of the Scott Owners' Club, membership of which is pretty obligatory if you become involved with these charismatic if exasperating machines. Aerco survives and releases existing stocks of spares via S. Pearce and Son in Bridgnorth, but the Club has a spares scheme by subscription that gets parts made up: it is for members only. There are 150 Birmingham Scotts on the registers, so with a springer one would not be alone (the beastly Rasselas suggested that so many Scotts survive because 'nobody has ever kept one running for long enough to wear it out', but that is an obvious calumny).

Expect to spend a lot of money, and not just on the purchase price: the pistons, for instance, are unique, with only two rings, and the entire skirt covered with oil-retaining grooves. A replacement radiator (and they can still be had) today will set you back in excess of £400—and it has to be the authentic, intricate brass honeycomb item with its hundred internal pipes, as according to marque enthusiast Jim Best, this is both more efficient and vibration-resistant than a car radiator. If the Scott radiator boils in traffic and you drive 20 ft, it stops boiling; but those who have substituted a modern car radiator core under those circumstances find out exactly what the difference is. It's just one of the idiosyncracies of involvement with the yowling two-stroke—but once you are involved, it seems that nothing else will do.

Scott: the 596 cc Flying Squirrel—dates and specifications

Production dates

596 cc Flying Squirrel (Shipley post-war)—1946–50
596 cc Flying Squirrel (Birmingham)—1956–78

Specifications
596 cc Flying Squirrel

Capacity, bore and stroke—596 cc (73 × 71.4)
Type of engine—Water-cooled two-stroke twin
Ignition—Coil
Weight—(1950) 375 lb, (1956) 395 lb rear sprung, 406 lb, rigid

A 1961 Birmingham Scott comes up for auction. All Scotts are sought-after.

Engine and Frame numbers

Shipley Scotts	Engine	Frame
1950	DPY 5370	5267
1951	DPY 5420	5322

Shipley-manufactured components, purchased when Aerco took over the original stock, were assembled into completed engines (commencing prefix DPY 5427) and were fitted into Birmingham Scotts up to 1959; they have also been sold subsequently, after the death of Matt Holder. (Last recorded Shipley number is DPY 5555.) The following number dating which represents commencing numbers for the year, is approximate only, as there are some inconsistencies and overlapping.

Birmingham Scotts	Engine	Frame
1956/57	DPY 5400 +	
	DMS 1001	S1001
1958	DMS 1090	S1120
1959	DPY 5500 +	
	DMS 1190	S1170
1960	DMS 2020	S1220
1961	—	—
1962	DMS 2090	S1290
1963	—	—
1964	DMS 2125	S1325
1965	DMS 2240	S1350
1978 (ends)	DMS 2279	S1536

Scott: colour schemes

1950 All black and chrome, with petrol tank thick outer, thin inner white lining for tank top and side panels. Cylinder barrels red.
1956-on As 1950 but with optional maroon for petrol and oil tanks, and mudguards.

Scott

Publications

The Scott Motorcycle: the yowling two-stroke by Jeff Clew (Haynes).

Spares

Sam Pearce & Son, Unit No 5, Stanley Lane Bridgnorth, Shropshire WV16 4SF.
Ken Lack, 5 Norton Lees Square, Sheffield, S. Yorks. Engine/gearbox overhauls and rebuilds.

Owners' club

Scott Owners' Club, Membership Secretary, Shirley Cumming, 22 Brendon Avenue, Chamberlain Road, Hull, S. Humberside.

Silk

Silk Engineering, Boar's Head Mill, Darley Abbey, Derby

The story of Silk is intimately connected with that of the previous marque, so the two sections should be read together.

From the time George Silk left school in 1958, he worked as an apprentice for five years with Scott specialist Tom Ward of Derby, who had known and worked at Shipley in the tool room with Alfred Scott himself. Soon Silk, whose father became treasurer of the Scott Owners' Club, began developing ideas for improving Scotts. These were effective: by 1969 his much-modified vintage racer, stretched to 620 cc capacity, clocked 102.3 mph on the Darley Moor circuit, with its owner in the saddle. This was no fluke because Ivan Rhodes rode the bike in the next race, clocking 101.4 mph.

At the job he had after working for Ward, he infected his new boss, Saab specialist Alan Cotterell with his own love of Scotts: so when working in that firm's precision engineering department, Silk was allowed to use the company's equipment to work on his ideas. Here, too, in a car engine project, he got to know aircraft industry man David Midgelow, whose experience of gas-flowing and other skills soon proved useful—he became Silk's designer. Then towards the end of the sixties George went into partnership with Maurice Patey to from Silk Engineering, marketing their own special parts at the same time as working on the overhaul and repair of Scotts at the rear of Tom Ward's premises.

The vintage racing involvement focused George's mind wonderfully on the weak points of the Scott layout, which race stresses revealed, and thence to the building of modified Scott-powered specials for Clubman racing. But to his credit, racing involvement did not turn him power-happy, or make him lose sight of the Scott big two-stroke twin virtues, the ideal of a flexible engine with good fuel consumption, and the advantages of lightness and good handling.

Crank failure was one of the obvious pitfalls; at first Silk could only fractionally increase web-width at stressed areas and have the cranks cold rolled, but it led him to contemplate a redesign of his own. Distortion and seizure of the deflector-type pistons was another. He did experiment unsuccessfully with variations in their shape; but rather than going over to flat-top pistons and the loop scavenge system with its thirst, pollution and peakiness, Silk preferred to stay with the deflector pistons with their pronounced rounded ridge running across the crown, and their good economy and bottom end performance. He recognized that previously inferior materials had been their flaw; die-cast Lo-Ex silicon alloy pistons from Hepolite would be his answer, with the pistons ported

to improve the gas flow to the transfer ports.

For further reliability in the area of the main bearings, he redesigned the Scott crankcase cups to accept a standard RLS parallel roller bearing, while the big ends got caged rollers. The old spring-loaded Scott metal-to-metal compression seals were modified to take modern counterparts. Power was raised by reducing crankcase volume by introducing stuffing blocks under the pistons.

But perhaps best of all was a throttle-controlled replacement for the dreaded Pilgrim oil pump. This was a system dubbed DUPU, and still featuring an engine-driven oil pump at the right-hand end of the crankshaft. It was a plunger-type pump with the piston driven by a cam, but there was also a contra-piston in the same cylinder which was controlled by the degree of throttle opening, and this governed the amount of oil drawn into the pump. Oil was force fed to a cylinder gallery and the main bearings: centrifugal force spun it out from there to the big-ends. No matter how small the throttle opening, a positive supply was there at all times. Throttle controlled oiling was already Japanese practice, but had its origins with the Velocette GTP models of the late twenties; in this instance, however, it was derived from a modified Tecalemit aircraft oil-metering pump. Such a system was both long overdue, and effective, for Scotts.

Silk also, despite initial oiling problems, successfully adapted the Velocette Venom four-speed gearbox in unit with the powerplant, by laying the box's internals on their back. The Clubman racing involvement led him to concentrate on lightness, and to seek out a modern chassis for the developed engine. This was provided by another young Derby firm, Bob Stevenson and Stuart Tiller's Spondon Engineering. In the world of erratically-handling Japanese two-stroke racers, their 1970 frame for 125 cc Yamahas was outstanding, a bronze-welded duplex construction of aircraft steel tubing, very strong and rigid especially in the steering head and swinging-arm areas. It featured eccentric rear chain adjustment, and Spondon also made their own forks, similar to Cerriani's but with more substantial stanchions, as well as their own brakes, both twin-leading shoe drums and cast-iron discs using Lockheed components. A scaled-up version of the Yamaha frame, together with forks, hubs and brakes, were supplied for the Silk Scott Specials, leaving George free to concentrate on the motor; 'at Silk Engineering we build engines,' as he would put it.

After an early 500 cc motor, he built one based on a 596 cc Flying Squirrel, opened out to 636 cc; this was getting close to the future production dimensions of 653 cc. Meanwhile the commercial basis for more ambitious things was being laid. Around 1972 George and Maurice Patey moved to the picturesque setting of an old mill on the river Derwent outside the city, where sub-

Right *A 636cc Scott Silk Special from early 1972.*

Left *The next stage. A 1972 Scott Silk Special.*

Left *Next stage again: A 1973 Silk Special.*

Right *A proud George Silk (holding bike) and one of the first of the 700S, in September 1975, outside the mill.*

contract general engineering work supported the motor-bike projects, and let them build up a workforce of around 25 including outworkers. David Midgelow was also very much in the picture as designer. The racer, it was realized, would never be quick enough to be truly competitive, but they did have the makings of a fine roadster. Negotiations began with Matt Holder for production rights to the Scott engine, but not entirely surprisingly, these fell through, and Silk decided to go it alone.

As the story so far will have indicated, George Silk is a personality of boundless enthusiasm and energy, as well as firm opinions on design matters, and he went about turning the dream of a perfected water-cooled two-stroke twin into marketable metal with tireless attention to detail. He and Midgelow had the intelligence to consign their completed work to the well-known two-stroke specialist Dr Gordon Blair of Queen's University, Belfast, and this was not the only resort they had to academic specialists. '[Design talent] is there if you use the universities and they're only too pleased,' said Silk. If Blair's forte was two-stroke porting and especially exhaust systems, Southampton University specialize in silencers and rubber mounting, and Loughborough in tribology, the study of friction and wear between bearing surfaces and the behaviour of oil on them.

The fruit of Blair's computer-assisted work for Silk was the optimizing of both the engine's 76 × 72 mm dimensions, and of a 'velocity contoured' charge/scavenge cycle for the cross-flow system dictated by the use of deflector-top pistons. Silk took out a British patent on the scavenge cycle. With that system there was already less risk of losing a portion of fresh charge down the exhaust port, and thus there was the basis for better fuel consumption. The underside of the cylinder head was designed to match the contour of the deflector piston top, maximizing the squish effect. The exhaust was still siamezed on the offside like a Scott, but the point where the two pipes joined was now located much further back for better gas-flow. The long, slim absorption-type silencer was the fruit of involvement with Southampton University. The end result was a tractable motor capable of speeds in excess of 100 mph, with overall mpg around the 55 mark; good in any modern 650, and remarkable in a two-stroke.

Around twenty Silk Scott Specials had been built by 1975, but the little firm was also capable of lateral thinking in the interests of surviving commercially, and a 1974 *MCN* piece on the third Silk prototype led with 'the fastest lawn-mower in the world'—the engine would be adapted to power large grass-cutters for football pitches etc. In the event, this was never taken up. Other applications for it were also considered, as well as a projected 1,000 cc 'Supersilk' triple variant, a Clubman racing twin with a reed-valve engine, and a 'halved'

330 single called the 'Macsilk' due to its monocoque frame being built by Macdonald Motorcycles of Macclesfield, which by 1979 got achingly close to production. I certainly saw the prototype perform impressively, and the engine would be adapted to power a championship-winning racing Hovercraft!

The 700S Silk did make it into production, and details of it will be found in the next section. Perhaps the most remarkable feature was its lightness: around 70 lb overall for the engine/ gearbox unit. The radiator, based on the Scott's honeycomb (after experiments with one from an LE Velocette) but with modified connections to the cylinder block and head, was said to weigh just 3 lb, and had a total liquid capacity of only ⅝ gallon. The cylinder was much lighter than an air-cooled one could be, and the head even more so, weighing a mere 1½ lb. Compare the overall 70 lb weight with the 130 lb of a 750 Triumph Bonneville, which produced around the same power as the Silk's claimed 47 bhp at 6,000 rpm. In conjunction with the use of fibreglass and light alloy (the 3 gallon version of the alloy petrol tanks, made by Ray Pettit who also did the silencer, was claimed to weigh less than a pound) this produced a claimed all-up dry weigh of 309 lb—which was less than most Japanese 250s then on the market.

Lest this narrative should take on too fairytale a quality, it should be said that the enterprise was beset by problems, and the machine was not without its faults. An early taste of the difficulties involved a three-month delay waiting for the arrival of an American-made Morse chain for the primary drive (gears had been rejected on the grounds of expense and noise). When it did arrive, the inverted-tooth chain, claimed to be self-adjusting, made the bike virtually unridable below 2,000 rpm, was noisy at low revs and caused violent snatch when changing down for corners; it was abandoned in favour of a duplex Renold chain. Unsuccessful experiments with an electric start system took up a further three months. But by late 1975 the show was on the road, at a cost of around £1,350—£650 less than a BMW R90S, but £500 more than that year's 750 Bonneville.

Some of the bike's early faults were the teething troubles inevitable with a new model, some were more serious, and a final one was more a limitation than a flaw. The

early styling was a little stuck-together, particularly at the front where the Lucas switchgear in an early instrument cowl struck an archaic note at odds with the Kawasaki-like tail-compartment, which itself was not perfectly integrated in appearance with the standard Lucas tail-light; a small concern could not afford to have its own ancillaries like lights designed for it. But there was never any undue impression of bulk from the polished radiator, while both ends were tidied up before long, and styling for the Mk IIs was commendably unified. Meanwhile any weakness in that department was compensated for by rider points, like the use of MZ bellows to protect the rear chain, and the beaky spats protecting the disc brake from the wet. Silk's questing intelligence also led him to develop a heated fairing, which he patented. There were some fiddles, such as the kickstart's forward operation, and the necessity of removing the lockable left-hand side-panel to turn the petrol on or to go to reserve (though the latter was later remedied). But on more important points such as the horizontally-split crankcase, the efficient Luminition electronic ignition and the quality of the finish, the Silk scored.

Some faults on press test bikes, detailed in the next section, indicated that ownership of this water-cooled two-stroke was still 'a test of enthusiasm'. But in enthusiastic hands it would perform impressively. In 1977 Hayden Rees, a Welsh dealer, rode his demo-model 700S, on which he went to work every day, down through France; and after a change to harder plugs, easily won the civilian 750 cc class of the testing Circuit des Pyrénées rally, finding the bike particularly good on the hills.

There could be some serious faults in operation. The single Spanish-made Amal Mk II carburettors were known to jam open sometimes, a disconcerting flaw which on at least one occasion sent a Silk owner up the road. Though Amal blamed the engine for this, Silk discovered the answer from speedway riders who had experienced the problem under even hairier circumstances. The cause was the weather, with certain conditions creating a vacuum above the slide. A $^{1}/_{16}$ in hole drilled in the top was the simple solution. More fundamental were problems with that brilliantly light radiator. It achieved its lightness partly by the absence of a thermostat or pump, as it relied on the 'thermosyphon' system, which was science-speak for hot water rising from the engine as it was displaced by cold from the radiator.

George Silk could talk a good fight for the necessity of water-cooling for *all* engines, pointing out the undeniable fact that an engine running at a constant temperature is more efficient thermally, as well as the benefits in terms of clean emissions. He considered that current Japanese offerings were comparatively crude, adding weight to an engine rather than making it lighter, and not (like his) having their water passages 'flowed' as gas passages are, and being narrow, of quite a small section and not deep. But in operation the Silk radiators were not universally efficient: they could boil up, and contribute to partial seizures. At least one owner fitted his own pump and thermostat; and for the extensively revised and restyled 1977 machine, now called the 700S Sabre, the cylinder block and heads were restyled with dummy finning to de-emphasize the Scott origins, and the block was redesigned and a larger radiator fitted, on rubber mountings.

Hopeful developments on the company front highlighted the first of the limitations, which was the fact that the little enterprise was dependent on indifferent large companies for component supplies, at a time when the last of the mainstream industry was crashing (see Vol 3, Norton, p113 on) and its support industry was consequently going to hell. In autumn 1976 Silk Engineering had been taken over by their

A finely finished 1977 Silk 700S Sabre.

largest stockholders, the Furmanite International group, manufacturers of leak-sealing equipment mostly related to the continuous process industries, and based in Kendal. Their chairman, Alan Forsyth, was extremely sympathetic to the motor cycle enterprise, and George Silk could begin to think in terms of less 'bespoke' products catering for individual customers' requirements, and of greater volume production.

This would involve a move to a development area, possibly Kendal, with the Boar's Head works being kept on as a design centre. The Mill's small size had had the advantages of everyone feeling involved, customers having direct contact with the builders and being able to choose particular components from the stores, and deliberate rotation of jobs to keep the work interesting (though there were exceptions, like the man who was expert at making up wiring looms; once Japanese switchgear had been adapted, Silk said he had got the job time down from a day to half an hour!). But the limitations on the tool room skills and atmosphere were tool room prices; competition machinery might command these, but for a roadster the way out was increased production. About thirty bikes had been built in 1976; later Silk would reckon ten a month was the minimum for profitability, while Alan Forsyth would put the figure much higher at 25 a week.

However, for greater production a steady supply of components was necessary. The smaller suppliers, Spondon in particular, and Avon tyres and the wheel builders, never let them down, on price, delivery, or quality. But as Alan Forsyth would put it, 'The manufacturers of electrical components, switch gear, instruments and lighting equipment have caused us nothing but anger and frustration and have thwarted all attempts to build a wholly British motor cycle.' Though leaving them unnamed, he was clearly referring to Lucas and Smiths. One example was the attempt to provide the up-to-date instruments which the high price of the 700S really demanded. Smiths were commissioned to produce a suitable electronic rev-counter, but after long months nothing emerged: the 1979 Mk II bikes fitted Italian Veglia instruments. On the electrical side, anyone familiar with British bikes knows the quality of Lucas switchgear, which Silk had also phased out in favour of Suzuki in 1969: in addition one owner's Zener diode blew several times, and one of the press biker's rectifier mountings snapped, causing it to arc against the body of the carburettor and create a potential fire hazard. These are some examples of what Forsyth was referring to when he spoke of 'the poor quality of their products [and] inadequate inspection'. George Silk would speak of 'problems of supply—bad, poor or none at all' slowing Silk production, which never reached more than seven a month, at a time when a network of twelve dealers had already been established.

There was also the cost of components, which was rather a vicious circle. While production manager Rob Sewell would admit that production methods were often slow and laborious as 'they couldn't afford the time or expense to replace rather outdated equipment. There's a lot of hand-building. . .', he also confirmed that 'parts were expensive, because we were never able to push quantities needed to the level where we could get them cheaper', something that was also being experienced, with the same major suppliers, by the Meriden Co-op. Sometimes, as in the case of the stainless steel control levers which they made themselves, Silk's hand-building was so as not to be held to ransom by suppliers; but that was not possible with electrical gear and instruments, and in my view there is some justice in Alan Forsyth's comments on how the 'total indifference to the needs of the small manufacturer reveals a malaise in the bigger companies which may be the root of many of our international problems. . .'

In the end, despite pegging away at the problems, and restyling and uprating the bike with developments like the move to left-hand shift to keep it competitive, production had to cease late in 1979. It was a chronically bad time for industry as a whole and for the remaining bike producers in particular, with a background of high inflation, and the cost of raw materials, particularly aluminium, soaring; that year Cotton went to the wall, and Triumph experienced a major contraction. The price of the 700S had risen from the original late-1975's to £1,355 to £2,197 in November 1978, to £2,482 by March 1979 with an imminent rise to £3,000 being spoken of. This clearly would not do. The bikes had never been profitable for the company; on Silk's own estimate, which was probably conservative, they were losing £200 on every bike sold at the later prices. This was something the parent company could not permit: the dealer network was terminated in March 1979, and after just twenty more had been made, the last complete machine was produced before Christmas 1979, bringing the total to 138 frames and 140 engines.

Silk Engineering kept their connection with motor cycles, continuing to produce spares for the 700S and to rebuild Scott engines. They also pegged away at the Trials machine, by 1981 reducing the capacity to 250 and putting it in Mk II form into a tubular frame; the cast aluminium swinging arm pivoted on the engine itself, and both UK and USA patents were taken out on the concentric drive for three-shaft motor cycle gearboxes as found on the Trials iron's eight-speed box, with its two levers, one each for the four higher and four lower gears. Work also continued on a 500 cc loop scavenge version of the twin, which was aimed both as a replacement for the 700 motor and for people wanting to put it in a racing frame. In 1981 Silk Engineering did move from the Mill to their present location on an industrial estate in Derby. In 1982 there was an attempt at a rebirth of the motor cycles by Wellingborough businessman Geoff Pedlar of Stainless Steel Systems, a company which had provided components for the 700S, but his attempts to raise the necessary £250,000, partly by offering shares to enthusiasts, did not succeed.

Though one thing might have led to another, the 700S Silk would probably never have been a big seller. The principal reason probably lay with the engine; people's most enthusiastic response to the bike was invariably reserved for the handling and brakes. The second ever bike to roll from Silk Enginering went to American Dave Roper, a classic racer who later won the first Historic TT race for the dedicated US Team Obsolete; he'd heard good reports about Silk and actually ended up working at the factory to help complete the bike, which he then raced (and dropped) scoring some success at Darley Moor before going back to the States and writing it off against a right-turning car. 'It was slow,' he recalls, 'but I could beat Yamaha RD 350s because it handled well and had lots of ground clearance.'

The price was understandably but undeniably high, and it was not a bike that many people would go broke for. It was in a sense never fully developed, and did not have the necessary outright performance, while in some earlier models there was a distinct lack of it; Peter Watson was one unimpressed journalist, and his judgements are usually worth taking seriously. Neither did it have the charisma of a big traditional four-stroke. It had a specialized appeal; many were sold to enthusiasts overseas, with one being crated up in 1979 for fifteen years, as its intended keeper was three years old at the time! It was an undeniably interesting machine, but for most not compulsive.

However this retrospective view should not blind us to either George Silk's enterprise, or the way in which he actively carried on and extended, and indeed continues to extend, a practical body of knowledge. This applied particularly in the fields of valve-controlled induction and of water-cooling, with their benefits in terms of quietness, economy and clean emission, in which his mentor Alfred Scott had shown the way to the world. If there is any future for a British motor cycle industry, it surely lies in such progressive minds and abilities; and last but not least, he and his team should be saluted, in a field long on talk and short on results, for what they actually achieved in the face of very considerable difficulties.

Silk: The 700S

The production Silk's 653 cc engine strongly resembled its Scott predecessors, but differed markedly at its heart. It was still an inclined parallel twin water-cooled two-stroke, but the overhung crakshaft with its small journals and proneness to fatigue had been designed out. The absence on Scotts of outer main bearings had meant that you could replace the big ends in minutes via the crankcase side doors; but it had also allowed the shaft to flex so that the existing bearings themselves needed replacing rather frequently, as Silk well knew from his racing experience.

So while the crankcase doors along with the big central flywheel were still in place, Silk's was a pressed-together crankshaft, still with 180° throws, but carried on four needle rollers, with one on either side of each crank flywheel, plus two extra ballraces for support. One of these was on the nearside, outboard of the crankshaft-mounted alternator, and the other on the offside, between the pickup for the Lumenition electronic ignition and the oil pump. It was the strength of these six bearings which permitted the engine's rev limit to be raised in safety.

The oil pump, which has been described in the previous section, was bolted to the right end of the crankshaft which drove it by worm, and was fitted inside a bolt-on guard, since it protruded; the union with the oil pipe there could be a source for leaks. It circulated oil from an alloy tank holding 3½ pints.

The crankshaft assembly weighed 25 lb, half of the total engine weight. It was counter-balanced, and perfectly matched to the paired Alpha con-rod and piston assemblies (as used on the Greeves Griffon Scrambler) with needle roller big ends and plain little ends, the latter being the only exception to the use of needle rollers throughout the engine. Compression ratio was 8:1 measured from the exhaust port closing. Primary drive was by duplex Renolds chains, one on each side of the central flywheel between the two crankcase compartments.

A single Amal 32 mm Mk II carburettor was fitted to the back of the inlet manifold: the manifold and the transfer passages were bolted to the rear of the cylinder block. The passages were fed through a piston-skirt window, and once in the chambers the pistons' humped crowns deflected the charge to the optimum position. On some but not all of the early bikes the water jackets as well as the engine castings were of polished alloy, not red as on a Scott or the previous Silk Specials. The exhausts were siamezed at a point close to the circular stainless steel silencer.

Bolted to the rear of the horizontally-split alloy cases was the squared-off shape of the gearbox. Internally the components and the ratios of its four speeds were those of the Velocette Venom. They were put together by a dedicated Velo expert on the team, and produced smooth changes once the box had loosened up. The kickstart operated forward, in an awkward manner, and the footrests were folding, to allow it do so. Another major area of redesign of the Scott by Silk had been the clutch, which was of the wet multiplate type, and impressively heavy-duty. It too ran on a massive 90 × 20 mm roller bearing, and it was supported at each side. The six plates used were readily available Triumph ones, which together with the substantial cast-iron pressure plate, finally

Above right *Evolution. One of the very first 1974 Silk own-brand Specials.*

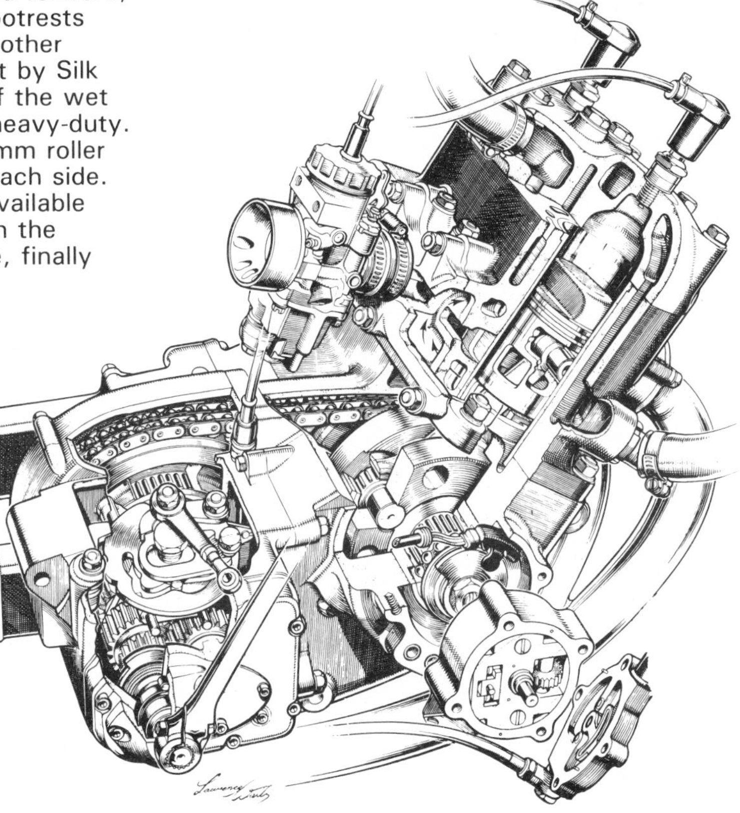

Right *Silk engine explored.*

Left *1975 Silk 700S with flamboyant finish.*

Right *An early 1977 Silk 700S, much revised.*

eliminated the characteristic plate-rattle when the clutch was withdrawn. This device was well up to handling the motor's power and torque, though slightly heavy in operation. Gear change was on the traditional right side, but with a left-hand change available if required.

The overall shape of the engine, gearbox, and radiator with its circular header tank has been compared to a lozenge with a bite taken out of it, and the Spondon duplex frame cradled the shape of the lozenge, holding the engine low down for excellent handling. The frame was heavily triangulated in a way Alfred Scott would have approved of. A general description of the chassis and of the high quality front forks, ungaitered at this stage and with matt black sliders, will be found in the preceding section. Rear suspension was by hydraulically-damped Girlings, sensibly shrouded. The swinging arm's tubes were closed at the rear, due to the snail cam adjustment for the rear chain provided at the eccentrically mounted swinging-arm pivot. The MZ gaiters fitted for the rear chain revealed the designers to be practical motor cyclists. The rear wheel was quickly detachable, one of several further rider points. Another was the engine's simple mountings, meaning that it could be removed from the frame in ten minutes. In the Scott tradition, it was a simple machine to work on.

The standard front brake on these early bikes was a single Spondon cast-iron 10 in disc, with a beak-shaped spat fitted above it to protect it from rain and keep disc-dust from spreading over the wheel. It used Lockheed hydraulic components, and there was the option of an additional disc or a Spondon TLS drum; the rear brake was a 7 in SLS drum, the disc/drum combination being a belt and braces compromise favoured by many at a time when disc performance in the wet was not reliable. Tyres and wheels were 3.50 × 18 in front and rear, with Borrani alloy rims on spoked wheels with stainless steel spokes, and the excellent Avon Roadrunner tyres. Early mudguards were alloy, later changing to fibreglass in the machine colours.

The ultra light alloy Ray Pettit petrol tank could be in either 3 or 4 gallon size; the only irritating point was the necessity of undoing the lockable side-panel, large and wedge-shaped, to turn on the petrol or switch to reserve. The seat, thinly padded and uncomfortable, was virtually for the rider only, and no pillion footrests were fitted. The space behind the seat was filled by a Kawasaki-like fibreglass tail compartment in the machine colours, and the main rests were in a semi-rearset position, usually matched by a semi-straight Vincent-type handlebar to give a riding position that encouraged high-speed cruising.

Finish on the early bikes was flamboyant, with the basic colour white, crossed with bands (on the tank and tailpiece) and wedges (on the side panels) of Scott purple, with thin gold lining just inside their outer rims. The tank badge was in bulbous red lettering outlined in yellow surrounded by white, like a sixties rock poster, and with the Silk name underlined by the shape of a con-rod in red. While well-finished and certainly different, the colours did not really suit either the heir to classic lines, or the machine's target audience of necessarily well-heeled but sporting older enthusiasts.

On some bikes the exhaust, silencer and radiator were not polished but in matt black. All the fasteners were in stainless steel, and everything else metal was polished alloy, including a massive handlebar clamp behind the fibreglass headlamp nacelle. The nacelle shielded the Lucas 7 in quartz-halogen headlamp, and contained the instruments, which did not run to a rev-counter, but included an ammeter, idiot lights and ignition switch.

Easy to start if the engine was kicked over a couple of times before switching on, the Silk's engine and gearbox needed around 3,000 miles before they began to loosen up properly. On the road the bike was a greyhound, light and low with a 28 in seat height, with an excellent power to weight ratio at 309 lb and 47 bhp at 6,000 rpm. It enjoyed a much wider rev range than the average two-stroke, with clean pulling from 1,500-3,000 rpm, the latter representing the peak torque figure as well as around 70 mph in top gear. Real power came from there on up, with the pleasant exhaust note, recognizably two-stroke but more of a baritone than others, going on the rise as top speed rose to around 110 mph, if the engine was a good one. But there was no peakiness, and power delivery at all times was notably smooth and progressive.

This was offset to some extent by the gears. The upper three ratios were close enough to make staying in the power band easy, and provided a nice long-legged feeling going through the gears, with the direct-drive top gear being quite tall. But since there were only four gears, the bottom one, which would take you up to 60, was much less responsive when pulling away than that of the average two-stroke, needing some slipping and the power feeding in smoothly rather than the zip-quick response of a modern multi; and this made the bike hard

work to use in town traffic. Snapping the throttle open at low speeds was not encouraged by the painful engine note and massive induction roar it produced, such roar on a lesser scale being a feature of the engine at all times. Otherwise mechanically it was outstandingly quiet. Progress in traffic was further impeded by an irritating habit of stalling, and the engine also four-stroked at tickover.

Suspension on these early race-bred bikes was hard, front and rear, giving notably good steering and handling but emphasizing the uncomfortable seat. One tester who took over the bike with the three-position Girlings on the top position found that that tyre had been scored by the oil tank top mounting bolt, which poked through the top of the mudguard; this encouraged the use of the hardest setting. (The same *Motorcyclist Illustrated* journalist found that his test hack had one bottom engine bolt loose, and both headsteady bolts gone.)

For the rider vibration only came in as an intensive buzz at very high revs, and otherwise the ride was smooth. But for most the dominant impression was of the bike's capabilities as a supreme scratcher. Wet or muddy roads presented no problems, and the light and ultra-responsive steering made fast twisty roads its preferred venue. Only the folding footrests touched down on tight bends, and there was no tendency for the machine to fall in. An owner writing in

Left *The fine lines of a 1977 Silk 700S Sabre shown off to advantage outside the mill.*

Right *A 1978 700S complete with optional fairing, alloy wheels, double discs.*

Classic Bike found that the precision steering compared favourably with that of a Ducati, with the only limit on the roadholding being the slim width of the machine and its forks. The chassis' agility allowed a change of line halfway through a bend, and encouraged leaving the use of the excellent brakes until later and later. He was not alone in concluding that the chassis out-performed the quite quick engine. Both the riding position and the smoothness also allowed fast touring at unobtrusively high average speeds.

During 1976, thirty or so bikes were produced, and carburettor size was increased from 32 to 34 mm (with some of the instruments being Mikunis) to try and improve tractability and bottom end punch. By September, new pistons, and a restyled petrol tank and deeper dual-seat were being employed, with pillion footrests now being fitted, and then the finalized model for 1977 was announced early in that year, under the title of 700S Sabre. The previously hand-finished alloy casings were now locally produced high-precision castings, the oil-pump too was of die-cast alloy, and to counter the boiling and partial seizure problems sometimes experienced, the cylinder block was revised and the radiator squared off, enlarged and rubber mounted, on mountings similar to those for the petrol tank. The size of the latter was standardized at 4 gallons. The radiator modifications were successful in curing the over-boiling.

For reasons of style and to get away from the Scott origins, the cylinders' water jackets and heads were given dummy ribs of polished alloy against a black background, with the black finish also applied to the gearbox cover. The larger carburettor was now paired with an exhaust pipe diameter enlarged from 1¾ to 2 in for a wider spread of power, and a new 72 decibel silencer tucked even further in for cornering.

At the rear the redesigned transmission housing now included mounting tunnels for the rear chain's gaiters, and there was a new light alloy casting with polished ribs, enclosing the rear wheel sprocket. A forward extension trigger was now fitted, to turn on the reserve petrol supply without having to open the side panel. At the front there was a new, black-painted Lucas headlamp unit, with, as on the Mk III Commandos, the ignition key, main beam switch, idiot lights, speedometer and ammeter separate on a rubber mounted console, with a conspicuous blank where the rev-counter they were waiting in vain for Smiths to develop would have been. At the rear the tail-lamp was now more stylishly blended with the rear compartment. This, like the glassfibre side-panels, seat-base and oil tank were by now made from new high-definition moulds, and looked it. The front forks were gaitered, and rather more sober colour schemes had been adopted, in metallic green, blue or Monza red, soon supplemented by classic black, and all with revised double pin-striping in gold. There was also a silver-grey option offered with blue lining. The old tank transfer had been replaced with a more angular black and gold diamond-shaped one, and for some machines a '700S' transfer for the side-panels.

Claimed power was up to 48 bhp, and altogether this was a much more handsome and suitable package. It was offered with a number of optional extras; a top fairing, clock and temperature gauge, as well as bronze Campagnola mag-alloy wheels, with at the front either the extra disc or a hydroconical brake, a triple pad conical brake drum, said to have the advantages of a disc. The bike could also be supplied in SPR production racing form, with a race fairing, and the engine in 'stage one' tune, if required. Four of these were built.

During 1978 the game changed again, so that by the end of that year when the 100th Silk was produced in November, it was in Mk II form. Going with the market, in mid-1978 this had adopted the previously optional left-hand shift as standard, and likewise standardized ARE die-cast alloy wheels, and the double disc front brake set-up, for all machines. The suspension had come in for some attention, with entirely new internal damping for the Spondon fork, and Girling gas shocks with exposed springs at the rear, a combination which provided a notably softer ride. There was slightly raised compression to 8.5:1, alterations to the porting, another increase in carburettor size to a 38 mm Amal Mk II, together with timing altered to less advance (another aid to smoothness) on a Lumenition system changed from the previous Mk 12 specification to an L16 set-up specifically tailored for Silk.

All this produced a claimed power increase to 54 bhp at 6,000 rpm, yet made for a more tractable machine that was said to be faster than its predecessors. The gearbox too had been modified, and a revised sprocket layout allowed the choice of 16, 17 or 18-tooth sprockets, as well as simplifying the job of threading the chains through the enclosure tunnels, a famous chore since Scott days. A grab-rail was fitted, fresh colours were also available, and now the handlebars were mildly raised and mounted in a new top yoke that brought them further rearward. In front of them were fixed a paired Veglia speedometer and rev-counter—Silk had got tired of waiting.

Titch Allen had tested the first Silk three years previously, and now found the 100th one a revelation, and a machine with a completely different feel, more docile, effortless, comfortable, and refined. He had assumed that the previous hard shocks and forks were the necessary price for the early bike's superb handling, so was surprised and delighted to find both the ride much softer and the handling even better. He did note that the kickstart/folding footrest set-up was as awkward as ever—the promised sickle-shaped kickstart couldn't be made to work; but this was balanced by the fact that tickover was now so reliable that the chances of stalling were greatly reduced. A rider of the old school, he loved the effortlessness and flexibility of the high, direct-drive top gear, and savoured the moment when the dogs locked the mainshaft to the final drive shaft 'and a great peace descended.'

The last twenty machines built during 1979 were to this specification, and that was that. Silks today fetch good but not outrageous money, currently around the £1,500 mark; and the same enthusiasm, together with spares, are on tap from the relocated team that designed and built them. Undoubtedly not for everyone, the light, fine-handling and distinctive 700S should nevertheless always be a valued part of the cavalcade of British motor cycles.

Silk: The 700S—dates and specifications

Production dates
700S—Late 1975–1979

Specifications
700S
Capacity, bore and stroke—653 cc (76 × 72 mm)
Type of engine—Water-cooled two-stroke twin
Ignition—Coil with Lumenition electronic
Weight—(1975) 309 lb (1979) 320 lb

Silk: The 700S—annual development and modifications

(In view of the low numbers produced, the amount of machines modified to customers' particular specifications, and the progressive nature of the introduction of changes, please see the text for details of 700S development and modifications.)

Silk: engine and frame numbers

Please note that production dates are not available but in some cases registration numbers are, which provides an approximate guide line: the P registration suffix represents August 1975-July 1976, R=August 1976-July 1977, S=August 1978-July 1979 and V=August 1979-July 1980:

Frame number	Engine number	Registration number
1	2	*KEC 1N*
2	3	*KVC 351P*
3	4	*KRC 2P*
4	5	*KRC 4P*
5	6	*KRC 1P*
6	7	*KFN 339P*
7	8	*MNN 904P*
8	9	*KRC 3P*
9	10	*MNN 905P*
10	11	*MNN 902P*
11	12	*MNN 901P*
12	14	*MNN 903P*
14	15	*MTO 789P*
15	16	*MTO 781P*
16	18	*NKU 497P*
17	21	*MTO 785P*
18	19	*MTO 786P*
19	20	*MEP 107P*
20	22	*MTO 787P*
21	23	*NKV 549P*
22	24	*NKV 584P*
23	25	Silk Prototype
24	26	*OAU 463P*
25	27	*PHP 482R*
26	28	—
27	29	*35 MAN*
28	30	*PHP 451R*
29	31	*OED 421R*
30	32	*PAU 410R*
31	33	*TBD 870R*
32	34	*PAU 409R*
33	35	*PAU 408R*
34	36	*PAU 407R*
35	37	*RAX 700R*
36	38	Racer
37	39	*PHP 965R*
38	40	*PAU 416R*
39	41	*PAU 415R*
40	42	*PAU 414R*
41	43	*PAU 412R*
42	44	*SDP 115S*
43	45	*UCH 75S*
44	46	*PAU 413R*
45	47	*UCH 71S*
46	48	*UCH 72S*
47	49	*ARA 54T*
48	50	—
49	51	*UCH 74S*
50	52	—
51	53	—
52	54	*UCH 73S*
53	55	*UCH 77S*
54	56	*UCH 76S*
55	57	*ARA 51T*
56	58	—
57	59	—
58	60	*UNB 731S*
59	61	—
60	62	*TAN 705S*
61	63	—

(From here on engine and frame numbers proceed in sequence with engine two figures later than frame throughout; details are therefore only provided of those machines for which registration numbers are available.)

Frame number	Engine number	Registration number
66	68	*XRP 850S*
70	72	*AWK 90T*
74	76	*UCH 78S*
76	78	*UAC 85S*
81	83	*XOH 40T*
84	86	*PFC 72T*
104	106	*ARA 53T*
126	128	*FNY 947V*
129	131	*ARA 58T*
130	132	*FNU 945V*
131	133	*ARA 59T*
133	135	*ARA 57T*
134	136	*FNU 948V*
136	138	*FNU 946V*
138	140	—

Silk: colour schemes

1975/6 Black frame, with tank, side-panels, tail-piece, and later mudguards (early were alloy) white, with coloured bands and wedges on side panels in Scott purple or Black, with thin gold lining just inside their edges.
1977 Black frame, with tank, side-panels, tail-piece and mudguards in metallic Pinewood Green, Neptune Blue, Monza Red or Black, with double gold lining.
Late 1978 As 1977, but colour Moss Green, Monza Red, Black, or White, all with gold lining as previously, or Platinum Grey with blue lining.

Silk
Spares Supplies and Specialists

Silk Engineering, 12 Cranmer Road, Meadows Industrial Estate, Derby. Tel: 0332 [Derby] 44375.

Sun

The Sun Cycle and Fittings Co Ltd, Aston Brook Street, Birmingham 6
Post-war the Sun concern were typical Birmingham manufacturers of bicycles, autocycles and lightweights, with the occasional foray into Villiers-engined competition machinery and a couple of scooters. But it had not always been so.

They had been in business since 1911, and in the early twenties were associated with a rotary disc 'bacon slicer' two-stroke engine which could have been a short-cut to the racing efficiency of modern times except that the company lost interest after modest TT results. They turned instead to JAP and Villiers power, and then with the Depression stopped motor cycle manufacture altogether between 1933 and 1940.

The company was under the long-time ownership of the Parkes family, and occupied a works on Aston Brook Street, which was just round the corner from Norton in Bracebridge Street. Aston Brook itself ran in a culvert through the middle of Sun's machine shop, and on occasion this led to temporary suspension of production due to flood!

The factory's output in the fifties was unexceptional, a utility range of which the 2T-engined Overlander described below was a logical progression. The heavily-panelled 250 shared the line-up for its three-year life span with the 98 cc Villiers-engined Geni scooter; but no one had explained to whoever rubbed the lamp to produce the Geni that spoked wheels really didn't make it on a scooter, and that a pressed steel hump looked faintly obscene between the skirted legs of the lady posed on it to extol the virtues of its optional extra shopping basket. Also nobody explained to the copy-writers that under 'Maintenance', putting just 'The maintenance of the Geni is simplicity itself' and leaving it at that produces a curious feeling of dissatisfaction.

At any rate, Sun was about to set, with motor cycle production ceasing again at the end of 1959. The scooters carried on for another couple of years until the governor Fred Parkes retired after 48 years with the company. The bicycle side went to Raleigh Industries and was moved out, and another of Britain's lightweight manufacturers had bitten the dust.

Sun: The Overlander Twin 250

For 1957 Sun adopted Villiers' new 250 twin two-stroke 2T engine, fitting it into cycle parts identical with their existing Wasp 9E-engined 200 cc single, to form the Overlander.

These cycle parts laid a heavy emphasis on weather protection, with at the sides and back, pressed-steel panels, decorated by three horizontal ribs, which encapsulated the tool and battery boxes and then swept rearward to become the rear mudguard. They were attached directly to the frame, and intended to protect the passenger's legs. At the front it looked as though the designer might have been reading *Hawkman* comics, with a beaky, well-valanced guard coming in to join the pressed-steel fork spats which concealed an Armstrong leading-link front fork.

The absence of stays both there and at the cantilever rear was seized on as a selling point—'no loose mudguard stays'. The swinging-arm rear also used Armstrong dampers. Chrome side-panels were optional extras for its 2¾ gallon tank. Villiers silencers were fitted, and a substantial-looking Dunlopillo-padded seat. At 280 lb, this was quite a heavy lightweight.

The Overlander's 2T engine will be found described fully in the Panther two-stroke section (see p.29). Its crankcase being larger than the 9E's meant a slightly longer wheelbase for its frame, but the same 7 in ground clearance as the Wasp. The 2T was a pleasant engine with quite useful power giving a 70mph top speed, and this fact was belatedly recognized for 1958 by substitution on the Overlander of 6 in brakes front and rear for the Wasp's 5 in jobs on the 19 in wheels. For 1959 the firm's obsession with weather-shielding found further expression as the rear enclosure was extended even more, losing the three ribs but now covering the shock absorbers. 'A very modern all weather motor cycle', they said, not forgetting to add

1958 250 Overlander Twin.

1959 Overlander, even better weather-shielded and not a mud-guard stay in sight.

'with not one mudguard stay to rattle.' But that was its last year.

Sun: dates and specifications

Production dates
Overlander Twin—1957–59

Specifications
Capacity, bore and stroke— 249 cc (50 × 63.5 mm)
Type of engine—Two-stroke twin
Ignition—Flywheel magneto
Weight—(1957) 280 lb

Sun: annual development and modifications

1958
For Overlander Twin
1 6 in brakes adopted front and rear.

1959
For Overlander Twin
2 Rear panelling lost its three styling ribs, and was extended to enclose rear dampers.

Sun: engine and frame numbers

For Overland Twin

	Engines numbered from	Frames numbered from
1957	950A	250 XMC-
1958	950A	250 YMC 42
1959	950A	250 YMC 326
	950A	250 ZMC 99

Sun: Colour schemes

1957: Overlander, all cycle parts Quaker Grey, with tank panels, tool and battery cases in Mushroom. Optional chromed tank panels. Chromed wheel rims.
1958: As 1957 but all cycle parts in Italian Red, with gold lining round shape of tank panel.
1959: as 1958.

Sun

Spares
Meeten and Ward, 360 Kingston Road, Ewell, Surrey (Tel: 01-393 5193), Villiers engine spares.
Alf Snell, 126 Boundary Road, London E17 (Tel: 01-250 5222), Villiers engine spares and service.
Dave Norridge, Brize Norton Road, Minster Lovell, Oxford (Tel: 0993 87613), Villiers engine spares.

Owners' club

The British Two-Stroke Owners' Club, membership secretary: Alan Abrahams, 38 Charles Drive, Cuxton, Nr Rochester, Kent ME2 1DR.

Sunbeam

Sunbeam Cycles Ltd, 48 Armoury Road, Small Heath, Birmingham 11
This one is really a sad story. The post-war Sunbeams represented the biggest manufacturer's first, and in a sense, their only all-new design. Its comparative failure, both technically and in the marketplace, must have had a discouraging effect on further innovation for an already somewhat monolithic and lethargic parent company, and hence for the industry as a whole.

Sunbeam's address for correspondence indicated which that parent company was: though the machines themselves were built at a satellite factory a few miles south in Redditch, soon alongside BSA Bantam engine/gearbox units. Sunbeam had been a highly-respected Wolverhampton-based cycle and motor cycle manufacturer, initially under the leadership of John Marston. The Marston Sunbeams were renowned for the legendary quality of their finish, and in the twenties for a line of highly competitive singles, TT-winners and record-breaking sprinters in the hands of their ace rider George Dance. But the thirties had taken their toll and in late 1936 the two-wheeled side had gone to the big AMC conglomerate in Plumstead, London.

BSA had acquired the Sunbeam name from

AMC in November 1943, and the company title indicates the initial reason: Small Heath had been concerned to get ahead of their competitors, Raleigh, in their other main market, bicycles, so it was only Sunbeam pedal power that passed to Birmingham. However, BSA had already received from the British government captured examples of the Wehrmacht's BMW R75 sidecar outfits. The Small Heath giant lacked a flagship, and reasoned that the proven R75 could form a sound basis for one; and that the Sunbeam name, traditionally identified as 'the gentleman's motor cycle', would be highly appropriate for a new machine whose initial tooling and production costs were going to put it in the upper end of the market.

So while Sunbeam (and BSA) managing director, James Leek, could speak publicly of 'a motor cycle as modern as tomorrow, but built in the famous tradition', and go on to say that 'within these limits the designer can start with a clean sheet of paper and really let himself go', he was in truth only talking about the detailing of the engine, as the concept of the shaft-driven four-stroke, with the gearbox bolted in unit behind it, as well as the wheel, brake and tyre design and sizes, the frame and the running-gear layout, the pancake dynamo in its characteristic protuberant circular housing at the front, and even details like the inverted handlebar levers with their cables inside the 'clean' handlebars, were all originally intended to derive directly from the R75.

The designer whom BSA selected was already working for the group, and had helped develop the successful Scout reconnaissance armoured car. Erling Poppe (the family name was Norwegian) had already been involved in motor cycle production in the twenties with the innovative P and P (Poppe and Packman) concern; this firm had enjoyed a good reputation, until Packman was killed during a fight at the works when a silencer, dislodged from a top shelf, fell on his head and cracked his skull. Erling, whose Coventry family firm of White and Poppe had built the first engines to power the 'Bullnose' Morris cars, then went to work on lorry engine design at Dennis Bros, and bus-building with Bristol

Tramways, before joining the BSA Group.

Because of its ultimate lack of success, it is easy to overlook the positive thinking embodied in Poppe's work. He laid out and saw through an all-alloy overhead-cam engine, the only new British roadster of that type to get into production post-war until the ill-fated Hesketh some 25 years later; and while, almost inevitably, it had its teething troubles, the Sunbeam's major problem was not associated with the engine. He was responsible for a handsome, designed-as-a-whole machine, which incorporated many useful and ingenious features. His motor cycle would provide a quiet and comfortable ride when barking bone-shakers were still the norm. At a time when the notion of neatness was alien to the thinking of the majority of motor cycle engineers (and riders), he oversaw an uncluttered machine with everything possible integrated and out of the weather.

His recent background in four-wheelers naturally led to the pursuit of car-type virtues. But the ideal of a two-wheeled car has always proved an elusive one, and for those who execrate the 'tin boxes', there may appear to be a certain justice in the fact that Poppe's original production motor cycle failed in exactly the areas one might expect from a four-wheel designer turning his hand to two wheels—it was overweight, it didn't handle and it lacked the ability to crack on.

Since so much else came off the BMW, it may have seemed perverse not to lift the flat-twin engine and its shaft-drive also. But BSA felt both that it would be a little too obvious, and that many of the young males of the motor cycling fraternity, currently in uniform, might have developed customer resistance to that engine configuration during A. Hitler's European tour. So while the overall concept of an all-alloy twin-cylinder engine with its crankshaft running on the line of the chassis was retained, Poppe thoroughly redesigned the engine. One source of ideas was an experimental BSA engine from 1928, the 'Line-Ahead Twin' (LAT), which Poppe had installed in his office. The notion of an in-line twin had a solid grounding in automotive practice, gave a very rigid bottom end, and had the appeal of keeping the bike slim; something which the adoption of an overhead cam, rather than pushrod valve gear, also ensured.

There was also the problem of the BMW kickstart, which on the German twins folded out unconventionally and was operated somewhat awkwardly at 90° to the engine. According to the Sunbeam marque's excellent historian Robert Cordon Champ, this was felt to be unacceptable to British riders. It led Poppe to design a new four-speed gearbox with a bevel-gear system to turn the kickstart through 90° and so to its customary position on the right. The new

History. A 1930's Sunbeam single on the island.

Left *The early Sunbeam S7.*

Right *The cause of the trouble: the underslung worm drive.*

box was a solid piece of engineering which would give no problems. However it did mean that the original BMW gearbox was abandoned, and with it their shaft-drive, one of the Bavarian beauty's strongest features; although since the first prototype chassis' rigid rear end was still like that of the German R75 bike, the line on which the drive-shaft emerged was similar to the BMW, being low down on the right side.

But then the shaft itself, with its proven crownwheel and bevel drive, was replaced by what would turn out to be the design's fatal flaw—underslung worm final drive, with the short, slim final driveshaft exposed, and a universal joint at each end. The necessity for this set-up was underlined when the first rigid prototypes had been augmented with plunger rear suspension (very probably also BMW-derived, as works racing machinery was part of the victor's spoils once Germany was occupied). Poppe's early, complex ohc cylinder-head meant a tall engine, and hence a crankshaft emerging substantially lower than on the powerplant of the compact BMWs. This might have been all right with a rigid rear end, but if any form of rear suspension went on full upward travel, the drive-shaft was pointed upwards at an angle dangerous for the previous design's universal joints.

The new design allowed the shaft to flex through as much as 20°, but the phosphor-bronze wheel and hardened steel worm, both mounted on ball-races and enclosed within the alloy cover that doubled as the rear brake-plate, would be the source of even greater trouble. Worm-drive is quiet and durable when rotational speed remains low and the load on it fairly constant, but neither of these conditions would obtain when it was used in a motor cycle. Once again we owe the explanation as to why this unsuitable arrangement was adopted to Robert Cordon Champ. It seems that it was at least partly to suit existing BSA Group production facilities, since the Daimler and Lanchester companies, also part of the Group, had used this form of rear-axle drive for years. The company would pay dear for this production economy, and there had already been an historical precedent to demonstrate the unsuitability of worm-drive for motor cycles. As long ago as 1910, Bob Currie writes, the Wilkinson Sword Company experienced it with their TAC in-line four, and on their later TMC models switched to crownwheel and bevel drive.

This unsuitability soon emerged in 1946, when prototype testing began. The original ohc engine was not the mild creation which was eventually produced for the public. It featured hemispherical combustion chambers with valves at 45° angles, and while the exhausts were always on the right, the prototype's larger carburettor was mounted on the left side, creating a 'cross-flow' head. This engine was good for a machine speed of over 90 mph, but problems quickly followed.

The worm-drive overheated, with its oil when drained turning to liquid gold from the bronze particles as the wheel wore away; they only lasted 5,000 miles. Likewise the handling was alarming, with initially sometimes unmanageable manifestations of torque-reaction, to which motor cycles with shaft drive and in-line crankshaft, not excluding BMWs, are prone. The short-stroke engine's power delivery was abrupt, and if the prototype was gunned or shut down quickly, the bike twitched badly to the right, more than once impelling testers on left-hand

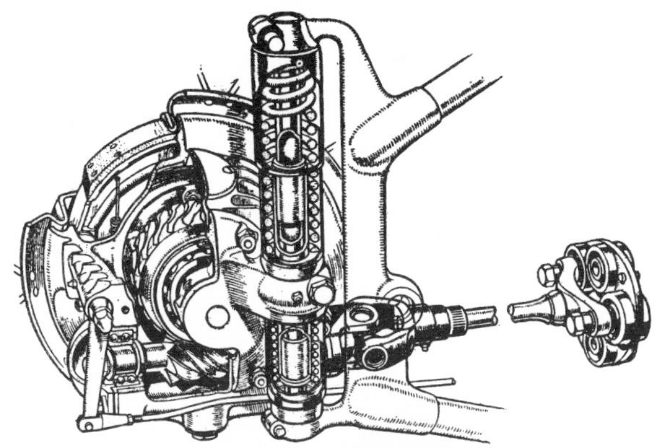

bends to leave the road on the high side.

In addition steering was uncertain, due to BSA's slavish imitation of the BMW's fat tyres, which they got Dunlop to make in 4.75 × 16 in size, block-pattern front and rear, and fitted on interchangeable wheels; it had apparently been forgotten that these were fitted to sidecar, not solo versions of the German bike. The result for the S7 was a machine which an *MCS* writer would describe as looking like 'a nice bit of motor trapped between two ring doughnuts.'

The tyres came in conjunction with Poppe's rather odd design of telescopic forks, with the two legs, their internals of wick-lubricated cotton-wool, being merely sliders: the main spring plus a small rebound spring were located centrally between them in a third, grease-lubricated housing, running down from the top yoke to a bridge-piece which retained the mudguard. These had to be revised after some breakages on test. Tyres and fork together made this a machine with less than hairline steering. Attempts were made to remedy matters by reducing front tyre width a tad to a ribbed-pattern 4.50 × 16 in; but all that really did was lose the chance of using one of the Sunbeam's rider points, the interchangeable front and rear wheels, which had really been another sidecar feature.

A final problem with the 'performance' engine was vibration; this was after all, a 360° parallel twin motor. The shakes were bad enough that even a later, low-powered S7 when turned over by a journalist to Triumph's hard-riding Ernie Nott, was pushed back with the engine dangling in the frame, all its mounting bolts broken by vibration.

These problems taken together led the company to revamp the machine in an unlikely way. Not, as one might have expected, by redesigning the shaft drive and the cycle parts—instead they chose to de-tune the engine by redesigning the cylinder head, and minimize the torque reaction by tilting the engine 3° backward in the frame. The latter measure was effective, and journalist Bruce Main-Smith would dismiss any further reputation for torque reaction problems on the model as 'old wives' tales'.

The head was recast to a 'squish' format, with valves now set at 22.5° and working in wedge-shaped combustion chambers. The operation of the overhead cam was simplified, and the inlet tract shifted to the right side of the head, so that the valves were now in-line, with inlet size and that of the carburettor reduced to a minimal 15/16 in. All this cut output to 23.6 bhp (a factory figure obtained by Champ, though the claimed figure on the production S7 was 25 bhp at 5,800 rpm). While the performance reduction minimized the handling problems and reduced wear on the worm-drive, it left the heavy machines (435 lb dry for the S7—the same as a 750 cc Norton Commando) severely underpowered, which is what they would remain for the rest of their lives.

The problem of vibration remained, but BSA swept it aside, as by now they were in a hurry. As far back as November 1944 an advert in *The Motor Cycle* had announced that 'The Sunbeam post-war programme is settled! Everything is ready! Planned. Agreed. Finalized. . .' Then there had been a somewhat contradictory release in June 1945 with an outline of the model and 'The Sunbeam Forum' inviting riders to let the company know the details they really wanted on the machines. In March 1946 *Motor Cycling* carried a description of the (already-abandoned) rigid prototype, test-ridden by Sunbeam legend George Dance. (The veteran was reported as returning, wreathed in smiles, with the comment 'It's *champion*' Robert Cordon Champ later ascertained from Dance what his actual comment on the prototype had been: though equally succint, it had not been nearly so complimentary.) But still nothing emerged for production until the end of that year, and with all the delay BSA were justifiably fearful that public interest was waning.

So in December 1946, an advance batch of production S7s was sent out to South

Africa to provide the Pretoria Police's escort for a visit by King George VI. They never saw that duty, however, being promptly returned as unridable, due to vibration. The factory, however, rallied quickly and effectively by rubber-mounting the engine, though on front and rear mountings which were rather crudely welded on the frame, plus snubbers to limit side-to-side movement, and with a tubular frame cross-loop inserted to preserve rigidity.

Details will be found later, but the effect was much as on the Norton Commando, with low-speed shakes when the engine was at rest, but rapidly smoothing out to give a notably vibration-free ride above 30 mph, a big part of the machine's overall comfort package. One flaw was the Flash Gordon-looking flexible joint between the exhaust and silencer, to stop the latter being shaken loose; it remained a prime point for wear and corrosion until the end.

Poppe had not been included in this work, which was done under BSA's David Munro. The company had been understandably dissatisfied with the original designer's results by now, and in the abrupt BSA way he had been given fifteen minutes to clear his desk and was then cast into the outer darkness: he subsequently went to work for Douglas in Bristol.

S7 production began slowly in 1947, and was matched by slow sales. For not only was there the shock of the new for customers in the ration-ridden post-war Age of Austerity; but 'The world's most magnificent motor cycle', as it was later billed, at £222 was at that time one of the three most expensive models on the market. There was plenty of theoretical interest; as Bert Hopwood would later write sourly, the Sunbeam 'was lauded by many cranks whose writings on the subject practically filled the gossip columns of the technical press, [but] none of these admirers were anxious to own one of these wonders. Very few were sold.'

Customer resistance hovered around legitimate points such as excessive weight, a low top speed (75 mph in a 1948 test), the absence of ground clearance (at 4½ in), poor brakes, the rather justified distrust of the massive tyres in terms of handling, especially in the wet, and the fuel economy which at 53 mpg overall sounds reasonable enough today, but less so in those rationed, pool fuel days when conventional 500 singles returned well over 70 to the gallon.

The model also developed a reputation for mechanical unreliability. Partly this was down to the design, with its inadequate 3-pint oil sump which could lead to overheating. It was aggravated by a tendency for oil to collect in the cylinder-head casting walls and, if the sump level dropped, mains could be starved and lead to bearing failure if high speeds were attempted. Another fault involved the pressed-in cylinder liners, which were often a poor fit, and cracked. Plugs oiled up and with only one oil ring per piston, oil consumption was high. Pistons overheated and clutch centre rubbers gave way (and were deleted as a consequence), the engine rubber mounts disintegrated, as did the cam and the rockers. A further complication sprang from a danger with any new design, as dealers' mechanics were often unfamiliar with the complications of setting up an ohc motor.

Then there was the bike's look. Overall the S7's appearance had certainly got away from the BMW. In broad outline it now resembled, rather superbly, the Yankee Harleys and Indians which the British had seen in Service

Nearside view of early type (1948) S7.

S7's quickly-detachable jam doughnut.

guise around the US bases. Fat tyres, bobbed fenders, the pan saddle with its patent adjustable cantilever springing, the wideish bars, the carburettor and air cleaner behind a tear-drop shield, even the flat, rather loud exhaust note, all related to the American Dream. Looking like a potential mount for lantern-jawed US motor cycle cops like Zip Nolan in *The Lion* comic did have its appeal; but unfortunately Yank bikes had an unshakable reputation on this side of the pond for 'hinged-in-the-middle' handling.

Only some 2,000 of the early S7s were made before March 1949, when the Redditch works with the development department under the direction of R. Harrison and still with the assistance of BSA's David Munro, attempted to turn around the model's fortunes with a last major redesign. A new and lighter 'Sports' version, the S8, was introduced, and many of the changes it incorporated were embodied two months later in the remaining heavier model, which from then on was titled the S7 De Luxe.

The engine was given an enlarged 4 pint oil sump, and the castings for it and the gearbox were revised so that the rubber-mounting lugs were not integral. The cylinder liners became a loose fit, and the head and gearbox stud mountings were changed, as were the oilways. A second scraper ring, positioned beneath the gudgeon pin, was fitted on the pistons to combat the problems of oil retention in the walls of the head; and the rear drive housing was fitted with a drain plug. The old and new engines were not interchangeable except as complete engine/gearbox units, suitably modified. Engine reliability increased considerably as a result of the changes, and Sunbeams driven suitably could see 100,000 miles without major attention, or even a rebore.

The differences between the S7 De Luxe and the S8, which was 30 lb lighter, will be detailed in the next section, but the suspension of both gained from the adoption of the Val Page-designed BSA/Ariel pattern hydraulically-damped front fork, for the S8 naked and unashamed, and with the BSA twin's 7 in front brake (with half an inch added to either side of the brake-hub to go with the wider yokes) and narrow-section wheels; but on the S7 De Luxe with its internals in wider set legs beneath the previous Sunbeam shrouds, and with the old 8 in brakes and fat tyres intact. The S8 had an inch more ground clearance, was about 5 mph quicker and put out a claimed 26 bhp at 5,800 rpm, the difference possibly being due to its minimally-baffled cast-aluminium silencer with an 'energetic' exhaust note, as well as to a slight rise in compression.

Production pushed ahead with these models, and their arrival was celebrated by the BSA Sunbeam's solitary triumph, with one-legged Trials sidecar ace Harold Taylor taking a Gold in the 1949 ISDT (though as Champ reveals, in the course of the competition the rear drive had had to be surreptitiously changed, three times!). Further publicity had been attempted by the presentation of an S7 to Field-Marshal Montgomery (a non-motor cyclist) at the 1948 Show, but this nearly backfired when

Left *G.G. Savage looks on again as 10,000th Sunbeam rolls off the line on 6 December 1951.*

Right *Gentleman player on gentleman's motor cycle. W. Landauer, BBC pianist, collects 1950 S7 De Luxe from Sunbeam sales manager G.G. Savage.*

Far right *Sportier 1953 S8 model.*

the press of onlookers collapsed the stand. By December 1952, the 10,000th 'Beam was rolling off the Redditch line.

The S8, some £25 cheaper, outsold the S7 De Luxe by around three to two. Among those tempted into purchasing one at the time, in his case by the lure of the shaft drive, was classic expert Titch Allen. He found starting easy, the gearchange slick, the clutch and transmission smooth. But for a spirited rider like Allen the crunch came, despite the motor being a high-revving, oversquare unit, when he whacked the throttle open—and nothing happened. 'No guts' was the damning judgement, and his bike was soon sold.

Yet on paper the model was only 2 bhp less powerful than BSA's other 500 twin, the redoubtable A7. Allen guessed that the main source of the performance discrepancy was once again that worm final drive, as after 50 miles of hard going its alloy casing was too hot to touch. 'You cannot heat something up that way without soaking up power,' he correctly observed, as the fast prototype builders had found too; adding that 'I am told that the American tuners who could make anything GO, even side-valves, were defeated by the Sunbeam.'

Titch concluded that it may have been a gentleman's machine, but he was no gentleman. But to me a 'gentleman's motor cycle' is a contradiction in terms anyway. If such a thing existed, it would be the truly 'magnificent' Vincent twins or pre-war Brough Superiors, which when the occasion demanded could use their gentleman's effortless superiority to blow everything else into the weeds!

From the late 1952 production peak onwards, the model stagnated, with output falling and development minimal. After-sales service to customers was reputed to be contemptuously brisk; whether or not this was a result of frustration from putting out a flawed machine, it was unforgivable, and once again cost the group dearly. There is some suggestion that Redditch was a pawn in the Dallas-type power games between BSA's down-to-earth MD James Leek, and the group chairman and his wife, Sir Bernard and Lady Docker (see Vol 2, BSA, p 17-18). Certainly several more hopeful-sounding prototype developments were strangled at birth, as was Hele and Hopwood's MC4 250, half an A7, which would have gone out under the Sunbeam name, and very possibly would have revitalized it. One experiment was a 600 cc version intended to redeem the undergunned motor's poor performance when pulling a sidecar, which had been another nail in the sales coffin. A second 600 cc version involved a water-cooled four-cylinder engine developed for use in a BSA light car, but when the car projected foundered on costing grounds, so did the four-pot bike. The most tantalizingly hopeful was the S10, as its rear drive was finally adapted to conventional

shaft-drive, while the motor was again expanded to near 600 cc adapted to a cross-flow head and overhead valves with internals from the trusty BSA A-range twins. The two prototypes built were said to be impressive, but the S10 too fell victim to BSA's internecine struggles.

The S7 and S8 followed it shortly. At the end of 1956 the Dockers were ousted by Jack Sangster and his lieutenant, Triumph's Edward Turner, and in the tightening-up process which immediately followed, Sunbeam twin production ceased forthwith. The lingering presence of unsold new Sunbeams for another two years suggests that it was not before time. Bert Hopwood's final words on the subject confirmed this. 'It would be true to say that [this beautiful but troublesome baby] was a heavy financial burden, mainly because the problems in service were due to fundamental design faults which could not be corrected without starting afresh.'

It really was a sad story, particularly since the S10 appeared to show that the fatal flaw could have been developed out, given the will. That other improvements were possible was demonstrated by a Japanese copy, the 250 cc TW Liner from Kitagawa Automobiles; it was introduced for 1954 very much in the S7 mould, but by 1958, as the TW III, featured swinging-arm suspension. The pity was that since 1949 Britain herself had been producing a modestly successful model with its drive-shaft in a swinging-arm, in the shape of the Velocette LE.

But enough of might-have-beens. What remains of the 15,000 or so S models produced is, within its limits, a well-engineered luxury tourer, stylish, quiet and comfortable, the S7 in particular delightfully easy on the eye, capable of reliable commuting in suitably restrained hands, always the centre of attention, and a refuge for those who like to 'do different'.

The last Sunbeam I saw was a metallic grey S8 in the thick of London traffic, ridden by a thin young figure in a crumpled tropical suit, sandals and designer stubble, smoking a Gauloise, with an elderly pudding basin helmet on his head and a large canvas satchel slung over one shoulder. In the hurly-burly of Tottenham Court road, man and machine appeared equally relaxed. If you possess a similarly unhurried approach to life and the road, these bikes could just be for you.

Sunbeam: The Model S7 De Luxe and S8

Description of the Sunbeam twins' development and of the early S7 (pre-March 1949) will be found in the preceding section, so here we will deal primarily with the 1949-and-later Model S7 De Luxe and the lighter, cheaper and sportier S8, which were

Right *Sunbeam all-alloy engine.*

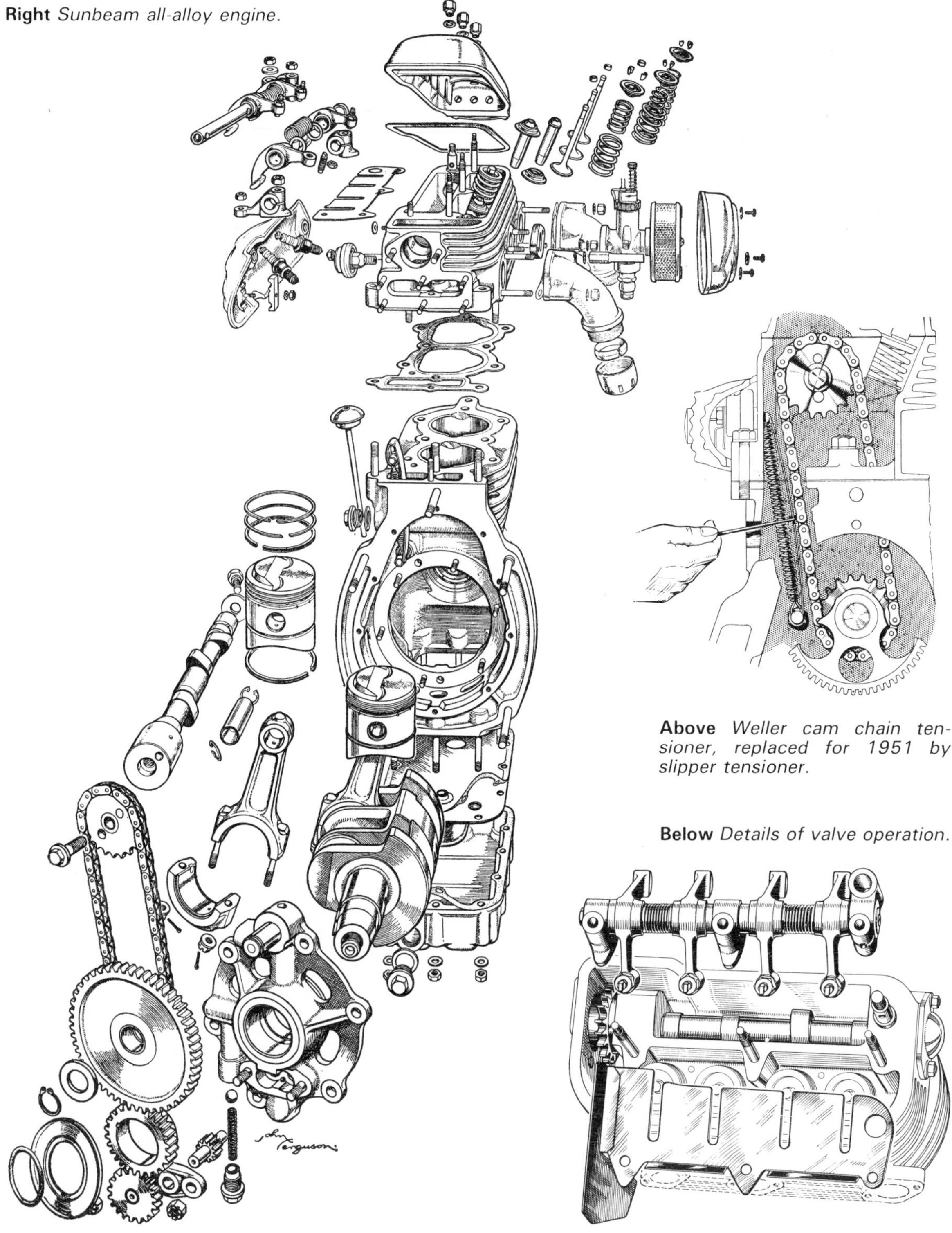

Above *Weller cam chain tensioner, replaced for 1951 by slipper tensioner.*

Below *Details of valve operation.*

identical in terms of their engines, but differed quite markedly as to cycle parts.

'Car-type' is the keyword when considering the Sunbeam power-plant. The use of a unit all-alloy engine with non-detachable cylinders cast en bloc with the crankcase, the gearbox bolted up in unit behind the motor, the wet-sump lubrication with the oil carried in an unstressed compartment bolted on beneath the engine, the coil electrics by pancake dynamo at the front and distributor behind the cylinders, and in a sense, even the overhead cam and the final shaft-drive with its underslung worm—all were derived from four wheel practice.

Also, just as importantly, the same applied to the design philosophy: what was aimed for being quietness, smoothness, neatness, comfort and convenience, the car virtues, rather than the speed and sports potential usually associated with 'cammy' motors.

To consider this unique engine further, the heads of the two in-line cylinders, like the crankcase/cylinder casting, were of alloy, and formed in one rigid unit, with shrunk-in valve seat inserts of austenitic iron. The valves were all 'in-line' on the offside, with the two exhaust parts emerging at flange-faces on the offside, into short bolted-on 'elbow' tubes of alloy (replacing the older S7's heat-prone iron ones). The 'elbows' led to the conventional chromed siamezed exhaust pipes, and were intended to prevent the pipes blueing. The two inlet ports united at a single flange for the small, side-mounted Amal 15/16 in Type 276 DO/3A carburettor, which on these later models was fitted as standard with a Vokes air-cleaner. The tear-drop shield behind which it sat was also revised to give adequate cooling for the carburettor, the later shields being identifiable by three fixing screws and by being painted in the machine's colour rather than the previous alloy finish.

The alloy cylinder head was secured by eleven bolts and studs, with some nuts rather inaccessibly placed between the fins; oil leaks and loss of compression could result if they were not carefully tightened. The overhead camshaft was mounted in the alloy cylinder head block, and ran fore and aft horizontally. It was driven by a single-strand chain, running up through a tunnel at the back of the cylinder block and operated by the timing gear. Initially the cam chain was tensioned by a Weller-type device, which involved a bow-shaped blade of flat spring-steel with its ends pulled together by a coil spring; for 1951 this was replaced by a spring-loaded pivoted slipper tensioner. The cam gear in the head lay readily accessible beneath a cast-aluminium cover secured by three nuts. Between the camshaft itself, on the nearside, and the valves, ran a second shaft with four rockers to work the valves; rocker adjustment was by screwed pin and locknut. The duplex valve springs were light, something which the layout permitted.

Valve angle was a modest 22.5°, and the combustion chambers were wedge-shaped for squish effect. Pistons were of aluminium alloy, and unusual in featuring a second scraper ring, below the fully-floating gudgeon pins, and near the bottom of the skirt. This had been part of the response to the pre-1949 machines' oiling problems. The notably short connecting-rods were also of RR56 light alloy, and helped keep down vibration. Big-ends were split, with car-type detachable steel-backed liners of indium-flashed lead-bronze.

The engine was oversquare with a bore of 70 mm and a 63.5 mm stroke, which in conjunction with the de-tuning at prototype stage had left the paradox of what was, for its time, a high-revving unit with a 6,000 rpm maximum, but a low road speed. One benefit of such short stroke was low piston speed, and consequently low wear; more than one instance was recorded of 100,000 miles being covered by Sunbeams before even a rebore was necessary. The alloy-iron cylinder liners were a loose fit, another revision for 1949. Compression for both S7 De Luxe and S8 was soon standardized at 6.5:1, though both the early S8's 6.8:1 and the export 7.2:1 remained available as options.

The fore-and-aft crankshaft was of Meehanite cast iron, and was inserted into the crankcase from the rear. It was a single-throw one-piece shaft (which use of the split big-ends permitted) with the crank journals separated by a substantial bobweight. It ran at the front on a large (1⅜ in diameter) deep-groove ball bearing, with a spring-loaded oil seal gland to protect the dynamo compartment at the front. This bearing would be replaced by a roller, and the crankshaft end-float revised, for 1954. At the rear the bearing was a 1½ in diameter plain lead-bronze item, and was fitted to a detachable

Left *Sectioned Sunbeam twin engine seen from offside.*

Right *1952 Sunbeam S7 De Luxe in non-standard black livery.*

cast-iron housing bolted on the rear crankcase wall. Behind it lay the timing gear, and the housing also functioned as the body of the gear-type oil pump. The pump was driven by the same half-time pinion (itself driven by a gear pressed and keyed on to the crankshaft) which operated the camshaft drive. The pump required no return side, as gravity took care of that.

Lubrication of the engine began with an extension pipe from the pump to the sump oil compartment, which drew oil up through a filter. Not unnaturally, if the sump level was allowed to drop too low, the pump, especially on bumpy going, would suck air, not oil. If all was well, though, oil was first delivered under pressure from the pump to an annular space surrounding the main bearing, where it divided. One stream went via a hole in the bearing, through the hollow crankshaft and out through radial holes to the big ends, where after lubricating them, and the cylinder walls by splash, it eventually returned to the sump.

The second stream passed up under pressure through vertical passages to the rear of the camshaft, which was also hollow. The oil passed through it to its far end, lubricated its front bearing and then went via a connecting passage into the hollow rocker shaft. It passed back down this, with some lubricant escaping through radial holes into the rocker bearings and through appropriate holes in these bearings, oil was projected on to the point of contact between rocker and cam. (This nevertheless remained a point of wear on the engine; and care had to be taken during a rebuild to position the rockers so that the holes did line up. There was no real provision for this, since the shaft went in a fixed position as it had cutaways for the studs, but after that the rockers had to be fitted as best they could.) After that the oil accumulated in a well below the camshaft, where a special splash plate had been incorporated to prevent too much oil spraying about. It then returned, via passages, down the cam-chain tunnel, to lubricate the timing gear and return to the sump.

The latter compartment was served by a filler cap on the nearside, with an external spring-steel strip bent at right angles, to retain it against crankcase pressure. The cap incorporated a dipstick, but there was still a risk of overfilling, as when it was on its centre-stand the machine was tilted forwards; filling to the top mark there would mean an over-filled sump when it returned to the level, with a consequent revival of the danger of oiling the bore. Also the use of straight SAE 50 is very much advised for the Sunbeam, as multigrades suit it even less

than they do other Brits: and oil must be changed no less than every 2,000 miles.

The oil-pump housing also contained a spring-loaded pressure-relief valve. This was supplemented by an engine-breather at the front of the cambox, which contained three small spring-loaded disc breathers. This engine-breather, which vented to the atmosphere, was less than adequate, and the hot-running Sunbeams proved quite prone to oil-leaks, especially if the sump was overfilled, or speeds of 60 mph-plus were maintained for long. A partial cure exists today in the form of a modified rocker-box front breather cover from Stewart Engineering, consisting of a sealed alloy collector box with a drain, and a big breather pipe routed down from it. But there are still persistent leak spots, such as the timing chain tensioner housing, and the pressure switch for the headlamp-mounted green oil-pressure warning light, which gave some warning if the sump level dropped too low. The switch, located halfway down the nearside of the engine, was mounted on a brass extension from March 1950 on, to prevent it overheating, and this also meant a cutaway on the finned alloy cover which concealed the sparking plugs.

At the rear of the crankcase was the gearbox, with the clutch bell housing forming part of the gearbox shell, and being bolted to the crankcase face by mounting studs which had been revised for the 1949-on bikes. There was a sheet-steel partition between the timing-gear and the clutch chamber, and this partition carried an oil seal to prevent leakage on to the clutch. The combined flywheel and clutch was coupled to the rear end of the crankshaft by taper and large nut. The flywheel was heavy, which contributed to engine smoothness, but permitted the removal of up to 4 lb of metal by those in pursuit of speed!

The clutch was unusual in being the car-type single-plate sort. Power was transmitted to it by two steel plates coupled to the flywheel, and six springs: while the 7 in diameter driven member had two Ferodo rings riveted together to it—one on each side. Today a favourite modification is the fitting of a Borg and Beck car plate, which embodies shock-absorber springs to help prevent the rivets from shearing. If the plate got contaminated by oil, replacement was the only answer; while a sudden increase in free play at the clutch lever indicated another possible calamity, failure of the race on which it ran. The drive to the gearbox was via an internal splined hole in the centre of the driven member, in which the splines on the gearbox mainshaft engaged. Clutch withdrawal was via a rod through the centre of the mainshaft, working on the steel plate nearest to the flywheel. When functioning well, this clutch was smooth and light in operation.

The gearbox too worked well, being a normal design which provided primary drive reduction between mainshaft and layshaft. Any alternative involving greater reduction at the worm drive, had been rejected on the grounds of bulk at the rear wheel. The box was novel, however, in featuring an easily-detached panel, on its nearside behind the toolbox. On the inside of this panel was mounted the selector gear, as well as one of the machine's special features. This was the kickstart quadrant, which by helical gearing, involving phosphor-bronze and steel skew gears coupled by a spring ratchet, turned the pedal operation through 90°. Hence, despite the in-line crankshaft, starting was by the 'normal' right foot backward kick, in line with the machine. The gearbox contained its own two-pint oil supply.

The shaft final drive, located on the offside, began with the 11½ in long chrome-molybdenum steel shaft itself: slim and exposed, this ran rearwards from the gearbox, above and parallel to the rod for the rear brake after it had crossed from the left side of the bike. The shaft ran at approximately half engine speed in top gear. It was coupled to the gearbox layshaft by a flexible, shock-absorbing Layrub universal joint, of synthetic wire-mesh reinforced rubber with bushes Vulcanized into them to take studs on the earlier ones and bolts on the later; the bushes were part of the inserts. This joint coped with deflection from the rear suspension. At the rear of the shaft was a Hardy-Spicer metal joint with needle-roller bearings. This joint was visible and accessible in front of the worm-drive casing, and it took care of bending stresses on the shaft as well as angularity between it and the worm-drive. Possibly stemming from the early troubles with the worm-drive, a myth grew up about the unreliability of the rear joint; but ironically it was actually the front one which could cause trouble. As the machines came on the second-hand market and passed into less gentlemanly hands in the late fifties, under prolonged thrashing the Layrub joint would sometimes distort, rip the centres out of the bolt's bushes, and break off.

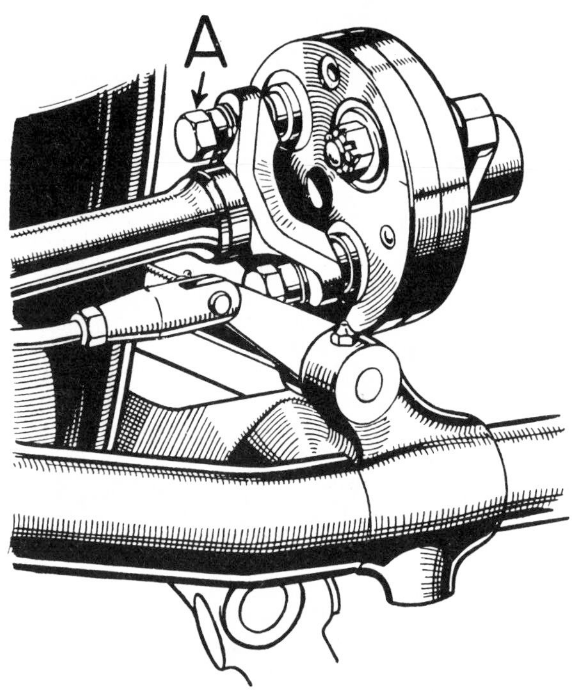

Within the substantial alloy rear hub casing, which doubled as the brake backplate, was housed the underslung steel worm, supported on ball-and-roller journal races. It had an oil seal at its front end, and a domed cap at its rear which bolted to the casing and enclosed the end location. The bronze worm-wheel, which the worm drove from beneath, was concentric with the rear wheel axis, and ran on two large-diameter ball-races.

The worm-wheel in turn drove the rear hub through a coupling, a steel sleeve with a wide, peripherally-serrated flange at each end. These serrations engaged at the sleeve's larger end in internal serrations on the worm-wheel, while at the other end they projected through the inner side of the worm-gear housing to engaage with internal splines in the wheel hub. The worm-drive gave a final reduction of 6 × 23 in standard form, but an alternative worm and wheel set could be supplied for sidecar use, giving a final reduction of 5 × 22 in. About half a pint of heavy gear oil filled the casing, which came equipped with an inspection cover, level plug and (new for the '49-on bikes) a drain plug at the bottom. A certain amount of 'gold' in the oil when drained is apparently no undue cause for alarm, and modern non-hypoy SAE 140 oil has improved the wear situation for the drive, though it still runs hot.

The Sunbeam electrics consisted of a 60 watt Lucas pancake dynamo in a circular protrusion from the front of the crankcase; of a 6 volt battery, coil and regulator concealed in the mid-section boxes; and of a Lucas AC564 distributor, flange-mounted behind the cylinder head and driven by a single dog from the end of the camshaft. The distributor was a car-type item, but by employing a single ignition coil with a contact-breaker connected in series with the primary winding, the system could use a simplified wiring harness and any excess sparking would happen at a time when it had no effect on the engine's running.

The distributor body contained the contact-breaker, the centrifugal automatic advance-retard mechanism (which was prone to wear) and the distributor itself, which ran on one ball-bearing and a bronze bush. It worked well; but today the distributors, though repairable, are unobtainable, and a point to watch when mounting the unit is to correctly locate the driving dog peg into the hole in the camshaft sprocket before tightening, as the alloy mounting flange 'ears' can break off if you fail to do so. The dynamo was mounted directly on the front of the crankshaft, and was a four-brush unit with four coils and a substantial output.

The engine was rubber-mounted in a frame which, like the suspension, was of good quality for its type. The looping chassis was of either Reynolds 531 or similar chrome-molybdenum tubing, a full-cradle item with duplex down-tubes and a single large diameter top tube, and brazed-on steel-stamped lugs. A bracing-piece ran across the front of the down-tubes at the bottom. For the '49-on bikes the rear plunger units and mounting lugs changed their dimensions to the type in use on other BSAs, with revised spring rates giving a claimed 3½ in of movement, and the previous two pairs of mounting lugs replaced by a single large forged-steel bracket on each side. The front forks will be described when detailing the differences between S7 De Luxe and S8.

How did the overall package measure up to the 'car-type' intensions of its makers? The design did score some remarkable successes. All-alloy engines are usually noisy; this one was not, with its short finning and effective quietening ramps for the overhead camshaft, as well as of course the absence of pushrod clatter. Twins with their cylinders in line have been known to run hot on the rear pot, but that was never to be a problem with the Sunbeam. Despite the comparatively light finning on the non-detachable head, though it was still true that the engine ran hot overall, this ceased to be a major problem after the 1949 revision of the lubrication system. The early S7s' 3 pint sump had been replaced by a deeper one with a capacity of about 4 pints, and a box filter projecting downwards, so that the oil pump could draw cooler oil from the lowest level. The worm-drive did get hot, as did the pancake dynamo; but the latter was never a problem, and with modern oils, if the engine is not abused, neither is the former.

As to the other intended aims, neatness was aided by the wet sump set-up, which eliminated all external oil lines. The electrics—battery on the nearside, ignition switch, coil, regulator, and unreadable-to-

Above left *Potential weak spot: Layrub joint at front end of drive shaft.*

Right *Lighter S8 Model for 1950.*

Left *A fine 1957 S7 De Luxe show model — but production had already ceased.*

Right *Detail of the S7's wishbone saddle mounting. The spring in the damper unit is concealed in the frame tube beneath the tank.*

Far right *1949 S7 De Luxe Sunbeam and matching S22/50 sidecar. Sadly, the low-powered bike was not really up to chair work.*

rider ammeter on the offside—were housed out of the weather in their own twin boxes, a concept very far from general in 1949, let alone 1946; while the flat 'lunch-box' compartment for tools, at crankcase level on the nearside, would never come undone as a side-panel commpartment could and scatter its contents down the road.

The ultra-clean black handlebars of the early S7, with its inverted control-levers, left-hand twistgrip headlamp dipper (unreliable in operation) and internal cables, had gone. But the S7 De Luxe's new chromed bars were still notably uncluttered by cables according to the standards of the day.

There was no air-lever and cable, as the spring-loaded choke control (altered from the earlier strangler lever) was down by the carburettor, neatly out of sight behind its teardrop shield. There was no advance-retard control cable either, as that function was taken care of automatically. Those that remained were routed thoughtfully, with the clutch cable being led through a steady slot on the crankcase casting. Only the placing of the horn, which on the early S7 had been symmetrically mounted high up between the front down-tubes, but was now located to the rear of the toolbox by the back mudguard, looked like an afterthought and seemed rather vulnerable.

The 120 mph Smith's speedometer was mounted in the headlamp shell, flanked by two 'idiot' lights for oil pressure and ignition, such lights then usually only being found on cars. This headlamp on the S7 De Luxe, as on its predecessor (but not on the S8) incorporated an integral mounting in its bracket for the road-tax licence, one less thing to bolt on. Even the sparking plugs were concealed behind the finned alloy cover on the nearside. Finally the shaft-drive eliminated the mess of an exposed rear chain. This was a genuinely uncluttered and well-integrated machine, and unusually for then, relatively easy to keep clean.

The engine's quietness has already been mentioned, and smoothness was ensured by the rubber mountings. These consisted firstly of two main pre-set mountings, to deal with low-frequency vibration. The rear one was low down at the back of the gearbox, and the forward one diagonally across from it, high up at the front of the cylinder block, in a mount that was still integral with the block for the 1949-on engines, but changed from the earlier twisted bracket to a parallel bracket which lined up the mounting. (While this was an improvement on the previous arrangement, today oil leaks from directly below these top front engine mountings are a critical point for a potential buyer to check; they can represent a cracked casting, which is expensive and awkward to repair.)

Next, for high-frequency shakes, there was a spring-loaded friction-type head-steady just above the distributor. Finally, to take care of side-to-side motion, the head-steady was combined with an adjustable rubber snubber, which was partnered by a second snubber mounted at the front of the engine beneath the dynamo casing. The clearances of these

snubbers, which could be set by owners, were vital for smooth running, and on the 1949 engines the rubbers had been enlarged. Adjustment was by thread and locknut, with a small bolt securing the two Tufnol (from 1949 on) crankcase inserts on the lower one. The rubbers needed replacing about every 100,000 miles, the bottom one being vulnerable to oil. The only really negative point about the rubber-mounting system was the necessity for the flexible exhaust-to-silencer joint, to prevent the silencer being tugged loose or fractured by the shakes: the joint itself proved vulnerable to rust and corrosion.

Otherwise comfort was further taken care of on the S7 by its patent adjustable saddle, which was replaced for the cheaper S8 by a conventional if long-nosed saddle with a pair of long exposed chromed springs, which are now difficult to obtain. The S7's had its helical spring in a damper unit concealed in the frame top tube, under the petrol tank, with a grease nipple to lubricate it. The saddle was set on a pivot at the front, and supported at the rear by a wishbone, which operated a plunger rod to the sprung damper in the frame tube. Adjustable for height and to three settings to cater for riders of different weights, while undoubtedly comfortable, the sprung saddle could add to a 'pogo' effect on bumpy surfaces induced by the S7's front forks (only damped one way) and plunger rear end. Pillion riders were less well catered for, with a saddle or pillion pad mounted on the rear mudguard being uncomfortable, and even more inclined to propel the passenger up into the air. A dual-seat was the answer there, though these were only offered as a factory option for 1955 on, and can spoil the line of the rear mudguard.

Other rider points were numerous. All controls, including the flat, custom-built footrests, were adjustable. This was particularly valuable for the gear pedal, which due to the location of the box, normally had to slope down quite sharply to be readily accessible to the foot. While for the S7 different section and type tyres (4.50 × 16 in ribbed front, 4.75 × 16 in block pattern rear) negated the use of the interchangeable wheels, at least both were very quickly removable, as were those of the non-interchangeable S8: the only tool necessary to do so in both cases was a tommy bar, and for the S7 a spanner to loosen the pinch bolt. The same went for the rear wheel's pinch bolt and the rear mudguard, while the various boxes were accessible via coin-slot fasteners, had lids with specially designed hinges and were fitted with check-stops. In general few tools were needed to work on the Sunbeam, with the only specialist items called for during a stripdown being a puller for the flywheel and another for the crankshaft gear. Whitworth bolt sizes were used throughout.

The early S7's ratchet centre stand with its variable control for height had gone, but while theoretically beneficial, in practice it had worn quickly, and could let the heavy bike fall once it had done so. For the 1949 bikes it was replaced by a roll-on centre stand, with an additional prop-stand for the S7 De Luxe, and for both still supplemented at the front by a lower front mudguard stay which doubled as a front stand. Though in practice sidecars, even their own brand S22/50 single-seater in colours to match the machine, made excessive demands of the Sunbeam, nevertheless, integral lugs were located at the front and centre of the frame, the rear mount being screwed into the pillion footrest hole and the lower front needing a special lug which screwed onto the front snubber in place of the nut; this broke off if it was run loose, so most people used a conventional bolt-round-the-frame lug at this point. These mountings permitted left or right-hand sidecar attachment; a steering damper was fitted as standard. A final thoughtful touch was the fitting of three bulb-holders inside the lid of the offside electrics box, to carry spare bulbs conveniently and safely.

While the S7 De Luxe and S8 may have had the same engine and basic layout, the somewhat sportier S8 was not only 35 lb lighter but also had a very diferent feel to it. The most noticeable variation was in the wheels and tyres, with the S8 opting for the conventional route with 3.25 × 19 in front and 4.00 × 18 in rear wheels, chromed rims against the S7's black paint and in the front hub, the BSA 7 in single-sided SLS brake with a pressed steel backplate, in contrast to the S8's all-enclosing saucepan lid alloy cover. The S8's rear brake was as on the S7, but both its front and rear mudguards were of narrower section, though the rear one was still wide enough and retained a graceful swelling curve.

The S7 De Luxe kept its 8 in brakes front and rear: as on the S8's rear brake also, the shoes of these were quickly adjustable for wear by a car-type click-stop fulcrum, operated by applying a spanner to a square head on the adjuster. The wheels were instantly detachable by removing a knock-out spindle, which left the brakes undisturbed. Regrettably the brakes themselves were not very efficient, suffering from lack of rigidity in their operating arms; a 1948 S7 test only managed to stop in 35 ft from 30 mph. Although the S8 did much better in one 1950 test, stopping in 25½ ft, closer scrutiny reveals that the test bike was credited with an 8 in brake, and in another test with the standard 7 in one in place, it only managed 33 ft. The BSA 7 in brake was never that clever, and thoughtful S8 owners prefer to substitute the Gold Star front stopper, which works better yet retains the period look. The S8's wheels did give it a useful edge in ground clearance, 5½ in against the S8's 4½ in, and naturally this helped cornering.

Another instant separator between the two models was the silencer. The S7 had a large and handsome circular chromed job with absorption-type internals and a diagonally slash-out central tail pipe: it gave a healthy but restrained exhaust note. The S8, by contrast, sported a flat-sided, cast aluminium item with its main body decorated by three linked ribs, and a tail-pipe, also slash-cut, secured by a pinch-bolt, and exiting from the top of the main body of the silencer. This one's internals were of the baffle type, and gave an exhaust note 'somewhat more energetic' as they put it at the time.

But perhaps the most significant difference

Left *Final look at a 1953 S8 in polychromatic gun-metal grey finish.*

Above right *A Stewart Engineering rebuild with an RM19 alternator conversion and extra chrome. Done in 1967, before prices made strict originality mandatory.*

for both models from the previous S7 was the front fork, though on the S7 De Luxe it was concealed beneath the old-style shrouds, and the legs were still set significantly wider apart. This was the Val Page design with helical internal springs and one-way hydraulic damping, and it was the biggest contribution to the improvement of handlng over their predecessor. The immediate external identifier was the chrome section at the top of the fork sliders, while a closer look would reveal the absence of the old S7's central spring unit. The steering head on both models had been altered to accommodate the new fork and it should be mentioned that although similar internally and in appearance to the fork on the contemporary BSA A, B and M ranges as well as the Ariels, the S8's undisguised version of the fork was nevertheless not identical to these others. Further detail differences between the two models included the headlamp, and the rear number plate mounting (conventional for the S8, but an adaptation of the previous circular rear light for use as a mounting on the S7 De Luxe).

The S7 De Luxe was finished in Mist Green, the same colour as that catalogued for the DI Bantam, though in practice the S7's shade had more blue in it. The colour, if not exactly inspiring, at least to someone of that generation is quintessentially fifties, like pillar-box red or Morris Minor grey; and was set off by the blue (to 1951) and then the yellow tank badges adopted for the revised models, the final badges being amber. The S8 retained the old black finish, but was also available at extra cost in the rather sombre Polychromatic Gun Metal Grey. On all machines the alloy of the engine, gearbox, drive castings and brake covers was left unpolished.

On the road, the S7, in David Munro's glorious circumlocution, could 'be ridden, if desired, with a profound disregard for its more ambitious performance at the higher speed ranges, and confined to the role of the luxurious potter-bus'; while the S8, if revved to its 6,000 rpm maximum through the gears, could attain 80 mph in 40 seconds, with a top speed of around 85. But good average journey speeds rather than high top speeds were where both the quite, smooth-running Sunbeams shone. They were and remain really comfortable, the S7's balloon tyres making it outstanding in that respect;

and in conjunction with good riding positions, this made possible anything up to the 500 miles in 24 hours mentioned in a *Motor Cycling* S8 test from racer Phil Heath, and with the rider reasonably fresh at the far end. The early reports of 53 mpg overall seem to have been over-pessimistic, with an overall 65 mpg being nearer the mark, which with a 3¼ gallon tank gave a useful range. Night riding was aided by the 8 in headlamp, a large size for its day, which gave fairly good service.

Starting was easy, and followed by the engine's unobtrusive tick-tock as it shuddered on its rubber mounts. The short-stroke engine was inevitably high-revving, and had to be wound up, even to 30 mph in first, 50 in second, and 65 in third, if reasonably fast forward motion was to be attained; but it was also flexible, so that one could potter at low speeds in top. The biggest drawback was probably mental; as an S8 rider interviewed in the Haynes Superprofile put it, 'the owner has to get used to the Sunbeam's peculiarities, and adapt his riding style to suit. The Sunbeam is rather short of power and the gear ratios are not well chosen. This impedes progress in hilly country or on twisting roads. The ideal riding medium is a flattish open road, and on this the bike is very pleasant'; he added that 'roadholding is good at normal speeds' though the machine (and this went double for the S7) was vulnerable to cross-winds. If ridden within their limits (ie, not taken much above 60 mph) the 'Beams are also fairly reliable; and with properly fettled brakes can hold their own in town traffic.

They have been well served by their marque historian, and continue to be by the one and only specialist and spares source, Stewart Engineering. Bob Stewart and his wife Chines cover the field pretty thoroughly. Any couple with the Stewart Sunbeam Sprint Special in their past (oversize valves, opened-out ports, 1¼ in fuel injector, polished internals, skimmed head, high compression, lightened clutch flywheel, Borg and Beck clutch internals, etc,) must know something about the strengths and weaknesses of the twins.

They offer several sensible modifications in addition to the ones already mentioned, and these include 12 volt conversions, electronic condensers, built-up reconditioned rocker arms, conversions to fit Concentric carburettors, plus mudguards, toolboxes and air filter covers in colour-impregnated plastic; they also undertake complete reconditioning and rebuilds. If the cost of items like worm-drive sets reflects the retail expense of small one-off runs, spares generally are no dearer than for a modern machine, and often rather more readily available. And what you do get with a Sunbeam are those intangibles, distinctiveness and style.

While the flawed but ultra-stylish early S7s are for committed rarity seekers only, the S8 with its more normal performance, access to modern tyres, and improvable braking, is still, as it was described at the time, the more practical of the two and with development so minimal, there is no real preference as to years of manufacture. But who could resist the S7 De Luxe's American aura, the magnificence of its wheels and fat tyres (even if they do give an unusual feel to the ride, bounce on bumpy surfaces and can slip on slime), the Rubenesque curves of its tank and mudguards, the sumptuous comfort of the saddle?

Well to tell the truth, I can, just, even though a good, original, low mileage one is on offer to me right this minute now. I can only run to one bike at a time presently, and I know it can't be one which won't respond on the rare but still compulsive moments when the badger gets loose and the throttle must be wound on. But if I was a *collector*. . . surely no collection could be complete without a Sunbeam.

Sunbeam: The S7 De Luxe and S8—dates and specifications

Production dates
S7 De Luxe—May 1949–56
S8—March 1949–56

Specifications
S7 De Luxe
Capacity, bore and stroke—487 cc (70 × 63.5 mm)
Type of engine—ohc twin
Ignition—Coil
Weight—(1950) 435 lb

S8
As S7 De Luxe, except
Weight—(1950) 400 lb

Sunbeam: The S7 De Luxe and S8—annual development and modifications

1950

For all models
1 Lucas MC45L 60-watt dynamo replaced previous Lucas MC45.
From February
2 Serial number of solo worm and wheel set, stamped on wheel edge and visible through inspection plate, changed to 89-5521 (Worm) and 89-5520 (wheel). (Sidecars were 89-5536 and 89-5535 respectively.)
3 Clutch operating lever no longer reversible to take up wear.
From March
4 Oil pressure switch now mounted on a brass extension piece to avoid overheating, which means a cutaway in the alloy sparking plug cover.

1951

For all models
1 Lucas 477-1 stop-tail lamp fitted.
2 Yellow tank badges replaced previous blue ones.
From April
3 Cam chain tensioner embodying spring-loaded pivotted slipper replaced previous Weller type. Conversion kit for prevous type available.

1952
For all models
1 Studs carrying the alloy sparking plug cover replaced by V-shaped brackets.
For S7 De Luxe
2 Handlebar clips now fully split, and clamped by twin bolts instead of one as previous.
3 Two grease nipples replace previous one for lubricating cantilever saddle.

1953
For all models
1 Lucas 525 stop/tail lamp fitted, and rear number plate now had enclosed sides.

1954
For all models
From January
1 Revised crankshaft front bearing, with roller-bearing replacing previous ball-race. Revised crankshaft end-float of 0.004 to 0.007 in, adjusted by shim.

1955
For all models
1 Dual-seat offered as option.

Sunbeam: engine and frame numbers

S7 De Luxe and S8, produced from May and March 1949 respectively, both have an S8 prefix to their engine numbers, but S7 frames kept on S7 prefix. Engine and frame numbers were not normally the same.

	Frame numbers
1949	
S7	from S7-2501
S8	from S8-101
1950	
S7	from S7-2900
S8	from S8-1350
1951	
S7	from S7-4500
S8	from S8-4500
1952	
S7	from S7-6000
S8	from S8-6000
1953	
S7	from S7-6700
S8	from S8-6800
1954	
S7	From S7-7000
S8	from S8-7400
1955	
S7	from S7-7500
S8	from S8-7850
1956	
S7	from S7-7800
S8	from S8-8300

Please note that these numbers are only approximate, and in many cases are contradicted by the register of actual machines held by the Sunbeam Owners' Fellowship. If in doubt, apply to them for more precise comparative dating.

Sunbeam: colour schemes

1949-56 *S7 De Luxe:* black frame and wheel rims, all other painted cycle parts Mist Green. Blue tank badges, changing to yellow for 1951, and later to amber.
S8: black frame and all other painted cycle parts black; yellow tank badges, or blue and gold. Alternative with frame black but painted parts Polychromatic Gun Metal Grey. Wheel rims chromed with black centre lining for both finishes, with a fine gold line each side of the black centre.

Sunbeam

Publications

The Sunbeam Motorcycle by Robert Cordon Champ (Haynes) (o/p)
Sunbeam S7 and S8 Superprofile by Robert Cordon Champ (Haynes)
The Sunbeam Owners Bedside Book (Workshop Manual) (Stewart Engineering)
Sunbeam Spares Catalogues (Stewart Engineering)
Sunbeam Motor Cycles by D. W. Munro (C. Arthur Pearson) (o/p)
The Book of the Sunbeam S7 and S8 by W. C. Haycraft (Pitmans) (o/p)

Reproduced factory handbook and spares list from Bruce Main-Smith Ltd., PO Box 20, Leatherhead, Surrey (Tel: [Leatherhead] 0372 375615)

Spares suppliers and specialists

Stewart Engineering, PO Box 7, Market Haborough, Leicestershire, LE16 8XL (Tel: [Kettering 0536 770926).

Owners' club

The Sunbeam Owners' Fellowship, 'Rotor, Stewart Engineering, PO Box 7, Market Harborough, Leics LE16 8XL.

Tandon

Tandon Motors Ltd, Colne Way, By-pass Road, Watford, Herts.
Here we may be in the presence of some kind of absolute. 'If a BBC (Bad Bike Club) were to be formed,' fulminated *Classic Motor Cycle*'s cantankerous scribe Rasselas, 'entry qualifications being slowness, dullness, and sheer bad workmanship, Tandon would be top of the list.' He went on to call these machines 'the ultimate in badly-made, badly-designed post-war ugliness.'

Never mind the quality, what about the names? Tandon's 9D Villiers-engined 125 was called the Supaglid—not Supa*glide*, but Supa*glid*, suggesting perhaps a model so smooth that by the time you were aware of it it had already glided through. . . And a firm that will call its competition machine the Kangaroo—that firm either completely lacked, or else possessed in abundance, a sense of the absurd. These machines issued from a works where the day began with a communal chant of 'Wonderful, wonderful Devdutt Tandon' (to the tune of *Wonderful, wonderful Copenhagen*); 'and even now,' writes Cyril Ayton, who recounted this curious procedure, 'uncertainty remains as to whether there was an ironic edge to the lyric.' Those were strange days indeed on the Watford by-pass.

It had all started with a fair amount of credibility. Indian businessman Tandon, based in the UK and previously the owner of a chain of photographic shops, worked out of 29 Ludgate Hill, EC4 in the City to set up production of the Milemaster, the firm's first 9D-engined utility model. This simple but strange-looking model had a bicycle-type seat on a pillar and a bolted-up frame of straight tubes and lugs, assembled solely by bolts and clamps. This was so that it could be exported in 'Completely Knocked Down' form, and re-erected with the simplest tools in the Indian sub-continent. One of the original employees at the factory could complete-assemble four bikes in eight hours. Pandit Nehru himself was invited astride one at a 1948 Caxton Hall reception. In Britain the machine was to be built under contract at Holgate Workshops in Bushey Hall Road, Watford.

But the export scheme never came to anything, and on the English market the Milemaster fared badly. A machine described

Left *Treading the light fantastic past Sadler's Wells, a younger Bob Currie pilots a 1955 322cc Tandon Viscount Twin on test.*

Right *1955 Twin Supreme. A rush job, with a slave tank and signs of recent surgery around the headstock.*

by one-time Tandon employee Dennis Howard as having 'the appearance of a rain-sodden partridge reluctant to rise to the guns,' it was priced about £10 over the odds for the utility market. Worse, it was a truly terrible design, with faults too numerous to catalogue, but fully bearing out Rasselas' harsh words. Before long there had been a falling out with the proprietor of Holgate Workshops, and with only 150 Milemasters assembled, the remaining components were thrown out for scrap.

But Tandon, a master of commercial brinkmanship, got to it again with a move to Colne Way, and with the help of a consultant designer and later staff man named Dicky Wright, further machines were produced with a variety of Villiers engines. Unique Tandon features remained, such as rear springing by means of a 14 in long synthetic rubber cartridge set horizontally under the back of the engine, and an undamped front fork which on one *Motor Cycle* test of a 197 Supaglid Supreme compressed sufficiently so that the front number plate smashed the headlight. On the same test while trying to obtain a best stopping figure from the brakes which 'lacked power' and exhibited a 'disconcerting sponginess', the nipple pulled off the brake cable.

Nevertheless, in 1954 the firm entered the larger capacity class with a 250, a British Anzani two-stroke twin in the cycle parts of the Monarch, their Villiers IH 225 cc single. Though no earthshaker, the heavier twin powerplant imposed alarming strains on both the Tandon front forks and rear suspension, for which were substituted an Armstrong leading link front fork and rear suspension units respectively. A few models were fitted even more ambitiously with the 322 cc version of the Anzani twin. But 1955 was to be the last year for the twins, as at the end of it the Commissioners of Customs and Excise obtained an order to wind up Tandon Motors. As is well known, you can't keep a good man down, and by 1956 the Tandon name had been bought by another of his companies, Indian Commerce and Industries Ltd, and until 1959 lightweights continued to be produced, though apparently more to the rhythm of Mr Tandon's complicated commercial necessities than any other discernible principle. Then production ceased, some 1,000 machines in all having been built over the twelve-year period. Devdutt Tandon died in 1980 at the ripe old age of 78.

Tandon: The Twin Supreme and Viscount

These were Tandon's top of the range

models, the 242 cc British Anzani-engined Twin Supreme coming first in 1954. That year the frame of their previous 8E-engined Imp Supreme had been redesigned with heavier tubing to take the 225 cc IH, and the IH-engined model, the Monarch, shared its cycle parts with the Twin Supreme. These included a centre stand with a locking device to prevent it collapsing (a problem that had arisen on previous Tandon models, sometimes in dealers showrooms with spectacular results).

The British Anzani engine will be found more fully described in the Greeves section of Vol 3 (p 13). They were converted marine outboard motors, simple 180° parallel twin two-strokes with rotary inlet valves, horizontally split crankcases and four-speed Albion gearboxes bolted to their rear. They were somewhat underpowered at just 9 bhp, and gave top speeds around the 60 mph mark.

It was soon evident that they imposed insupportable stresses on Tandon's quaint own-brand undamped telescopic forks and rubber-block swinging-arm rear suspension, and these were replaced by 1955 with Armstrong leading-link forks, and the rear suspension also adapted to take Armstrong units. The frames were also revised, the size of the petrol tank was increased from 2¼ to 2½ gallons, and on the 19 in wheels, in the British Hub Company full-width hubs, the size of the brakes was increased from 5 to 6 in front and rear. Also for 1955 a few examples of the 322 cc Anzani-engined Viscount went into the same cycle parts. This motor resembled the 242 cc but featured piston-controlled inlet ports in addition to the rotary valve. Both models were discontinued at the end of the year.

In Armstrong-forked form these machines would probably not be as awful as the name Tandon suggests. With bought-in forks, suspension units, hubs and Dunlop wheels, and with the engines carrying their own magneto electrics, the Colne Road works really only made the frame, and the later frames' handling was said to be tolerable. They were also very light, if the Twin Supreme's claimed weight of 209 lb can be believed; but that was recorded in 1954, before the heavier Armstrong suspension arrived. Apart from total unavailability of cycle parts and chronic absence of British Anzani spares, owning a beige-coloured Tandon twin could be grounds in British bike circles for dubious but definite distinction.

Tandon—dates and specifications

Production dates

Twin Supreme—1954–55
Viscount—1955

Specifications

Twin Supreme

Capacity, bore and stroke—242 cc (52 × 57 mm)
Type of engine—Two-stroke twin
Ignition—Magneto
Weight—(1954) 209 lb

Viscount

As Twin Supreme, except
Capacity, bore and stroke—322 cc (60 × 57)
Weight—(1955) 260 lb

Tandon: annual development and modifications

1955

For Twin Supreme

1 Armstrong leading-link forks and rear suspension units adopted.
2 Petrol tank size increased from 2¼ to 2½ gallons.
3 Brake diameter increased from 5 in to 6 in, front and rear.

Tandon: Colour schemes

1954: Twin Supreme, Beige frame, forks, chainguard, tank, mudguards, toolbox, suspension units painted portion.
1955: Twin Supreme, as 1954. Viscount, as Twin Supreme but red panel on tank sides, and optional black finish with ivory tank sides.

Tandon

Owners' club

British Two-Stroke Owners Club, Membership Secretary, Alan Abrahams, 38 Charles Drive, Cuxton, Rochester, Kent ME2 1DR.